NAPOLEON IN HIS TIME

NAPOLEON
IN HIS TIME

BY
JEAN SAVANT

Translated from the French by
KATHERINE JOHN

*

THOMAS NELSON & SONS
NEW YORK

First published in France as
Napoleon: raconté par les témoins de sa vie
1954
First English edition
1958
© *by Putnam & Co., Ltd. 1958*

Printed in Great Britain by Richard Clay and Company, Ltd.,
Bungay, Suffolk

Contents

CONTENTS

Illustrations

NAPOLEON IN HIS TIME

FIRST STAGE

From Ajaccio to Castiglione

(1769–1796)

Can one be revolutionary enough? Marat and Robespierre, those are my Saints!

BUONAPARTE

FROM THE CRADLE TO BRIENNE

On the 15th of August, 1769, Letizia, the very handsome, very young wife of the illustrissimo signore Carlo Buonaparte, gave birth to her fourth child in the city of Ajaccio, which had been French for a twelve-month. It is said that the family was of Greek origin; and the child received a Greek name, signifying: Lion of the valley.

What Napoleon's history might have been if France had not purchased Corsica from the Genoese the year before he was born is an open, though vain question. The island became French; and Carlo Buonaparte hastened to improve the new situation, paying court to the governor and getting everything he requested for himself and his progeny (twelve children, four of whom died young). The little ones went off in succession to the schools of Louis XVI, where they were brought up free of charge.

Napoleon thought nothing of that. Though the French interest prevailed in his own home, there was strong resistance outside; and at play with other little boys, Carlo's son picked up the violent anti-French feeling of his countrymen at large.

It may be added that he could not speak French, and could barely read and write Corsican when he was shipped off to France at the end of 1778. He was nine years old.

AT BRIENNE

Napoleon did not go straight to the Royal Military School at Brienne, where Louis XVI had granted him a free place. First he spent three or four months at the college of Autun, where his elder brother Giuseppe was a pupil, and where he had his first lessons in reading and writing French. Finally, in May, 1779, he arrived at Brienne, for a stay of five years.

To this period relates our first eye-witness account of Napoleon. It comes from one of his schoolfellows, Louis de Bourrienne, who will reappear in his orbit more than once.

We were scarcely nine years old, Bonaparte and I, when our association began. It soon became very intimate.

I was one of the pupils who managed best to fall in with his saturnine and stern temper. His self-absorption, his reflections on the conquest of his country, and the impressions he had received in early childhood of the ills endured by Corsica and his family, led him to court solitude and made him, but in appearance only, very disagreeable of approach.

Being of the same age, we started as classmates in literature and mathematics. From the moment of entering the school, he showed a decided wish to learn. As he spoke only the Corsican dialect, and already excited the most lively interest on that account, Monsieur Dupuis, who was then vice-principal, undertook to give him private lessons in French. The pupil was so responsive to his pains that in a very short space of time he was being grounded in the elements of Latin. The young Napoleon had such an aversion to this study that at the age of fifteen he was still very low in the fourth form.

I left that class very early, but remained his classmate in mathematics, at which to my mind he was indubitably the best in the school. Sometimes he would furnish me with the solution of the problems we were set, at which he arrived at once with an ease that always astonished me, in exchange for compositions and translations, to which he absolutely refused to apply himself.

Bonaparte was distinguished at Brienne by his complexion, much altered by the French climate in later years, by his piercing and searching glance, by the tone of his conversation with his masters and comrades. There was always something acid in his remarks. He was by no means affectionate.

The pupils were invited to the principal's table in rotation. When it was Bonaparte's turn, masters who knew his admiration for Paoli made a show of decrying him.

'Paoli,' retorted Bonaparte, 'was a great man. He loved his country. And I will never forgive my father, who had been his adjutant, for helping to unite Corsica with France. He ought to have followed his fortunes and shared his fate.'

Bonaparte was on the whole unpopular with his schoolmates, in whom he certainly had no flatterers. He had little to do with them and rarely took part in their games. His country's subjection to France was always reviving in his young mind a painful feeling, which alienated him from the noisy sports of his comrades.

I was nearly always with him. As soon as recreation time came he would run off to the library, where he devoured works of history, especially Polybius and Plutarch.

The young Corsican's temper was further embittered by the jeers of the pupils, who often chaffed him about his Christian name of Napoleon and about his country. More than once he said to me angrily:

'I will do you French all the harm I can.'

LIEUTENANT OF ARTILLERY

From the school at Brienne, Napoleon went on to the military school at Paris (facing the Champs de Mars) in October, 1784, to pass out the following year as a second lieutenant of artillery.

For this period we have only a few words to be found in the Recollections of his schoolmate Alexandre des Mazis (Figaro littéraire, 8th May, 1954), in which Buonaparte appears as quarrelsome, violent and rather idle.

On leaving the military school, the young officer joined his regiment and was stationed first at Valence, then at Auxonne. Stendhal, who admired Napoleon without reserve, has set down what was told him by one of Lieutenant Buonaparte's brother officers.

A very distinguished officer, a man of the old regime and perfectly amiable, said one day in Berlin that, frankly, nothing had amazed him so much as to find M. Bonaparte winning battles.

At first he had thought it must be another officer of the same name, a brother of Napoleon. From his acquaintance with the latter at Valence, and afterwards at Auxonne, he had carried away only the impression of a young windbag, plunging into interminable arguments in and out of season and for ever bent on reforming everything in the state.

'I have known a score of ranters like that since I joined the service!' added the officer.

As for his figure and appearance, his figure had neither grace nor ease, and his face, but for its extreme singularity, would have passed for ugly. But he was saved by the ladies' verdict.

'I think,' said the Berlin officer, 'they were fascinated by his sombre and intent, Italian glance. No doubt they imagined those were the eyes of a great lover.'

BACK IN CORSICA

Lieutenant Bonaparte was passionately fond of his arm, but not of his duties. He took or obtained a staggering amount of leave: approximately 50 months' holiday to 30 months with the regiment. (Which was no bar to promotion.) As a rule he was to be found in Corsica, sometimes in Paris.

At home he had the joy of reunion with his family, now diminished by the early death of his father and increased by little brothers and sisters born since he first left the island. He had four brothers, Giuseppe, Lucciano, Luigi and Girolamo, and three sisters, Maria-Anna, Paoletta and Maria-Nunziata. The eldest girl was a pupil at Saint-Cyr.

Napoleon's own regiment had a company stationed in Corsica. One of its young officers, Félix de Romain, son of the seigneur of La Possonnière, near Angers, has left a record of his encounters with Napoleon Buonaparte, then (and for some years to come) violently anti-French.

In 1788 M. Buonaparte arrived in Corsica on furlough. He held a commission in our regiment. By this right he called on us all, and, as was usual, we took it in turns to ask him to dinner, so as to improve the acquaintance.

He was slightly younger than myself, and had entered the corps two years later.

I did not care for his looks, still less for his personality; and his turn of mind was so dry and so sententious for a young man of his age, a French officer, that it never occurred to me to make friends with him.

My knowledge of governments ancient and modern was too slight for me to engage him in this, his favourite topic of conversation.

Therefore, when it was my turn to have him to dinner, which occurred three or four times that year, I used to withdraw after coffee, leaving him at grips with one of our captains, who was much fitter to break a lance with so valiant a champion.

My brother officers, like myself, saw nothing in this but absurdity and pedantry. We even thought the lofty tone he adopted was innocuous, till one day when he held forth with such vigour on the rights of nations in general, even including his own, *Stupete gentes!*, that we could not get over our astonishment:

especially when he said, speaking of their national assemblies, which there was talk of convoking, though M. de Barrin hoped to delay this step, that *it was very strange that M. de Barrin should think of denying them the right to debate their interests*. And he added in a threatening tone:

'M. de Barrin does not know the Corsicans. He will see what they are made of.'

These chance words gave away his character.

One of us replied:

'Would you draw your sword against the King's deputy?'

He made no answer.

We parted coldly, and that was the last time this *ci-devant* comrade did me the honour of dining with me.

REVOLUTION

One of his prolonged spells of absence, and the risings he directed against the French authorities in Corsica, led to his discharge, and the year 1792 found him in Paris, where he witnessed the mobbing of the Tuileries and slaughter of the Swiss Guards. This was the time of his next meeting with Bourrienne, *his old classmate.*

In April, 1792, I reached Paris, where I met Bonaparte again. We found our schoolboy friendship intact. I was not very prosperous, he was weighed down by adversity. Often he was penniless. We passed our time like other young men of twenty-three who have nothing to do and very little to spend. He had even less than I. Every day brought forth new schemes. We were in search of some profitable speculation. At one time he thought we should rent several houses that were being built in the rue Montholon, which we would then sublet. We considered the owners' demands excessive. We were in want of everything.

Meanwhile he was soliciting employment from the War Office and I from the Foreign Office.

This rather vagabond way of life brought us to the 20th of June, sombre prelude to the 10th of August.

We had appointed to meet for our daily excursions at an eating-house in the rue Saint-Honoré, near the Palais-Royal. As we came out, we saw approaching from the Halles what Bonaparte reckoned to be a crowd of five or six thousand men, ragged and

grotesquely armed, vociferating, howling the grossest insults and
making rapidly for the Tuileries. These were clearly the vilest and
most abject denizens of the suburbs.

'Let's keep an eye on that rabble,' said Bonaparte.

We went on ahead and began strolling on the terrace by the
water. It was from there he saw the shameful scenes that took
place. It would be hard to depict the surprise and indignation
they excited in him. He could not get over such a display of
weakness and long-suffering. But when the King appeared at one
of the windows overlooking the garden, in the red cap a man of
the people had just put on his head, Bonaparte's indignation became irrepressible.

'*Che coglione!*' he exclaimed out loud. 'How could they let that
rabble in? They should have swept away four or five hundred
with cannon, and the others would still be running.'

THE SIEGE OF TOULON

*Having been lucky enough to get himself reinstated in the army and even
promoted captain, Napoleon hastened, not to his regiment, but to Corsica,
where he tried in vain, and for the last time, to act a political part.
Threatened with death and pursued by his own countrymen, he fled with
his family to France. After that he made every effort to get back into the
service, and succeeded not long before the bloody incidents in the South.
In the course of a mission to Avignon, he published a pamphlet, 'Le
Souper de Beaucaire'. He was then a savage Robespierrist, and was
shortly to become intimate with Robespierre's brother.*

*However, his most effectual patron, the man who is said to have
'invented Bonaparte', was Paul Barras, soon to bring about Robespierre's fall. It was Barras, as a Commissioner of the Convention, who
discovered Napoleon Buonaparte at the siege of Toulon, and secured
him a general's epaulettes at twenty-four.*

*Here he describes the beginning of his acquaintance with the young
Corsican gunner.*

I thought we should first give serious attention to that part of
the Provençal coast where fresh enemy landings might take place.
I needed an officer who could reconnoitre and place batteries. An
intelligent lieutenant would have been enough. I chose one of the
youngest officers. He fulfilled his mission with promptitude and

dispatch. Satisfied with the report he submitted on my return, I said:

'Thank you, captain.'

That was Bonaparte's first interview with me.

On my arrival at Ollioules, I was struck with the confusion reigning in Carteaux's division. I discussed this with my colleague Saliceti. He agreed with me that no time should be lost in sending Carteaux back to his paint-brushes. (*He was an artist by profession.*) We communicated our findings to the Committee of Public Safety, and Dr Doppet was appointed commander-in-chief at Toulon.

Carteaux was doubtless what people are in the habit of calling a worthy man, when they mean to describe a second-rate man, but he had no experience of war. Into the bargain he had a conceited wife, who wanted to have a hand in administration and indeed in the war itself. According to some officers, especially the young artillery captain, who was already, in point of fact, little inclined to say or hear a good word for anyone, and who, while ingratiating himself with Carteaux and his wife, jeered at them continually, it was Mme Carteaux who drew up the orders of the day, and went so far as to sign them, whether from simplicity or impudence: '*femme Carteaux.*'

On my tour of Carteaux's camp, since I was dissatisfied with the general and could get no proper intelligence from him, I made it my business to visit the outposts. I was escorted by the young artillery officer, who had taken to following me about since my arrival.

'Everything is going wrong,' he told me. 'I feel obliged, citizen commissioner, to let you know the state of affairs. Your loyalty and your military rank assure me that you will welcome my observations. I am,' he continued, 'up against the Corsican faction, the arrogance of Carteaux and his wife. I believe myself to have some knowledge of the artillery arm. I appeal to your judgment: every useful suggestion of·mine is dismissed. I beg your support; my zeal shall be answerable to the protection you will bestow on me when you have scrutinised everything.'

As he talked in this style, Bonaparte presented me with several copies of a pamphlet he had just composed and printed in Avignon (*Le Souper de Beaucaire*), and asked my leave to distribute it to the officers and even the men of the republican army. Laden with a great bale, he would say, while handing the copies out one by one:

'This will show what a patriot I am! Can one be revolutionary enough? Marat and Robespierre, those are my saints!'

He was not drawing the long bow in his profession of faith. It is impossible to conceive anything more ultra-Jacobin than the principles of that hellish tract.

Even at our first meeting I was struck by his activity. His attention to duty inclined me in his favour. Intimacies are quickly formed in a life of common danger; I lost no time in securing for the young Corsican all that he desired and that interested him personally. I allayed Saliceti's prejudice. I showed my goodwill to him in public. During the preparations for the siege we had frequent talks. He was soon admitted to my table, and was always placed next me.

We are apt in general to feel a kindness, and even a certain admiration, for any man who, in a weak frame, displays more vigour than nature seems to have granted him. We feel that his spirit has overcome his body, and that we owe him gratitude for a double triumph. Independently of this cause, which may have been at work unknown to me, I had a peculiar reason, of which I shall make no secret, for being attracted to this young artillery officer.

It was not only the merit, in his small person, of that zealous activity, that perpetual motion, that physical restlessness which, compact of force, began in the head and did not stop even at the last extremities! There was also, in the whole manifestation, a striking resemblance to one of the most famous, or even the most famous of all the revolutionaries to have appeared on the republican stage.

This *other Bonaparte* was Marat.

I had frequently seen the latter in his place in the Convention, and even earlier. It was impossible that I should feel more sympathy with him than was inspired and permitted by his everlasting violence and his appeals for carnage. Nevertheless, without seeking to justify or explain his methods as a publicist, I was far from believing Marat such a grisly fiend as he has been and will always be thought.

My predilection for Bonaparte silenced his enemies. Meanwhile the Committee of Public Safety, appreciating the soundness

of our reflections on the inefficiency of Carteaux and Doppet,
replaced both of them by General Dugommier.

Bonaparte was present on the arrival of the new commander-
in-chief. Dugommier at once showed the greatest confidence in
the man he called, and who was proud to be called, 'my little
protégé'. Bonaparte was not slow to abuse it. He soon took a
peremptory and dogmatic tone which displeased the commander-
in-chief. Dugommier, with his reputation and character, was not
to be dominated. Losing patience with his criticism and insinua-
tions, alternately sycophantic and violent, Dugommier invited
Bonaparte to restrict himself to the sphere of his own command; he
ordered him to do so, in a firm tone which allowed no rejoinder.

After the siege of Toulon, he [Bonaparte] was appointed
brigadier-general, with orders to join the army of Italy, under
General Dumerbion. It was there he made friends with the
younger Robespierre, Ricord and his wife, who were to become
his patrons. From his first period of Italian service, when, as a
very junior commander, he was already longing and planning to
rise by every means, Bonaparte, who believed women to be a
powerful one, paid assiduous court to Ricord's wife, knowing the
deputy to have great influence with the younger Robespierre, his
colleague. He dogged Mme Ricord with attentions, picking up
her gloves and fan, holding her bridle and stirrup with deep respect when she got on horseback, escorting her on her walks hat
in hand, and seeming to be in constant terror lest she should meet
with an accident.

Before the departure of the generals and representatives of the
people who had retaken Toulon, the revolutionary committees
were to give us a banquet of friendship and fraternity. I said to
him: 'You will come and dine with the commissioners.' Bonaparte declined, showing me the holes in his elbows.

'Go and change,' I said, 'at the military stores. I will give the
commissary an order.'

Bonaparte reappeared in a twinkling with a whole outfit, newly
equipped from top to toe, keeping the most respectful distance
from the commissioners, and hat in hand all the time. He carried
it as low as his arm could reach.

The dinner went off as usual in those days: patriotism in
abundance, very fiery talk, in which Bonaparte joined at intervals
with the greatest vivacity. Yet, already acting the double part

which was in his nature, he found time to oscillate between the commissioners' dinner, where he was so happy and proud to be, and that of the sans-culottes in the other room, going in to apologise, as it were, for not being with them, and carry on the sort of Italian flirtation which may be seen here in its beginnings.

THE CANONESS

Napoleon Buonaparte, now a general and in command of artillery in the army of Italy, spent the year 1794 and the beginning of 1795 on the Côte d'Azur and the Riviera. On the fall of Robespierre he was compromised, but quite shortly regained the saddle. Then, after a lull of several months, he received orders to join the army of the West (May, 1795). Along with an aide-de-camp (Junot), an officer (Marmont) and his brother Louis (ex-Luigi), he set out for Paris.

At Châtillon-sur-Seine he stayed a few days with Marmont, who introduced him into local society. Among the neighbours was Victorine de Chastenay, *a canoness and a witty girl. Here is her account of him.*

General Bonaparte was accompanied by his brother Louis, then aged sixteen, whom he was educating himself. This young man seemed good-natured, and in no way remarkable. I can only remember that his brother having set him to calculate the logarithm of 44, he was not allowed to come with us to the forge of Sainte-Colombe till Mamma begged him off, for he had not done his task, and the stern mentor would not excuse him.

Everyone has seen Bonaparte. He was then thin and pale, and his appearance was all the more distinctive. Mme de Marmont brought him to call on us the very day after his arrival. The good lady could not think what to do with her guest, whose complete and uniform taciturnity was driving her to despair.

During his first visit, to pass the time, I was asked to play the piano. The general seemed pleased, but his compliments were brief. I was called on to sing. I chose an Italian song which I had just set to music. I asked him if my pronunciation was good. He simply said no.

I had been struck by his countenance. Next day we dined at the Châtelot, in the general's honour. Our usual hour in those days was about two o'clock. We sat long at table, and afterwards, eager to converse with the general, whose monosyllables had impressed me differently from the rest of the company, I went up to him. I asked a question about Corsica, and our conversation began. I think it lasted more than four hours.

We were both standing, leaning on a marble console between the two windows of the drawing-room. Parties were made up, people came and went, and it was not till Mamma gave the signal for departure that our talk came to an end. I regret not having written it down. Now I can recall only fragments. It had keenly interested and amused me.

I was not long in perceiving that the republican general had no republican principles or beliefs. This took me aback, but he was completely frank on the subject.

I believe (and Bonaparte cared very little for the suspicion)—I believe that he would have emigrated, if that course had really offered any chance of success. Toulon might have had him as its defender, if business interest had not made its defeat an element in his plans. This young soldier had then his fortune to make. He was still an adventurer, and was never to take an unsuccessful step.

Bonaparte spoke of Ossian's poems, for which he was an enthusiast. I have always remembered that the novel also had its place in our talk. Bonaparte said that the tragic end of *Paul and Virginia* was the main cause of the interest their story excited.

We talked of happiness. He said that for a man it must lie in the greatest possible development of his faculties. At the time I did not know Condillac had said this, and I thought it dazzling.

We met every day, at the Châtelot or in my own home. I can still see him helping me to make a bouquet of cornflowers. At that time I had been translating a little Italian poem on the fan, and I mentioned it to him. He said he had made a detailed study of the character of the fan. He saw in its fluctuations all those that swayed women themselves, and he had verified and confirmed his findings at the Théâtre-Français, watching the acting of Mlle Contat.

At the Châtelot we played parlour games, and in claiming a forfeit, I saw that man on his knees to me who was soon to see Europe at his. We danced rounds. Our compatriot Junot, then the general's aide-de-camp, later a general himself and Duke of Abrantès, bellowed the well-known round *Mon berger n'est-il pas drôle?* and the glee was boisterous.

DISCHARGE

In Paris the authorities had decided there was a plethora of generals. Till the 9th of Thermidor.* the consumption had been large, for stars were freely distributed, but careers were comet-like and reached a hasty end on the scaffold. However, since the fall of Robespierre the generals had been staying alive, to their great astonishment. And so their number, above all in the artillery, was reckoned to be excessive. The youngest, Buonaparte, was therefore asked to serve in the infantry. But he wished neither to serve in the Vendée nor to change his arm. To gain time he reported sick.

At this moment Bourrienne returned to Paris from a diplomatic mission in Germany.

We resumed our usual intercourse. He gave me all the details of the recent campaign in the South. At this time he made a great point of his *Souper de Beaucaire*, and was far from wishing to repudiate it as he has done since.

He was fond of repeating and describing his feats of arms at Toulon and with the army of Italy. In talking of his first successes he renewed the pleasure and satisfaction they had afforded him.

The then government had wished to send him to the Vendée as brigadier-general of infantry. The young Bonaparte had two reasons for refusing to go. He regarded that theatre as unworthy of his talents and the transfer as a kind of insult. His second and stronger motive was reluctance to change his arm. This was the only one he advanced officially.

The Committee of Republic Safety then made the following order, of which he was notified by Pille.

LIBERTY, EQUALITY

The Committee of Public Safety decrees that Brigadier-General Buonaparte be removed from the list of general officers on active service, in view of his refusal to proceed to the station assigned him. The ninth commission is charged with the execution of the present decree.

On this unexpected blow, Bonaparte retired into private life, and an enforced idleness hardly to be borne by that fiery nature, which was still in the heat of youth.

* See Republican Calendar page 419.

He was lodging at a hotel in the Rue du Mail, near the Place des Victoires. We fell back into our manner of life in 1792, before he went off to Corsica. With a struggle, he made up his mind to await the end of the prejudice with which he was then regarded by the men in power. It was his hope that this same power, being in perpetual motion, would pass into the hands of others more friendly to him.

He came very often to dine and spend the evening with me and my elder brother. He always made these hours pleasant to us by his agreeable manners and the charm of his conversation.

Nearly every morning I went to see him. There I might find several persons eminent in their day, among them Saliceti, with whom he had very animated conversations and who often showed a desire to be left alone with him. Saliceti once gave him three thousand francs in assignats, as the price of his carriage, which he had been forced to get rid of. I soon noticed that our young friend was privy, or at least hoping to be privy, to some political intrigue. Indeed I believe myself to have noticed that Saliceti had sworn him in, and that he had engaged to say nothing of what was hatching.

He was always thoughtful, often depressed and anxious. Every day he was obviously impatient for Saliceti to arrive. Sometimes, reverting to more civilian views, he would envy Joseph, whose marriage to Mlle Clary, daughter of a rich merchant of Marseilles, had just taken place there.

'That rascal Joseph has all the luck!'

It was his usual formula for the fits of grudging at others' good to which he was prone.

Time went by without his achieving anything. None of his schemes prospered. None of his requests were listened to. Injustice embittered his temper. He was tortured by the need to be doing something. He found it intolerable to remain in the crowd.

He resolved to leave France, and the pet idea which has haunted him ever since, that the East is a fine field for glory, prompted him to go to Constantinople and devote himself to the service of the Grand Turk. What dreams he dreamt! What gigantic schemes he brought forth in the heat of his imagination!

He asked whether I would come with him. I replied in the negative. I looked upon him as a young madman, driven to absurd ventures, to desperate resolutions, by the irritation of his mind, the injustice he was meeting with, his irresistible need to act, and, be it said, want of money.

He did not blame me, but said he would take Junot and several other young officers he had met at Toulon, and who would follow his fortunes. Marmont was another he named.

A CLEVER WOMAN'S VIEW

It is in 1795 that contemporary impressions begin to multiply. For Napoleon Buonaparte was on the eve of a leading role, and then people would at once remember meeting this little Corsican whose looks were against him. Among them, in the spring of 1795, was a girl who became a clever woman, and who afterwards wrote down her impressions for Stendhal.

He was certainly the thinnest and strangest being I had ever met in my life. In the fashion of the time, he wore immense 'spaniel's ears' right down to his shoulders. Italian eyes, with their peculiar and often rather gloomy look, do not go with this prodigality of hair. Instead of getting the notion of a talented man full of fire, one is too apt to think of someone it would be unpleasant to meet near a wood at night.

General Bonaparte's get-up was not reassuring. The great-coat he wore was so threadbare, he had such a seedy look, that at first I could hardly believe this man was a general. But I felt at once that he was a talented man, or at least a very remarkable one.

On meeting the general with the queer name for the third or fourth time, I forgave him his absurd 'spaniel's ears'. I thought of a provincial who overdoes the fashions, and who, in spite of this little folly, may be an able man. Young Bonaparte had very fine eyes, which grew animated as he talked.

If he had not been so thin that it gave him a sickly air and was painful to see, one would have noticed great delicacy of feature. The lines of his mouth, especially, were full of charm. A painter, a pupil of David, told me he had a Grecian cast of feature, and this led me to respect him.

Some months later, after the revolution of Vendémiaire, we heard that the general had been presented to Mme Tallien, then the queen of fashion, and that she had been struck by his eyes. We were not surprised.

The fact is that all he needed, to win a favourable verdict, was to be less wretchedly clad. And yet at that time, when the Terror was newly over, people were not exacting judges of dress.

I still remember that the general talked very well about the siege of Toulon, or at least he captured our interest. He talked a great deal, with increasing animation. But there were other days when he never emerged from a gloomy silence.

He was said to be very poor, and proud as a Scot.

He had not at all a military, dashing, swaggering, vulgar air. Today I feel one could read in the lines of his mouth, which was so delicate, so sensitive, so firmly cut, that he despised danger and that danger did not put him in a passion.

A LITTLE ITALIAN, PALE, FRAIL AND SICKLY . . .

In his unceasing solicitations, Napoleon Buonaparte came to knock at many doors, and many times at the same doors. For the Committee of Public Safety had sixteen members, a quarter of whom were replaced every month. Aubry, chairman of the sub-committee for war, was succeeded by Pontécoulant, who had special designs for the Italian front.

One evening when he was discussing his problem with Boissy d'Anglas, the latter mentioned to him, as a source of all the intelligence he needed, a young general from the army of Italy, who, being now in Paris without employment, was applying to the government for leave to go to Constantinople and offer his services to the Grand Turk or the Bey of Tunis.

'A little Italian, pale, frail and sickly, but remarkable for the audacity of his views and the vigour and firmness of his language.' He was to be found knocking at every door, said Boissy d'Anglas. And as his temper seemed to be rather factious and indiscreet, he was telling everyone of his schemes and the wrongs he said had been done him.

The very next day M. de Pontécoulant made a point of sending for this young officer. And he was presently confronted by a young man, modestly turned out, to say the least of it, with a haggard and ghastly countenance, a stooping frame, a feeble,

sickly appearance, but with an eagle eye brightening as he talked,
and seeming to shoot forth lightning at the words *army*, *battle* and
victory.

Bonaparte had attended the committee some days before, to
appeal against the decision which had recalled him from the army
of Italy and removed his name from the artillery list. He had
emerged from that interview sad, disheartened, and with his mind
almost made up to offer his unvalued services abroad. But Aubry
was no longer chairman of the committee. M. de Pontécoulant
had taken his place, and, instead of an envious and biased judge,
Bonaparte found a hearer equally benevolent and enlightened.
As a result he soon gave full rein to the ardour of his southern
imagination, and passing beyond the sphere marked out by the
questions which were addressed to him, he spread before his
astonished listener a whole wonderful plan of conquest and invasion, which seemed to have been long fermenting in his brain, and
came shooting out like lava bursting from the compression of the
volcano.

AT THE THEATRE AND AMONG HIS FRIENDS

*This period of unemployment was very short: about four months.
Napoleon spent the time visiting his friends and going to the theatre, for
he was stage-mad. Mme de Bourrienne remembered her husband's old
schoolfellow as he had been in those days.*

The day after our second return from Germany, in May, 1795,
we met Bonaparte at the Palais-Royal. He embraced Bourrienne
as though he were fond of him and glad to see him again.

We went to the Théâtre-Français, where they were giving a
tragedy, followed by *Le Sourd ou l'Auberge pleine*. The whole
house was in fits of laughter. The bursts of laughter were such
that the actor often had to break off.

Bonaparte alone, and I was much struck by this, maintained a
frigid silence. I observed at this period that his temper was cold,
and often gloomy. His smile was false, and often very ill-timed.
And in this connection, I remember that at the same period, very
shortly after our return, he had one of those moods of fierce
hilarity which distressed me and made it hard for me to like him.

He told us, with a delightful gaiety, that when he was in com-

mand of artillery before Toulon, one of his subordinate officers
had a visit from his wife, to whom he was newly married and
fondly attached. A few days later he had orders to make a fresh
attack on the town, and this officer was detailed. His wife approached Bonaparte and begged him, with tears in her eyes, to
exempt her husband from duty that day. Bonaparte was unmoved, as he told us himself with charming and savage gaiety.
The hour came for the attack, and this officer, whose gallantry,
according to Bonaparte himself, had always been extraordinary,
felt a presentiment that his end was near. He turned pale, he
trembled. He was next to the general, and at a moment of very
heavy fire from the town, Bonaparte called out:

'Mind that bomb!' .

The officer, he added, instead of moving aside, bent down and
was cut in two. Bonaparte laughed heartily as he named the part
which was taken off.

At that time we used to see him nearly every day. He often
dined with us. And as there was a shortage of bread and sometimes we were allotted only two ounces a day, it was usual to tell
guests to bring their own bread. He and his younger brother
Louis, who was his aide-de-camp, a gentle, amiable young man,
used to bring their ration bread, which was black and full of bran.
And I am sorry to say that it was the aide-de-camp who ate all of
it, while we gave the general some very white bread, which we
procured by getting a pastry-cook to make it in secret, with flour
that had come illicitly from Sens, where my husband had an
estate.

We remained in Paris for six weeks, and often went with him
to the play and to Garat's concerts. These were the first brilliant
gatherings since the death of Robespierre. There was always
something eccentric in Bonaparte's style. For he would often
disappear from our house without a word, and when we did not
know he was in the theatre, we would see him in the second or
third gallery, alone in a box, as though he were sulking.

Before going down to Sens, we looked about for more spacious
and cheerful quarters than we had in the Rue Grenier-Saint-
Lazare. Bonaparte came with us, and we hired the first floor of
a fine new house in the Rue des Marais.

He had a fancy to settle in Paris, and went to look at a house
opposite ours. He formed the idea of renting it along with his

uncle Fesch, the future cardinal, and Father Patrault, one of his teachers at the military school, and one day he said to us:

'This house, with my friends, you two over the way, and a gig, and I shall be the happiest man alive.'

RESORT TO BARRAS

He was neglecting none of the contacts formed at Toulon. Members of the Convention like Ricord, Turreau de Linières and Fréron (the lover of his sister Pauline, ex-Paoletta) gave him their support, but could do nothing for him with the Committee of Public Safety. Even Barras, though regarded as the victor of Thermidor, had not yet the power he was to derive from the coup of the 13th Vendémiaire, which was slowly preparing. But it was possible that General Barras would be the man of tomorrow, and Buonaparte, fearing that his patron might have forgotten him, called with a letter of recommendation.

Here are the circumstances to which I owed his return and visit.

In the course of operations at Toulon, I had been in a position to use the services of men from my own part of the country. I gave a contract for the supply of meat to a citizen who had already been employed in this way. I had only to treat this person with a certain familiarity, for Bonaparte to take mental note of him as a man who might have some access to me.

Soon after the 9th of Thermidor, Bonaparte, discharged and under suspicion as a terrorist, went to see M. Pierrugues, the contractor, at Nice. He was accompanied by a Marseillais named Ardisson, who was his particular acquaintance. They had heard of the eminent, I might say brilliant, position in which I had been placed by the 9th of Thermidor and my subsequent conduct. They asked M. Pierrugues for a letter of recommendation to 'citizen representative of the people Barras'.

They explained to him, in the greatest detail and with the greatest modesty, the full unhappiness of their situation. 'They were being accused of terrorism because they were patriots! It was essential that they should go to Paris to vindicate themselves.' Pierrugues gave them the letter they were begging for, Bonaparte rushed up to Paris, and it was with this letter, dated from Nice, that he presented himself.

I told him I had no difficulty in recognising my 'little captain' of the siege of Toulon.

'Perhaps,' I added, 'it was not so very unfair that you should be thought something of a terrorist, for I remember we actually had to restrain you at the time of the military executions. But after all, we need men of execution. The terrorists of royalty are pressing upon us: those of the Republic must be up to the mark. Meanwhile, captain, do me the favour of dining with me.'

THE FAIR MME TALLIEN

While Barras had directed operations on the 9th of Thermidor, the overthrow of Robespierre had been partly due to a woman—Tallien's mistress, whom he afterwards married. She was known as 'Our Lady of Thermidor', and gathered about her a new society of influential men and pretty women. Here the banker Ouvrard, the most brilliant financier of the day, first encountered Napoleon Buonaparte.

General Barras dominated this society. Another of its members was General Hoche, whose ardent soul and indomitable spirit were reflected in an expressive countenance.

Mme de Beauharnais adorned these circles by the sweetness of her nature and the charms of her mind. It was there that fortune, which was to raise her to such heights, made her acquainted with Bonaparte, then only commander of an artillery brigade, but already, on the occasions when his frigid reserve forsook him, betraying the profundity of his schemes and the burning ambition which filled his soul.

It was some time before the 13th of Vendémiaire that Bonaparte was introduced into Mme Tallien's circle. Of all those composing it, he was perhaps the least prominent and the least favoured by fortune.

Politics furnished the usual stuff of conversation, but did not altogether engross it. Often, in the middle of the liveliest discussions, little groups would form in the drawing-room, where people were chatting frivolously to forget the grave interests which had too often preoccupied them.

Bonaparte rarely joined in. But when he did so, it was with a kind of abandon. He then exhibited a gaiety full of fire and wit. One evening he assumed the tone and manner of a fortune-teller, seized Mme Tallien's hand and talked a flood of nonsense. Then all wanted to have their hands read. But when it was Hoche's turn, his mood seemed to change. He studied carefully the lines of the hand offered him, and said in a solemn voice, clearly with malicious intent:

'General, you will die in your bed.'

For a moment Hoche's face kindled with generous anger, but a sally from Mme Beauharnais dispersed the cloud, and revived the gaiety which had been chilled by this incident.

The equality prevailing in those days was chiefly based on a feeling of goodwill which over-rode differences in wealth and standing. The revolution had demolished such brilliant lives, it had taught us to put so little faith in the stability of the present, that no one could either blush for his distress or pride himself on his affluence.

A decree of the Committee of Public Safety dated Fructidor, year III, made officers on active service a grant of cloth for a uniform coat, waistcoat and breeches. Bonaparte applied for the benefit of this order. But as he had no right to it, not being on the active list, he was refused. Mme Tallien gave him a letter to M. Lefèvre, quartermaster of the seventeenth division, and shortly before the famous day of Vendémiaire, the commissary acknowledged Mme Tallien's recommendation by a grant of cloth to Bonaparte.

IN QUEST OF A DOWRY

On various occasions he had wanted to marry. As a young lieutenant at Auxonne he was courting Manesca Pillet. Just after his promotion to general, he hoped to win Emilie Laurenti. A little later, he fixed on Désirée Clary, who had become his mistress and was sister to Joseph's wife.

In Paris, some time before the 13th of Vendémiaire, he lent a willing ear to Barras's proposal of Montansier, a woman of the theatre who had been a friend of Marie-Antoinette, and was now of course of ripe years, but well preserved. We have confirmation of this marriage project, related by Barras.

As he paid me an informal call every morning, he would breakfast with me. Then, after breakfast, I used to say: 'You will dine with us.' He never missed.

'As far as I am concerned,' he said one day, 'I could wait patiently. A man does not need much. But I have a family in the utmost distress. I know we shall get the better of misfortune. In a revolution there must be bread for everyone, and the aristocrats have engrossed the fruits of the earth long enough. Our turn must surely come. Meanwhile life is hard for us.'

I could not oppugn a complaint grounded on such a trying personal position. I said:

'You have talent, ability, courage, patriotism. All that will come into its own a few days sooner or later. Patience!'

And as the word 'patience' seemed to grate on his ear:

'Well,' I said, laughing, 'do you want to go faster yet? I will find you a way. Marriage. That was our way in the old regime. I have often seen it done. All our nobles who were ruined, or who had never had a chance to be ruined, since they were born poor—they all settled their affairs like that. They looked out for the daughters of merchants, bankers, financiers. They never missed one. If only I have a little time to look and consider, I can get you fixed up.'

As I talked to Bonaparte in this strain, Mlle Montansier was announced. She often looked in on me without ceremony, in the informal dress of a neighbour. Addressing me, with an impulse of trust and of flattering dependence, she spoke of the unrest making itself felt in Paris, of the disturbance in the sections.

'Still you citizens will come through,' said she. 'You are men, you are soldiers. . . . Think what it is for us lonely, unprotected women . . .'

As she spoke, she ran her soft eyes over me and the little soldier who was closeted with me.

'Then madame has not a husband,' said Bonaparte to Mlle Montansier in a tone of great interest. 'At least she is certain to find plenty of arms to defend her.'

'You can hear,' I said, 'that madame has not a husband, since she is a demoiselle. This is Mlle Montansier, who was arrested before the 9th of Thermidor because she is rich, because they still owe her more than a million . . .'

'Alas, yes,' said Mlle Montansier with a melancholy air, 'I was in prison, and I may well have been about to perish, like so many others who had deserved it as little as I, when Barras at last delivered us from that demon Robespierre, and enabled us to breathe again. It is to Barras I owe my life. So I am doubly happy that he

c

should have consented to lodge under my roof; I feel he is still
protecting me, like a lightning-conductor.'

'Mademoiselle,' replied Bonaparte, 'who would not be flat-
tered and honoured to be your defender? Citizen Barras will
never lack friends who would be charmed to do likewise.'

Mlle Montansier bent a sweet smile on the little officer who was
so politely spoken. . . .

Bonaparte had pricked up his ears when I alluded to Mlle
Montansier's fortune.

'Well, citizen representative,' he said the next day, 'you have
placed me on flirting terms with Mlle Montansier. One really
would not suspect that woman's age. She is very gay, she is kind
and good-natured, she is always bent on putting everyone at his
ease.'

'Have done with your compliments,' I replied, laughing. 'I
was talking marriage with you a little while ago. You have not
forgotten. Can you be thinking of following up my idea? Cards
on the table: do you want to marry Mlle Montansier?'

'Citizen representative,' said Bonaparte, lowering his eyes, 'it
is worth thinking over. I find nothing distasteful in mademoiselle's person; the disparity of age is like many other things
one has no time to consider in revolutions. But is the fortune you
spoke of as solid as it was before her troubles? When it comes to
a serious affair like marriage, one must know what one is building
on.'

'I can't answer your questions, which are those of a more
sensible man than myself,' said I, 'for I got married myself about
twenty years ago, without stopping to think of these things. It's
true that if I contracted marriage precipitately, I abandoned it
even more precipitately, for two days after the wedding I left for
the Indies, and I have never seen my wife since.'

'That,' said Bonaparte, 'is a thing one may also look forward
to, in a given case. There is nothing to prevent a man from
serving abroad, once his affairs are settled.'

'Very well, I undertake to ask Mlle Montansier the questions
whose solution may favour your suit. To begin at the beginning,
not to put the cart before the horse, I must first know whether
she wants to marry, whether she would have you as a husband.
After that I'll get on to the subject of her fortune, and how matters
stand now.'

Bonaparte thanked me most humbly. I kept my word. Mlle Montansier replied with no beating about the bush that 'she would be very glad to marry, so as to have done (she said frankly), and also to have a protector, which was twice as important to a woman getting on in years'.

'A soldier is what you need,' I said sympathetically.

She took my hand; I pressed hers, and said:

'I can put you on to the very thing. . . .'

Next moment I asked how much of her fortune had gone, after all her tribulations. She said she had still at least 1,200,000 francs. She could prove it to me . . .

And she hastened to ask, who was this very thing?

'A young soldier you got a glimpse of in my lodging, who noticed you very particularly. He thought you charming, and is ready to prove it.'

'Can you mean that young man I saw, who paid me such flattering compliments?'

'Well, why not?'

'But he can't be thirty. I might be his mother!'

'That young man may not be quite thirty, but he is far ahead of his years in reason, in forethought. At first glance one may form rather a slight opinion of him, on account of his exiguity. But he's a brave officer, who has shown his mettle already at the siege of Toulon, and who will distinguish himself, believe me. I have heard him called "leather-breeches" by those who don't know him, and his character and talents raise him above these gibes. I am sure the woman he marries will be happy and respected.'

I was to bring the future couple together at dinner. I engaged them for that same day. Both accepted with equal alacrity.

We rose from table. The lovers drew near each other, fell into very intimate talk. I moved away. I could hear them saying: 'We will do this, we will do that.' *We* every moment. Bonaparte spoke of his family, which he hoped to make known to Mlle Montansier. His mother, all his brothers, would appreciate such a distinguished woman. He wished, as soon as it became feasible, to take her to Corsica. The climate was excellent. It was a land of longevity, a new country, where with a little capital one could make a fortune in no time, double it in a very few years, etc. He was building his bride castles in Corsica, which were as good as castles in Spain.

But in those days it was impossible to spend an evening quietly at home, indulging some private fancies. Just as I was going to mingle in the conversation of the two turtle-doves, there came a message that there was trouble in Paris, and my colleagues on the Committee of Public Safety had sent for me.

'I leave you in charge of the house,' I said to Bonaparte and Mlle Montansier.

And I left them together.

IN QUEST OF A DOWRY (CONT.)

He had views on another woman, recently widowed, and said to be very rich: a friend and compatriot of his mother's, Mme Permon, née Stéphanopoli-Comnène. Mme Permon's daughter Laure afterwards married Junot and became Duchess of Abrantès. In 1795 she was not old enough to be married. But she had a brother, on whom Napoleon fancied he might bestow his sister Pauline. Thus the whole of the Permon fortune would pass to the Buonapartes.

Napoleon, who was on visiting terms with the family, paid an official call, and began, says the Duchess of Abrantès, *by offering his sister's hand to the son of the house.*

He added, kissing my mother's hand, that he was resolved to ask her to initiate the union of the two families by a marriage with himself, as soon as the proprieties of mourning allowed.

My mother described this strange scene to me so often that I am as familiar with it as though I had been the leading actress.

For a few seconds she looked at Bonaparte with an amazement bordering on stupefaction, then she burst into such peals of laughter that three or four of us heard her in the next room.

Bonaparte was highly affronted at this way of receiving a proposal he thought wholly natural. My mother noticed this, and quickly explained that she was not laughing at him, that it was she who cut such an absurd figure.

'My dear Napoleon,' she said, when she had stopped laughing, 'let us be serious. You believe you know how old I am? Well, you don't. I shall not tell you, because it's my little weakness. I shall just say that I might be not only your mother, but Joseph's. We won't joke of it any more; you make me uncomfortable.'

Bonaparte insisted that it was not a joke at all, from his point of view; that he would not care about the age of the woman he married if, like herself, she did not look thirty; that he was addressing her after mature thought; and he added these remarkable words:

'I want to marry. I have been offered a woman who is charming, good-natured, agreeable and connected with the faubourg Saint-Germain. My Paris friends urge this marriage. My older friends are against it. As for me, I want to marry, and what I suggest to you would suit me in many ways. Think it over.'

My mother broke off the conversation by saying with a laugh that she had no need to think; that as for my brother, she would have a talk with him . . . and she hoped their friendship would not be disturbed by this little incident.

'But at least think it over,' Bonaparte persisted.

'Very well, I will think it over,' replied my mother, laughing harder than ever.

THE 'WHIFF OF GRAPESHOT'

While he indulged in these matrimonial projects, the plight of the Convention was getting worse. The reactionaries threw off the mask and took the offensive. Barras, the man of vigorous measures, was appointed commander-in-chief of the army of the interior. He began by suspending a general, Menou, who had thought fit to parley with the insurgents.

He decided at once to make use of Buonaparte, and likewise employed another officer, Murat, then in disgrace and to become famous.

We have an account of these events from the principal actor, Barras. It is corroborated by several witnesses, and by Napoleon's own evidence at the end of his life.

When Menou gave way in our hands, and the Committee of Public Safety was at its wits' end, I said:

'There is nothing easier than to replace Menou. I have the man you want: a little Corsican officer who will be less finicking . . .'

The Committee, at my suggestion, at once agreed to place Bonaparte on the active list. I spoke of him in these terms, thinking I could answer for him, after all his overtures to me in the last few days. But that day, the 12th, when he ought to have been attending me with other soldiers and patriots, I had not had a glimpse of him all morning. As there was still no sign of him when I had secured approval of his appointment, I sent to his lodging. He was not there, not at any of his usual cafés or eating-houses.

It was almost nine o'clock when he finally appeared at the Carrousel, which I had made my headquarters. I upbraided him for being so slow. Every day till now he had been making me such eager, and even fulsome offers of service against the enemies of the Republic!

He came from the Le Pellettier section, where it seems he had held numerous *pourparlers*. In the revolutionary guilelessness we had not yet lost, I was far from suspecting a soldier as emphatically republican as Bonaparte of being uncertain what to do at this juncture: still less that his suspense might be the wavering of treachery, that he was bargaining with both sides at once, and came down on ours only because there was too little to be got from the other.

'I was waiting for orders,' replied Bonaparte, with an air of confusion in strong contrast to the very decided manner I was familiar with. 'What post,' he went on, 'have you actually assigned to me in this struggle?'

'All my positions,' I told him, 'are commanded by the officers who got here first. You will be one of my aides-de-camp.'

I returned to the Committee of Public Safety. Bonaparte came with me. I sent for Menou. He was still under arrest in a private room in the Tuileries. I asked him to tell me very briefly whatever we ought to know. Nothing could have been less auspicious than his whole statement: our enemies were in the proportion of eight to one. It turned out that the force at my disposal did not exceed five thousand men of all arms. There were forty pieces of cannon at the Sablons, guarded by fifteen men. It was midnight, and I had various intimations that we should be attacked at four in the morning. I said to Bonaparte:

'You see how much time we have, and whether you deserved scolding for being so long. I want those cannon fetched straight away, and brought back to the Tuileries double quick.'

Bonaparte saw to this immediately. Murat set off with three hundred horses. In another moment it would have been too late.

SECOND IN COMMAND

This was when his name first appeared in the newspapers. (They spelt it Buonaparté or Buona-Parté.) Barras wanted him to be made general of division forthwith, and appointed his own successor in command. There was strong resistance.

When I attended the Committee of Public Safety to offer my resignation, I saw the point was being taken with some alacrity by several members, Carnot in particular. It is not the way of republicans, any more than of kings, to spin out their gratitude for services rendered once the peril is over. And though, as a citizen, Carnot should perhaps have been grateful to the 'general of the 13th Vendémiaire', he felt somewhat uneasy with me owing to the different parts we had played before and after the 9th of Thermidor.

He was therefore the first to speak, and he said:

'Our colleague might usefully be succeeded by General Beaufort.'

It was pointed out to Carnot that he had been known to make happier selections. Beaufort was notoriously the most depraved and the most incompetent man in the army. Combating this unseemly suggestion, I said:

'I propose my chief-of-staff, Bonaparte.'

Yet he had been only my aide-de-camp. But by investing him with an important office, to which he had certainly no title, I meant to raise his status and effect a kind of transition from inferior rank to the highest.

Hardly had I made this proposal, when I heard people whispering:

'It's a creature of his.'

I left the room. The Convention was sitting. I went straight back there. I began again by announcing once more that all was quiet in Paris; that being vested with the dangerous powers of a dictator, I felt anxious and obliged to lay down the fasces by resigning from my command; as my successor, I offered the National Convention my senior aide-de-camp, Bonaparte, who had acted as my chief-of-staff, and I spoke in high praise of his military talents.

Not knowing the man in question even by name, the

Convention hesitated. I guaranteed the choice by consenting not to take leave of the armed forces, but to continue in charge of them as representative of the people.

The Convention gave its assent to both my proposals by a large majority. I was to retain the title of general of the army of the interior. Bonaparte was therefore, by a decree of the 18th Vendémiaire, appointed second in command of the army of the interior, in spite of the committees.

He approached me respectfully, looking and voicing the keenest gratitude.

'You overwhelm me,' said he. 'My whole family was already steeped in your kindness.'

It will be seen later what the gratitude of Bonaparte and his family was like.

HE HAD BECOME A GREAT PERSONAGE

Barras did not give up. Some days later he returned to the charge, and secured for his protégé the rank of lieutenant-general (16th October, 1795) and command of the army of the interior (26th October). In reality this was only a division, the 17th. Nevertheless it was undreamed-of promotion for the little Corsican officer discharged a few months before, and though it was not a gunner's job he made no objection to it.

Furthermore, the 13th of Vendémiaire had yielded Barras's second in command a large sum of money. It had also given birth to a new regime, the Directory, in which Barras held sway, and Buonaparte could consider himself one of the founders of this new order.

As for his attitude, those who had known him a few weeks earlier were struck dumb. Mme de Bourrienne describes the change.

The school friend had become a great personage. He held the command of Paris as a reward for the day of Vendémiaire. The little house in the Rue des Marais had turned into a magnificent hotel in the Rue des Capucines, the modest gig had become a superb equipage, and he himself was another man. Friends of his boyhood were still received in the morning. They were invited to sumptuous breakfasts, where there were sometimes ladies, among others the beautiful Mme Tallien and her friend the graceful Mme de Beauharnais, to whom he was becoming attentive.

He showed little concern for his friends, and he had already stopped calling them *tu*. I will mention only M. de Rey, a gentle, pleasing young man and a devoted royalist. He was another we saw every day. He called on his old school friend, but could not bring himself to say *vous*. So Bonaparte turned his back, and when he came again, did not speak to him.

After the 13th of Vendémiaire, M. de Bourrienne saw Bonaparte only at long intervals. But in February, 1796, my husband was arrested at seven in the morning, as a returned émigré, by a troop of men armed with muskets. They tore him away from his wife and a child six months old, without giving him time to dress.

His wife and friends rushed all over the town to enlist help for him, and among those they went to was Bonaparte. They had great difficulty in seeing him. Mme de Bourrienne, along with a friend of her husband's, waited for the commander of Paris till midnight. He did not come home. She returned the following morning very early. She told him what had befallen her husband (at that period, his head was at stake). He was very little affected by his friend's situation. However, he went so far as to write to the minister of justice, Merlin. Mme de Bourrienne delivered this letter herself. She met the great man on the stairs, on his way to the Directory. He was in full dress, tricked out in a quantity of feathers and a Henri IV hat, in singular contrast with his person. He opened the letter, and, possibly because the general was no more congenial to him than the cause of M. de Bourrienne's arrest, replied that the case was out of his hands, it was now a matter for the public prosecutor.

THE WIDOW BEAUHARNAIS

As Mme de Bourrienne observed, General Buonaparte was becoming attentive to another widow, Rose-Josephine Tascher de la Pagerie, whose husband, the Vicomte de Beauharnais, had been guillotined under Robespierre.

This Creole (she had been born in Martinique) then ranked among the great courtesans of the day. The fieriest of Napoleon-worshipping historians, Frédéric Masson, was obliged to admit that Barras, in the following revelations, had not slandered Josephine. Indeed some of her letters to him have been found, her affair with Hoche has been verified, and letters to another of her lovers have come to light.

Napoleon fell back on her on being shown the door by another of Barras's mistresses, Mme Tallien.

I had introduced him into the society of Mmes Tallien, Château-Renaud and de Staël, and several other houses where he found a welcome and a dinner. His advances to Mme Tallien were fruitless; they encountered only rebuffs which made him a laughing-stock.

Bonaparte had heard me say: 'Women are of some use in the world; they are more obliging than men.' Among the ladies who called on me most frequently at the Luxembourg he had noticed the widow Beauharnais, a woman of rather appealing manners, very complaisant, who would sometimes treat me more intimately than others. Mme Beauharnais was believed to have some influence with me; some thought she had been my mistress, others that she still was so. It is at least certain that she had previously, as a matter of public knowledge, been that of General Hoche, and of Tom, Dick and Harry. Not but what she may really have had a preference for General Hoche; one could understand it. He was our foremost warrior and one of our handsomest men, rather on the model of Hercules than of Apollo. Possibly from ambition, yet more than love, since she deceived him like anyone else, Mme Beauharnais had carried her views on Hoche to the point of urging him to get a divorce and marry her. But Hoche had still a tender regard for his young and virtuous wife. He was capable of neglecting her, but not of deserting and forgetting her for a transient intrigue, such as had sprung from his prison acquaintance with the widow Beauharnais. He had therefore repelled this proposal with disgust, saying firmly to Mme Beauharnais that 'a man might occasionally fancy a slut as his mistress, but not as his lawful wife'. Hoche told me, rather indiscreetly perhaps, that to win him round, Mme Beauharnais had tried to broach the subject of fortune and influence: it was in her power to speak for him to the new government, and especially to me, 'with whom,' she added, 'she could do a great deal.'

Hoche, a proud man who did not choose to owe his glory and fortune to anyone but himself, would have none of that. Before these discussions, he had been in a position to realise that Mme Beauharnais did not even respect the sentiment with which she seemed most imbued, and that the passion which allowed her every mercenary design likewise forbade her none of the amusements of infidelity; he had had frequent assurance of it, in particular from one of his aides-de-camp, who, when delivering a letter to Mme Beauharnais, had been tempted by her, like Joseph by Mme Potiphar, and had not left his garment behind.

General Hoche could accuse Mme Beauharnais of even less refined fancies—dare I say it, and would it be thought possible, if it were not borne out by a letter in his own hand:

'*As for Rose* [Rose, one of Mlle Tascher-Lapagerie's Christian names, was the one we called her by; Bonaparte afterwards substituted that of Josephine, thinking it less homely, not so staled by the past, loftier and better adapted to a great destiny, just as he afterwards changed his own name of Buonaparte into Bonaparte, and then Bonaparte into Napoleon, when it struck him as more sonorous and resonant]—*as for Rose*,' wrote Hoche, '*from now on she can leave me in peace; I give her up to Vanakre* [Van Acker], *my groom.*'

This was an Alsatian, keeper of the stable, who was included in Hoche's escorts to lead the horses of the commander-in-chief; this man, of colossal stature and proportionate vigour, had received special notice from Mme Beauharnais, who had even secretly made him presents, such as her portrait in a gold locket, and a chain of the same metal.

Hoche, no less indignant than mortified at this partnership, and wishing to justify some former dealings with Mme Beauharnais, said to me not without shame:

'It was only in prison, before the 9th of Thermidor, that one could have grown so intimate with her; it would be inexcusable once a man was restored to freedom.'

This break with Hoche and the tale of Tom, Dick and Harry were all over the town.

THE IMPROVISATORE

Success and financial ease modified Napoleon's disposition and revealed an undoubted gift, noted and admired by many contemporaries, who had heard him indulge it in society even at the height of his glory. He must certainly have practised it as a junior officer, but we have our first recorded instances under the Directory. Barras is the narrator.

In the period between the 13th of Vendémiaire and the month of Ventôse, when we appointed him to command the army of Italy, and when he was married, he often called on me. I received him on an intimate footing.

He had long been taciturn, up to the moment when it was settled that his marriage would take place, and that he was to command the army of Italy.

Then it was as though he went mad with joy, and whenever he had been dining with me and felt more or less at home in his company, he would ask me to have the door closed so that he could give us a play.

In this play, which was always a genuine improvisation, sometimes on a given theme, he would furnish the dialogue impromptu, taking several parts and acting them all at the same time. He would ask my leave to take off his coat, gather up napkins and table-cloths, make himself different costumes, and, after getting behind armchairs to deck himself out, emerge suddenly in the most grotesque disguises.

Though the delivery of his improvisations was not very fluent, he would adopt every tone to vary the different scenes, and with complete success.

Another evening there would be tales in the manner of Boccaccio or of Ariosto's episodes, which he began without knowing, he said, what was going to follow. Yet it followed on to the end, with inexhaustible copiousness.

What was equally droll, and perhaps more so than all the rest, was that, of the very thing he had just created and been the first to laugh at, he would gravely say in conclusion:

'You know, it's quite true, it really happened.'

He appeared disposed to take offence if one doubted it, and more than once he talked in the most domineering, and even the grossest style to those who were not paying earnest homage to his veracity.

HORTENSE DOES NOT WANT A STEPFATHER

Josephine had two children, Eugene and Hortense, from whom she concealed her way of life. But her relation with Napoleon was too intimate to be hidden for long. Indeed he spent the night with her oftener than at home. She was counting on marriage. For all these reasons she wished

*to bring her daughter and the general together, and she decided to take
Hortense to one of Barras's large dinner-parties (21st January, 1796).*

*All her life Hortense, like a good daughter, exerted herself to wipe
out the traces of her mother's scandalous past. They could not all be
wiped out, and sometimes she had to resort to interpretation. Here it will
be seen how she explains Josephine's connection with Barras, Tallien and
others.*

My mother could only resign herself to the separation from my
brother and me by recalling us on frequent visits.

On one of these she told us that she was going to dine with
Director Barras, and would take us with her.

'What, mother!' I burst out. 'You visit people like that! Are
you forgetting our misfortunes?'

'My child,' she replied with the gentleness which never forsook
her, 'you must remember that since your father's death I have
spent my whole time appealing for the remains of his fortune,
which it was thought you would never see. Should I not be
grateful to those who have helped and protected me?'

I felt myself in the wrong. I begged pardon, and I accompanied
my mother to the Directory, which had its seat in the Luxembourg palace.

Barras had invited a large company. Tallien and his wife were
the only people I knew.

At table, I found myself between my mother and a general who
kept leaning forward to speak to her, with such briskness and
perseverance that he exhausted me and forced me to draw back.
Thus I could not help studying his face, which was handsome,
very expressive, but strikingly pale. He talked eagerly and
seemed wholly preoccupied with my mother.

It was General Bonaparte.

Whatever might be the cause of the general's marked attentions, they put it into my head that my mother would perhaps
marry again, and this idea made me sad.

'Then she won't love us so much,' I told my brother, on imparting my observations to him.

When the general came to see my mother, he noticed a certain
chill on our part. He took some pains to dispel it, but in a style
which did him no good with me. He liked to tease me by speaking ill of women, and the warmer I grew in their defence, the

more briskly he attacked them. I was preparing for my first communion. He maintained that I was pious, and when I retorted: 'You must have done it, why shouldn't I?' he laughed heartily at having annoyed me. And as it never occurred to me that he was making fun, I took everything he said seriously, and formed a bad opinion of him.

Every time I returned from Saint-Germain I found him in closer attendance on my mother. He appeared to be the life and soul of her little circle, which consisted of Mmes de Lameth, d'Aiguillon, de la Gallisonnière and Tallien and several men.

His conversation always had something striking about it, and even the ghost stories he sometimes told were made interesting by the originality with which he narrated them. In short, the little group evidently admired him so much that I could not hide from my mother the fears engrossing me. Her disclaimers were faint. Then I begged her with tears not to marry again, especially a man whose situation would take her away from us. But the general had already more influence than I. Yet I know that my distress kept her undecided for a long time. She gave way only at the moment of parting. He had just been appointed commander-in-chief of the army of Italy.

THE COMEDY BEFORE MARRIAGE

Lover and mistress had separate views. Or rather it was the same view, but the reckoning was different. Both were thinking of marriage; both were hoping to make a good thing out of it. They opened their hearts to Barras, turn about. Napoleon was first on the scene, and Barras started by teasing him, for he had heard—like everyone else—that his protégé was heaping the Creole with gifts.

'It appears that you've been mistaking the Beauharnais for one of the soldiers of the 13th Vendémiaire, and including her in the bounty. It would have been better to send that money to your family, which needs it, and which I've just been helping again.'

Bonaparte blushed, but did not deny that he had made her substantial gifts. As I was chaffing him on his generosity, fearing it might be due to unbridled passion, he also began to laugh, and said:

'I've not been giving presents to my mistress. I've not been trying to seduce a virgin. I am the kind of man who would rather find love ready-made than have to make it. Suppose these gifts you find fault with were wedding gifts, citizen director, would you have anything against it?'

'Do you really mean that?' I asked. 'The idea of marriage has occurred to me; it strikes me as less absurd than it did at first.'

'To start with, Mme Beauharnais is rich,' returned Bonaparte impetuously.

The lady's display of opulence had taken him in.

'Oh, in that case,' I said, 'as you're consulting me seriously, I will answer in your own words: why not? You are isolated, with no connections. Your brother Joseph has given you a lead; he is now a made man, thanks to the Clary dowry. Yes, do marry. A married man has social position, he offers rather more surface and resistance to his enemies.'

A few days later Mme Beauharnais called to confide in me in her turn. Guided by motives of interest, she was quite frank with me in putting them first. She began by emphasising that it was not the heart which inclined her to this new tie. That little 'puss in boots' was the very last man she could care for; he was not at all to her taste. He belonged to a mendicant family, in low esteem wherever they went. But he had a brother who had made a great marriage, at Marseilles, and who promised to assist the others himself. Mme de Beauharnais owned to me that he had made her presents so splendid as to suggest that his means were larger than might appear.

'For my part,' she said, 'I felt it would be unwise to let him into the secret of my cruelly embarrassed circumstances. He believes me to have some fortune now, and he thinks I have great expectations from Martinique. Don't let out anything to the contrary, dear friend; you would spoil it all. There can be nothing against this match, you understand, seeing that I don't love him; you are the one I shall always love, you may depend on it. Rose will always be yours, always ready, whenever you make a sign. But I know you don't love me any more,' she went on, suddenly shedding a flood of tears, which she had at command. 'That's the greatest of my sorrows. Do what I may, I shall never get over it. When one has loved a man like you, Barras, can one ever care for anyone else?'

'And Hoche,' I replied with very little emotion, and almost

laughing, 'you doted on him as well, without prejudice to the aide-de-camp—and Vanakre—and Tom, Dick and Harry! What a humbug you are, my dear.'

I sent one of my aides-de-camp to escort her home. Her tears were then dry. And the aide-de-camp reported to me that when the carriage drew up before her house, Bonaparte was already waiting there. He was at the door.

Mme Beauharnais jumped out of the carriage, asked Bonaparte for his arm to lean on, and told him hurriedly, in front of my aide-de-camp, calling him to witness, that she had just had a fainting-fit at my house; she had been so ill that I would not let her go home alone; she was not herself again yet.

'Tell Barras how grateful I am,' she added, dismissing my aide-de-camp. 'Tell him that you left me with the best of friends.'

The best of friends was impatient to learn the result of an overture which had been his own idea. Everything was got up between them, but they were also deceiving each other in concert, with remarkable adroitness.

After what she had just told Bonaparte of her so-called illness, it became necessary to give some reason for it. According to her, I had long been courting her to no purpose. I had been more pressing than ever . . . she had fainted.

Bonaparte showed the liveliest emotion at this tissue of fibs. He flew into a great rage with me. Mme Beauharnais soothed him with caresses and speeches:

'We must take things and men as they are. Barras is very good-natured, very obliging, he is faithful in friendship, and any-one he has taken up can be sure that he won't desert them and will serve them warmly. Can Barras be of use to us, in our circumstances? Undoubtedly he can, of the utmost use.'

'Oh!' cried Bonaparte with rapture, 'if he'll give me command of the army of Italy, I forgive him everything. I'll be the first to show myself the most grateful of men. I'll do credit to the appointment, and we'll be in clover. I guarantee we'll soon be rolling in gold.'

FROM THE HIGHEST SOURCE

There is no questioning Barras's evidence, for Napoleon was kind enough to confirm it almost in articulo mortis. *Nor was he unaware*

*of his mistress's past, for he also said at St Helena that 'he had no doubt
Josephine had come to him straight from an assignation'. But here is
what he told* General Bertrand:

I really did love her; I had no respect for her. She was too much
of a liar. But there was something taking about her. She was a
true woman. She had the prettiest little tail imaginable.
I often had it in mind to divorce her. Her conduct was not
very steady . . .
Actually, I married Josephine only because I thought she had a
large fortune. She said so. There was no truth in it. And then, I
wanted to seem older. All the same, I knew before our marriage
what to believe. Father Patrault advised me to go and see a deputy, M. Emmery, a merchant of Dunkirk, who had estates in
San Domingo. I asked him for particulars of Josephine's fortune.
Emmery told me that it was not a large fortune. Mme La Pagerie,
whose only daughter she was, had a plantation bringing in perhaps fifty thousand francs a year. It was a respectable family.
Josephine's first husband was a general of the Revolution. In
short, it was a good stroke of business for me. A family purely
French was just the thing for me as a Corsican.

*At St Helena, Napoleon confirmed Barras's statement on another
point. The authority is* General Gourgaud:

Barras did me a good turn when he advised me to marry her,
saying she had ties with the old regime and the new. That would
give me standing. Her house was the best in Paris, and I should
get rid of my label of Corsican. In short, it was a union that
would make me quite French.

Finally, a statement of Napoleon's brother, Lucien Bonaparte:

This woman, who had never been a beauty and was well past
her prime, bewitched him to the point of offering marriage. It
is true that Barras saw to her dowry, which was the supreme
command of the army of Italy.

THE FIRST TRIUMPH

*Napoleon married Josephine on the 9th of March, 1796. Barras and
Tallien were the witnesses.*

D

On the 11th the general left Paris, to take command of the army of Italy at Nice. It was at this point that he dropped the u from his name. Henceforth he was to be called Bonaparte.

At Antibes he met his chief of staff, Berthier. And at once his military genius declared itself. Within a very short time he had beaten his immediate adversary, the King of Sardinia, who sent him two plenipotentiaries, Baron de La Tour and Marquis Henry Costa de Beauregard. This was the first time he dictated peace. The interview took place at Cherasco on the 28th April, 1796, little more than a fortnight after the opening of the campaign. We have the details from Costa de Beauregard.

The commissioners reached Cherasco at half past ten in the evening and alighted at headquarters, which had been set up in Count Salmatoris' palace.

There was no guard at the approaches to the house, and hardly any lights showed. All one could see were a few soldiers asleep on the threshold and the staircase. No horses, waggons or draught mules. No servants. Silence and calm seemed to prevail in the rest of the town.

A young man attached to the staff showed Baron de La Tour and Marquis Henry into a reception-room where a large fire was burning, and went to inform Lieutenant-General Berthier, the chief-of-staff, who presented himself without delay. When the commissioners had acquainted him with their business, he went into the next room, where the commander-in-chief was resting, and remained closeted with him for nearly half an hour.

At last Bonaparte appeared. He was in commanding officer's uniform and high boots, but without his sword, hat or sash. His bearing was grave and cold. He listened in silence to the Piedmontese general's opening remarks, and, in reply, merely asked whether he had not a copy of the terms that had been proposed, whether the King had not accepted these terms. And on some complaints relative to the harshness of these terms, he added:

'Since offering them I have taken Cherasco, I have taken Fossano, I have taken Alba. I am not raising my original demands; you should think me moderate.'

On the fear that His Majesty might be forced, with regard to his present allies, into some measures contrary to the delicacy and integrity of his principles, Bonaparte exclaimed in a solemn voice:

'God forbid that I should exact of you anything opposed to the laws of honour!'

To the attempts which were made to show him how little advantage he would gain by certain of the required concessions, he rejoined rather tartly:

'My Republic, in entrusting me with the command of an army, credited me with judgment enough to decide what would suit its interests, without recourse to the advice of my enemy.'

Apart from this slight sarcasm, when his voice rose and sounded bitter and hard, Bonaparte was uniformly cold, polite and laconic throughout that part of the meeting which preceded the drafting of the articles.

At one o'clock in the morning, seeing that the discussions were dragging on with no decisive result, he pulled out his watch.

'Gentlemen,' he said to the commissioners, 'I warn you that the general assault is ordered for two o'clock, and that unless I am certain Coni will be placed in my hands before nightfall, that assault will not be deferred by a moment. I may come to lose battles, but I shall never be found losing minutes, either from confidence or sloth.'

The drafting began.

When the articles had been signed, Murat, Marmont, General Despinay and two or three staff officers made their appearance.

There was a move to the dining-room, where a kind of *medianoche* was waiting on a table laden with a multitude of candles.

The central dish was a tureen of clear soup. There were also two or three plain meat dishes, some very indifferent side-dishes and ration bread. The most conspicuous dish was a pyramid of ring-biscuits, which the nuns of Cherasco had presented to the victor on his arrival. Several bottles of Asti wine filled up the great gaps of this table.

THE SECOND TRIUMPH

Having beaten the Piedmontese, he harried the Austrians, entered Milan, and soon forced the Neapolitans to give up the struggle (5th June, 1796). The truce was signed at Brescia, by Prince Belmonte-Pignatelli. He had arrived with the French envoy to Tuscany, Miot de Mélito, who recalls his own meeting with Bonaparte.

On the 17th of Prairial, Bonaparte reached Brescia. He was on the way back to Milan, and I encountered him within a few seconds of his alighting.

I was strangely taken aback by his appearance. Nothing could have been more unlike the image that I had conjured up. I saw, in the midst of a numerous staff, a man under the middle height and extremely thin. His powdered hair, cut in an unusual style, square below the ears, fell to his shoulders. He was wearing a straight coat buttoned right up, adorned with a very narrow strip of gold braid, and had a tricolour feather in his hat.

At first glance he did not strike me as handsome. But marked features, a quick and probing eye, lively and abrupt gestures revealed an ardent spirit, and a broad and sober brow a profound thinker.

He made me sit by him, and we talked of Italy.

He expressed himself curtly, and, in those days, very incorrectly.

He said nothing would be over till we held Mantua. That there was no doubt Austria would raise an army to relieve a stronghold of such importance, but time would be required to levy this army. That we had therefore a month before us, which he wished to turn to account by advancing on central Italy and making himself master of it, so as to be at ease in that quarter when the campaign in upper Italy reopened.

These remarks naturally led me to speak of the overtures Prince Belmonte-Pignatelli had made to me in Florence. I acquainted him with that negotiator's presence in Brescia and my desire to present him.

He told me that it was welcome news, and that, like me, he saw no objection to discussing an armistice.

(He used the word *amnesty*, and throughout the conversation nearly always made that mistake.)

I proposed stipulating, as an article of the treaty, that the ports of the kingdom of Naples should be closed to the English.

'Ah!' he replied brusquely, 'these are a diplomat's notions. What we have to stipulate at the moment is that Naples should at once recall the troops she has in the Austrian army. The infantry is no good. But let me tell you they have four excellent cavalry regiments which have given me a lot of trouble, and which I want to be quit of as soon as possible. Bring M. de Belmonte to see me. The treaty will be soon made.'

And in fact this instrument was drafted and signed in less than two hours. Nevertheless I managed to get in a clause stipulating that the Neapolitan vessels should part company with the English squadron as soon as they could.

THE MONOPOLY OF GLORY

As the years went by, more and more was to be heard of Napoleon's zeal in playing down or hushing up the ability of his associates, and even disparaging them, in the very act of loading them with riches and honours. There were to be dramatic scenes as a result, for some of the marshals would not submit quietly to this monopoly.

Berthier did, however. He had become attached to Napoleon. Twelve years after this he had still nothing to say when Napoleon, fulminating against chiefs of staff in general, declared in public:

'I've only to call in young Marbeuf, the orderly officer, who is in the outer drawing-room, and I'll have a chief of staff.'

A couple of incidents, noted by Denniée *and* Miot de Mélito, *reveal Bonaparte's attitude and Berthier's self-effacement.*

One day at the same period, when the French army was making its first entry into Milan, General Berthier and the quartermaster-general, a friend of his, were in conference with Bonaparte.

The latter, during the discussion with his chief of staff, flew into a violent rage.

When the meeting was over, General Berthier's friend said feelingly:

'You know, that man's temper is really insufferable!'

'Yes, my dear Denniée, but remember that one day it will be a fine thing to be second to that man.'

Bonaparte, as he had promised, sent me word of his arrival at Bologna, and on the 4th of Messidor I went there to see him.

He was talking with General Berthier when I was shown in.

Berthier, like myself, had been born at Versailles. I had been great friends with him as a boy, and this long intimacy appeared in our manner of speech. We called each other *tu*. Bonaparte noticed the fact. He dismissed Berthier, saying he wished to see me in private, and before opening the conversation, he asked me:

'Where did you meet Berthier? How do you come to know each other so well?'

I explained briefly.

'Very good,' he replied. 'But do you believe, as so many people do, and as I have read in the gazettes here, that I owe my successes to Berthier, that it is he who directs my plans and that I merely carry out the ideas he puts forward?'

'By no means,' I replied. 'I know him well enough not to credit him with abilities he does not possess. If he did, he would certainly not leave you the glory.'

'No, indeed,' returned Bonaparte with great vivacity. 'Berthier is not fit to command a battalion.'

A POET AT BONAPARTE'S COURT

It was at Milan that Bonaparte came to realise his value and his power. Thenceforth he adopted the attitude of a chief of state who has taken command of the armed forces. He occupied a sumptuous palace. He held court and played the sovereign. Josephine, who had at last, after endless entreaties, been prevailed on to join her husband in Italy, did the honours of the palace. She had a companion, a kind of lady-in-waiting, in Berthier's mistress, the Marchesa Visconti. She had taken the precaution of bringing along her current lover, Hippolyte Charles, a 'strapping punster' whom Bonaparte did not suspect as yet, though one of his sisters did. For the Bonapartes were there in full strength, immersed in speculation, traffic and—in Uncle Fesch's case—even usury.

From France, as well as Italy, people came running to 'contemplate Bonaparte in all his glory'. (It was an age of grandiloquence, and the hyperboles of the day have had their share in magnifying Bonaparte.) One day, among the arrivals from Paris, there appeared the well-known poet Arnault, brother-in-law to Regnault de Saint-Jean d'Angély (who was to be one of the greatest of Napoleon's associates). Arnault lost no time in hitching himself to Bonaparte's chariot. He has described his 'campaigns' in Italy and Egypt in the Souvenirs d'un Sexagénaire, *from which we take this account of his arrival in Milan.*

After breakfasting and making our toilet at Turin, we went on to Milan.

The commander-in-chief, General Bonaparte, had just arrived. He was residing in the Palazzo Serbelloni. Leclerc went straight there. I had myself driven to the Casa Greppi, where Regnault de Saint-Jean d'Angély, who had been acting as director-general of hospitals for the past six months, was then living with his wife. I was received like a brother.

Regnault, being at the head of a department, was in constant touch with the commander-in-chief. On reporting to him for orders that evening, he mentioned that I had come, and spoke of my wish to be presented to him.

'Bring him here at once, if he is not too tired,' replied the victor of Rivoli.

He was just as eager to talk with a man fresh from Paris as I was to see the man of whom all Paris was talking. Almost as I alighted, therefore, I saw before me the greatest of French generals, the greatest general of the age, the general on whose genius all the reputations in Austria had just been wrecked.

The Palazzo Serbelloni is one of the most splendid in Milan. The granite courses which form the base of this edifice, and rise to a considerable height above ground, are rose-coloured and studded with grains of crystal, which were sparkling in the sun; they might have been blocks of sugar-candy. Such must have been the palace of the King of Cocagne.

The general's reception-room was divided by pillars, I seem to remember, into three compartments, like the foyer of the Opera House in Paris; those at either end were drawing-rooms, perfectly square; in the middle was a long and broad gallery.

In the drawing-room by which I entered, Mme Bonaparte was sitting with Mme Visconti, Mme Léopold Berthier and Mme Yvan. Joking and laughing with these ladies, on a settee which ran round the walls, was a young page, Eugène de Beauharnais; of all the men present, he was the only one sitting down. Beyond the arch forming an entrance to the gallery was the general.

Around him, but at a distance, were the senior officers, the heads of military departments, the magistrates of the town, and several envoys of Italian governments, all standing like himself.

Nothing was so striking to me as the attitude of this little man, in the midst of giants dominated by his personality. His attitude was not one of pride, but one could detect in it the self-assurance of a man who knows his value and feels himself in his place. Bonaparte was not standing on tiptoe to be on a level with his company. They already spared him the trouble. None of those with whom he entered into conversation seemed bigger than he was. Berthier, Kilmaine, Clarke, Villemanzy, Augereau himself, silently waited for him to speak to them, a favour not granted to all on that occasion. Never has headquarters been more like a court. It was what the Tuileries became afterwards.

As a rule, anyone presenting himself to General Bonaparte in the wake of some reputation was received with a politeness not free from coquetry, either because the merit of the man he hoped to win over was incontestable, or because he ascribed to him more than he really had: *the power of the unknown*, he would say, when he chose to express himself on the subject.

Probably I exerted this power on him that evening, for I was the object of his particular attention. Taking me off to the gallery with Regnault, he questioned me as we walked about. First of all on the state of Paris.

MADAME'S DOG

Arnault *became one of the regulars at the Palazzo Serbelloni. The ladies made a fuss of him. The general often talked with him. One day, he spoke of the 'bane' of his married life.*

After dinner, when I returned to the drawing-room, it had filled up again. Mme Bonaparte and Mme Berthier were there with pretty 'Paulette', in those days more impatient to be Mme Leclerc than she was afterwards to be Princess Borghese.

Close to Mme Bonaparte, on the same settee, was 'Fortuné', the favourite which had made the journey from Paris between her and her son. The affection she bore him had not decreased, and this affection, which she did not hesitate to display even in public, was of the liveliest. Let us forgive her. Let us not be more severe than her husband was.

'Do you see that gentleman?' said the general. 'That's my rival. He was in possession of Madame's bed when I married her. I tried to turn him out. Vain pretension. I was notified that I could either make up my mind to sleep elsewhere or consent to go halves. I found that rather vexatious. But it was all or nothing. I resigned myself. The favourite was not so accommodating; I have a proof of it on this leg.'

THE IMPROVISATORE AGAIN

Arnault *was often present at the general's improvisations. One of them struck him by its ironic allusion to a third person, the Austrian plenipotentiary.*

Bonaparte referred everything to tactics and policy. Insensibly he brought all conversations round to them, whatever the original subject had been. Even the tales he improvised were linked up with them.

One day, after dinner, the guests were assembled in the drawing-room.

'Everyone,' he said, 'must tell a story. You first, M. de Gallo.'

M. de Gallo begged to be excused. The plenipotentiary had not by a long way, in this sphere at least, the same readiness of mind as M. de Cobentzel, who later became his colleague.

'Well, since you won't tell us a story, I will give you a fable.'

And before this minister, festooned with ribbons and entrusted with the gravest negotiation, he began improvising an allegory on the futility of human concerns, on the nothingness of grandeur, on the vanity of decorations.

He compared life to a bridge over a fast-flowing river. Travellers are crossing it. Some with lingering steps, others at the double. Some in a straight line, some weaving from side to side. Some are empty-handed, and pause to sleep or to watch the water flow. Some are laden and take no rest, but wear themselves out in pursuit of soap-bubbles, bubbles of every colour. Charlatans on richly ornamented stages are blowing these up and launching them into space, where they disappear, dirtying the hand that clutches them.

The theme of this satire, the malice of which was enhanced by a crowd of pungent sarcasms, had escaped no one, for no one was smiling except M. de Gallo, which proves that if the diplomat could not make a joke, he knew how to take one.

This was droll. But is it not also droll that within a few years the author of the fable should have blown so many bubbles himself, to replace all the bubbles he was then scoffing at?

SECOND STAGE

From Castiglione to Marengo

(1796–1800)

I have always been fortunate. My fate has never withstood my will.

BONAPARTE

ON JOSEPHINE'S LAP . . . STORY OF A FAMOUS PICTURE

Just after the Austrian defeat at Castiglione (3rd August, 1796), the general made a new recruit. From the opening of the campaign, he had been at work to build up a following, a squad of satellites. Few of these were to be as blindly devoted as young Lavallette, who had been recommended by General Baraguey d'Hilliers, and came to possess Napoleon's whole trust and many of his secrets.

He was first sent to the general as an aide-de-camp.

I reported myself to the commander-in-chief, then resident in the Palazzo Serbelloni. He was giving audience. The room was crowded with officers of all ranks, and high officials of the country. His air was gracious, but his glance was so steady and so intent that I felt myself turning pale when he spoke to me.

I stammered my name and a few words of thanks, to which he listened in silence, his eyes fixed on me with a stern expression which abashed me completely. At last he said:

'Come back at six o'clock, and put on the scarf.'

This scarf, which distinguished the commander-in-chief's aides-de-camp, was of red and white silk and was worn on the left arm.

When I returned to the palace at the appointed hour, the duty officer showed me into the aides-de-camp's room.

These were my new comrades, with whom I struck up an acquaintance while awaiting the commander-in-chief. He arrived about seven, and we sat down to table. He ordered me to sit next him. All those present shared my astonishment at this signal favour. But I was not long in doubt of the motives I had to thank for it; the general wished to form an opinion of the new acquisition he had just made so lightly.

His questions began with the first course, and did not cease till we left the table; that is to say, they lasted three-quarters of an hour.

'Where have you served? With what army, at what time did you begin the war? Under which generals have you fought?

61

What was the strength of the army of the Rhine? What was its position before Mayence? Which of its generals have the highest reputation? What was the strength of the enemy on the 13th of October, and when the lines were retaken?'

He listened carefully to each answer, and summarised them when they were too long.

I soon saw from his brief comments that he knew the whole history of the army of the Rhine. The distance and situation of the places, the skill of the generals, their methods, their mistakes, all was familiar to him.

After dinner he did not speak to me again. I was afraid he had been dissatisfied with my answers. However, I took comfort in reflecting that the test of the battlefield would be less unfavourable to me.

We remained in Milan about a fortnight.

The commander-in-chief was then in the full ecstasy of his marriage. Mme Bonaparte was charming, and all the anxieties of command, all the cares of the government of Italy, could not prevent her husband from giving free rein to his domestic happiness.

It was during this brief stay at Milan that the young painter Gros, afterwards so famous, made the first portrait we have of the general. He represented him on the bridge at Lodi, at the moment when, flag in hand, he dashes forward to encourage the troops.

The painter could not obtain a moment's audience. Mme Bonaparte used to take him on her lap, after breakfast, and keep him still for a few minutes.

I was present at three of these sittings. The couple's age, the modesty of the painter and his enthusiasm for the hero excused this familiarity. The portrait was then amazingly like.

ON PARADE

Already he loved to strike the imagination of the crowd by reiterated displays of his power. And no one will deny him an acute sense of stage effect. Even soldiers, observing him on such an occasion for the first time, were strongly affected. Carrion-Nisas, who was both soldier and politician, kept a journal of the Italian campaign. The following page refers to the parade of 20th June, 1797.

(Five years earlier, on 20th June, 1792, Bourrienne and Lieutenant

Bonaparte, then discharged, had been watching the invasion of the Tuileries.)

After the review, Bonaparte and his whole staff line up under the arches of the Corso, where he takes the salute of the Guard. I make my way through the crowd, and study him at my ease and from close at hand.

What! Is that the Bonaparte whose name rings through Europe, whose hand weighs the fate of empires, whose fortune and genius have made him the arbiter of kings, and the hope of nations! How unlike the figment of my imagination! On those pale and faded cheeks, in that drawn visage, under those fixed, melancholy eyes, I look in vain for the semblance of the hero-conqueror I had conjured up. That brow, furrowed with wrinkles and anxiety, is the brow of the victor! His head, so thickly shaded with laurel, bends under the weight of care, and his soul seems lost in a gaze in which I read sadness, profound thought.

I turn away deeply moved by this spectacle.

THE RESIDENCE OF MONTEBELLO

Bonaparte had now forsaken the Palazzo Serbelloni for a more princely dwelling at Montebello.

The opinions he expressed were likewise assuming a more princely character. Miot de Mélito *was stupefied.*

It was in the superb mansion of Montebello that I found Bonaparte on the 13th of Prairial, rather in the midst of a brilliant court than at the headquarters of an army.

He was already surrounded by a strict etiquette. His aides-de-camp and officers were no longer admitted to his table, and he was particular in his choice of those he received there. It was an honour much coveted and difficult to obtain.

He dined, so to speak, in public. During the meal, natives of the country were ushered into his dining-hall and allowed to run greedy eyes over his person.

Moreover, he showed no diffidence or embarrassment at these profuse honours, but received them as though he had never known anything else.

His drawing-rooms and a huge tent that had been pitched in front of the mansion, on the garden side, were invariably swarming with generals, administrators and great contractors, as well as with the highest nobility and the most distinguished men of Italy, who came to entreat the favour of a glance or a word.

In short, everything had bowed down to the lustre of his victories and the haughtiness of his manners. He had already ceased to be the general of a triumphant republic, and become a conqueror in his own right, prescribing laws to the vanquished.

I always found him as remote as possible from republican methods and ideas; he treated them all as day-dreams. He even showed his hand more than ever on a particular occasion, which I cannot pass over in silence.

Among the crowd surrounding and rushing after him, he had appeared to me to distinguish M. de Melzi, a Milanese noble and one of the most enlightened and respectable citizens of Lombardy.

One day I was with him at Montebello, and Bonaparte took us both for a walk in the spacious gardens of that fine residence. It went on for about two hours, during which the general talked almost without stopping; and whether he were led by his confidence in us to speak freely, or urged on by the need he often felt to vent the surging tumult of his ideas on the first person he met with, he dissembled none of his views for the future.

'What I have done so far,' he told us, 'is a mere nothing. I am only at the outset of the career in store for me. Do you think my triumphs in Italy are meant to aggrandise the lawyers of the Directory, the Carnots and Barrases? Do you think they're meant to found a republic? What an idea! a republic of thirty million men! with our manners, our vices! How should it be possible? It's a chimera the French have run mad for, which will pass like so many others. What they need is glory, the satisfactions of vanity. But as for liberty, it means nothing to them. Look at the army! The victories we have been winning, our triumphs, have already restored the French soldier to his true self. I am everything to him. Let the Directory just try to take away my command, and see if it has the power. The nation wants a chief, a chief in the blaze of glory, and not theories which mean nothing to the French. Let them have baubles, that's all they ask. They will play with them and follow on, always provided one is clever enough to conceal where they are being taken.'

Bonaparte at Arcole, 1796, by Gros

General Bonaparte, c. 1800, by Appiani engraved by Bartolozzi

REPORT TO THE DIRECTORY

Independent as Bonaparte gave himself out to be, he could not ignore his dependence on the French government. And though Barras was still entirely his, the other Directors had become uneasy at his goings-on. To be sure, he was sending millions upon millions (in gold) to Paris, but rumour accused him of keeping some for himself. The enrichment of his family had got abroad. In all things, military and diplomatic, he took his own way. The Directory therefore sent General Clarke to his headquarters as a spy. However, Bonaparte quickly found him out, and made haste to buy him. (He was to pay much more for him in a few years, by creating him count, duke and minister for war.)

After that, Clarke sent in reports on judicious lines (adulatory, with some concessions to truth), of which the following is a sample:

This general has rendered the most important services. Advanced by you to his present glorious post, he shows himself worthy of it. He is the man of the Republic.

Several times the fate of Italy has hung on his masterly planning. There is no one here but looks on him as a man of genius, as indeed he is. He is feared, loved and respected in Italy. All the petty resources of intrigue are foiled by his penetration. He has a great ascendancy over the individuals composing the republican army, because he divines or understands from the first their ideas or temper, and directs them skilfully to the point where they can be most useful.

Bonaparte would achieve success in more than one sphere of action. His knowledge and exceptional talents give him the means to do so. I believe him attached to the Republic, and without any ambition but to preserve the glory he has won. It would be an error to suppose him a party man. He belongs neither to the royalists, who slander him, nor to the anarchists, whom he dislikes. The Constitution is his guide. Staunch to that and to the Directory which maintains it, he will, I think, always be useful and never dangerous to his country. Do not imagine, Citizen Directors, that I speak from enthusiasm. I am writing calmly, and have no object but to acquaint you with the truth. Bonaparte will be ranked by posterity with the greatest men.

I have ascertained here that the government commissioner, Garreau, did not mean it to be understood that this general had

been wanting in probity. He is too careful of his glory, too careless of petty matters to have thought of enriching himself. The
persons I have consulted, such as Citizen Garreau and General
Berthier, confirm this view. Quartermaster-General Denniée,
whose probity is here regarded as strict, gave me a similar assurance. I have myself questioned Bonaparte on this head; he replied
in a style which I thought frank, and which puts suspicion to
flight. He seemed to me not unaware that there were men who
had gained too much by the conquest, but I know that those he
suspects enjoy only so much of his esteem as they may have
earned by other, more useful qualities.

It has been murmured here that the commander-in-chief of the
army of Italy employed men of straw as contractors. Time has
not allowed me to probe these charges. I have studied them, however, and they struck me as groundless.

If General Bonaparte should have misappropriated funds, I
would remind you, Citizen Directors, of Marshal de Villars and
his hundred thousand crowns' worth of vinegar.

Nevertheless, General Bonaparte has his faults. He drives men
too hard. He does not always address members of the army who
approach him with the restraint befitting his character. He is
sometimes harsh, impatient, precipitate or imperious. Often he is
too hasty in requiring difficult things. And his manner of requiring what may be good in itself debars those in contact with him
from suggesting a better way to carry out his intention.

RE-ENTER BOURRIENNE

*For months Bonaparte, wanting the right kind of secretary, had been
sending message after message to his old schoolfellow, later a diplomat,
and then prosecuted as we have seen. At last, in the spring of 1797,
Bourrienne gave way and started for Italy.*

I joined Bonaparte at Leoben on the 19th of April, the day after
the preliminaries of peace had been signed.

These preliminaries bore no resemblance to the final treaty of
Campo Formio. The fall of the State of Venice being incomplete, it
did not as yet afford a prey to divide. That was set right later. Woe
to the small States that lie in the path of two fighting giants!

This is the end of my relations with Bonaparte as an equal and

comrade, and the beginning of the period when I knew him
suddenly great, powerful, lapped in homage and glory.

I did not accost him in my old way. I was too much alive to his
personal importance. Thanks to his position, the social gulf between us was now so wide that I could not but feel the need to
conform my greeting to it.

I made with pleasure, and unrepining, what was indeed the
very easy sacrifice of familiarity, the use of *tu*, and other small
freedoms. When I entered the drawing-room where he was surrounded by a glittering staff, he called out aloud:

'*Te voilà donc, enfin!*'

But as soon as we were alone he gave me to understand that he
was pleased by my own reserve and felt obliged to me.

I was at once installed as his principal secretary.

That same evening I talked of the rising in Venetia, the dangers
run by the French, those I had just escaped, etc.

'Never fear,' said he, 'those rascals will pay for it. They've had
their Republic.'

THE GENERAL AT WORK

Hostilities were suspended. Money was coming in from all sides. The
Pope had provided thirty millions (in gold) and countless art treasures.
Peace was being negotiated. Or rather, Bonaparte was negotiating, or
shamming, as he saw fit, regardless of his instructions from the Directory.
It was at this point (October, 1797) that Carrion-Nisas saw him again.

After waiting five or six hours, I secured an audience of five or
six minutes. Bonaparte was reading my papers and I was looking
at him.

I had not eyes enough, not ears enough, to take in his features,
his gestures, his glances, his lightest words. Here before me is
Bonaparte! I touch him, I see him, I hear him! An unutterable
tremor, a religious thrill, made my heart beat, and I felt a nameless
disorder of my whole being.

Genius, glory, virtue, how great is your dominion, how strong
your hold on mankind! This is the same face that struck me so
powerfully at Milan, it is the same drawn countenance. But I
admire a feeling and profound gaze, tinged with gravity and
gloom. Content has not its abode in that soul. It is banished for

many a day to come, perhaps for ever! O human wretchedness! Bonaparte is not and will not be happy.

The most favourable time for speaking to Bonaparte is after dinner. Then it is easy to approach and converse with him. When he has conferences, they start in the evening and go on into the night. Sometimes he goes to bed at four or five in the morning and gets up about noon. He works till four or five in the evening and dines at six or seven. It is during this morning work that business is done, and that one can clinch matters with him. But he is then almost unapproachable.

Berthier approaches him fairly freely. He works hard, has a passive role, is not in every secret, receives orders and obeys.

With Bonaparte, one never knows what is happening; he alone knows what is going to happen.

Mme Bonaparte is not young or pretty. She is extremely polite and complaisant. She is very caressing to her husband, who seems attached to her. She cries often, several times a day, for trivial reasons. It must be dreary for her at Passariano, and no doubt she is longing to get away.

WELL, WE MUST MAKE PEACE . . .

So far he had been chiefly playing at negotiation, for his ambition urged him to push on to Vienna. But he could not do it alone. The support of the French armies on the Rhine would be essential. He was still hoping for this support when one morning Bourrienne *brought him a piece of news, trifling in appearance but disastrous to his schemes.*

On the 13th of October I opened my windows at daybreak to find the mountains covered with snow. Yesterday's weather had been superb, and till now there had been promise of a fine and late autumn.

As usual, I entered the general's bedroom at seven o'clock. I woke him, and told him what I had just seen. At first he pretended not to believe me, jumped out of bed, and ran to the window. Then, seeing this abrupt change of temperature for himself, he very calmly pronounced these words:

'Before mid-October! What a country! Well, we must make peace.'

He dressed hastily, while I read him the newspapers, as I did every day. He paid little attention. Shutting himself up with me in his study, he reviewed the whole situation of his army with the greatest care, and then said:

'The armies of the Rhine will need more than a month to second me, if they are able, and within a fortnight the roads and passes will be blocked with snow. That's that, I shall make peace. Venice will pay for the war and the Rhine frontier. The Directory and the lawyers can say what they please.'

Fourteen years later, an equally early winter, in a more severe climate, was to oppose him with more deadly effect. Why had he not the same forethought?

POPULARITY ON THE WANE

It was more than eighteen months since Bonaparte had invaded Italy, giving out that he came only to make the Italians independent and to fight for their happiness. Since then, a rich country had been feeling the evils of an interminable occupation. Requisitioning and war taxes were exhausting public and private funds. On the eve of Campo Formio, Carrion-Nisas witnessed the people's estrangement from the 'liberator' of Italy.

On drawing near his capital, I saw a numerous train of horses and vehicles. The fiery victor, who had focused the eyes of the world and the hope of nations, was going away, escorted by his officers and by troopers ranged round him and his baggage-train.

A woman at his side was blazing with diamonds, and complacently enjoying her vain splendour.

He was gloomy and abstracted. But his cold and immobile visage displayed neither remorse, nor grief, nor emotion. Insensibility was written on his brow in letters of ice.

There was now an end to the shouts and cheers, the cohort of blessings and acclamation, with which the peoples used to surround his laurel-strewn car when he was crossing the plains in the time of conflict.

Silence reigned afar. The farm-hand, the workman turned away at sight of him, and fell back without a word. Their gestures and looks proclaimed the indignation and scorn their mouths dared not utter.

One of the waggons following his chariot happened to overturn in the middle of the road, and at once a host of little gold pieces spilled out on the ground, and in an instant covered the highway. The officers flung themselves from horseback and leapt avidly on the spoil. It was as though they had not moments enough to fill their pockets, and they were never satisfied, even when sinking under the weight.

I moved on, shuddering with horror and pity.

COME ALONG, GENERAL. HERE IS A PEN . . .

When peace was signed, Bonaparte returned to France. To take command of another army? He was not keen. His object was the Directory. He meant to be one of the Five. However, he was under the required age, and if all the victorious generals had made this claim, the Directory would have had twenty members. None the less he tried everything, flattery and threats, intrigue and frontal attack; but the Directors, especially Rewbell and Barras, were unmoved. In later years Napoleon was more than once to acknowledge the setback. Thus confirmed, Barras's account has great value.

From the first moment of his return from Italy, Bonaparte had cast on France an eye of ambition one could hardly misread. But to avert attention from his designs on his real prey, he was trying to fix it on other points.

To us, naturally as he might be prompted to talk of Italy, after being so active there for two years, it was obvious that on many occasions when he referred to it, his harangues were only roundabout ways of addressing strictures or compliments to France. We could not have failed to detect this ulterior view in many of his proceedings in Italy, in the phantom constitutions he had bestowed on different parts of that country, and even in his parting words to the Italians.

Rewbell and I were keeping our eyes open, and were not hoodwinked. Nor did we scruple to let him know it. Whenever he called upon us at the Directory he seemed to be quivering, and he danced with impatience if he were kept waiting a moment or two. Now and then we actually let him wait a little on purpose.

When, on being shown in, he made to seat himself directorially at our table, like a colleague, we repelled his familiarity with an excess of courtesy, giving him a seat apart from ours.

It would have been hard to miss the gleam of fury that crossed his features, but instead of being daunted by it, we were not far from being diverted.

In my own apartments of an evening I was less formal, and accorded him the honours of the sofa; but I often placed others there as well, so as to give him a few lessons in the equality he appeared so much inclined to forget and trample.

One evening, impelled by his need to be constantly talking of himself, when he could no longer, as in Italy, do it by bulletins and proclamations, he was holding forth to me, in no connection, but with singular animation, on 'the docility of the Italian peoples, the ascendancy he had over them'. They had wished to make him 'Duke of Milan, King of Italy'.

I could not restrain what I felt from the very outset of this speech. Bonaparte, noting with his incomparable quickness that I had fathomed him, caught himself up and said, as though in continuation:

'But I think of nothing like that in any country.'

'You are wise not to think of it in France,' I replied, 'for if the Directory were to send you to the Temple tomorrow in recognition of the idea, not four persons would think of objecting. You must not forget this is a Republic.'

Bonaparte, who had hitherto been acting the guileless narrator, apparently of something far off and long ago, seemed convulsed by a vexation he could not repress. Bounding to his feet like a wild animal, he dashed from the sofa to the fireplace—but had soon resumed that air of specious composure which is one of the most refined Italian gambits, and might in fact be called the triumph of knavery.

Once when he was trying as usual to force our hands, and talked of sending in his resignation, Rewbell, who had just informed him that it was not his place to seat himself among the Directors, answered:

'Come along, general. Here is a pen. The Directory awaits your letter.'

François de Neufchâteau and I intervened. And Bonaparte, far from signing his resignation, made the most formal apologies to the Directory and to Rewbell himself.

OFF TO EGYPT

From Barras, who had still a good deal of fondness for him even now, he secured an exceptional command: the leadership of an expedition to Egypt which had been his own idea. Nothing was stinted: neither gold, soldiers nor ships. He had just been made a member of the Institute, and, recalling Choiseul-Gouffier's pompous embassy before the Revolution, decided to imitate it by taking along a whole tribe of scholars and scientists.

The fleet sailed from Toulon on the 19th of May, 1798.

Arnault, classed among the scholars of the expedition, acted as librarian.

Boredom was the greatest evil most of the passengers had to contend with. For the first few days they had recourse to play. But as the play was anything but moderate and the gamesters' means were not inexhaustible, all the money had soon collected in a few pockets, where it remained. Then they fell back on reading, and the bookcase proved a great standby. I had the key. I became an important man.

When he gave it me, the day after we embarked, the general had also given me his instructions. I was to lend books to such persons as he admitted into the council-chamber which served him as a drawing-room, but they were to be read there and not to be taken away.

'Lend only novels,' he added. 'We'll keep the history for ourselves.'

At first few demands were made on me. I have explained why. But as soon as the unlucky gamesters took it into their heads to seek consolation in philosophy, I grew rather busier. Our collections of novels barely sufficed. It was the time between breakfast and dinner they devoted to reading, stretched out on the settee that went round the room.

Now and then the general would emerge from his cabin and make a circuit, usually tilting with one and another: that is to say, pulling their ears or ruffling their hair, which he could permit himself without inconvenience, all, as is well known, having followed Berthier in adopting the heroic style.

On one of these circuits, he took a fancy to know what they were all reading.

'What have you got there, Bessières?'

'A novel!'

'And you, Eugène?'

'A novel!'

'And you, Bourrienne?'

'A novel!'

M. de Bourrienne had *Paul and Virginia*, a work which, by the way, he considered execrable. Duroc was likewise reading a novel, and so was Berthier, who, chancing just then to appear from his little cabin next to the general's, had asked me for something very sentimental, and had gone to sleep over the passions of young Werther.

'Lady's-maids' reading,' said the general testily. (Just then he was feeling sea-sick.) 'Give them nothing but history. Men should never read anything else.'

'For whom shall we keep the novels, general, for we have no lady's-maids here?'

He retired without answering me, and I did not scruple to neglect this injunction. Otherwise the bookcase would have been merely an ornament.

EVENINGS AT THE INSTITUTE

Bonaparte also relieved the tedium of this crossing by holding a daily meeting of 'his' savants, 'his' institute, which was to become the Egyptian Institute. Arnault was always present.

In the evening, when he had had his walk on the deck, Bonaparte gave himself up to society and gathered about the council-table what he called his Institute. Then, under his chairmanship, there would be formal debates, in which he took little part except to reanimate them when they were inclined to die down; in these lists he preferred the role of judge to that of champion.

A few farcical incidents had now and then tempered the gravity of these meetings, which were not to everyone's taste, and which the commander-in-chief had almost ordered everyone to attend. They were nearly all caused by Junot, to whom the general allowed a great deal of licence, and who took a great deal.

'General,' he said to the chairman on the opening day, 'why is Lannes' (and he did not pronounce the *a* short), 'why is Lannes not a member of the Institute? Shouldn't he get in on his name?'

During the same session he pretended to fall asleep, or perhaps did so.

'What's that snoring?' asked the general.

'Junot,' replied Lannes, who did not snore, but who, even while getting his own back, held much the same view of savants as his comrade was rather blatantly expressing.

'Wake him up.'

Junot was woken up, and next moment was snoring louder than ever.

'Wake him up, I tell you.'

Then, with some impatience:

'What's making you snore like that?'

'General, it's this blasted Institute of yours that sends everyone to sleep but yourself.'

'Go and sleep in your bed.'

'That's what I want to do,' said the aide-de-camp, getting up. And taking this leave of absence as final, he thought himself authorised to attend no more of our meetings.

NEWS OF JOSEPHINE

The landing took place without a hitch, on the 13th of July. Only the Mamelukes, masters of the country, put up a resistance, which was short-lived; they were horsemen, and Bonaparte mowed them down with his powerful artillery. But soon the luck had turned. The English destroyed the French fleet at Aboukir (13th August). Thenceforth Bonaparte became as it were 'a prisoner of his conquest'. The army was demoralised. The chiefs were grumbling. And in these circumstances Bonaparte heard that Josephine was deceiving him afresh. For he had found out; he had forgiven her, she had promised to behave, and now Junot told him that she had renewed her affair with Hippolyte Charles. Bourrienne witnessed this painful scene.

One day I saw Bonaparte walking alone with Junot, as he did fairly frequently. I was a little way off, and I cannot tell what had fixed my eyes on him during this conversation.

The general's face, always very pale, had for some reason turned paler than ordinary. There was something convulsive in his features, something wild in his looks, and he several times struck himself on the head.

After a quarter of an hour's talk, he left Junot and came walking back. I had never seen him look so displeased, so preoccupied. I walked to meet him, and as soon as we were together:

'You are not attached to me,' he said in a brusque and harsh voice. 'Women! . . . Josephine! . . . If you were attached to me, you would have told me all I have just heard from Junot. There's a true friend. Josephine! . . . and I am six hundred leagues away. You should have told me! Josephine! . . . To deceive me like that! . . . She! Woe betide them! I'll exterminate that race of whipper-snappers and fops! . . . As for her, divorce! Yes, divorce! A public, resounding divorce! . . . I must write! I know all! . . . Divorce must part us for ever! . . . I will not be the butt of every loafer in Paris! I shall write to Joseph: he will procure a divorce!'

These sharp, spasmodic ejaculations, his distorted features, his broken voice made it all too clear what had been the subject of his conversation with Junot.

THE PLAGUE

Everything was going wrong, and to create a diversion and give his troops something to do, he undertook the conquest of Syria. This also went wrong. The Turks barred his way. He had to retreat from Acre. Plague began to ravage his army. This time discouragement was complete. And at this point we have the scene celebrated by a famous painting, The Plague-Stricken at Jaffa (Gros): Bonaparte, braving the epidemic, mingles with the plague-stricken to revive the courage of his men, and, of course, takes care to spread it about that this disease is not the plague. The point is noted by Brigadier Détroye.

Several days ago a sickness made its appearance in the army, especially in Bon's division. It is a high fever accompanied by swellings, and death occurs very quickly. Many soldiers have succumbed to it, and even died suddenly. This malady was thought to be the plague, and the view has become so widespread that some men attacked by it have killed themselves.

As the assurances of the surgeon-general failed to convince that it was not the plague, the commander-in-chief has been to visit the hospital in person, touched the principal sufferers, and helped to move the body of a soldier with swellings who had just died. This stroke of profound policy is having the best effects. Misgivings have been allayed.

The illustrious Desgenettes, *surgeon-general to the army of the East, can speak with most authority at this juncture.*

On the 21st of Ventôse the commander-in-chief, attended by his staff, came to visit the hospitals. Just before he left camp, the rumour was heard even in his tent that several soldiers had dropped dead while walking on the quay. The simple fact is that men who had died in hospital during the night were to have been thrown into the sea, but the Turkish hospital attendants had been content with setting them down at the gate.

The general went through both hospitals, spoke to nearly all the men, and spent more than an hour and a half reviewing all the details of organisation. In a narrow and very congested room, he helped to move the loathsome corpse of a soldier whose ragged clothes were soiled by the bursting of an inflamed bubo.

After making unobtrusive attempts to escort the general back to the gate, I gave him to understand that it would now be worse than useless to linger. In spite of which, the army has often murmured against me for not objecting more categorically to this prolonged visit from the commander-in-chief. He can be little known to those who think it such an easy matter to change his resolutions, or intimidate him by threats of danger.

Did Bonaparte, at this stage, have opium given to the sick to expedite their release? The worshippers have denied it. Here is the exact story, according to Desgenettes:

On the 27th of Floréal, very early in the morning, General Bonaparte had summoned me to his tent, where he was alone with his chief of staff.

After a short preamble on our medical situation, he said:

'In your place, I should bring to an end both the sufferings of our plague-stricken and the dangers with which they threaten us, by giving them opium.'

I replied simply:

'My own duty is to preserve them.'

Then the general developed his idea with the greatest composure, saying that what he recommended for others was what in a similar case he would wish for himself. He also desired me to take note that it was his business, more than anyone's, to preserve our army, and *therefore* to prevent the sick we abandoned from being cut down alive by Turkish scimitars.

'I am not trying,' he went on, 'to overcome your distaste, but I believe I shall find persons to appreciate my intentions.'

General Berthier remained silent during this interview. But a moment later he made it clear that he approved my refusal.

To conclude, it was only on our return to Jaffa, and nowhere else, that to my certain knowledge plague patients, to the number of twenty-five or thirty, were given rather a strong dose of laudanum. Some got rid of it by vomiting, found relief, recovered and told the whole story.

THE MAMELUKE ROUSTAM

Bonaparte was beaten, and had lost more than 20,000 men; he backed out, abandoned Syria and returned to Cairo. His dream—to found in the East a kingdom comparable with Alexander's—plainly could not be realised. Still, he had been spellbound by the East. For him it was all seduction, promise, enchantment. He was fascinated by its magnificos in their pomp. He had seen the haughty Beys, escorted each by a Mameluke in glittering attire. And he wanted one of his own, to create a sensation on his return to France.

In the household of an Egyptian prince there was a young Mameluke, a native of Armenia (the Mamelukes were recruited from slave-markets), bearing the name of Roustam, son of Raza. In Egypt he had had to embrace the religion of the Prophet and change his name.

It was an officer named Elias, an interpreter, who found him for Bonaparte. Henceforth Roustam was to attend Napoleon like his shadow. He was an average man, for whom Napoleon's private life had no secrets. But he was never to plumb those of the French language. This is obvious from his Recollections.

M. Elias takes me to the general, who received me in his drawing-room. First thing he does to me, he pulls my ears. He says to me if I can ride. I say yes. He asks me also if I can give sabre-cuts. I say:

'Yes, even I have more than once sabred the Arabs.'

He says to me:

'Very good. What is your name?'

I say:

'Yahia.'

Says:

'But it's a Turkish name. But the name you had in Georgia?'

I say:

'My name is Roustam.'

'I do not want you to be called the Turkish name. I want you to be called Roustam.'

After his return to his bedroom, he brings me a Damascus sabre, on the hilt six big diamonds, and a pair of pistols fitted with gold. He says:

'Here, this is yours! I give it you and I will take care of you.'

He takes me into a room filled with papers. He makes me take all away to his study. I brought in his dinner, the same day, at eight o'clock in the evening. After dinner, he asked for his carriage to drive round about the town. He asks for M. Lavigne, his groom, to give me a good Arab horse and a fine Turkish saddle, and we went to drive, that I was placed by his carriage door.

The very evening he says to me:

'There is my bedroom. I want you to sleep at my door, and you let no one in. I rely on you.'

I say, by M. Elias, who was beside me:

'I feel happy to have his confidence, and I would die rather than leave my door and let people into the room. You can rely on me.'

OFF TO FRANCE

These were Bonaparte's last days in Egypt. Almost furtively, he was planning to get back to France. One or two ships had escaped the destruction of the fleet, and were to carry him and his satellites. One may say his accomplices. For he was not absconding solely because the position in Egypt was desperate. He had had stimulating news from Europe: news of a strong anti-French coalition, of defeats on the Rhine and in Italy (where his successor Joubert was killed in action), and of internal revolt and discord. He had the impression that the pear was ripe, and meant this time to achieve power by hook or crook.

Accordingly, he was about to desert his army, leaving the command to

*Kléber. He transferred it at the last moment, and by letter; if he had
spoken to Kléber, the Alsatian would not have let him go aboard. Of
course Roustam was of the party.*

They did not say to us we were going to France. I heard that
very long after. Several days after I entered the general's service,
the valet comes, at midnight, to dress the general. He says to
me:
'We are going to leave for Alexandria, because a Turkish and
English army is coming.'
So we left in a hurry. I had not time even to go and get my
things.
We left Grand Cairo on . . . (*sic*) and came in the evening to
Menouf. The general dined there, and we left, next morning, for
Alexandria, as they said.
On the way we met a great lot of Arabs who were blocking our
way. I asked the general's permission to charge on the Arabs with
the Guides who were the general's escort. He said to me:
'Yes, go, and take care that the Arabs do not take you, for they
won't be gentle with you!'
I had a very good horse, I was afraid of nothing, and I was well
armed: I had two pairs of pistols, a sabre, a blunderbuss and a
truncheon on my saddle.
After the charge, the general asked M. Barbanègre, who was
commanding the charge, if I behaved well. He said:
'Yes, he's a brave soldier; he wounded two Arabs.'
After that, the general he has me given a dagger of honour, the
same day, which gave me the greatest pleasure. Since that time,
it has never left me.
We slept, that day, in the desert, on the sand. The same evening
M. Elias arrives from Grand Cairo, in dispatch for the general.
Same time, he has brought me water-melons, which did me the
utmost good, for it was very hot, and he was saying to me:
'There is not the Turkish or English army, as they say up to
now, and you are going another journey.'
Not saying any more. So he has gone back to Grand Cairo.
The next day we arrived at ten o'clock in the evening between
Alexandria and Aboukir, by the side of the Mediterranean sea.
The tents were put up, and there were orders to get the dinner.
I see two frigates in the roads. I ask M. Eugène, who was aide-

de-camp to the commander-in-chief, what were these two frigates, who they belonged to. He said they belonged to the Turks. He had still hidden the secret, for it was two French frigates that were waiting, in the roads, after the general and his escort. But I heard not till the evening. In between then it was so hot that I went and bathed in the seaside.

I come to the tent, and I dine. After that I see everyone very glad and very merry. The soldiers were making their packs jump and the horsemen were leaving their horses to those who were still staying in the country.

I spoke to M. Jaubert, interpreter, a Frenchman, one of the general's interpreters:

'Why is this, I see everyone very glad?'

He said:

'We are going away to Paris. It is a good country and big town. The two frigates we see from here, that is to take us to France.'

So I have gone with several officers about a quarter of a mile from the tent to get into the launches, to go to the frigates. The sea was very rough. The waves beat on our heads. The launches were filled with water. Everyone was ill with that little crossing. But I was not ill, not at all.

We arrived very late in the evening in the frigate, and we sailed away at once; everyone very glad.

I was a whole day without seeing the general. He had gone in another dinghy from mine. I was very worried. I was seventeen and a half. All the gentlemen, to tease me, were saying that when I arrived in France I would have my head cut off, because when the Mamelukes took the French soldiers they had their heads cut off the same thing; that made me worry a little.

When we had been aboard three days, I asked to speak to the general through M. Jaubert, who spoke Arabic. Well, he makes me speak the same day. The general says to me:

'There you are, Roustam! How are you?'

I say:

'Very well, but very worried about my fate.'

He says:

'But why?'

I say:

'Everyone says that when I arrive in France, my head will be

Napoleon at Malmaison, 1802(?), by Isabey engraved by C. L. Lingée and Godefroy

Napoleon with plague victims at Jaffa, by Gros

cut off. If they are saying the truth, I would like it to be now, and not have to suffer until France!'

He says, with his usual kindness, still pulling my ears, as every day:

'Those who told you that are blockheads. Fear nothing. We shall soon come to Paris, and we shall find many pretty women and much money. So you see we shall be well off, much better than in Egypt!'

ABOARD THE MUIRON

Lavallette, *who was there as the general's confidant, is a weightier informant.*

At ten o'clock in the evening the commander-in-chief, attended by his staff, embarked on the *Muiron*. Those he admitted to it were Generals Berthier and Ganteaume, MM Monge and Berthollet, his aides-de-camp Eugène Beauharnais, Duroc, Merlin and myself and his private secretary.

The crossing presented many difficulties. When I was talking with Sir Sidney Smith's secretary, he had let slip the remark that it was much better to blockade out of sight. We might therefore expect to find the English commodore on our route. In that case, the *Carrère* had orders to engage and give the *Muiron* time to escape. But these two frigates were Venetian and bad sailers.

We had therefore to avoid notice by stratagem. Admiral Ganteaume's device was to spend thirty days hugging the flat African coast, which no vessels ever patrol, and to make short tacks of half a league, never standing out on the high seas.

We all found this period very long, for, as it would have been rash to light up at night, we had to go to bed with the sun.

So the days passed in reading or in discussion. The inexhaustible learning of the two savants filled our days very agreeably. Often Plutarch came to our aid. And sometimes, in our long evenings, the commander-in-chief would tell us ghost stories, a form of narrative at which he excelled.

The situation and future of France were often the object of his reflections. He expressed himself on the Directory government with a severity bordering on contempt. As yet nothing appeared in his talk of what he was going to do. But certain chance words,

F

certain musings and covert innuendoes gave us much food for thought. His administration of Egypt had been pure, his military operations full of genius. But was that enough to absolve him in the eyes of the Directory, which viewed him with fear and with no good-will? He would be obliged to make war again. But must he bow to the plans of a government lacking military discernment, which might place him in an awkward position and give his rivals means of success which would perhaps be denied to himself? All these ideas occupied him profoundly.

At last a steady east wind began to blow. We passed Cape Bon during the night, and arrived speedily at Ajaccio.

Among the tumultuous throng in the boats surrounding the poop cabin was an old woman dressed in black, stretching her arms up to the general and crying '*Caro figlio!*', but unable to catch his eye. At last he caught sight of her, and began shouting: *Madre!*

It was his old nurse.

ROUSTAM IN CORSICA

The general went ashore an hour after coming into the roads, afterwards lodged in the house where he was born. The general he says to ask how I like his native country. I say:

'Very well, it's a good country.'

He says:

'It's nothing. When we come to Paris, it's a different story!'

When we arrived in Corsica, they were vintaging. There were plenty of grapes and fine figs.

There were several pretty women, who were very kind to me, as being a foreigner.

We went back on board the frigate, to sail for Toulon, but the weather was so bad, we were obliged to return again to Corsica, and we were there a whole day, and we left, the day after, for Toulon.

On the way, the general and General Berthier begin to laugh when they see me, saying:

'Why! You are cleverer than us! You have had the women in France already, and we, we have had none yet!'

BONAPARTE CROSSES SWORDS

As soon as he reached Paris, on the 24th of Vendémiaire, Year VIII (16th October, 1799), Bonaparte made contact with the Directory.

Gohier was now president. Of the other Directors, Barras was still his man (and was to mollify his anger with Josephine, pointing out that she could be uncommonly useful). But the remaining three (Moulins, Sieyès, Roger-Ducos) distrusted him. And the 'situation of France' had changed rather awkwardly; while Bonaparte was avoiding Nelson's ships, the home government had been suppressing revolt, winning battles and recovering lost ground.

Nevertheless, before taking any secret political action he renewed his bid for a place among the Five. Gohier received him politely. But he said no; and his narrative points us to the eve of the coup d'état.

On the morning of the 24th of Vendémiaire, Bonaparte, who had been met neither by his wife nor his brothers, reached Paris, drove to his little house in the Rue Chantereine, and at once went to see the chairman of the Directory, together with Monge, my old colleague and friend.

'How happy I am, my dear president,' said Monge, embracing me, 'to find the republic triumphant on our return!'

'I am delighted too,' said Bonaparte with a slightly embarrassed air. 'The news that reached us in Egypt was so startling that I had no hesitation in leaving my army to come and share your perils!'

'General,' I replied, 'they were great, but we have weathered them gloriously. You are just in time to rejoice with us at the many triumphs of your comrades-in-arms, and to console us for the loss of the young warrior who learnt by your side to fight and conquer.'

His call was brief. As the account of the state in which he had left Egypt was to be submitted to the Directory at a special meeting, we fixed a day and hour for receiving him.

On the following day, the 25th, Bonaparte waited upon the Directory as we had arranged.

On being ushered into our council-chamber, he began with his victories in Egypt and the good spirit which prevailed in his army, spoke in just praise of the general to whom he had transferred its command, and then sought excuse for his desertion in the intelligence of our successive defeats, in the indignation with which he had learnt that our frontiers were being threatened by the foreigner. What he had felt most keenly was that our misfortunes were being ascribed to his absence. That had been enough, he added, to induce him to come and share our perils, to determine him on sailing.

'Citizen directors,' he exclaimed (*laying his hand on the pommel of his sword*), 'I swear that it will never be drawn save in defence of the republic and of its government.'

As chairman of the Directory, I replied:

'Citizen general, the executive Directory has viewed your unforeseen return with the mingled pleasure and surprise it must have caused throughout France. Only the enemies of your glory, whom we shall always regard as ours, could give an adverse interpretation to the motives of patriotism which have induced you momentarily to desert your colours, and which you have so vigorously expressed. You came, we can have no doubt, to share our perils, and you find France victorious. And what must surely rejoice you yet more, your presence revives in every French heart the glorious consciousness of liberty. They were no less flattering than well-earned, those acclamations that burst out on your arrival and along your path. It was with shouts of "Long live the Republic!" that Bonaparte was, and was rightly, welcomed. The triumphs which have just been won by your old comrades-in-arms have saved the republic, but there are laurels yet to reap in the fields made famous by your memorable exploits. The conqueror of Italy will not think it enough to mourn with us the young hero he himself found worthy to take his place.'

The ceremony concluded with the fraternal embrace, which was neither given nor received very fraternally.

A few days after his return, Bonaparte dined at my house with several members of the Institute he had asked me to invite. I did not feel I could leave out Sieyès, who was also a member.

'What have you done?' said Mme Bonaparte, catching sight of him in my drawing-room. 'Bonaparte loathes Sieyès of all men. He's his pet aversion!'

And in fact, Bonaparte did not speak a word to Sieyès. He even affected not to look at him.

When dinner was over, Sieyès left the room in a fury.

'Did you notice,' he asked me, 'how that insolent little man treated a member of a body which ought to have had him shot?'

Bonaparte, detesting Sieyès himself, formed a plan to relieve the Directory of him, and at first thought himself sure of the vacant place.

Calling on me a few days after the dinner-party:

'I was,' he said, 'nearly as amazed to find Sieyès in your drawing-room as I had been on landing to find him in the Directory. If you are not careful, president, that cunning priest will betray you to the foreigner.'

I was then far from dreaming that the *foreigner* would be Bonaparte himself.

'When I arrived here,' he went on, 'any number of good citizens assured me that on Rewbell's retirement, it had been regretted that I was not in France. But if it was a misfortune, it could easily be set right.'

'There is no doubt,' said I, 'that you would have obtained every voice, if there were not a definite clause in the constitution to prevent your being chosen. But our social covenant absolutely requires a member of the Directory to be forty years old.'

'And you yourself would hold strictly to that statutory arrangement?'

'In my eyes, general, nothing could excuse an infringement of it.'

'President, you are clinging to the letter that kills!'

THE COUP D'ÉTAT

The ablest of his fellow-conspirators was Talleyrand, who had lately been dismissed from the Foreign Office. It was he who convinced Bonaparte of the folly of despising Sieyès. For the abbé, as a political theorist, was himself a declared enemy to the Constitution, and he had a considerable following, which included a fellow-director, Roger-Ducos. The addition of Barras's voice (without his knowledge) gave a pseudo-majority of Directors. It only remained to transfer the legislative Councils (the Ancients and the Five Hundred) to Saint-Cloud, out of the way of Paris and insurrection. This was done on the pretext of a 'Jacobin plot'. At Saint-Cloud, it was thought, the legislators would be easy to handle, and would vote as required: especially since Lucien Bonaparte was chairman of the Five Hundred.

The 18th of Brumaire (9th November, 1799) passed off without a ripple. But the 19th, at Saint-Cloud, was another story. The Five Hundred actually turned on Bonaparte, with catcalls, physical assault, and cries of 'Outlaw!', and he had to be 'rescued'. And in spite of the lavish distribution of money, and the exertions of Lucien Bonaparte, the coup d'état would have failed, but for the bayonets of the Grenadiers.

The many accounts of this famous day are all more or less at one. Bonaparte's confusion in face of the assemblies: incoherence of his language, jeers of his comrades—'A nice figure you cut!' Augereau flung at him. For admirers of Napoleon, it was always to be a painful memory. So it was with Thibaudeau, *an ex-Conventionnel and future State councillor and 'grand prefect' of the Empire: also, a warmly devoted chronicler.*

On the 18th of Brumaire, at seven in the morning, the Council of Ancients met in extraordinary session, issued a decree transferring the legislative body to the commune of Saint-Cloud, entrusted General Bonaparte with its execution and gave him command of the armed forces. He walked up to the bar of the Council and took the oath. In the gallery there were only a handful of spectators. A few quite small groups had formed in the Tuileries gardens.

This first act of the drama went off as easily as possible. It was neither booed nor cheered. A step or two from the palace, no one knew it was happening.

On the 19th I went to Saint-Cloud, to observe the sequel and denouement of the play of which I had seen the first act at the Council of Ancients. A mere onlooker with no personal stake, I listened and watched. In the courtyards full of troops and general officers, and inside the château, there were many sightseers like myself, awaiting the issue of the event in store. Most of them had no idea what was planned. Those who were in the secret spoke of it only in vague terms. They were going to save the Republic, according to some; to destroy it, said others. The atmosphere was highly excited, and this excitement increased with waiting.

At last the Councils began their session. I went back and forth, to hear the speeches and see what would come of the debates. I followed Bonaparte, I heard him address the Council of Ancients. I shall not retrace the different scenes; they are described faithfully in the *Moniteur*. When Bonaparte was driven from the Council of Five Hundred, his escort of Grenadiers fell back in disorder, carrying him from the hall and back to the staircase, by which they returned to the courtyard. All this was the work of a moment. In the lobby of the Council-chamber, such was the confusion that some of the Grenadiers lost their busbies and their arms. To avoid being wounded, smothered or swept away in a retreat very like a rout, I climbed on a big table which served me and several others as a rampart.

I followed Bonaparte to the courtyard. There was some confusion. He was, they say, gloomy and nonplussed. It was dark, and I could not get near enough to study his expression. He was on horseback. Several generals appeared to be torn by indecision, and I thought some of the men were shaken. But presently the first moment of stupor was succeeded by a burst of shouting. This was in response to Bonaparte, who was addressing the troops. Then, with the arrival and forceful eloquence of his brother Lucien, all hesitation was dispelled and each took fresh heart.

I returned to the Council of Five Hundred. Instead of taking vigorous action against Bonaparte on his repulse from the hall, they had been wasting time in vain threats, in trifling and unseasonable debates. They were still wasting it. What they needed was one of those commanding speakers whose voices can rouse and control assemblies. But there was no such man in the Council. With a decree of outlawry, Augereau and Jourdan, who were at hand, and Bernadotte, who was privily awaiting the outcome, would probably have declared themselves, and might have carried with them the assembly's guard of grenadiers, which had not the spirit of the army, and shaken the other troops.

Thus the issue of the day hung on a decree of one line, or a dagger-thrust. The Council's idleness and improvidence were the more baffling, in that it soon learnt of the intention to dissolve it by force. The deputies thought it majestic to sit in their curule chairs and await death, or rather the bayonets that were shortly to turn them out. They did not wait long. I heard the drums beating the charge, I saw the soldiers breaking into the sanctuary of the laws, the spectators making off through a cloud of dust, and most of the deputies withdrawing, before a soldiery deaf to their protests, by the windows which were on garden level.

With this violent dissolution, the question was decided in Bonaparte's favour.

Morally and physically exhausted, I returned to Paris. The road was thronged with carriages taking the deputies home. On the way I thought of the sorry spectacle I had just witnessed. I had neither liking nor esteem for the Directory, I was far from edified by the conduct of the Councils and the whole attitude of the government which had just collapsed. Yet there was no blinking the fact that its defeat entailed the downfall of the constitution of which I had been a founder, and dealt a mortal blow to the representative system. As a Frenchman and a citizen, I was shocked by the ease with which it had been possible to overthrow in an instant a building erected at great cost, at the price of so much labour and sacrifice. The scene at Saint-Cloud struck me as even more ignoble than the shameful revolutions of the seraglio, or at the court of the Tsars.

THE BEGINNINGS OF THE CONSULATE

About thirty deputies, rounded up on the highway and in the cafés and restaurants of Saint-Cloud, were made to vote the establishment of a consular commission, which would rule from now on. The Directory was no more.

The Consulate took shape. The three provisional consuls were Sieyès, Roger-Ducos and Bonaparte (in that order). Sieyès got to work on his Constitution, a complex bureaucratic machine, which Bonaparte promptly simplified into a near-absolutism. The First Consul was supreme; the two others were otiose. A few weeks later, Sieyès preferred a gilded retirement (considerable capital, country estate, etc.) to the impossible task of collaboration. Roger-Ducos went with him, and they were succeeded by Cambacérès and Lebrun. Bonaparte then assumed the title of First Consul.

He had been installed in the Luxembourg since the 20th of Brumaire (11th November, 1799). He was to remain there a hundred days, trying his hand at dictatorship, but with infinite circumspection. In law, the consuls were officials of a democracy, chosen for ten years, though re-eligible. The time for frankness had not yet come.

Bourrienne *had the only complete view of this transition phase.*

The most important transactions of the Consulate were confined to his closet in the Luxembourg.

At the Luxembourg his principal occupation, next to the business involved in setting up the consular government, and perhaps even before such business, was the quest for money. He also kept up a very brisk correspondence with foreign courts, to engage some of them to make peace, so that it might be easier to fall on the others.

Bonaparte had his quarters on the ground floor of the little Luxembourg. His closet was near a hidden staircase leading to the first floor, where Josephine was installed. I had the apartments above.

After breakfast, which was at ten o'clock, Bonaparte would have a brief chat with those who had shared the meal: that is to say his aides-de-camp, persons he had invited, and myself, who never left him.

Among his most welcome callers were his brothers Joseph and Lucien. He conversed familiarly with them.

Cambacérès often called on him about noon and stayed a long time, often a whole hour. Visits from Lebrun were rare.

When Bonaparte rose from the breakfast table, bidding good-day to Josephine and her daughter Hortense, he would nearly always add:

'Come along, Bourrienne, to work.'

After the morning levee, I remained with Bonaparte, either reading to him or writing to his dictation. Or he might attend the Council, which he did three or four times a week.

On leaving the Council, he would return to his closet singing, heaven knows how tunelessly! He would look over the work he had ordered, sign a few letters, stretch himself in his armchair and read the letters of yesterday and the pamphlets of the day.

When there was no council he remained in his closet, chatting with me, singing all the time, cutting up the arm of his chair as usual, sometimes reminding one of a little boy. Then, suddenly waking up, he would outline the plan of a public building to be erected, or dictate vast matters which have astonished or terrified the world.

Five o'clock was the dinner hour. After dinner the First Consul would go up to Josephine's apartments, where he was in the habit of receiving the ministers, and always welcomed the minister for foreign affairs, especially now that the portfolio had been restored to M. de Talleyrand.

At midnight, and often earlier, he would give the signal for retirement by saying abruptly:

'Let's go to bed.'

Bonaparte had beautiful hands, and set great store by this beauty. So he took particular care of them, and would sometimes eye them complacently as he talked.

When he was walking about, either alone or with a companion, in his apartments or his gardens, he held himself slightly bent, his hands crossed behind his back. He often made an involuntary movement of the right shoulder, raising it a little, and at the same time jerking his mouth from left to right. If one had not known that these two muscular movements were only a habit, one might have supposed them to be convulsive.

When walking with anyone he treated familiarly, he was accustomed to take his arm and lean on it.

Bonaparte often said to me:

'You see, Bourrienne, how abstemious and slender I am. Well, nothing will get it out of my head that at forty I shall become a great eater, and that I shall get very fat. I foresee that my constitution will change, and yet I take plenty of exercise. But there you are; it's a presentiment, it is bound to happen.'

This idea worried him a great deal.

For his bath he had an absolute passion, which he regarded as a need. I have known him regularly spend two hours in it. Meanwhile I would be reading him extracts from the newspapers or some new pamphlets, for he would have liked to hear everything, know everything, see everything for himself. All the time he was in his bath he was constantly turning on the hot-water tap, raising the temperature to a point where I would find myself enveloped in steam so thick that I could not see to go on reading. Then there was nothing for it but to open the door.

If his enemies have sought to stigmatise him by imputing to him a grave periodic infirmity, his flatterers, evidently from an idea that sleep is incompatible with greatness, have talked just as falsely of his alleged sleepless nights.

Bonaparte kept others awake, but he slept, and slept well. He had told me to wake him at seven o'clock every morning. I was therefore the first to enter his room. But when I woke him, often enough he would say to me, still half asleep:

'Oh, Bourrienne, do let me sleep a little longer!'

When there was nothing very urgent, I did not return till eight. In general, he slept seven hours of the twenty-four and had a short nap in the afternoon.

As soon as Bonaparte was up, his valet would shave him and arrange his hair. While he was being shaved I read him the newspapers, always starting with the *Moniteur*. He gave his attention only to the German and English newspapers.

'Go on, go on,' he would say when I was reading the French ones, 'I know all this, they only say what I choose.'

I was often amazed that the valet did not cut him during these readings, for whenever he heard anything striking he would turn sharply towards me.

When Bonaparte's toilet was finished, and he made it with great care, being immaculately neat, we went down to his closet together. There he would sign the comments on important petitions of which I had made an abstract the day before.

Bonaparte had two genuine passions: glory and war. He was never more cheerful than in camp, never moodier than in repose.

Bonaparte said to me more than once:

'A great reputation is a great noise. The more one makes the further it carries. Laws, institutions, monuments, nations, all have their day. But noise remains, and resounds in other ages.'

This was one of his favourite ideas.

'My power,' he would say again, 'derives from my glory, and my glory from the victories I have won. My authority would collapse if I failed to base it on more glory and fresh victories. Conquest has made me what I am, conquest alone can maintain me.'

Bonaparte was not inclined by temperament to think well of human nature. He despised it the more, the more he saw of it. He would often say:

'There are two levers to move mankind: fear and interest.'

It was one of Bonaparte's greatest misfortunes not to believe in friendship or experience the need to love, which is the sweetest sentiment given to man. How often I have heard him say:

'Friendship is only a word. I care for nobody.'

His grave insults, his sharp apostrophes, his bursts of rage, all these were calculated and prepared in advance. When he had to show anyone his displeasure, the presence of witnesses encouraged him. Then his language was always harsh, pungent, humiliating.

When he was intending to make a scene with someone in private, he always wanted a third party as witness. I often noticed how it emboldened him. And in fact, if one were alone with him and understood his ways, by dint of great coolness, frankness and impassiveness one was certain to get the better of him. When he was expecting someone, he would tell me beforehand:

'Bourrienne, you will stay.'

And if anyone were announced that he was not expecting, such as a minister or general, as I made to withdraw he would say in an undertone:

'Stay where you are.'

Bonaparte had some curious habits and tastes. Whenever he was crossed or absorbed in some unpleasant idea, he used to hum what was not a tune or anything like one, his voice, as I said before, being so unmusical. He would sit down at his desk, and then tilt his chair till I frequently had to warn him he might fall over backwards.

In this posture he would vent his ill-humour on the right arm of the chair, mutilating it with his penknife, which he used for no other purpose.

Politeness to women was not one of Bonaparte's habitual traits. He rarely had anything pleasant to say to them. Indeed he was often uncivil to them, or would say the most outrageous things. It might be:

'Goodness, what red arms you have!'

Or:

'How frightful your hair looks! Who made such a frump of you?'

Or again:

'That's a very dirty gown you have on! Do you never wear any other? I've seen you in that twenty times.'

Never did Bonaparte say: 'I was in the wrong.'

MALMAISON IN ITS HEYDAY

While her husband was in Egypt, Josephine had bought the château of
Malmaison as a love-nest. On his return, Bonaparte stayed there and
took a liking to it. For several years he was to spend there, first his Sat-
urdays and Sundays, then several days a week, and finally weeks on end.

He was still young (about thirty), and his suite of aides-de-camp,
friendly generals and their wives was also very young. They played
there like children. Bonaparte led the life of a wealthy landowner. To
one of his associates, Roederer, he said outright:

'After being in so many wars, willy-nilly one is bound to have some
fortune. I have 80 or 100,000 francs a year [thirty of our millions], a
town house and a country house.'

The chronicler of Malmaison and its simple gaiety is the Duchess of
Abrantès, *in those days not a duchess but plain Mme Junot. Bonaparte's*
aide-de-camp had just married her.

On Wednesdays there was an almost formal dinner at Malmaison. The guests were the second consul (the third scarcely
ever left home, and led a very retired life), councillors of state,
ministers, a few generals in particular esteem, and women of spot-
less reputation. For at that time, Napoleon was rigid in his choice
of society for Mme Bonaparte.

Mlle de Beauharnais and Mme Bonaparte had forewarned me
that there would be theatricals, and that I should have to play the
soubrettes. Junot was our leading talent, along with Bourrienne
and Eugène de Beauharnais.

'Citizen Cambacérès,' said the First Consul one evening, 'you
ought to join our troupe of young men. You would play the
heavy fathers.'

'Don't imagine you are joking, citizen consul,' returned Cambacérès, 'I have appeared, and I may add not without success, as
Montauciel in the *Deserter*.'

'Really!' said the First Consul. 'Well, it proves one should
never say: This is impossible.'

We had the honour of being the sole actors on the Malmaison
stage, and at the outset this had its pains. It was no trifling matter
to be playing not only before three hundred persons, but before
the First Consul. For my part, I confess that I would rather have
had the audience doubled. Indeed it is rather curious that while I

was unquestionably bolder with him than anyone else at Malmaison, and readier to answer him back, sometimes even too smartly, yet I could not endure his strictures on my rendering of a part, even though quite convinced he was wrong.

Dinner was at six o'clock. On fine days, the First Consul ordered it to be served in the park. We were not long at table, and the First Consul thought the dinner protracted if it took half an hour.

When he was in a good humour, when the weather was fine, and he was able to spare a few minutes from the unbroken toil which was then killing him, he used to join us at prisoner's base. He cheated, as he did at *reversis*, for instance, making us laugh like maniacs. On these occasions Napoleon took off his coat and ran like a hare, or rather like the gazelle to which he would give all the snuff in his box, telling it to run at us—and the wretched beast used to tear our gowns and very often our legs.

MARENGO, OR A WAR FOR DICTATORSHIP

On his return from Egypt, when President Gohier was talking of peace in the near future, Bonaparte had objected:

'Would you be in favour of a general peace? You would be wrong, president. A republic should make only partial peace. One must always have some little war in reserve, to keep up the military spirit.'

However, he did not make war simply for war's sake. Over and above the reason advanced to Gohier, he had also made it an axiom that war pays. Relatively, that is to say in the short run, this was true. Now, at the beginning of the Consulate, he was chafing for absolute power, but could not assume it, because the Treasury was empty.

It was from Ouvrard he sought supplies for the army he was to lead against Austria, which would secure him the victory of Marengo (14th June, 1800), in other words the dictatorship. Ouvrard undertook the task, in spite of Bonaparte's former treatment of him; he had had the financier thrown into prison for refusing him twelve million.

Ouvrard has left his own account of their dealings (to which one may add that the banker had succeeded with Mme Tallien, when the general had not).

My fortune was made, and Bonaparte [*just after the 13th of Vendémiaire*] had his to make. Already impatient of superiority in any form, he could ill disguise the chagrin he felt at this difference of standing. Since then I have had only too much cause to perceive that neither the First Consul nor the Emperor had forgotten anything of this first impression.

When the revolution of the 18th Brumaire was accomplished, Barras retired to Grosbois, doubtful whether the pledges made him would not be broken. I went to see him. I found him still alone, deserted by his courtiers, on his guard, well armed. My visit to Grosbois reached the ears of the First Consul. The touchiness he felt at my position led him to ascribe a political motive to a step which was one of mere duty and politeness.

A few days later, the First Consul sent for me to ask for a loan of twelve million. The state of my affairs would have allowed me to accede to his request. However, I refused. He convoked a meeting of bankers, to whom he made the same proposal, with no better success. Whether because he viewed this outcome as a sort of conspiracy, or because want of money, at such a decisive juncture, upset some of his plans, his attitude to me became hostile.

When, shortly afterwards, I applied for payment of the ten million I had advanced to the Directory, my demand had the air of a new offence against his authority.

[*It was at this point that Bonaparte had him imprisoned.*]

The First Consul's most intimate advisers remonstrated with him, and when M. Collot, now director of the mint, whom I did not know, ventured to say: 'It's a bad start, general, to unsettle everyone like this', Bonaparte revealed the motives of his conduct in these words:

'A man who has thirty million he doesn't care about is too dangerous to my position.'

Bonaparte's vanity was keenly wounded when he found out that I had lent Mme Bonaparte certain sums of money during the campaign in Egypt, for Malmaison and for her personal expenses. This mortified the First Consul's pride, and his ill-will towards me became more pronounced.

The scope and prosperity of my affairs had turned my offices into a kind of ministry; the legal department was entrusted to M. Cambacérès, later arch-chancellor of the Empire.

I asked M. de Talleyrand to secure me a passport from the Consul. But instead of granting it, Bonaparte a few days later instructed the minister of war, General Berthier, to bring me before the council.

'Well, M. Ouvrard,' said he, 'will you give me twelve million?'
'General,' I replied, 'I should like the four million owing to me.'
We were, as may be seen, at cross-purposes.

However, after a long explanation and a great many figures, he handed me an order for four million.

Beguiled by this show of fair dealing, by his promises, and perhaps yet more by my taste for large operations, I made myself responsible for his services, every branch of which was at a standstill. An irretrievable blunder, which I should not have committed if I had then heard of his reply to M. Collot.

In this way Ouvrard promoted Bonaparte's campaign of 1800. Yet the news of Marengo did not, according to the Marquise de la Tour du Pin, *excite the expected raptures.*

There was one thing by which my husband and I had been greatly struck: the coldness with which the Paris crowds, so easily fired, received the news of the battle of Marengo. In company with M. de Poix, we went to see the 14th of July celebrations in the Champ de Mars. After the review of the national guard and the garrison, a little squad of a hundred men in dirty and tattered clothes, some with arms in a sling, others with heads swathed in bandages, carrying the standards and colours taken from the Austrians at Marengo, entered the enclosure. I was expecting frantic and well-justified applause. On the contrary: not a cheer, and very few signs of joy. We were no less surprised than indignant.

THIRD STAGE

From Marengo to Austerlitz

(1800–1805)

Given five hundred thousand men, one can do anything.

NAPOLEON

THE FIRST CONSUL AT THE THEATRE

Bonaparte was indifferent to the lack of enthusiasm. He had gained his point; rich, and at the head of a victorious army, he could now dictate his orders. His latest victory, though secured by a miracle (but this was not public knowledge), magnified his fame. From several countries of Europe travellers were hastening to Paris to view this soldier of fortune who had so thrillingly made good. He had long since quitted the Luxembourg for the Tuileries. Soon he was to adopt Saint-Cloud, Compiègne, Fontainebleau, the Elysée, Rambouillet, etc.

The German Kotzebue, some of whose plays had already been given in Paris, was among those who admired him during his consulate.

On reaching Paris I felt the liveliest curiosity to see the hero of the age. For some days I was unable to gratify my wish. At last, one evening, at the Théâtre Français, the piece was interrupted by loud and general applause, and all eyes turned to Bonaparte's box, which was a stage-box.

From my own, unluckily, he could not be seen, but I hastened to make use of the privilege very kindly granted me by the directors of the theatre, and flew round to the stage, where (from the wings facing his box) I might survey this astonishing man at my ease.

Already I had more than once availed myself of this permission without let or hindrance. What, then, was my amazement to find the first three wings filled with consular guards, who were turning away all comers. Not even the maid of Mlle Duchesnois, who was playing that day, could get leave to pass. However, through the intercession of MM Lafon and Monvel, who were present, the order was revoked, both for me and the maid.

I am at a loss to account for this rigorous interdiction. Merely as a security measure, I should think it inadequate. Perhaps Bonaparte dislikes being looked full in the face? He may be right, but he should inure himself, for it is a thing inseparable from the position he occupies. But the order may not have come directly from him. Perhaps he even objected to it? For since then I cannot remember seeing any guards in the wings.

At the play he maintains a grave and calm attitude, and gives no sign of approval or disapproval. He appears very attentive, and does not address any of his suite, who stand respectfully behind his armchair. The pit never fails to greet him with clamorous applause, but seems otherwise to disregard him, and does not surrender the right to hiss and to make a noise. I have even been present when a new piece, of which Bonaparte was attending the first performance, could not be played to the end.

He sits through the whole uproar with perfect calm, doubtless remembering that the Parisians, like the Romans, are quite content as long as they get their *Panem & Circenses*.

THE CARROUSEL THEATRE

The crowd had been untouched by the sight of the Marengo wounded, because it hated the war. But in time of peace the Parisians were always thrilled by troops marching past. During his consulate, therefore, Bonaparte multiplied these parades, gave them an impressive setting, and always commanded them in person, in the Place du Carrousel. All observers are unanimous. 'One of the most amazing sights in the world,' said the Comte de Mérode-Westerloo.

Kotzebue thought likewise, and was able to watch the whole parade from a window of the Tuileries.

I have twice been present at the grand parade, which is just now one of the most curious sights of Paris. It is truly an imposing spectacle. I was stationed with several others on the first floor of the palace, in a large room through which Bonaparte was to pass.

Soon he appeared, in a group of generals and aides-de-camp all magnificently dressed, while Bonaparte wore the plainest of uniforms, without embroidery, without any glitter, and a hat with no braid or plume. He went quickly by, a little cane in his hand. At the foot of the perron he mounted a dapple-grey horse and rode along the ranks, attended by a brilliant crowd. Having inspected the infantry, he entered the Place du Carrousel to review the cavalry.

In this square, besides the troops, there was a host of spectators, and, as far as I could see, anyone might approach him. I have often heard of the great precautions taken for his safety, but today at least there was no such thing, for as he passed through the crowd his life would have been at the mercy of a determined villain.

When he rode back into the courtyard I saw him stopped several times, even by women, who actually went right up to him, spoke to him and held out petitions. He took these, and I thought handed them to his aides-de-camp. I saw one of these suppliants (that is, unless my eyes deceived me) lay hold of his horse's bridle as she offered her petition. Bonaparte took it, opened and quickly read it, then made the woman a short answer.

Throughout this review his faithful mameluke, superbly attired, was not close behind him, as we are so often told in Germany, but merely in his train, behind the generals.

The hero came back and stopped near the entrance to the palace, a few paces from where I was. Here the Turkish ambassador presented him with two horses from the Sultan. No doubt they were fine ones. But they were screened by large caparisons richly embroidered with gold and pearls, which prevented the eye from distinguishing their shape. That they were frisky and spirited I can bear witness, for one of the Turkish riders who were showing them off in the square was very soon unseated and thrown to the ground. But he seemed accustomed to the mishap, for he was immediately on his feet again and vaulted lightly back into the saddle.

Bonaparte, who, during the display, took many pinches of snuff from a very plain tortoise-shell box, did not honour this gift with much attention. He scarcely threw it an occasional, unmoved glance. On the other hand, he seemed greatly occupied with the troops, and made each regiment perform several evolutions.

RECEPTION OF THE DIPLOMATIC CORPS

After the parade Bonaparte usually received the diplomatic corps, together with the distinguished foreigners. Kotzebue was of the number.

On the consul's return, and before he entered the building, we went quickly downstairs and into the ambassadors' hall, or rather quite a plain drawing-room which is so called. There we found the diplomatic corps, along with all the foreigners who were to be presented.

Just then the doors of the audience-hall—which has its finest adornment in picturesque groups of flags—were thrown open.

Bonaparte was between the second and third consuls, who wore scarlet coats richly embroidered, and cut in the French style. The chief justice was also present, in his robes which strongly suggest a cardinal's.

As soon as the circle was formed, Bonaparte stepped forward, addressing first the electoral prince of Wurtemberg and then, in order of rank, the ambassadors and ministers of the different courts, who presented their countrymen with the same ceremonial used for presenting foreigners to kings and princes.

None of the pictures I have seen of him, whether in Germany or France, is a perfect likeness, and most are not like at all. David's famous painting is among the latter. Isabey is the one who has hit him off best. He has painted him full-length. But what seems even more like him is his effigy on the new five-franc pieces of the year XII. Whenever I see one, the consul himself rises before me.

Recently he has put on weight, which does not become a man like Bonaparte. For one is so accustomed to thinking of him as pure genius that the imagination flatly refuses him any larger casing of matter than is required to be the instrument of mind. I wager that no one can fancy Bonaparte grown stout. And yet he is stoutish, nowadays. And perhaps he looks more so, because of his small stature? His profile is that of an ancient Roman, grave, noble, expressive.

If he were always silent, this gravity would have something cold in it, and a frightening air of sternness. But the moment he speaks, a kindly smile imparts a gracious line to his mouth, and inspires confidence. It was exactly the same with Paul I, whose graciousness was irresistible.

Having mentioned Paul I, I cannot omit to say that the First Consul spoke to me of that unfortunate monarch, and candidly evinced his regard for him. He said, among other things, that Paul I had an effervescent brain, but an excellent heart.

A few steps from me was the American envoy, to whom, if I understood him aright, he spoke of his country's trade. In this connection, the envoy expressed a slight wish for peace. The First Consul gave a shrug of the shoulders, as if to say: 'It's not my fault!'

He talked very wittily, easily and fluently on all manner of subjects, and when he came up to me for the second time, the theatre was again spoken of.

He bestowed on the Germans the epithet of 'melancholy', and said of the 'pathetic' drama that it encroached rather too far on the domain of French tragedy, and that he was not fond of shedding tears.

Bonaparte, having made his round, went back to his place between the two consuls, who had been standing motionless all this while. Then he bowed, and this was the signal for departure, but he did not move till the whole diplomatic corps had withdrawn.

DINNER WITH THE FIRST CONSUL

Another foreign visitor was Elisabeth Petrovna Divov, *née Buturlin, wife of an officer in the horse guards, chamberlain to the Tsar and director of the French theatrical company at the Hermitage.*

In her eyes, the parade was 'sublime'—but to be asked to dinner was very Heaven.

I was presented at the Tuileries drawing-room, before the dinner to which my husband, my son and I were invited. It was at half-past five that Count Morkov introduced me. The First Consul came up and said that he knew I had come from Berlin, that he was much beholden to me for the letters I had given Frenchmen who were going to Russia, for my kindness to the unhappy Frenchmen living in Russia as émigrés, and that he should be charmed to see me prolong my stay in France. Among other things, I shall never forget that he said:

'Don't you think, madam, that the dancing is better here than in Berlin? If I may venture to say so, our young ladies and our young gentlemen dance too well.'

I laughed heartily.

The hall used for drawing-rooms in the Tuileries is enormous, and it is at the far end, near a fireplace, that my dear, kind Mme Bonaparte sits in an armchair. When I entered the room, the prefect of the palace took my hand and led me straight up to her. The generals, senators, etc. (all those connected with the government) were arriving with their wives and conducting them straight to Mme Bonaparte.

When, at six o'clock, the door opened and an usher cried: 'The

First Consul!', I can safely say that if a fly had crossed the room, it would have been heard.

Everyone rose to greet him, and it was at that moment that I was presented to him. He spent a few minutes chatting with me most kindly, and all went in to dinner. Each gentleman gave his arm to a lady. Joseph Bonaparte was my partner, and I was placed between him and his younger brother Lucien, whom I found by his conversation to be excessively agreeable and witty. I was very well entertained, for though Joseph is not such a brilliant talker as Lucien, he is very agreeable, sweet-tempered and polite, and people may say what they choose, I shall always say he is a charming man in society.

In less than an hour, the whole dinner was over.

The First Consul says himself:

'Those who want a quick meal should dine with me. A good meal, with the second consul. And a bad one, with the third consul.'

Then we returned to the same drawing-room to take coffee.

The First Consul, at table, had behind him his faithful Mameluke whom he brought from Egypt, and was served entirely by him. On one side of him was the Papal nuncio, on the other a French minister. At dinner he spoke only to his neighbours.

A DIFFERENT VIEW

Foreigners met him when he was 'on show', as it were. On Frenchmen who knew him better, he did not invariably make such a good impression.

L.-A. Pichon, later French chargé d'affaires in the United States, consul-general, councillor of state, and chief commissioner of the West-phalian Treasury, is distinctly hostile. It should be noted, however, that all the sayings and characteristics he mentions are attested by many witnesses.

The trait that first strikes one in his character is that violent, saturnine, fortune-hunting temper which creates usurpers and raises them up amid the turmoil of revolutions.

In Napoleon this temper never relaxed for a moment, and a thousand sallies of the violent gusto which never forsook him show the degree to which he was constantly inspired by it. These sallies, broadcast by flattery, were presented to the stupefied nation as sublimely great, when they were only revelations of the most sickening ferocity or the most insulting contempt for mankind and for his contemporaries.

One day he said to an admirer who, in Italy, had made certain payments out of army funds, and was pleading orders from the Directory:

'Don't you know that there's not one of those directors or ministers but would kiss my boot for twenty thousand francs?'

Before some of the tribunes, when the tribunate was opposing the establishment of special courts:

'What should stop me from having them all flung into the Seine? And all Paris would applaud.'

To someone who pointed out that public opinion would be against a measure:

'I shall wall up your public opinion when I choose.'

He took pleasure in mixing irony with violence.

'Are you not afraid,' said Lucien, 'that France may rebel against your shameful abuse of power?'

'Never fear,' he replied, 'I shall bleed her so white that she'll be incapable of it for a long time to come.'

The most ominous of his sayings:

'Europe is an old, rotten whore. I have eight hundred thousand men. I shall do what I please with her.'

All his speeches had their source in a basic vanity which, with so much power, was bound to produce the most fatal results. He set up to know everything. Was he not encouraged by legal experts in the council of state to go through the farce of debating the civil code? This vanity laid him open to flatterers, to prompters of every rank, who managed to engross him. It is inconceivable how they cried him up. They went so far as to tell him, in an official report, that the Treasury owed him the introduction of book-keeping by double entry, and that he had decided on this after mature and expert consideration: which was certainly carrying flattery to the point of burlesque.

It had become a maxim that everything was Napoleon's idea, when as a rule nothing was his idea. Each was indulging the oppressions and tyrannies of his neighbour. And thus the councils were reduced to a comedy staged by the ministers among themselves, of the ministers against Napoleon, so that, like a fiery charger made to exhaust itself by pawing the sand, he would be worn out after a debate in which his servants, having reached agreement in advance by dint of small parlour-compromises, sported very gravely with his absurd eagerness to hear and sift everything.

VOLNEY KICKED OUT

Some of his partisans were breaking away: like Volney, at the time of the discussions preceding the Concordat.

The learned Volney was one of Bonaparte's oldest friends. They had been on intimate terms in Corsica when Bonaparte was still a young lieutenant. At that time one could say anything to him. But times had changed. The breach is described by François-Yves Besnard.

It seems that the First Consul had formed a very high opinion of Volney, since Volney was the first to whom he offered the ministry of the interior. Volney declined it, after the twenty-four hours he had asked to be allowed for consideration. At the time his refusal made no change in the regard of the one or the devotion of the other, who was immediately appointed a senator. For more than a year, Volney was constantly seen at the Tuileries and at Malmaison, and indeed fairly often dined at these residences.

When Bonaparte, discussing with Volney the Concordat of 1801, said it was his intention to restore Catholic worship and to pay the clergy, Volney strongly condemned this scheme, declaring that it would be enough to restore general freedom of worship, and leave each sect the responsibility of maintaining and paying its own ministers.

'But,' said Bonaparte, 'France is calling on me to do both.'

'I see,' returned Volney (perhaps with that supercilious air which was not unwonted), 'and if France called on you to restore the Bourbons, would you oblige?'

At these words Bonaparte was beside himself, and, yielding to one of the passions in which he is said to have indulged fairly frequently, he struck Volney in the belly with his foot, hard enough to knock him over. Then, after ringing for someone to pick him up, he coldly gave orders for him to be seen to his carriage.

Next day Volney sent in his resignation from the senate, and, though the First Consul had the good feeling not to accept it, they have never subsequently been reconciled. Volney's philosophy inclined him to liberal ideas, and he took a dislike to the course of the consular government, as he saw it moving further away from them.

'What can one think of a man,' he once said to me, 'who asserts that with money men can be had, and with men money can be had!'

THE COUNCIL OF STATE

The consular machine of government was made up of four assemblies: the senate, the legislative body, the tribunate and the council of state. The first two were paid to be dumb, the third was to be suppressed for its independence. The only one that mattered to Bonaparte was the council of state. There, throughout the consulate and then during the Empire, he was regularly seen and heard. The councillors were of his own choice, and it was they who elaborated or completed all the great consular undertakings. The council had no seat of its own; it met wherever the Consul was residing.

State councillor Pelet (de la Lozère), *who made a collection of Napoleon's utterances from 1800 to 1814, gives a general view of him at these sessions.*

Napoleon sometimes had himself announced in advance. At other times he would appear unexpectedly. The drum beating the general salute on the Tuileries staircase announced his arrival. He was ushered in by his chamberlain, and followed by the aide-de-camp on duty. Both stationed themselves behind him.

His armchair, raised one step above the floor, was at the end of the room. On his right and left were the princes and great dignitaries, and before him, on either side, the long tables at which the councillors of state were seated.

Napoleon's chair kept its place even when he was in the field. The arch-chancellor, on his right, presided in his absence.

Business made little headway when Napoleon was in the chair, since he would now and then fall into deep abstraction, during which the debate languished, or embark on political divagations foreign to the subject. But these divagations were highly interesting, as symptoms of his state of mind, or as a disclosure of his policy and his plans.

The meetings, made longer by Napoleon's digressions, were never too long for him. At Saint-Cloud he often kept us from nine in the morning till five in the afternoon, with a quarter of an hour's break, during which he retired to his apartments and we into the great gallery, where a snack was waiting. The arch-chancellor had always to let him know when it was too late in the day for the session to be continued, and he chaffed him about these warnings, affecting to think them premature.

Princes of his family who were in Paris attended the meetings. He also admitted foreign princes who were visiting him. For quite a while the princes of Baden and Bavaria could be seen, as though dispatched to the great man's school to learn the art of reigning.

Woe betide him who arrived when the session had begun! The door was barred, and there was no further access, either for prince or subject, without special authorisation.

Anyone might ask leave to speak. Napoleon often called upon others, whose opinions he wished to know. Speeches had to be simple and straightforward.

The council of state had its most arduous days during the con-sulate and the beginning of the Empire.

The Duc de Broglie, another councillor of state, was more struck by the incorrectness of the master's language.

As a rule, Napoleon would preside at two of the three weekly meetings. He would arrive about an hour after the opening, that is, about half-past one, interrupting the debate; there was a copy of the agenda on his desk, and he would call the item on which it suited him to have a discussion.

He was a patient and attentive listener. He was a ready and frequent inquirer, mostly interrogating Regnault de Saint-Jean d'Angély, Defermon, Treilhard and above all the arch-chancellor. When the discussion had lasted some time, he would intervene. He spoke at great length, with little sequence in his ideas, and very incorrectly, harking back again and again to the same turns of phrase, and in all humility I am bound to confess that I never noticed, in his rambling and often vulgar eloquence, those high qualities of which he has given proof in the memoirs dictated by him to Generals Bertrand and Montholon.

However, I must admit that at the time of which I am speaking, at the summit of his power, an object of adoration and almost of idolatry, he was far from applying to public business that watchful and potent activity which had marked the early days of his reign. The official records of the discussion on the civil code do him more honour than the meetings at which I was present, and the contemptible servility of the admiration roused by his lightest words may have made me unjust to him.

The solemnity of these council meetings was not always unbroken. In the papers of Réal, *councillor of state and one of the highest police officials of the consulate and Empire, we get a glimpse of the lighter side.*

At the council of state he had in front of him a desk with one drawer. At the end of the session, as he got up, he would shut this drawer and turn the key. No one ever opened it in his absence. When he was not presiding at the council, his place remained empty.

He used to come in with a snuff-box in his hand, and, as soon as the chamberlain on duty, who was standing behind his chair, perceived this snuff-box to be exhausted, he would slip him another. But that was not enough. If Napoleon heard the sound of a box being opened somewhere in the room, he would turn his eyes to what he thought was the point of origin, and make a sign with his hand. The usher immediately went after the box and brought it to him. After helping himself twice or thrice, he would fling it on his desk or, more often, into his drawer. In that case the snuff-box was for ever lost to its owner.

Once informed, the councillors of state avoided the trap. They had their council snuff-boxes. These were of cardboard, and when they incurred confiscation the loss did not exceed fifteen or twenty sous.

Several members of council had the habit, fairly common with men absorbed in thought, of scribbling as they listened to the debate.

If one of them chanced to turn out something really odd, he would pass the paper to his neighbour. Napoleon often caught sight of this byplay, and would sign for the paper to be brought to him, throw it an absent glance, and crumple it up with a shrug of the shoulders.

Once only, he said to M. de L . . ., whose masterpiece he had just attached, and who, on a point of legislation, was expressing himself rather obscurely:

'All this, sir, does not prove that you will ever become a famous artist.'

In order to avoid any disturbance of his habits, he had contrived not to form any. He had no fixed hours either for his meals, for going to bed or for getting up. If he awoke in the night he would get up, call for his secretary and set to work.

But nature is not to be defrauded, and the next day, overcome with fatigue, he would fall asleep wherever he was.

A good many times it befell him to drop off in the middle of a discussion in the council of state.

When that happened, the members would quietly withdraw.

One day, when the meeting had already lasted two hours, he fell asleep in his chair. As usual, the councillors went away.

He remained fast asleep for five hours.

On returning to his apartments, he found Josephine surprised at this long delay, and curious to know what the meeting had been about.

'It was about,' he replied, only half awake, 'it was about . . . seven hours.'

HESITANCY OF A FUTURE MINISTER

In the council of state Bonaparte's explosions were rare. In the council of ministers they were habitual. Those who got a glimpse of them went away dumbfounded.

Mollien was an official of the old school, with vast experience; before the revolution he had worked under Necker, Terray, Turgot, etc. In 1806 Bonaparte was to put him in charge of the Treasury. In 1801 he wished to make him director-general of the sinking-fund. Mollien had therefore been invited to a cabinet meeting to talk it over, and had witnessed one of Bonaparte's volcanic rages.

On reviewing all the circumstances of the scene at which I had been present, I realised that the First Consul, in his very lively peroration, and in the course of some unjust criticisms, had also displayed great shrewdness, a rare talent for divining, as it were, conclusions ordinary men have to reach by a slow process of observation: the power of foreseeing and forestalling objections: above all, that of raising doubts in the mind of his hearers on what they had always regarded as indisputable inferences, of stunning

their imagination, and reducing their real strength to swell his
own.

His eyes, his features, his every movement, the vividness, the
singularity of his expressions, even the incorrectness of some, the
peremptory tone of his decisions, all seemed to announce that at
such moments, those about him had nothing to do but submit in
silence.

Such was at least the impression made on me, all the more
sharply since I was not expecting it.

At other times, when his instinct for domination was allowed
to sleep, as it were, he carried the virtue of patient listening to
excess, and I had learnt this at my first interview.

But though I saw very worthy men exposing themselves to this
alternation, I own that I was rather less willing to take the risk,
and so I explained next day to the finance minister.

He had almost forgotten the tempest of the day before.

'It would be very foolish,' he said, 'to attach more importance
to these sallies than their author does. You will get used to them.
They are not infrequent, but they leave no trace. The First Consul
is the first to tax himself with them, and he expects one to forget
them, as he does himself.'

THE DESPOTIC HUSBAND

*Here we have the famous ordeal of the barouche. Bonaparte spares Mme
Junot, who is pregnant, but has no mercy on Josephine, who will never
be pregnant again.*

*He felt his whole achievement would vanish if he had no son. For a
long time he had kept up hope. Treatments by his doctor, Corvisart, had
induced a kind of miracle, and one morning Bonaparte had entered his
study in high glee, rubbing his hands and saying to his secretary: 'All's
well, my wife's courses have started!' But the illusion was short-lived.
And he lost no chance of overwhelming her with sarcasms on her
sterility.*

All this is reflected in Duchess of Abrantès's *narrative.*

Josephine had one of those frightful migraines that so often
tortured her, poor woman. They were so painful that there was
nothing to be done but get her to bed and let her sleep.

'Nonsense, come along!' said the First Consul. 'The fresh air will do you good. It's the sovereign cure for all aches and pains.'

Mme Bonaparte dared not go on refusing. She sent for a shawl and hat and, with Mme de Lavallette and myself, got into the barouche, a basket-shaped carriage in charge of a young postilion riding one of the horses.

Napoleon was in front of us with Bourrienne. Not even the aide-de-camp on duty had been required for this outing, with which the First Consul was as charmed as a little boy on holiday. He was on horseback, galloping ahead of us, then coming back to take his wife's hand, just as a child running on ahead of his mother goes and comes, is off again, back to give her another kiss, then racing away afresh.

No words can describe Mme Bonaparte's terror when driving. Nor can I find any to express my impatience when I see others intolerant of such weaknesses. They are tiresome, I know, but it is the upbringing that should be blamed, not the person so unhappy as to be going through positive martyrdom. Napoleon did not quite share my way of thinking, he felt no pity for his wife and made no concession to her.

That day, as it was the first time we had gone to Le Butard, the postilion did not know the road. He came to a gully, or rather a brook with very high banks which made it awkward for the barouche to cross. No sooner had Mme Bonaparte caught sight of this precipice, as she called it, than she exclaimed that he was not to go any further. The outrider, whom she questioned and who knew of her timidity, replied that the crossing might really be dangerous.

'You see!' she cried. 'I won't go to Le Butard by this road. Go and tell the First Consul that I'm going back to the château, unless he knows a different way.'

She ordered the postilion to turn round, and we retraced our steps. But we had not covered a dozen, when the First Consul overtook the barouche.

'What's this?' he said, with the expression only his face could wear, when something affected him disagreeably. 'What fresh whim is this? Go back where you came from,' he added, tapping the postilion's shoulder with the end of his riding-whip.

And, setting spurs to his horse, he dashed off again. We found him on the edge of the fatal brook, eyeing the banks, which were really high. But since he had just crossed this same brook on horseback, everyone had to cross it. This little scene was the pattern of a great deal that I observed later.

'Come,' said Napoleon to the lad who was guiding the barouche, 'a good start, then give the horses their heads, and you'll be across.'

Mme Bonaparte uttered a piercing scream, which made the woods ring.

'Never will I consent to stay in the barouche. Let me get out! . . . Bonaparte! . . . for pity's sake, let me get out! let me get out!'

She clasped her hands, weeping; she was truly piteous. Napoleon looked at her, but, far from being touched, he shrugged his shoulders, and ordered her rather harshly to be quiet.

'This is childishness. You will cross! and in the barouche . . . Come, don't you hear me?' he said to the postilion with an oath.

I saw it was time to intervene on my own behalf, hoping also that the diversion might make him aware of behaving badly, as indeed he was just then. I was pregnant, and did not mean to stake my child's life on a safe crossing in this barouche. We might overturn, and as the least result of Napoleon's stubbornness the barouche would be smashed.

'General,' I said, signing to the outrider to open the carriage door, 'I am responsible for another life. I cannot stay here. There will be a terrible jolt, which might be very bad for me, it might even kill me,' I said laughing, 'and you don't want that, do you, general?'

'I!' he exclaimed. 'Do *you* any harm in the world! Get out; you are right, a jolt might be very bad for you.'

And he came up to the barouche to help me out, for he had dismounted at the beginning of the scene. Encouraged by the perfectly good-humoured, and indeed more than kindly look in his face, I ventured to say, rather absurdly perhaps, as he was supporting me:

'But perhaps a jolt might be very bad for Mme Bonaparte, general? You know, if she should be like me . . .'

I leave it to those who are good at riddles to interpret this one. The First Consul looked at me with such a drolly stupefied air that instead of jumping down I remained on the step, laughing like the young madcap I was. And suddenly he chimed in, only once, but with such a shout of laughter that it gave us a start. At last I jumped to the ground, and Napoleon, who had regained his

H

gravity the next moment, pointed out that I had taken a risk in
jumping like that. Then, as though fearing he had not been bitter
enough to show his displeasure with his wife:

'Put up the step, and drive on!' he said in a tone that admitted of
no reply.

Mme Bonaparte was so pale, she had felt so wretched even
when we set out, that I could not help saying to Napoleon:

'General, one would think you ill-natured, yet you are not
really. Mme Bonaparte is ill, she is feverish. I beseech you, let her
get out!'

He eyed me without a word, but in a manner that turned me
cold, if I may so express it.

'Madame Junot, I was never fond of remonstrances even as a
child. The Signora Letizia and Mme Permon will tell you that.
Judge how likely I am to have grown more pliable!'

Then, observing that what he said and above all his tone of
voice, his look, almost frightened me:

'Come along, let me help you over this dreadful river, this
appalling precipice!'

Bourrienne had likewise got off his horse. They both helped
me across the brook by a row of stepping-stones. When we got
to the other side, Napoleon saw that the barouche was not moving. For indeed Josephine, weeping as she would have wept on
being led to the gallows, was begging the postilion to wait a
moment, like a condemned man begging a respite.

'What, you rascal,' said the First Consul, 'won't you do as
you're told!'

And this time it was not lightly, but with all the strength of his
beautiful little pink-and-white hand, that he brought down his
riding-whip on the postilion's back. Immediately, lashing the two
horses, he set them off at a gallop, and the barouche got across the
stream, but to be frank, with such difficulty and such a violent jolt
that one of the swan-necks was broken, a pin came out, and the
little body of the barouche was so damaged by the wheels as to be
of no further use.

As for Mme Bonaparte, she came off still worse in this unlucky
crossing. Josephine was a wreck. What he showed was more than
ill-humour. It was rage. He pulled her almost brutally from the
carriage and took her a little distance into the woods, where we
could hear that he was still scolding her.

IN THE CONSUL'S STUDY

In his study, Bonaparte could no longer idle and chat as he had done with Bourrienne, before coming into absolute power. Moreover, Bourrienne left in 1802, and was replaced by a young man who had been keeping Joseph Bonaparte's books in order. At St Helena, Napoleon was to say of Méneval that he was only 'a clerk who could hardly spell'. This was published after Méneval's death, or it might have qualified his own memoirs.

Méneval, after the fall and death of Napoleon, had remained an ardent Bonapartist, and was writing to serve the cause. This was no more than proper; his services to Napoleon brought him a salary of 24,000 francs, and about as much again in bonds and gratuities. (Roughly fifteen of our millions a year.) On his marriage he received an additional 300,000 gold francs (90 of our millions). Etc., etc. To Méneval, therefore, Napoleon was a kind of god.

Napoleon was of middling height (about five feet two inches), and well made, though rather long in the bust. He had a big head and a highly developed skull. His neck was short and his shoulders broad. The volume of his chest indicated a robust constitution, less strong, however, than his moral faculties. His legs were shapely, his feet small and well-formed. His hands, of which he was slightly vain, were delicate and plump, with taper fingers. He had a high and broad forehead, grey eyes, piercing and uncommonly mobile, a straight, well-formed nose, and rather fine teeth; his mouth was perfectly moulded, the upper lip turning down a little at the corners, and his chin slightly prominent. His skin was smooth and his complexion pale, but beneath this pallor one was aware of the blood circulating. His very fine chestnut hair, which he had worn long, cut square and covering his ears up to the time of his expedition to Egypt, was now cut short. On the upper part of his head it was thin, and exposed the brow, seat of high thoughts. The contour of his face and the features taken together were strikingly regular. In short, the nobility and dignity of his head and bust were unsurpassed by the finest antique busts we possess.

When he was excited by some violent passion, his face became stern and even terrible. There was a distinct rotary movement of the forehead and between the eyebrows. His eyes hurled lightning. The wings of his nose dilated, swollen by the tempest within. But these passing fits, whatever their cause, failed to disorder his mind. He seemed to have full control over explosions which, besides, were to be increasingly rare as time went on. His head remained cool, the blood never rose to it. It always surged back to the heart.

In daily life his expression was composed, thoughtful and mildly grave. It was lit up by the most gracious smile; his whole countenance was sweet and winning when it was relaxed by good-humour or the wish to please.

In private, he had a loud, bantering laugh.

He was not much at home in the spelling and pronunciation of proper names. He never recalled them very accurately. But if the names escaped him, the sound of them was enough to conjure up in his mind a vivid image of the person or place. Once he had seen a man or visited a locality he never forgot them.

Napoleon did not, like the pythoness, remain glued to his tripod. He would abstract himself. Attention, focused on the subject under review, would seize his whole mind. He would get up without haste. He would begin slowly to pace the room where he was, covering it from end to end.

This walk went on all the time he was dictating.

His utterance was grave and emphatic, but was never suspended. As he got deeper into the subject, inspiration made itself felt. It was revealed by a livelier tone, and a nervous habit of twisting his right arm and pulling at the coat-cuff. However, his delivery was not hurried by this excitement. His tread remained equally slow and measured.

Expressions offered themselves easily to convey his thought. Though they were sometimes incorrect, these very mistakes increased the energy of his language, and always rendered his meaning wonderfully vivid.

Napoleon seldom wrote with his own hand. Writing was a weariness to him. His hand could not keep pace with the rapidity of his thoughts. He never took up a pen unless he were alone and wanted to commit to paper the first sketch of an idea. But after a few lines he would stop and throw down the pen.

Then he would leave the room to summon his usual secretary, or in his absence the second secretary, or the secretary of state, or General Duroc, or at times the aide-de-camp on duty, according to the nature of his employment. He would greet the first to answer the call without annoyance, and indeed with visible satisfaction at being rescued.

His handwriting was a collection of isolated and illegible symbols. The words had half their letters left out. He either could not read them himself, or would not trouble to do so. If he were asked to explain anything, he would take back his rough copy, which he tore up or threw in the fire, and dictate a fresh one. The ideas would be the same, but differently expressed and arranged.

His own spelling was incorrect, though he was well able to point out the mistakes of others. With him it was a habit of carelessness. He did not choose to give the spelling an attention that might confuse or break the thread of his ideas.

In figures, where correctness is absolute and positive, Napoleon likewise made mistakes. He rarely got a sum right.

MME DE STAËL'S VIEW

Bonaparte already had favourites, especially in the army. 'I like only fighting men,' he would say. He had also his victims.

One of these was Mme de Staël. He once remarked: 'She talks neither of politics nor of me, so they make out. But somehow people are always less attached to me when they have been with her.' He persecuted her unceasingly, exiled her and had her books pulped. She did not deserve this martyrdom. Lavallette, though accustomed to say amen to Napoleon's every whim, wrote in high praise of her superior mind, 'allied with a nobility and goodness of heart which have been too little understood'.

A priori, one might question the evidence of such a victim. All the same, this is a voice to be heard. And in practice, what she says here is hardly debatable.

I was invited to General Berthier's on a day when the First Consul was to be there. And as I knew he spoke very ill of me, it came into my head that he might accost me with some of those rude speeches it often amused him to make to women, even those who were paying court to him, and before going to the party I wrote down haphazard various proud and cutting answers I might make, according to what he said to me. I did not wish to be at a loss if he took the liberty of affronting me, for that would have shown lack of spirit even more than of wit. And as no one can swear to avoid discomposure in the presence of such a man, I had my defiance ready in advance.

Happily it was needless; all I heard from him was the tritest of questions.

It was the same with such of his opponents as he thought capable of answering him. In every field he attacks only when he feels himself much the stronger.

During supper the First Consul was standing behind Mme Bonaparte's chair, rocking from one foot to the other, like the princes of the house of Bourbon. I pointed out to my neighbour the vocation for royalty which was already so conspicuous.

The hallmark of Bonaparte's rule is a profound contempt for all the intellectual riches of human nature. Virtue, dignity of feeling, religion, enthusiasm—these are in his eyes, and to use his favourite expression, 'the eternal enemies of the continent'.

I do not think Bonaparte, on reaching the head of affairs, had formed the project of universal monarchy. But I believe his system was what he declared himself to a friend of mine, a few days after the 18th of Brumaire.

'One must,' said he, 'do something fresh every three months to captivate the imagination of the French people. With them, whoever fails to move on is lost.'

He had promised himself to encroach day by day on the liberty of France and the independence of Europe. But without losing sight of the goal, he could adapt himself to circumstances.

It was by the art of alternating trickery and force that he subdued Europe.

For that matter, Europe is a big word. Of what did it then consist? Of a number of ministers, none of them as able as many men picked at random from the nations they ruled.

The thrones of Europe, at the time when Bonaparte determined to overset them, were all filled by sovereigns who were very decent men. The political and military genius of that world was extinct, but its peoples were happy. And though in most states the principle of free institutions was not admitted, the philosophical ideas which had prevailed in Europe for half a century had at least the merit of preventing intolerance and softening despotism.

But what had Bonaparte in his gift? Was he bringing greater

liberty to the people of foreign countries? Not a monarch in
Europe would have allowed himself in a year the sum of tyrannic
insolence with which he filled every day. He came only to make
them exchange their tranquillity, their independence, their language, their laws, their fortunes, their blood, their children for the
misfortune and shame of being annihilated as nations and despised as men. He was embarking, in short, on his venture of
universal monarchy, the greatest scourge that can threaten the
human race, and the certain cause of war everlasting.

Meanwhile monarchical institutions were making strides in the
shadow of the republic. A pretorian guard was being formed.
The crown diamonds were being used to adorn the sword of the
First Consul, and in his get-up, as in the political situation of the
day, one observed a mixture of the old regime and the new. He
had garments of gold and straight hair, a little body and a big
head, something awkward and arrogant, contemptuous and
sheepish about him which seemed to combine all the uncouthness
of a parvenu with all the impudence of a tyrant. His smile has
been cried up as agreeable; for my part, I feel sure it would have
been disliked in anyone else, for that smile, which began and
ended in gravity, was more like the working of a spring than of a
natural impulse, and the expression of his eyes never agreed with
that of his mouth. But since his smile had the effect of reassuring
those about him, the relief he caused by it was taken for charm.

THE CONSULAR COURT

*In different terms, and from another point of view, Mollien writes of the
new society Bonaparte was organising, as a trial sketch for the imperial
court which would soon follow.*

He wished to make himself popular in the salons. He had great
faith in his direct influence on men. He wished to extend its scope.
It was impossible that with his serious temper, his restless and
brooding mind, he should care for large routs and noisy gaieties,
or for the witticisms, the playful talk, the exchange of subtle
pleasantries and elegant trifling, which were once regarded in
France as the charm of society, a tradition certain circles hoped to
revive. But he was always ready to sacrifice his mere tastes to a

greater interest. He wished to gain a fresh hold on the younger
generation, by seeming to join in the amusements of their age; to
reconcile all views, by bringing all ranks together in the name of
pleasure; to encourage young soldiers, who would follow him in
the hope that one day, when they had gained some glory, they
might ally themselves with the daughters of wealthy or once
illustrious families they were meeting socially. So his leading
generals, his ministers, his brothers and sisters, all those he had
raised in the world received his command to open their houses to
all who were conspicuous in Paris for talent or wealth, old names
or recent services, and to ambassadors and accredited foreigners.

THE VOICE OF THE OPPOSITION

*Mme de Staël's view was the expression of a personal philosophy and
referred mainly to personal character. She did not speak for the opposition. For there was, and was always to be, a strong opposition to the
regime of force imposed by Bonaparte.*

*Its worthiest, best qualified, best informed and most levelheaded
spokesman is the deputy J-Ch. Bailleul.*

This course of success and prosperity is imposing. But let us
raise the veil and take a closer look at the facts.

The reign of Napoleon Bonaparte has found great admirers,
and detractors who have perhaps been yet more extravagant in
heaping abuse on him.

His ideas on the history of the revolution were extraordinarily
superficial and defective. He had chosen to grasp only so much
of it as he needed to contrive a regime which was neither the old
nor the new. This misapprehension, wilful or involuntary, of men
and things had the most deadly influence on his fortunes.

What, in actual fact, was the character of this reign, in which all
the elements of liberty were, not destroyed, but invaded by
despotism?

If I told the whole truth, I should stir up a great volume of
hatred. Here are a few glimpses. Impartial history will do the
rest.

Napoleon Bonaparte achieved everything at home by great
daring on his own part and great meanness on the part of his most
loyal agents and supporters. No passion was too despicable for

him to enlist on his side. To be sure there were some honourable men, even about his person. But these were not the most influential. So much for men who had reached a certain age. Later there arose a class of young enthusiasts whose views were no longer of the same nature.

He achieved everything abroad through his own great daring and the courage of our armies.

At home, meanness could at times sink to a degree of abasement which was not fictitious. There is the well-known remark of one prefect:

'You are my friend. If the Emperor ordered me to throw you into the river at noon, you would be there at a quarter to.'

Everyone has passed on these words from a speech by another prefect: 'God created Bonaparte, and rested.'

Was he a great man, as some voices have already proclaimed?

To me it seems that before giving a man the title of great, one should really know why.

In the past men have been called great who had scarcely any merit but that of astonishing the world: if such titles are enough, Napoleon Bonaparte astonished the world.

But if true greatness required him to achieve, without departing from the laws of duty and conscience, an end useful to his country and to humanity, all the world is convinced that frankness and honesty were not the familiar virtues of the man in question. Even in his most trivial relations he displayed the most unfailing and refined machiavellism. Far from achieving the end marked out by the revolution, to which he had fallen heir, he did not even catch sight of it. The outcome of all his wars, and of what he called his glory, has been to deprive us of conquests rightfully made before his name was heard in the armies, and deliver us up to two invasions by all the nations of Europe.

At one of the first meetings of the Tribunate, the tribune Duveyrier, for some reason or rather without any, for I think it was a question of turning the restaurant-keeper Février out of apartments he occupied on the ground floor under our assembly hall—Duveyrier produced an antithesis, in which he contrasted a tyrant of fifteen days with a tyranny of fifteen centuries.

Bonaparte thought the tyrant of fifteen days was himself.

I had not been to see him since his installation as First Consul.

I went the day after this meeting. It was at the little Luxembourg.
The room was full of generals forming a rather large oval, in
which Bonaparte was walking about alone. He greeted me, but
had not made two rounds when, addressing himself to me, he
set about poor Duveyrier and called him everything.

From Duveyrier he went on to the Tribunate. It was a natural
transition. But he must have had something further on his mind,
for he interrupted himself to say:

'It's like the idea that I am going to be governed by whores.
No, I am not going to be governed by whores.'

Then he returned to Duveyrier:

'I was in my bath,' said he, 'when that sentence was read to me.
It was midnight. So-and-so, my aide-de-camp, wanted to go at
once and cut off his ears. I would not let him.'

Everyone kept silence. I was the only speaker. I defended
Duveyrier as best I could.

'The very fact that he uttered that sentence, general,' I said,
'proves that he did not think of it as insulting to you——' etc.

When it was the Tribunate's turn, he repeated:

'With fifty of my grenadiers, I can kick the Tribunate into the
river.'

'You may, general, but it will not be your finest exploit.'

THE HOSTILE BROTHERS

*At the beginning of the consulate, Napoleon had given a ministerial post
to his brother Lucien (one of the artificers of the coup d'état). But he had
very soon taken umbrage at his brother's activity and withdrawn his
portfolio—sending him, however, to get rich in Spain in the role of
ambassador.*

*Lucien, married during the revolution, had lost his wife. He fell in
love with a very pretty woman, and remarried without telling the First
Consul, who had an ugly princess in view for him. From that moment
until 1815, they were to be at daggers drawn.*

*The chemist Chaptal, minister of the interior, witnessed the following
scene with the notary who had registered the marriage.*

I have never seen Bonaparte in such a rage as came over him
at the news that his brother Lucien had been married at Senlis to
the widow of Jouberthon, a Paris stockbroker. He ordered me to

send for the notary and tell him to bring his register, which was done.

The notary arrived. I took him to Saint-Cloud, at nine in the morning. Here, word for word, is the dialogue between the First Consul and the notary:

Bonaparte: Was it you, sir, who registered my brother's marriage contract?

Notary: Yes, Citizen First Consul.

Bonaparte: So you were unaware that he was my brother?

Notary: No, Citizen First Consul.

Bonaparte: Then you did not know my consent was needed to validate the contract?

Notary: I think not. Your brother has long been of age. He has held great offices. He has been a minister and ambassador. He has no father. He is a free agent.

Bonaparte: But he has a mother whose consent was required.

Notary: No, he is of age and a widower.

Bonaparte: But I am head of the state, and my consent was required as such.

Notary: You are its head only for ten years, and have no prerogative in respect to your family.

Bonaparte: Show me this marriage contract.

Notary: Here it is!

The First Consul read the entry, and nearly tore the page as he shut the book.

Bonaparte: I shall have this contract annulled.

Notary: That will be difficult, for it is well cemented, and everything is provided for.

Bonaparte: Go away!

The notary went off with his register, having been unruffled throughout.

Bonaparte took Lucien sharply to task for his marriage, and the clash grew so heated that he even reproached him with marrying a widow. To which Lucien replied:

'So did you marry a widow. But mine is not old or smelly!'

AN AUDIENCE AT SAINT-CLOUD

What staggered those who were meeting Bonaparte for the first time was the fire of questions he kept up. Practically, he said little. It was the others who had to talk. But when they left him, it was nearly always with cries of: 'What a genius! He knows everything!'

Norvins, *the author of a famous* Memorial, *was not as simple as that. None the less, on his admission to the First Consul's study he felt the charm. He was just back from San Domingo (Haiti), where the expeditionary force against Toussaint l'Ouverture and his black republic, commanded by Pauline Bonaparte's husband, had been wiped out by yellow fever. Leclerc himself was dead. Norvins had returned gravely ill. However, he dragged himself out to wait on Bonaparte at Saint-Cloud.*

It was the 12th of April, 1803. I reached Saint-Cloud and had my name given to the aide-de-camp on duty. By good luck it was my old school friend Lauriston. He came downstairs four at a time, and took me at first for one of the mummies he had seen so many of in Egypt. Still he had the shocking courage to embrace me, and, when he got to the outer drawing-room, settled me in a big easy-chair, the one he slept in at night.

'The First Consul is asleep,' said Lauriston. 'He's been out hunting. As soon as you are rested, I'll go and scratch at the door of his study. You'll be well received, I promise you.'

Half an hour later, he got up and scratched at the door.

'Come in! What is it?'

'It's Citizen Norvins, the secretary-general, back from the Cape.'

'Send him in!'

I went in, though my legs would hardly carry me. And I knew one might not sit down before the First Consul. I made him a low bow.

'Come along, Citizen Norvins. I am very glad to see you.'

I handed him the dispatches in silence. Emboldened by his welcome, I retreated upon the chimney-piece, to the right of which the First Consul was sitting at his desk, in a green morocco armchair. I therefore based myself skilfully on the chimney-corner, so as to have a three-quarter view of him; that was enough to start with.

What followed was not a talk, but, as it should have been, an examination, a general and private inquiry. I can still recall the main points, as well as the seeming disorder in which the genius, who was then so young, so mighty and eager to know everything at once, placed and displaced his questions.

'What is the army doing at San Domingo?'

'It is dead.'

'What! And the fourteen thousand men I have just sent?'

'There were not more than eight thousand under arms when I left. Now there are far less.'

'How did the Tortuga rising come about?'

'By sea.'

'How?'

'The negroes arrived by night on barges from Terra Grande.'

'Then there was no naval patrol?'

'Yes, general.'

'Well, then?'

'It was English.'

'Then what are the twenty warships doing?'

'Staying in port or sailing elsewhere. It was different under your brother-in-law.'

'How many vessels of war are there in Jamaica?'

'So many.'

'And troops?'

'So many.'

'That's right. You are well informed.'

'I have always dealt with the correspondence.'

'True—you served my brother-in-law well.'

'I did, general.'

And a thrill of visible emotion passed from my face to his.

'I am pleased with you. I shall have an appointment for you. Get your health back. Count on me, Citizen Norvins.'

Then the First Consul leant both hands on the arms of his chair, thus hoisting himself for a half-bow, which I gave him back entire.

I was happy; I had seen the great man, and he had adopted me. So I thought then.

THE CONSUL AND THE ACTRESS

On another evening of the same year, Bonaparte was welcoming to Saint-Cloud a princess of the theatre, a queen of beauty. This was Mlle George, *a very young actress of the Comédie Française. She had been born Joséphine-Marguerite Weimer; Bonaparte was to give her the pet name of Georgina.*

The night before, after the performance, he had sent his valet to ask her out to Saint-Cloud the next day. At eight in the evening the valet called for her in a carriage.

I found Constant at the foot of the stairs by the stage door. This Constant was laughing heartily, which I thought rather impertinent.

'Make yourself easy. You will see how good the consul is. You'll very soon get over your fright. So don't worry. He is waiting very impatiently, etc. . . . Ah, here we are! Come, mademoiselle, make yourself easy, yes, and go on trembling.'

We went through the Orangery, then we came to the window of the bedroom opening on the terrace where Roustam was waiting for us. He drew back the curtain, shut the window after me, went into another room. Constant said:

'I'm going to tell the First Consul.'

So I was alone in this big room. A huge bed at the far end, and, opposite the windows, heavy curtains of green silk, a big enlarged divan, etc.

I hear a slight movement. Ah, how my heart beats! It is he. The consul comes in by the door next the fireplace, a door leading to the library.

The consul was in silk stockings, white satin breeches, green uniform with red facings and collar, his hat under his arm. I rose. He came up to me, looked at me with that charming smile which was his alone, took me by the hand and made me sit down on that enormous sofa, lifting my veil, which he threw on the floor without more ado.

'How your hand trembles! So you're afraid of me? You think me terrifying? *I* thought you very fine last night, madam, and I wanted to congratulate you. So you see, I am kinder and more polite than you are.'

'In what way, sir?'

'In what way! I sent you 3,000 francs [*900,000 of our francs*] after your performance as Emilie. I was hoping you would ask leave to come and thank me. But the fair and haughty Emilie did not come.'

I stammered. I did not know what to say.

'But I didn't know, I dared not take such a liberty.'

'A poor excuse! So you were afraid of me?'

'Yes.'

'And now?'

'More than ever.'

The consul burst into a hearty laugh.

Thus the routine is apparent. He fancies an actress. He sends her a little fortune, expecting her to come and pay him in kind. If she hangs back, he sends his valet to fetch her. For all that, with a girl as young as George he can be good-natured and even playful.

I parted from the consul at seven in the morning. But, ashamed of the charming disorder left by the night, I did not conceal how it abashed me.

'May I tidy up?'

'Yes, my dear Georgina. I will even give you a hand.'

And he was kind enough to look as though he were helping me to tidy the bed, witness of so many forgettings and caresses.

For the first fifteen days he gratified my scrupulous delicacy, and, I venture to say, my modesty, by repairing the disorder of the nights, by seeming to make the bed.

He dressed me, put on my shoes, and, as I had buckled garters, which he found tiresome, even ordered me closed garters, to be slipped over the foot.

Then we have the parting scene.

I was called for at eight in the evening. I went into the room adjoining the bedroom. It was the first time I had seen this apartment, which was the library. The consul came in directly.

'I sent for you early, my dear Georgina. I wanted to see you before I left.'

'Oh, dear, are you going away?'

'Yes, at eleven in the morning, to Boulogne. It's still a secret.'

He began joking and playing with me, and made me run after him. To escape being caught, he climbed the ladder used for getting the books, and as this was on castors and very light, I began wheeling it right up and down the room. He was laughing and shouting:

'You'll hurt yourself. Stop it, or I'll be cross.'

That night the consul stuffed into my bosom a thick parcel of bank-notes.

'Gracious, why are you giving me all that?'

'I don't want my Georgina to be short of money while I'm away.'

There were forty thousand francs [*twelve of our millions*].

MORE THAN A CRIME: A MISTAKE!

He had something besides dalliance on his mind, in that winter and early spring of 1803–4. He was resolved to strike a great blow which would terrorise Europe, and open a new phase of his career. In France the royalist party would crumble, while the more extreme revolutionaries would welcome the step as a pledge of faith.

At that time the young Duc d'Enghien, the last Bourbon of the house of Condé, was living at Ettenheim in Baden. Napoleon found an excuse in conspiracies that were being hatched against his own person—some of them on his instructions. He then ordered Generals Caulaincourt and Ordener to make a raid into Baden, kidnap the young duke, bring him post-haste to Vincennes and have him shot the same night. He was punctually obeyed. Before daybreak on the 20th of March, 1804, the innocent young man was dispatched by a firing-squad.

Napoleon asserted his responsibility for this act to the last gasp, and never showed the least feeling about it. He reopened his testament to congratulate himself on it. Even at St Helena, when one of the faithful spoke of it, he replied: 'What, the Enghien affair? Pooh! what is one man, after all?'

In any case, he had consulted no one, and would listen to no arguments against the murder. Fouché, who was then the only statesman in France, tried in vain to reason with him.

I flew to Malmaison, where the First Consul then was. Arriving at nine in the morning, I found him restless, walking alone in the park.

'I can see,' he said, 'what has brought you. Today I am striking a great and necessary blow.'

I then pointed out that he would rouse France and Europe, unless he furnished indisputable proof that the duke was conspiring against his person at Ettenheim.

'Where is the need of proof?' he exclaimed. 'Is he not a Bourbon, and the most dangerous of the lot?'

I persevered, urging political motives that should outweigh the reason of state. It was in vain. He concluded by saying testily:

'Haven't you and your like told me a hundred times that in the end I would be the Monk of France and restore the Bourbons? Well, now there will be no going back. What stronger guarantee can I give the Revolution you cemented with the blood of a king?

Besides, it's time to have done. I am surrounded by plots. I must strike terror or perish.'

As he spoke these last words with which hope was extinct, he had been walking towards the château. I saw M. de Talleyrand drive up, and a moment later the two consuls Cambacérès and Lebrun. I returned to my carriage and went home in dismay.

Next day I heard that there had been a council after I left, and that, during the night, Savary had proceeded to execute the unhappy prince.

The indignation I had foreseen burst out with the utmost fury. I was not the least forthright in condemning this outrage on the law of nations and of humanity.

'It's more than a crime,' I said, 'it's a mistake!'

Words which I set down because they have been repeated and attributed to others.

THEY WERE CRYING IN THE STREETS . . .

It was like a tremor that rocked the whole of Europe. Henceforth there could be no sense of safety. Anywhere, a gang sent by Bonaparte might loom up to seize, kidnap and shoot anyone who had annoyed the First Consul. Or rather the Emperor—for when the blow was struck, Bonaparte had himself proclaimed Emperor of the French. Josephine became an empress. Generals who did not flinch were created marshals. Generals he was afraid of were imprisoned and sentenced. (One of them, Pichegru, was found strangled in his dungeon.)

The Marquise de Nadaillac *describes the reaction in Paris.*

Next day they were crying in the streets: 'Execution of the Duc d'Enghien!' His arrest had transpired the day before. It is only right to say that the degradation of the French people did not prevent them from feeling and abominating this horrid crime. In every true heart in France, hatred of Bonaparte was increased. The violation of foreign territory, the kidnapping, the murder of a young prince beloved by all Europe, excited universal disgust.

M. de Caulaincourt, whose family had largely owed their position to the house of Condé in the old days, received the bloodmoney, and was heaped with favours by the Corsican.

I

It has often been asked what made Bonaparte commit such a useless crime. In my view his only reason was to get rid of a Bourbon. He desired and hoped to wipe them all out one after another.

Two months later appeared the senatus-consultum proclaiming Napoleon Bonaparte Emperor of the French. The nation that had shed so much blood to found a republic flung itself unreservedly at the feet of the most violent and despotic of usurpers. All the regicides turned courtiers in a moment!

This event produced the following quatrain:

> On loans and alms I long supported life,
> I fawned on Barras, took his drab to wife;
> I strangled Pichegru, shot Enghien down,
> And for so many crimes received a crown.

VENDETTA CORSICA . . .

It may be objected that the Marquise de Nadaillac was a royalist. Then let us see what the Bonapartists thought of Enghien's execution. The most authoritative is the 'black' secretary Lavallette.

Another motive, and the most decisive, lies in the character of Bonaparte, his impetuosity, and the eagerness for revenge that might well be known as *vendetta corsica*.

To be sure, this feeling was just then inflamed to the highest pitch by his enemies.

'Let them set all Europe on me,' I heard him say a few days later, 'it's up to me to defend myself. It's legitimate attack. But that they should blow up a whole district, that they should not shrink from killing or maiming more than a hundred people to get at me, that now they should be sending forty ruffians to murder me, that's too much. I'll make them shed tears of blood. They'll find out to their cost what it is to legitimise murder.'

Revenge is only a vulgar passion, yet it is the one most common to rulers. The First Consul was worthy to have risen above it. I should have liked him to have had the Duc d'Enghien arrested and condemned, but to have sent for him after the verdict, confronted him (as he could) with proof of conspiracy, and immediately sent him away to England.

It is my faith that the prince's heart was too noble not to have been affected by such a display of magnanimity. And if his family were to reign, Bonaparte would not have found him an enemy, nor found in his heart a reproach he will never silence.*

I may add, this act has been made the basis of all the horror with which France and Europe have been urged to regard him. But without quoting all the princes, respected by mankind, who have similar faults to deplore, did not the greatest and wisest of our own writers, Montesquieu, say of Alexander: 'He burnt Persepolis and killed Clitus, but', etc.?

I went to Saint-Cloud a few days after the sentence. While waiting to be called into the First Consul's study, I used to pass my time in the library with a young man named Ripault, who looked after his books.

He told me that the day before, as he was leaving this room, Bonaparte had noticed a bust of the great Condé, in a passage leading to his study. He said to Ripault, brusquely and in an agitated voice:

'Move that somewhere else.'

News of the prince's arrival and of his death reached the palace at the same time.

A GENERAL ESTIMATE

So much for the consulate, now for the empire. After four years of power, Bonaparte could be judged, especially by one who had seen him every day, shared in his labours, and occupied a high position in the state.

This was the case with Chaptal, for four years minister of the interior. Chaptal was also a man of science; his high intelligence enabled him to appraise Bonaparte, and he could do so impartially, for he had not to endure either fits of rage, disgrace or insults.

When Bonaparte took the reins of government, not only was he profoundly ignorant of the principles of administration, of jurisprudence, of geography etc., but he knew nothing whatever of the government that had existed before the revolution. Bonaparte had ruminated a great deal, but had never studied. And the knowledge of mathematics which has been made so much of was very slight. Military glory alone had carried him to the supreme

* *Written while Napoleon was at St Helena.*

eminence. That alone surrounded him with all the glamour of
enthusiasm and illusion. And it supported him to the end.

Bonaparte had one virtue which is more unusual the higher a
man has risen. He was not ashamed of knowing so little of the
details of general administration. He put many questions, asking
the definition and sense of the most ordinary words. He incited
discussion, and kept it going till his opinion was formed. It was
common for him to mistake words the first time they were used
in his hearing, and then he would ever afterwards reproduce them
as he had picked them up. Thus, he would regularly say *îles
Philippiques* for *Philippines*, *section* for *session*, *point fuminant* for
point culminant, *rentes voyagères* for *rentes viagères*, *armistice* for
amnistie, etc.

In the four years of his consulate he held several councils every
day. There all questions of administration, finance and jurisprudence were debated in turn. And as he was gifted with great
acumen, he would often throw in profound comments, judicious
reflections, which astonished those who had most experience in
these matters.

The councils often went on till five in the morning, since he was
never known to abandon a question till his opinion was formed.
And on this head he was somewhat difficult, rarely contenting
himself with the one offered him by his most enlightened advisers. At that time the ministers and the council of state had some
power over him. As his judgment was not yet formed on most
subjects, he permitted argument, and it was then possible to
enlighten him, and even to carry the opinion one expressed in his
presence. Accordingly, this period was marked by achievements
in statute law, administration and finance which have been
admired by all Europe and will long be the pride of France.

But as soon as Bonaparte had acquired settled views, right or
wrong, on all questions of government, he ceased to consult anyone, or if he did so, it was no longer to embrace the opinions
offered him. He always followed his own ideas. His opinion was
his one rule of conduct. He made bitter game of all who expressed
a view different from his. He tried to hold them up to ridicule,
and would often say, tapping himself on the head, that 'this sound
instrument was more useful to him than the advice of men who
were supposed to be educated and experienced'.

Only those who observed this period of four years can have a just idea of the changes that took place in the First Consul. Till then he had sought to gather round him the ablest minds of every party. Soon he began to think the choice of his agents immaterial. So he called indiscriminately to his council and to leading posts in the government those whom favour or intrigue might suggest, thinking himself strong enough to rule and govern single-handed. He even made a point of removing all who had ability or charac-ter enough to be irksome. He wanted flunkeys and not advisers, and had thus managed to isolate himself completely. By now the ministers were only head clerks. The council of state was reduced to shaping decrees of which he was sole author. He governed even in the most petty details. All about him were timid and passive. They studied the will of the oracle and performed it blindly.

Once he had reached the point of concentrating the whole government in himself and taking counsel only with himself, Bonaparte hit on the idea of moulding a generation of satellites. He often said that men of forty were imbued with the principles of the old regime, and therefore could not be devoted to his own person or principles. He took a dislike to them, and from that moment started a nursery of five or six hundred young men, whom he appointed in turn to every office. One saw a young man of twenty-two placed at the head of a department; others set to administer conquered territory; another, barely thirty years old, and without any previous study, discharging the important func-tions of supreme judge and minister of justice. Not all these young men had either the capacity, or the prestige, or the decorum required. But he thought them devoted to his person and govern-ment, and that was enough. He had applied the same principles to the organisation of the army. The glory of our elder generals irked him, their advice offended him, and in his last years his aim was much less to make use of ability than to reward devotion to his person.

This conduct of Bonaparte's had no small share in alienating the minds of the French. A department placed under the direction of a schoolboy feels humiliated by such a choice. Its confidence in the head of the government is weakened. Its respect for the magistrature is at an end.

Napoleon was unceasingly on guard against the ambition of the generals and the discontent of the people, and was always engaged in stifling the one and forestalling the other. At every period he was seen to maintain the greatest reserve with his generals. He always kept them at a great distance. He hardly spoke to them, and then only on trifling matters. They knew nothing of his orders till it was time to go and carry them out. If they distinguished themselves, he merely said they had done their duty. Only now and then did he give them honourable mention in his bulletins. If they were unlucky, it was all their own fault, and was never due to the inferiority of the troops he had put under their command, nor to the bad positions in which this inferiority had placed them.

And so, with the exception of two or three who had known him in his youth and retained a certain liberty with him, they approached him trembling, and could not say they had ever enjoyed a moment's freedom with him. He loaded them with affluence, granting them titles and estates in the conquered countries, first because he needed wealthy houses at court, where there were none, and also to bind them more intimately to his fate and interest them in the maintenance of his conquests.

I never caught Napoleon speaking in praise of any general, and I have often heard him criticising them sharply, now for want of talent, now for want of conduct. Used as he was to relate everything to himself, to see only himself, to admire only himself, Napoleon paralysed all about him. He wished for no glory but his own. He believed in no ability but his own.

That was why, both in the field and in council, he engrossed everything, he arrogated everything to himself.

There was another factor at work to swell his triumphs and abate those of his generals. He ventured all because he depended on no one, and could sacrifice men and material without fear of blame, whereas his generals calculated losses and were always in dread of falling into disgrace, which made them timorous and less daring.

Marshal Lannes was the only one who preserved his frankness and independence. Though dotingly fond of Napoleon, he never subscribed to his master's whims, never dissembled or concealed his way of thinking. Whether on the battlefield or at court, he told him the whole truth. As a result they were nearly always at odds or rather sulking. For the most perfect reconciliation would occur at first sight, and the marshal nearly always wound it up by saying pettishly that he was very unlucky to have such an ill-

starred passion for 'that trollop'. Napoleon laughed at these outbursts, knowing that the marshal would always be there when he
was wanted.

I shall not speak of a number of henchmen he had gathered
round him. These men had the loyalty of fanatics, that is to say
they obeyed his orders without thinking, and were alert for his
every whim so as to have the merit of anticipating it and forcing
on the action they were ordered to take. Napoleon was not fond
of them, still less did he respect them. But, naturally distrustful,
he saw himself obeyed blindly and was enabled, by the ease with
which he could get his orders carried out, to delude himself on
their atrociousness. These men were all the more dangerous in
that Napoleon's first thoughts were terrifying. His most violent
decisions came on the spur of the moment, and he plunged into
the blackest excesses on finding satellites always ready to obey.
A police report, an incident of which he was told, threw him
into furies it was impossible to curb, and the most discreet in-
tervention only exasperated him. In these first moments he would
dictate the most violent steps and order them to be carried out.

One man who never really gave in to Bonaparte, but who
neither served, nor crossed, nor enlightened him, was Consul
Lebrun. He stood up to him only when his vanity was wounded.
One day, in a council of ministers, Bonaparte asked his opinion.
This contradicted his own. Bonaparte then said nothing was to
be expected of an old fogey of sixty-eight.
'Yes,' retorted Lebrun, 'that's what children say.'
Another day, Bonaparte was criticising his translation of
Jerusalem Delivered with regard to the style. Lebrun replied:
'You'd better learn the French language before passing judg-
ment on it.'
I have said how terrible were Napoleon's first resolutions. At
first he gave himself up wholly to the promptings of a touchy and
vindictive nature. He attempted neither to clear up the facts, nor
to discover the forms laid down by law for the prosecution and
trial of those who were charged with an offence.

It was from policy or ostentation that he encouraged the arts,
never from the feeling which leads us to judge a country and its

civilisation by its monuments and works of genius. I have more than once heard him say that of all the objects that had struck him in his life, those he found most wonderful were the pyramids of Egypt and the height of the giant Frion. It was curious to observe him walking through the fine art gallery of his capital. He confronted the masterpieces of every age with uniform impassivity. He never stopped before any of them. And if his attention were directed to one, he would ask frigidly: 'Whose is that?' without venturing any comment or displaying the slightest reaction.

He had been told that David was the first painter of the age. He believed this and repeated it, but never entering into the least detail on the nature of his talent, or venturing on any comparison with other artists of the day. One could easily see the constraint he was under whenever he found himself in this kind of situation, and his eagerness to escape as quickly as possible from a state of penance.

Napoleon placed agriculture in the forefront of the useful arts. Yet it was a subject he had no knowledge of. Indeed his ignorance of it passed all bounds. He could never see, for instance, that cultivated meadows were not usurping the place of corn. And it was vain to tell him that cultivated meadows provide fodder, that fodder provides livestock, that livestock provides manure, and that manure trebles the produce of the fields; all he could see was the place of corn being taken by cultivated meadows. He went so far on this wrong track as to let fall several times that he was tempted to forbid cultivated meadows in agriculture. But as he had only a hazy idea of such things, he never risked making up his mind to it.

Napoleon was afraid of the masses. He dreaded insurrection, and this fear was always driving him to wrong measures. He made it a principle that corn should be very cheap, because riots are nearly always due to the high price or scarcity of bread. As a result, he never allowed the export of grain till farmers threatened to stop growing it. No one could get it into his head that since the price of all commodities had risen by a third or half since the revolution, it was natural for corn to follow on. He did not see that well-to-do farmers mean a wealthy nation, since then they consume the manufactures they are able to buy. No, he wanted corn to be cheap, and dried up national prosperity at the source.

Napoleon never knew a generous feeling. That was what made him such arid company. That was the reason he had no friend. He regarded men as base coin, or as the tools with which he was to gratify his whims and ambition. A Russian minister, Prince Kourakin, talked of his country's resources for keeping the army up to strength.

'I admit that,' said he, 'but can your master afford twenty-five thousand men a month as I can?'

In a battle the issue of which hung on a good cavalry charge, ordering General Nansouty to charge with the horse guards, he said:

'Break the enemy line if it costs them all, I didn't gild them for their sakes.'

On being told that General de Latour-Maubourg had just had his leg shot off, he returned only the chilly question:

'Who replaces him?'

Walking on the battlefield of Eylau, covered with twenty-nine thousand corpses, he turned some of them over with his foot, saying to the generals around him:

'Small change.'

Back from the rout of Leipzig, he accosted M. Laplace:

'Why, you've got very thin!'

'Sire, I've lost my daughter.'

'Oh, that's nothing to get thin about! You are a geometer. Apply the calculus, and you'll see that all that equals zero.'

We have already remarked that Napoleon was quite un-educated. The Greek and Latin authors were almost unknown to him. He had gone quickly through some historians and retained some of their facts. He had formed an opinion offhand. And the most respectable authorities, the unanimous approval of the ages, were powerless to make any change in his ideas. Tacitus, he declared, was the worst historian of antiquity. Perhaps his view had been based on the picture of Tiberius he found in this author. Horace was only fit for sybarites. Homer alone had his suffrage. Among the moderns, he thought little of Voltaire, Racine or Rousseau. Corneille was the French poet he ranked highest.

Napoleon spoke no language well. His native language was Corsican, which is an Italian dialect, and when he was talking French one could easily see that he was a foreigner.

THE EMPEROR'S OFFICIAL LIFE

The 18th of May, 1804, gave the signal for a huge transformation scene. The admirable simplicity of the consulate was trodden underfoot. The new sovereign, likewise abjuring the name of Bonaparte to adopt that of Napoleon, meant to give the world an exhibition of regal pomp. For Napoleon, a man of the past, was chiefly concerned to tread in the steps of the kings of France.

His personal household multiplied. Coats were overlaid with gold and silver trimming: men, with high-flown titles. Cambacérès and Lebrun went up from consuls to princes. Talleyrand and Berthier likewise became princes. Napoleon's brothers were princes, with key dignities: Louis, High Constable; Joseph, Grand Elector. Murat, who had married Caroline Bonaparte, became a prince and Grand Admiral, etc., etc.

The aide-de-camp Duroc received the title of Grand Marshal of the palace. Caulaincourt was Master of the Horse. There were chamberlains, and twenty more classes of dignitaries.

One of them, Bausset, *prefect of the palace, made himself the chronicler of Napoleon's days in the midst of his household.*

At nine o'clock every morning, Napoleon would leave his private apartments, dressed as he was to be all day.

The orderly officers were the first to be admitted. Napoleon gave his orders for the day.

Immediately afterwards, the *grandes entrées* were shown in. These were composed of personages of the highest rank, either in virtue of their office, or by special favour. Officers of the imperial household who were not on duty had likewise the privilege of admission.

Many who now seem to have forgotten the fact were then very eager in making use of such a flattering distinction. Napoleon addressed himself to each in turn, and listened benevolently to all they might wish to say. On finishing his round he bowed and those present withdrew.

At half-past nine Napoleon's breakfast was served. The prefect of the palace went to announce it, ushered him into the breakfast apartment, and remained in sole attendance, along with the head butler who performed all the active duties.

Napoleon breakfasted at a small pedestal table of mahogany, covered with a cloth. The prefect of the palace stood by this little table, with his hat under his arm. Napoleon, as abstemious a man as ever lived, had often finished his breakfast within eight minutes.

But when he felt the need to 'close his office', as he now and then called it with a smile, breakfast would be fairly prolonged, and then nothing could equal the genial gaiety and charm of his conversation. His utterance was rapid, positive and picturesque. To this aspect of my service I owe the pleasantest hours of my life.

Very often I suggested his receiving at breakfast time a number of persons to whom he had granted that privilege. These were mostly scholars and scientific men of the first rank. Some of them survive, and I am confident they will all agree with me that nothing could equal Napoleon's graciousness and amiability. It was in these unreserved moments of easy talk that he surprised and delighted most.

Returning to his study, Napoleon began work and received ministers or heads of departments, arriving with their portfolios. These different labours went on till six in the evening, and were never interrupted except for meetings of the council of ministers or the council of state.

Dinner was served punctually at six.

At the Tuileries and Saint-Cloud their majesties dined alone, except on Sundays, when the whole imperial family was admitted to the banquet. The Emperor, the Empress and Madame Mère were seated in armchairs, while the others, kings, queens, princes or princesses, etc., had only dining-room chairs.

There was only one course, set off by dessert. The simplest dishes were those Napoleon preferred. He drank nothing but Chambertin wine, and rarely without water. It was the pages who waited at table, seconded by the valets, butlers and carvers, never the liveried staff. Dinner usually lasted fifteen or twenty minutes. He never drank dessert wine or liqueur. Every day he had two cups of pure coffee, one in the morning after breakfast and the other after dinner. All that has been said of his indulgence in coffee is false and absurd. During dinner the prefect of the palace had only to keep an eye on the service and answer questions addressed to him.

It must not be supposed that the style of living was shabby or parsimonious. Napoleon's tastes were simple and modest, but he liked glitter and magnificence around him.

Back in the drawing-room, a page presented to the Emperor a silver-gilt salver on which were a cup and a sugar-bowl. The head butler poured out the coffee. The Empress took the Emperor's cup. The page and the head butler withdrew. I waited till the Empress had poured the coffee into the saucer and handed it to Napoleon. His Majesty so often forgot to drink it at the right time that the Empress Josephine, and after her the Empress Marie-Louise, had thought out this pleasing remedy for the little hitch.

I withdrew. Soon afterwards Napoleon returned to his study and set to work again, for, as he said, he rarely put off till to-morrow what should be done today. The Empress went down to her own apartments by a private stair. Entering her drawing-room, she found there the *dames du palais* who were on duty, some other privileged ladies and the officers of her household. Card-tables were set out as a matter of form, and to break the gravity of a 'circle'. Sometimes Napoleon would come in through the Empress's private apartments, and chat with equal simplicity and unreserve, either with the *dames du palais* or one of us. But as a rule he did not stay long.

The officers on duty with him went back upstairs to attend the audience of the *coucher*, and receive his orders for the next day.

Such was the life regularly led by the Emperor at the Tuileries. Its uniformity was never disturbed, unless by a concert, play or hunt.

THE IMPERIAL COURT

First an emperor, and the etiquette of an imperial household; then a court and court etiquette. It was audacious to hark back in this way, so soon after the revolution. But in Gordon's words: 'If the plague had places and money to dispose of, courtiers would flock round it.'

Paul-Louis Courier wrote:

'*So much for our news. Tell me about your part of the country, and how the farce of founding the empire went off there. Much the same, I dare say.*

Each, trembling, kisses the enchaining hand.

'*By the poet's leave, that is false. They are not trembling. They want money, and are simply kissing the hand that pays.*'

From Pelet *we get a glimpse of the stage management.*

However, this court had to be arranged on a proper footing. All the books on the subject were exhumed from the dust of libraries. An old gentleman, formerly page to the king, was summoned from the country to impart the traditions of Versailles. His appearance in the Tuileries drawing-room was an event. It was long since anyone had seen, off the stage, the personages of the old court, with their powdered and curled locks, their consequential and frivolous air. This one presented himself like an oracle about to reveal the secret of the ages and knit up, as has been said, the chain of time.

With his aid, it was found possible to compile a volume as extensive as that of the civil code. There were now chamberlains, equerries, a great master of ceremonies, a grand huntsman. Each learnt what was his proper station in the long sequence of palace halls. Every dignity, every office, acquired its distinctive costume. Napoleon himself settled what the Empress should wear, and saw it tried on.

Countess Potocka *was ruthless in her judgment of the imperial court.*

This court, so magnificent from a distance, would not bear close inspection. One observed in it a kind of muddle and discord which dispelled the aura of majesty and brilliance one had a right to expect. It was a scene of gross incongruity. One might have thought oneself at a rehearsal to which the actors had come to try on their costumes and run through their parts.

NAPOLEON IN THE MIDST OF HIS COURT

If the court was severely judged, so was Napoleon's behaviour in it. What Chaptal *says on this point is nowhere contradicted.*

It was especially during the four years of Bonaparte's consulate that one had a chance of studying that extraordinary character. In those days he was accessible to everyone. He showed himself openly. He admitted to his table almost all who saw much of him. He would then receive his ministers and foreigners in boots and plain clothes. One very frequently passed whole days with him at his country house of Malmaison, and the time was all spent in walks, games and conversation.

Then Bonaparte was truly great and esteemed. And if he could

have been satisfied with that, he would still be on the throne of
France, encompassed with public blessings.

But Providence willed otherwise. The modest title of First
Consul seemed to him below his pretensions. He had to establish
a dynasty and found an empire.

He cut himself off from the men who had hitherto enjoyed a
kind of intimacy with him. He established a strict etiquette at his
court. He created there, for his courtiers, an extravagance of
costume the most sumptuous courts had never displayed.

These innovations wrought a disastrous change in public
opinion. The men who thought scarcely less of him than of their
country drew away, and thenceforth he had only flatterers about
him.

Those who saw little of Napoleon or saw him only for a few
moments are bound to judge him very unfavourably. At the outset his bearing was cold and his remarks trifling or uncivil. He had
not the agreeable ways that come of social experience or a good
upbringing. Was he speaking to an ambassador:

'Are you pleased with Paris? Have you heard from your country?'

Such were his usual formulae. If he were greeting a senator or
a councillor of state:

'How do you do, Monsieur le . . .? It is hot today, it is cold or
wet.'

In a gathering of women he would ask each one her name, often
including those he had known for years, and, once in a long while,
might add some compliment on a gown, a diamond, etc.

Indeed he was often uncivil and boorish. At a fête in the
Hôtel de Ville he said to Mme . . ., who had just told him her
name:

'Goodness, I heard you were pretty!'

To another:

'It's a fine time for you when your husband is in the field.'

To old men:

'At your age one has not long to live.'

To young girls:

'Have you any children?'

In general, Napoleon had the manners of an ill-bred young
lieutenant, and at first blush one would not have suspected him
either of parts or of the least knowledge of the world. I have

known him, at small receptions, come out of his study whistling, accost women without breaking off his music, and go back again humming an Italian song.

Often he summoned six or eight hundred people to court and did not appear. Often he invited ten or fifteen people to dinner, and left the table before the soup had been taken away.

Yet there was undeniably a great deal of wit and a great deal of pungency in Napoleon's talk, but these gifts never came out except in discussion. He could even be very eloquent when he warmed up or wanted to carry an opinion. I have heard him say a number of things that would make the fortune of a wit.

Napoleon was at times free and easy in conversation. But if the other person took advantage of this to criticise him or attack any of his principles, he abruptly changed his tone, resumed all his ascendancy and set out to humiliate rather than argue with him. One had to be constantly on guard against his false air of good-nature. The men who knew him best, those who were his most regular companions, like Duroc and Berthier, never deviated from the proprieties. He played frequently at all sorts of games, but he was always cheating. He required to be paid, but used to give back the money his conscience told him had been unfairly won.

No one was at ease in dealing with Napoleon, because no one could rely on a spirit of kindliness or indulgence. The smallest mishap, the slightest negligence sent him into a fury, and he had no consideration for those who were in daily touch with him, so that they were always on thorns, afraid of displeasing or of taking responsibility for decisions that might annoy him. As a result they spent their whole time getting his orders on the most trifling points, and executing them without modification, and even then might think themselves lucky if they had not to bear the blame for the ineptitude of some measures he had ordered himself.

His court was truly a slave-galley, where every man pulled as he was bid.

Mme de Rémusat, *dame du palais, confidante of Josephine and wife of a chamberlain, had for ten years spent every day of her life at this court.*

It is quite true to say that he would have liked to be the sole master of reputations, and make and unmake them at pleasure. He would compromise a man or tarnish a woman for a word, with no sort of caution. But he took it greatly amiss that the public should dare to observe and criticise the conduct of those he had given shelter within the halo surrounding him.

One day when a good many of us *dames du palais* were breakfasting with the Empress, Bonaparte suddenly came into the dining-room, looking rather gleeful, leaned on the back of his wife's chair and made some trivial remarks to one and another of us. Then, questioning us all on the life we led, he made known, at first in hints, that there were some of us who were being publicly talked of. The Empress, who understood her husband and was conscious that, from one word to another, he might go very far, tried to change the subject. But Napoleon kept it up, and in another minute or two had contrived to make it sufficiently embarrassing.

'Yes, ladies,' said he, 'the good people of the faubourg Saint-Germain are taken up with you. They are saying, for instance, that you, Madame . . ., have such a connection with M. . . .; that you, Madame . . .'—and so on, addressing two or three of us in turn.

It can easily be imagined how awkward we all felt at this strain of talk. Truly, I still believe Napoleon was enjoying the discomfort he excited.

'But,' he added suddenly, 'let no one think I approve of such gossip! To attack my court is to attack me. I will not have anyone saying a word either against me, or my family, or my court.'

And then, with a darkening countenance and in harsher tones, he went into a long diatribe on those social circles in Paris that were still refractory, saying he would banish any woman who uttered a word against a *dame du palais*, and working himself up on this text absolutely unaided, for none of us was tempted to make the responses. The Empress cut short the meal to put an end to this scene. The bustle stopped Napoleon's harangue, and he left as he had come.

One of our ladies, a devout admirer of *all* Bonaparte, was all but in tears over the kindness of a master who intended our reputation to be something sacred. But Mme de . . ., a very clever woman, answered impatiently:

'Yes, madam, let the Emperor speak up for us like that again, and we shall be ruined!'

He was much surprised when the Empress pointed out the

absurdity of this scene, and still insisted that we ought to feel obliged to him for the warmth of his indignation when we were attacked.

NAPOLEON'S TOILET

In private, out of sight of his court, Napoleon was a different man, whom no one knew better than his principal valet, Constant.

It was the Emperor's habit to begin the day with a cup of tea or orange-water. If he were taking a bath, he did so immediately on rising, and there a secretary read him his dispatches and news-papers. When he took no bath he would sit by the fire while they were read to him, or very often read them himself.

He dictated to the secretary his replies and the remarks sug-gested by his reading of his papers. As he got through them he would throw them haphazard on the floor. Afterwards the secretary picked them up and arranged them for removal to the private study.

Before making his toilet Napoleon slipped on, in summer, trousers of white piqué and a dressing-gown to match. In winter, trousers and dressing-gown of thick flannel. On his head was a madras knotted on the forehead, and with the other two corners hanging down over the back of his neck. Napoleon put this on himself at night. After his bath a fresh madras was brought to him, for, as he twisted and turned incessantly, his own always got wet.

Having had his bath or read his dispatches he began his toilet. I used to shave him, till I had taught him to shave himself. On first acquiring this habit, like everyone else he used a looking-glass attached to the window. But he stood so close to it and lathered his face so abruptly that the glass, the window-panes, the cur-tains, the washstand and himself were deluged. The staff called a conference on this difficulty, and it was settled that Roustam should hold the glass. When the Emperor had finished one side he turned the other side to the light, and made Roustam cross over from left to right or from right to left, according to the side he had started with.

The washstand was also moved about. After shaving, the Emperor washed his face and hands and carefully trimmed his

K

nails. Then I took off his flannel vest and his shirt, and rubbed his whole bust with a silk brush, extremely soft. I then massaged him with eau de cologne, of which he used up a great deal, for the same brushing and massage was performed daily. It was in the East that he had learnt this hygienic practice, which he found invigorating.

When all these preliminaries were over, I dressed him in light slippers of flannel or cashmere, white silk stockings (he wore no other kind), drawers of very fine linen or fustian, and sometimes white kerseymere breeches and soft riding-boots, sometimes close-fitting trousers of the same material and colour, with small English boots reaching to mid-calf. These were fitted with tiny silver spurs, not more than half an inch long. All his boots had these spurs attached.

I then put on his flannel vest and his shirt, a very thin muslin necktie, and over it a black silk collar. Finally a waistcoat of white piqué, and the coat either of a chasseur or a grenadier, but usually the former.

His toilet complete, he received his handkerchief, his snuff-box, and a small tortoise-shell box of liquorice flavoured with aniseed, cut very fine.

It will appear from all this that the Emperor had himself dressed from head to foot. He never lifted a finger, submitting like a child and meanwhile busying himself on his affairs. I have forgotten to say that for his teeth he used a boxwood pick and a brush dipped in toothpaste. Napoleon had been born, so to speak, a man of manservants. As a general, he had no less than three, and was waited on as elaborately as at the height of fortune.

Napoleon had no fixed hour for going to bed. He was soon undressed, for on reaching his bedroom he was accustomed to fling everything he had on in all directions: his coat on the floor, his *grand cordon* on the carpet, his watch at random on the bed, his hat on a distant piece of furniture, and so with all his clothes one after the other.

When he was in a good humour he would summon me in a loud voice, with a kind of halloo: 'Ohé! oh! oh!' At other times, when he was not pleased, it would be: 'Monsieur! Monsieur Constant!' All the year round his bed had to be warmed. It was only in very hot weather that he did without.

Owing to his hurried way of undressing, when I came in I had often very little to do but present his madras. I then lit his night-light, which was of silver-gilt, covered to subdue the flame.

When he was not going to sleep at once, he sent for one of his secretaries or for the Empress Josephine to read to him.

By order, there were little silver-gilt censers in his bedroom, burning now aloes wood, now sugar or vinegar. Almost through-out the year there had to be fires in all his apartments; he was habitually very sensitive to cold.

When he wished to sleep, I returned for his candlestick and went up to my own room.

NAPOLEON AND HIS DOCTOR

Roustam *was always in attendance in these private apartments. He shows us Napoleon chatting with his head physician, Corvisart.*

M. Corvisart was there every two or three days at Napoleon's toilet. One day, M. Corvisart is announced. He says to come in.

'There you are, great quack! Have you killed many people today?'

'Not many, sire.'

His Majesty: 'Corvisart, I shall not live long. I feel weaker than five or six years ago!'

He said this laughing.

Corvisart says: 'Sire, am I not here to prevent you?'

His Majesty pulls his ears, laughing.

'You think that, Corvisart? I shall bury you!'

Corvisart says: 'I'm sure, sire, me and plenty more!'

His Majesty says smiling: 'Hold your tongue, quack! What's that in your hand?'

'It's my walking-cane, sire.'

'It's very ugly! It is not nice. How can a man like you carry an ugly stick like that?'

'Sire, this stick, it costs me a lot, and I had it very cheap.'

'Well, Corvisart, how much did it cost?'

'Fifteen hundred francs, sire. That is not dear.'

His Majesty says: 'What! Fifteen hundred francs! Show it me, that ugly stick!'

His Majesty examines the stick in small detail. He sees the

portrait, in gilded medallion, of Jean-Jacques Rousseau, on the knob of the stick.

'Tell me, Corvisart, is it Jean-Jacques' cane? Where did you get it? I suppose one of your clients made you this present? Indeed, this is a pretty keepsake you have!'

Corvisart says: 'Excuse me, sire, it cost me fifteen hundred francs!'

His Majesty: 'After all, Corvisart, it is worth more, for he was a great man, that's to say a great quack like Corvisart!'

Corvisart was laughing.

His Majesty says: 'After all, Corvisart, he was a great man in his way. He did some fine things.'

After that, he pulls M. Corvisart's ears and says: 'Corvisart, you want to mimic Jean-Jacques!'

After that, His Majesty says: 'Corvisart, are there many sick people in Paris?'

He answers: 'Why, not too many, sire.'

'Tell me, Corvisart, how much money did you earn yesterday, in the morning?'

'Why, sire, I haven't counted!'

'You earned, at least, two hundred francs.'

'Not so much, sire.'

'But, Corvisart, you don't take less than twenty francs a visit!'

'Excuse me, sire, I have no fixed sum. I was taking even three francs.'

'Well done, you are humane.'

Just then His Majesty was dressing to go shooting in the forest of Saint-Germain.

'Corvisart, shall I have fine weather for my shoot?'

'Yes, sire, it's a splendid day.'

'Do you shoot, Corvisart?'

'Yes, sire, I do sometimes.'

'And then you let your patients die! Where do you shoot, Corvisart?'

'At Chatou, sire, on the Duc de Montebello's estate.'

'Corvisart, I want you to come shooting with me. I want to see whether you're a good shot.'

'Sire, it is a great honour. I have not my guns.'

'You shall have my guns. Do you hear, Roustam?'

'Sire, I shan't be able to use Your Majesty's guns.'

'Why not, quack?'

'Because I am left-handed.'

'Never mind, I want you to come, there is no time to send for your guns.'

Corvisart got into the Master of the Horse's carriage and set off for Saint-Germain.

That was the only time M. Corvisart went shooting with His Majesty.

NAPOLEON THE MUNIFICENT

Napoleon was growing richer every day, and soon his fortune would be colossal. From policy, and from good-nature as well, he gave largely to those who served him. It would be easy to multiply examples like the following, from the papers of Réal.

Napoleon gave a great deal. His giving was opportune, and remarkably gracious. What he gave was always a just reward for good and long service.

He had a great liking and regard for Count Mollien, minister of the Treasury. On the 1st of January, Mollien called to pay his respects. Napoleon had risen in a good humour. He received Mollien with most particular kindness.

'Monsieur Mollien,' said he, 'does Mme Mollien like chocolate?'

'Yes, sire, she takes it sometimes.'

'I have received some very good chocolate. I want her to have some of it for the New Year. You will take it to her, and say I made a point of her trying it today, and preparing it herself. Here are a few packets. You must tell her to be careful of it. It is very scarce. But let her taste it, and she will be surprised.'

Mollien went home to his wife, delivered the present, and acquainted her with Napoleon's rather odd injunction. Mme Mollien hastened to obey, and unsealed the packets of chocolate. Under the wrapping she found a considerable sum in banknotes.

WHEN I NEED SOMEONE

He not only tried to attach men by his munificence, but did his utmost to talk them over and bring them to share his views. Generally speaking, he would stick at nothing in pursuit of a man he really wanted.

Caulaincourt, *who was Master of the Horse, minister and ambassador under Napoleon, shrewdly observed this policy and recorded a phrase which sums it up.*

This persistence derived, I believe, from the habit he had formed, even to excess, of imparting his conviction to others or imposing it on them. There is no doubt that the successes he was used to obtaining in this field were the cause of his partiality for interviews with sovereigns, and his practice of negotiating the most delicate and important business directly with the ministers and ambassadors of foreign powers.

He had, when he chose, in his voice and countenance, as in his manners, something winning and persuasive which gave him as great an advantage over the person with whom he was talking as the superiority and flexibility of his mind.

No woman ever had more adroitness in making others wish and consent to what he desired, when he thought it his interest to persuade or merely wished to do so.

These reflections put me in mind of a phrase I heard from him on one such occasion, which expresses, better than any other words, the value he set on prevailing.

'When I need someone,' said he, 'I am not squeamish; I would kiss his arse.'

THE MASTER'S VOICE

On the other hand, there was no quarter for what he considered sins against his authority. He must have forgotten his own youthful absences without leave when he addressed to General Gouvion Saint-Cyr the threat of which Chaptal—*among others—was an astounded witness.*

One day General Gouvion Saint-Cyr appeared at the levee in the Tuileries.

Napoleon addressed him in a composed voice:

Napoleon: General, you are just back from Naples?

Gouvion: Yes, sire, I surrendered the command to General Perignon, whom you sent to replace me.

Napoleon: No doubt you had leave of absence from the minister for war?

Gouvion: No, sire, but I had nothing further to do at Naples.

Napoleon: If you are not on your way to Naples in two hours, before noon you will be shot on the plain of Grenelle.

I saw him behave in the same way to General Loison, who had left his command at Liège to spend a couple of days in Paris on urgent business.

Sometimes this will to be obeyed at all costs took a sensational form, as at Boulogne on the 20th of July, 1804. Constant's *account of the incident is staggering.*

One morning, as he mounted his horse, Napoleon announced that he was going to review the naval forces, and gave orders for the ships lying at anchor to quit their moorings, saying that he meant to inspect them in the open sea. He set off with Roustam for his usual ride, expressing the wish to find everything ready on his return, at an hour he mentioned.

Everyone knew that Napoleon's wish was his will. During his absence this one was conveyed to Admiral Bruix, who replied with imperturbable coolness that he was very sorry, but the review would not take place that day. In consequence, not a vessel moved.

On his return Napoleon asked whether all was ready. He was told what the admiral had said. This reply, so unfamiliar in tone, had to be twice repeated to him, and, with a violent stamp of his foot, he sent for the admiral, who waited on him directly.

Napoleon, as the admiral was not quick enough for his liking, went to meet him half way from the hut. His Majesty was attended by the staff, who gathered round him in silence. His eyes were flashing fire.

'Admiral,' he said in a choked voice, 'why have you not carried out my orders?'

'Sire,' replied Admiral Bruix with respectful firmness, 'there is a frightful storm getting up. Your Majesty can see that as well as I. Your Majesty does not wish to expose so many brave fellows to needless danger?'

And in fact the heaviness of the air and the low rumbling that could be heard in the distance bore out the admiral's fears only too well.

'Sir,' returned Napoleon with increasing irritation, 'I gave an order. Once more, why did you not carry it out? I am the sole judge of consequences. Obey!'

'Sire, I shall not obey!'

'You are insolent, sir!'

And Napoleon, who was still carrying his riding-whip, advanced on the admiral with a threatening gesture. Admiral Bruix fell back a step, laying his hand on his sword-hilt.

'Sire,' he said, turning pale, 'be careful!'

All who stood by were frozen with terror. For some time Napoleon remained motionless, his hand raised, and his eyes fixed on the admiral, who, on his side, retained his terrible posture.

At last Napoleon threw down his whip. Bruix let go his sword-hilt, and awaited bareheaded and in silence the outcome of this horrible scene.

'Rear-Admiral Magon,' said Napoleon, 'you will instantly carry out the movement I ordered. As for you, sir,' he went on, looking once more at Admiral Bruix, 'you will leave Boulogne within twenty-four hours and retire to Holland. Go.'

Napoleon immediately walked off. As they went, some officers, but only a very few, clasped the admiral's outstretched hand.

Meanwhile Rear-Admiral Magon was putting the fleet through the fatal movement Napoleon had insisted on.

Hardly had the first arrangements been made when the sea became dreadful to behold. The sky, dense with black clouds, was streaked with lightning, thunder rolled continually, and the gale broke all the lines. In short, what the admiral had foreseen took place, and the most appalling storm scattered the vessels till it seemed there could be no hope for them.

Napoleon, with head bent and folded arms, was anxiously pacing the beach, when suddenly dreadful cries were heard. More than twenty gunboats full of soldiers and sailors had been flung on the rocks, and the unhappy men on board, struggling with the raging waves, were crying for help no one dared to give.

Napoleon saw his generals and officers shuddering with horror around him.

FAMILY SEDITION

Napoleon's authority, however, was being constantly flouted by his brothers and sisters. For them his thunderbolts had no terror. He railed, threatened, but did nothing; and he never stopped paying. (One of

Joseph's salaries, as Grand Elector, brought him two million, or six million of our money.)

He did not always tackle them direct; third persons were used as envoys and negotiators between him and his family.

In November, 1804, Napoleon was awaiting the Pope, whom he had requested (in a manner of speaking) to come and crown him in Paris. Now, the Bonaparte family did not want Josephine to be crowned. Further, they thought the succession to the throne should revert to Joseph, who was the eldest, and who therefore held that Napoleon had robbed him of his birthright by becoming emperor. (Into the bargain, his 'great marriage', once the pride of the family, was now sadly eclipsed by Louis's union with Hortense Beauharnais, the Emperor's stepdaughter.)

Napoleon being childless, the imperial succession became a problem. Roederer, councillor of state, had to draw up a report on the subject, which was followed by a striking interview with the Emperor.

On Saturday the 12th of Brumaire (3rd November, 1804) I submitted to the Emperor my draft of a report (on the votes cast in the Senate for an imperial dynasty). I had not shown it to anyone. Maret was told to read it aloud. He said of the first two or three pages:

'That's good. That's very good.'

He stretched himself on a sofa, and heard the rest in silence. When Maret had finished, he said:

'Don't you see this report is hostile to me? It puts Joseph almost above me. It means to give him fictitious rights.'

Then he complained of his brother's conduct. He said it was factious. He appeared distressed at encountering opposition, perhaps ill-feeling, in the bosom of his family. Maret said that he did not believe I had meant any harm. Then the Emperor told him to see me, to make sure that I was not trying to *give battle*, and if not, to bring me with him tomorrow.

On Sunday (November 4th) I called on Maret, at ten o'clock. I told him that though the Emperor had been unjust to me at the distribution of places in the Legion of Honour, and the prince his brother treated me with great confidence, I had made the Senate a conscientious report; moreover, I had not shown it to anyone, only the Emperor had seen it; thus the report was not even in existence.

'That's what I thought,' replied Maret. 'I'll get dressed, and we'll go to the Emperor together.'

Here is what the Emperor said to me, and the substance of my replies. All the expressions of any moment are literal.

'Well, this report of yours—tell me the truth, did you make it for me or against me?'

'I swear that no one has seen it but Your Majesty, to whom I took the liberty of submitting it for Your Majesty's own decision. I swear it . . .'

'I believe you. But how, then, did you come to put Joseph on the same footing as myself? What's the meaning of this eulogy you make such a parade of? What! you present him as the object of the nation's wish for a dynasty equally with myself? Apparently you forget that my brothers are nothing except through me; that they are great only because I made them great. All that the French people know of them is what they have heard from me. There are thousands of men in France who have rendered more service to the state. You yourself are among the number. You have done more than they have. And then, you don't say a word of Louis. Why this injustice to Louis? He has been more useful to me than all the rest. Joseph is only what I have made him. If I wrote a letter commending him to the Senate, next time I will write just as strongly to commend Louis. I can't have them placed beside me on the same footing. Nor does the system require it. I am fair-minded. Since I began to govern I have always been fair. It was out of fairness that I refused to divorce. My interest, indeed that of the system, called on me to marry again. But I said: Am I to cast off this good wife, simply on becoming greater? If I had been thrown into prison or banished, she would have shared my fortunes. And because I am growing powerful, I am to cast her off? No, that is beyond my strength. I have the heart of a man. It was not a tigress that gave birth to me. When she dies I shall marry again, and I may have children. But I will not make her wretched. I have been equally fair to Joseph. When I left for Egypt I entrusted him with my whole property. He has not yet rendered an account of it. But I have grown too great to think of such things. . . . I never looked on my brothers as being the natural heirs of power. I regarded them as fit men to save the power from collapsing when it became vacant, under a minority. That is the only right they derive from the senatus-consultum.

For a hereditary claim to thrive, it must pass to children born in the purple. If he should have sons, I may adopt one. I shall not be unfair to him. But his wife brings no more sons than mine . . .

'He thought it strange of me to assign the title of "monseigneur" to a certain number of places—for instance, to the marshals of the empire. And a host of people are exclaiming against it as unnecessary and absurd. You yourself, Monsieur Roederer (*planting himself opposite me*), you have not the kindness to credit me with a little wit, a slight glimmering of wit. Yet you ought to understand my reason for giving the "monseigneur" to the marshals of France, that is, to the men with the strongest attachment to republican principles; it was to ensure that the imperial dignity should have the title of "majesty". They were in no position to refuse it, or yield it with a bad grace, when they found an exalted title had come their own way. You have not the kindness to allow me a little wit and common sense. Isn't that so? You think I have no judgment, eh?'

'Sire, I admit the principles you have just laid down.'

'Then why do you dictate the opposite to Joseph?'

'Sire, I think your Majesty has been misinformed.'

'I think you are loyal to me, you should be, but you are an unruly fellow . . .'

He was then facing me, and, laughing, he slapped one side of my face with the flat of his hand.

'. . . you are an unruly fellow, eh?

'Lucien, who has parts, was more consistent than Joseph. He said to me:

'"I am married, will you acknowledge my wife?"

'I replied:

'"No."

'"May I expect that you will acknowledge her one day?"

'"Never."

'Well! he left me. He went to Rome . . .

'But what does Joseph want? What is he aiming at? He's setting himself in opposition to me, rallying my enemies! Who is working him up? He doesn't want to be a prince. Does he think the state should give him two million for lounging about the streets of Paris in a dress-coat and a round hat? Does he think he can wrestle with me for power? I am founded on rock. . . . Power doesn't make *me* ill, for I'm growing fat on it. My health is better than ever. But you are wrong about what's disturbing Joseph. He declared himself to me outright, in front of Cambacérès and Lebrun, who were dumbfounded. A few days ago we were talking of my wife's coronation: if Lebrun, Cambacérès, you, the council, had all said to me: "No, she must not be crowned", it would not have angered me in the least. I realise what can be said for and against. But that Joseph should dare to tell me that her coronation is against his "interests", that it tends to give Louis's children higher claims than his own, that it prejudices the rights of his children by making Louis's children the grandsons of an empress, while his own will be the sons of a bourgoise; that he should talk of his rights, and of his "interests", to me, and even in front of his brother, that is wounding me in my sore spot. Nothing can wipe that from my memory; it was like telling a passionate lover that he had kissed his mistress, or merely that he was hoping to succeed with her. After that confession it would be useless for him to back out next day and call it a joke; the harm would be done. My mistress is power. I have done too much for her sake to let anyone steal her from me or even cast an eye on her. You may say that power came to me of its own accord, but I know the pains, the sleepless nights, the scheming it cost me. A fortnight ago I should never have thought of being unjust to him. Now I have no indulgence for him. I shall smile at him from the teeth out. But he kissed my mistress.

'The Senate, the council of state could oppose me for ten years without making a tyrant of me. To make me a tyrant, only an outbreak from my family is needed.

'They are jealous of my wife, of Eugène, of Hortense, of everyone about me. Well, my wife has diamonds and debts, that's all. Eugène has not 20,000 francs a year. I like those children because they're always eager to please me. If a gun is fired, it's Eugène who goes to see what's happening. If I have a ditch to cross, it's he who gives me a hand. Joseph's daughters don't know yet that I am called emperor; they call me consul. They believe I beat their mother. Whereas little Napoleon [Louis's son], when he's passing the grenadiers in the garden, shouts, "Long live Nonon the soldier!" I love Hortense; yes, I love her. She and her brother always take my side, even against their mother, when she flares up over a wench or some such trumpery. They say:

"'Well, he's a young man! You are in the wrong. He has plenty to put up with. We have plenty to thank him for."

'If Hortense were to ask for me while I was in council, I should go out and see her. If Mme Murat [*his sister Caroline*] were asking for me, I shouldn't go. With her I always have to get into battle array. To impress my views on one little woman of my own family I should have to make as long speeches as to the Senate and the council of state. They say that my wife is sly and that her children's attentions are affected. Well, so be it! They treat me like an old uncle. It's the comfort of my life notwithstanding. I'm getting old. I am thirty-six. I want some peace.

'They say I mean to give Italy to Eugène. Well, I have more sense than that! I think myself quite capable of ruling Italy and even the state of Venice. Italy brings me in twenty million. If I gave it away, there would be endless haggling before I could get fifteen. My wife is a good-natured woman, who does them no harm. All she wants is to play the empress a little, to have diamonds, handsome gowns, the trumpery of her age. Yes, she shall be crowned! She shall be crowned, if it should cost me 200,000 men!'

PAULINE AND HORTENSE

Napoleon used to say: 'One should wash one's dirty linen in private.' As we have just seen, he neglected to practise what he preached. Too many third parties were in the secret of his jangling with his brothers. Too many people had a chance of observing, not without surprise, the liberties he took with his sister Pauline. (In Italy, before his guests, he would calmly slip his hand into Josephine's bodice.) It was whispered that he was the lover of Josephine's daughter Hortense, and the father of little Napoleon.

Many of these statements are in the nature of tittle-tattle, but what we hear from Baros Mounier *secretary to the Emperor, peer of France, etc., cannot be ignored.*

A few days before leaving Paris I dined with M. de Sémonville. He told us stories of Princess Pauline:

'I was one of her lovers. There were five of us sharing her favours in the same household, before she went off to San Domingo.'

He did not give the names, but I assume that he, Macdonald and Montholon were three of them.

Of Macdonald he told us that Pauline had been mad for him, that for three days they had been shut up at Saint-Leu (Pauline and Macdonald) with a stock of food and had not admitted a living soul.

Soon afterwards they quarrelled.

M. de Sémonville talked, as though it were a commonplace, of how Napoleon slept with his sisters.

'Pauline was the greatest hussy, but the most tempting imaginable.'

The match with Leclerc had been made like this:

General Bonaparte was working in his study at Milan. Leclerc was a staff officer. He took the opportunity of a folding-screen to set about Pauline. General Bonaparte heard a noise, got up, and saw.

The wedding ceremony was performed without a moment's delay.

It was the same man (Sémonville) who told me that Pauline Bonaparte, then Mme Leclerc, had said to him shortly after the 18th of Brumaire:

'I'm on very good terms with my brother. He's slept with me twice already.'

M. de Sémonville had been one of her thousand lovers, and had remained friendly with her.

Bourrienne sets up to prove in his Memoirs that there was no amatory relation between Napoleon and his stepdaughter (Hortense). That seems to me quite untrue.

I often heard M. Lespérut talk of it as a *recognised* thing. It was the same in the imperial household.

Louis's—so called—son was generally regarded as being Napoleon's. He meant to adopt this boy and appoint him his successor. I remember seeing Napoleon myself, at the beginning of 1806, leading him by the hand through the gallery at Saint-Cloud. Satisfaction and pride were written on his face. The child was handsome, and distinctly resembled him. As long as that child was alive, plans for a divorce were turned down because he had an heir.

M. Capelle told me the other day that when Josephine, after her fall, was spending a few months at Geneva he had long conversations with her. In one of these she acknowledged that her daughter had had intimate relations with her husband. Speaking of which, M. Capelle also told me how, at the same period, he had heard from Josephine that Napoleon had meant to play a trick on his brother Jerome by welcoming his betrothed in his place; that for this purpose he had arranged matters so that the Princess of Wurtemberg would be left alone with him; Jerome had been given a false itinerary, but suspecting the fraud and the scheme, had set out in time, met his betrothed and remained with her.

I find the story hard to believe, but it shows what Josephine thought or wished others to think of Napoleon.

I recall being told by members of the imperial household, during the empire, that Napoleon had intended to adopt little Louis and proclaim the child his heir, but his brother Louis declared that in that case he would throw himself into the Seine.

This anecdote seems to me well-grounded.

As for Napoleon's intimacy with his sisters, MM Lespérut and Capelle made no doubt of it, nor M. Beugnot, who, as head of the police immediately after the empire, looked into all that, if only to amuse the King. Besides, M. Lespérut had owned the fact to us as early as 1807.

Beugnot told me at Ghent that while he was in charge of the police, from 1814 to 1815, they intercepted letters written from Elba by Pauline. She said:

'Since I've been here I've had only this rotten old man' [*her brother Napoleon*].

THE CORONATION

The 2nd of December, 1804. The great day had dawned. The Pope was awaiting the Emperor at Notre Dame.

We are told that before setting out from the Tuileries, Napoleon took his brother Joseph by the arm, walked him up to a looking-glass and said:

'*Joseph! if our father could see us!*'

Mme de Rémusat *describes the occasion in all its pomp.*

The weather was cold, but dry and fine. The streets of Paris were thronged. The crowds, rather curious than excited. The Guards under arms, a flawless spectacle.

The Pope preceded the Emperor by several hours, and showed himself wonderfully patient, sitting all this while on a throne that had been prepared for him in the church, without a murmur either at the cold or at the tedium of the hours that went by before the arrival of the procession. The church of Notre Dame was decorated with taste and magnificence. At the far end a stately throne had been raised for the Emperor, where he could appear in the midst of the whole court.

Before leaving for Notre Dame we were ushered into the Empress's apartment. Our dress was very brilliant, but its lustre paled before that of the imperial family. The Empress especially, blazing with diamonds, her hair in a thousand ringlets in the Louis XIV style, did not look more than twenty-five. She was wearing a court dress and mantle of white satin, embroidered in a mixture of gold and silver. She had a diamond fillet, necklace, earrings and girdle of the highest value, and wore all this with her usual grace. Her sisters-in-law were also sparkling with an infinite number of precious stones, and Napoleon, inspecting us all one by one, smiled at this opulence, which was, like all the rest, the sudden creation of his will. He also was brilliantly attired. Since his imperial robes were only to be put on at the church, he wore a French coat of red velvet embroidered in gold, a white sash, a short cloak spangled with bees, a hat turned up in front with a diamond clasp and surmounted with white feathers, and the collar of the Legion of Honour in diamonds. The entire costume suited him very well.

The whole court were in velvet mantles embroidered with silver. We were showing off to each other a little, it must be owned, but the show was really beautiful.

Napoleon took his place in a gilt coach with seven windows, along with his wife and his two brothers, Joseph and Louis. Then everyone repaired to the carriage allotted him, and the long cortège made its way at a walking pace to Notre Dame.

There were plenty of cheers as we went by. They were not the rapturous outbursts that might have been wished by a sovereign anxious for a token of his subjects' love, but they might content the vanity of a master with more pride than sensibility.

At Notre Dame, Napoleon remained some time in the archbishop's palace to don his ceremonial robes, by which he seemed rather crushed. His small figure melted away under the huge ermine mantle. A plain laurel crown encircled his head. He looked like an antique medal. But he was intensely pale, genuinely moved, and his eyes appeared to have a stern and rather troubled expression.

The whole ceremony was most impressive and beautiful. The crowning of the Empress excited a general stir of admiration, not because of the act itself, but she went through it so becomingly, she walked so gracefully to the altar, she knelt down with a motion so elegant, and yet simple, as to please every eye.

When it was time to walk from the altar to the throne, she had a brief dispute with her sisters-in-law, who were carrying her train with such reluctance that I thought the new-made empress would be brought to a standstill. Napoleon perceived this, and spoke a few dry, firm words to his sisters that set everyone in motion.

The Pope, throughout this whole ceremony, had something like the air of a resigned victim, but resigned nobly of his own will, for a great and useful purpose.

About two or three o'clock we started off again in procession to the Tuileries, and arrived after dark, which comes early in the month of December, lighted by the illuminations and by an infinite number of torches attending our progress.

We dined at the palace, with the grand marshal, and afterwards the Emperor wished to see those of his court who had not retired. He was gay, and delighted with the ceremony. He thought us all pretty, exclaimed on the way women are embellished by finery, and told us with a smile:

'You have me to thank, ladies, for being so charming.'

He had made the Empress keep her crown on, though she had dined alone with him, and he complimented her on her manner of wearing the diadem. At last he dismissed us.

JOSEPHINE UNVEILED

He could not have too much of a good thing. After crowning himself Emperor of the French, he hastened over the Alps to crown himself King of Italy.

There were one or two comic incidents en route. The narrator is Thiard, once an emigré in the Condé corps, now an imperial chamberlain.

L

On reaching Turin before the Pope, Napoleon decided to go over the palace, which he did not know. No one could tell him what was meant to be the function of a kind of drawing-room, lighted from above. Conjecture was running riot.

'Ask M. de Thiard,' said the Emperor with a bitter smile. 'He was here with his princes. He can tell you what it was.'

'No, sire,' I replied. 'I was not here. I only joined them at Worms.'

All through the visit he found fault with everything I had done. At last, coming to a door I had had screwed up, he had it forced open. What was the result?

The result was that when the Pope had arrived, and the Empress had retired to change her dress, an old papal chamberlain, seeing this open door, entered the dressing-room where she was in a state of nature.

The Emperor was at once informed, and was probably about to upbraid me when I forestalled him with the reminder that he had restored the communication himself.

The Empress laughed a great deal at this adventure, which, by the way, had no sequel.

TREMBLING À PROPOS

Thiard *is still the narrator, and the scene is Genoa.*

Two days after the Emperor's arrival I was on duty when M. de Ségur, the grand master of ceremonies, came and told me that Cardinal Maury would be visiting the palace; that he had induced the Emperor to grant him an audience, and would like me to announce him as soon as he presented himself.

When the cardinal appeared he was in a state of extreme agitation. I expressed my surprise at this, assuring him that he would be received by the Emperor with a distinction and affability he did not seem to expect.

Napoleon also observed it, and said:

'Calm yourself, my lord cardinal.'

'Sire,' replied the Abbé Maury, 'I did not tremble to confront a great nation, but I tremble to confront a great man.'

I have never been quite sure whether the agitation was not designed to lead up to the reply.

It is certain, at any rate, that in Paris the semi-official newspaper [the *Moniteur*] reported this emotion in such a way as to suggest that it had not been taken amiss.

GOD GAVE IT ME . . .

And so he crowned himself for the second time. In Milan cathedral, Mlle Avrillon, Josephine's principal maid, was well placed and did not miss anything.

The ceremony was gorgeous. The Empress looked on from a gallery commanding a perfect view. I was seated a little lower, in front of this gallery, with some of her household.

The iron crown, which was said to have been used for Charlemagne's coronation and was used for that of the Emperor, had been lodged at Monza. It was fetched with great pomp, and taken back the following day. At the moment of coronation the Emperor took the crown in both hands, rammed it boldly down, rather than set it on his head, and exclaimed in a loud, ringing voice:

'God gave it me, woe to him who touches it!'

Everyone has heard that, and no one is unaware that these words became the motto of the order of the iron crown, which the Emperor founded at the time, or soon after. But what they cannot know, what no one can imagine, is the expression on the Emperor's face at that moment; it was radiant with joy.

On our return to the palace I was busy in the Empress's room when the Emperor came in. He was wild with glee. He was laughing. He was rubbing his hands. And his good humour led him to speak to me.

'Well, mademoiselle,' said he, 'had you a good view of the ceremony? Could you hear what I said as I placed the crown on my head?'

And then he repeated, almost in the same tone as when pronouncing it in the cathedral:

'God gave it me, woe to him who touches it!'

I replied that nothing had escaped me. He was excessively pleasant to me, and I very often noticed that when the Emperor had nothing to vex him, he was very familiar with the domestic staff. He would talk to us with a kind of good-nature, of unconstraint, as though he had been our equal. But when he spoke to us in this way it was always to ask questions, and to avoid displeasing him one had to answer without showing too much confusion.

Sometimes he would give us a slap or pull our ears—and we could estimate the degree of his good humour by how much he hurt us.

One day, when he was obviously better pleased than usual, he pinched my cheek so hard that I could not repress a scream, and, as I was plump, for several days I retained a visible mark of His Majesty's satisfaction.

He had no idea of the pain he was inflicting. Very often he caused as much to the Empress while we were dressing her. He would give her slaps . . . by preference on the shoulders. In vain she would say: 'Do stop it, do stop it, Bonaparte!'—he went on as long as it amused him. The Empress did her best to laugh, but I more than once caught sight of tears in her eyes.

JOSEPHINE'S SWANS

He did not confine his teasing to Josephine's shoulders. One day, Roustam found himself in a cruel dilemma.

One morning, at Malmaison, the Emperor was making his toilet. His window looked out on a little canal, opposite the château. There were swans.

His Majesty asked for his carbine. I brought it. He fired at the swans.

The Empress was in her boudoir, who was dressing. She hears the shot. She comes running in her shift, wound up in a big shawl. She flings herself on the Emperor, saying:

'Bonaparte, don't shoot at my swans, pray!'

The Emperor persisted, saying:

'Josephine, do let me be. It amuses me.'

Then, she takes hold of my arm and says:

'Roustam, don't give the carbine.'

The Emperor says:

'Give it me.'

The Empress sees me in difficulty and takes the carbine out of my hands, which she carries off.

The Emperor was in fits of laughter.

AND AGAIN, WAR . . .

*He had not, actually, been at peace. All this time his Grand Army
at Boulogne was supposed to be on the point of invading England. But
now, by his proceedings in Italy, and above all his annexation of Genoa
(the Ligurian Republic), he made sure of another continental war.
Some French circles, at least, held the view that his goading of Austria
and Russia was timed to disguise the failure of his invasion scheme.
'The new coalition,' says Marbot, 'came just at the right moment.'*

*There is also the wider view, that he could not stop. On this subject,
Mounier wrote:*

*'We talked of Napoleon's character, and of his aversion to peace at all
times. M. de Sémonville (senator, peer, etc.) told us that at the signature
of the treaty of Amiens, M. de Talleyrand entered the First Consul's
room to find him bent over the map and fairly beside himself with irritation. He thought the negotiations must have broken down.*

*'No,' said Napoleon, 'your f—— peace is signed. What's to become
of me?'*

*At the outset of this campaign, Thiard had a characteristic interview
with him.*

Besides the Empress's own chamberlains, Napoleon had chosen
four of his to remain with her at Strasbourg. I was one. Napoleon
had been kind enough to give me this fresh mark of his satisfaction. As M. de Talleyrand would not consent to ask permission
for me to refuse it, I returned to the palace and was admitted
without delay.

I took the liberty of telling the Emperor that I had been a
soldier all my life. That it would be incessant torture to find myself, as it were, in the midst of a camp without sharing its pleasures
or incurring its dangers. That it would be impossible for me to
endure this constraint, and that I implored his permission to set
off for Pierres [*his father's château*] on the day he crossed the
Rhine.

'If you like,' said he, with a gracious air which was not customary, 'I shall be very glad to take you with me.'

And without awaiting my reply, which he could easily guess
from the satisfaction written on my face:

'I don't know,' he went on, 'what rank to give you. I am not
master of the army as people think. I have to treat it with great

circumspection. You are known to have served in the Condé corps!'

And he added words which were flattering to me, certainly, but in which he found yet another reason why there should be some difficulty in my joining the army.

'I cannot put you higher than captain . . .'

I replied that I felt all the value of what he was offering me, but that if he saw any objection to granting me even that rank, there was a way out: it was to allow me to wear the trefoil on my shoulder [*badge of other ranks in the Guard*], and then after the first battle he could give me, before the army, whatever rank he thought fit.

'No, no,' he replied. 'I don't want to go so far. Since that is agreeable to you, you shall be a captain in the mounted grenadiers of my Guard, and you will not leave me.'

My face immediately clouded.

'Why, what's wrong?'

I am a little ashamed to confess it, as I was to say it, but such is my nature, and I replied that I had always served with light troops, that, therefore, I was not sure I could get used to the heavy squad. He smiled and said:

'Well, no matter. In the light cavalry.'

That was how I opened another door to the emigration.

STAGE EFFECT

This campaign developed as a series of victories by Murat, Lannes, Ney. Napoleon occupied Vienna. Prussia was hesitating to draw the sword. When a Prussian minister arrived at French headquarters, it was a case for intimidation; and Napoleon's handling of it is described by Marbot, one of the actors.

As the Emperor knew that M. d'Haugwitz sent off a courier to Berlin every evening, he decided that Prussia should learn through him of the defeat and capture of Field-Marshal Jellachich's army corps, which must still be unknown there, such was the hurry of events at this period.

This is how the Emperor set about it.

The marshal of the palace, Duroc, after acquainting us with what we had to do, secretly returned to the quarters I shared with

Massy all the Austrian flags we had brought from Bregenz. Then, a few hours later, while the Emperor was conversing with M. d'Haugwitz in his study, we repeated the ceremony of handing over the flags, exactly as it had been the first time.

The Emperor, on hearing the band in the courtyard of his palace, affected surprise, went to the window with the ambassador at his heels, and, seeing the trophies carried by non-commissioned officers, summoned the aide-de-camp on duty and asked him what it was all about.

The aide-de-camp having replied that Marshal Augereau had sent two of his aides-de-camp to the Emperor with the flags of Jellachich's Austrian corps, captured at Bregenz, we were shown in, and Napoleon unblinkingly, and as though he had not seen us before, took Marshal Augereau's letter, which had been resealed, and read it through, though he had known what was in it for four days.

Then he questioned us, making us enter into the greatest detail. Duroc had warned us that we should have to speak loud, since the Prussian ambassador was rather hard of hearing. This came about very inopportunely for my friend Massy, the head of the mission, who was suffering from an almost total loss of voice. So it was I who replied to the Emperor, and, understanding his design, I painted in the liveliest hues the defeat of the Austrians, their dejection, and the enthusiasm of the French troops. Then, presenting the trophies one by one, I named all the enemy regiments they had belonged to. I stressed two in particular, since their capture was likely to produce a greater effect on the Prussian envoy.

'Here,' I said, 'are the colours of the infantry regiment of H.M. the Emperor of Austria, and here is the standard of the Uhlans of Archduke Charles, his brother.'

Napoleon's eyes were sparkling, seeming to say: 'Very good, young man!'

Finally he dismissed us, and as we went out we heard him say to the ambassador:

'You see, Count, my armies are triumphant at every point . . . the Austrian army is annihilated, and soon it will be the same with the Russians.'

M. d'Haugwitz looked shattered, and Duroc said to us, when we got outside:

'This evening he will write to Berlin to inform his government of the destruction of Jellachich's corps; which will cool down spirits inclined to make war on us, and give the King of Prussia fresh reasons for temporizing. Now that is just what the Emperor wishes.'

THE EVEN OF AUSTERLITZ

The following day's battle (fought on 2nd December, 1805, the anniversary of the coronation) was to be decisive, and to turn the map of Europe upside down. Napoleon awaited it with an easy mind. Thiard gives an account of the scene.

I have rarely seen Napoleon as cheerful, as contented, as he was all that day. More than once I caught him rubbing his hands joyfully, as though saying to himself: 'I've got them', or 'They shan't escape me'. This confidence was shared by the whole army, and anyone suspecting the possibility of a reverse would have been thought out of his mind. The day before a battle is a great day, when one has faith in the general. There is only one finer—the day of action.

Supper showed the influence of this happy frame of mind. The conversation was never brisker or more lively. At first it turned on the theatres of the capital, to which it had been led by a feuilleton we had received in the morning. From there it moved on to the respective rank which should be assigned to our three great tragic dramatists. Junot, who had as much education as mother wit, took a large part in it. There was no argument except on Voltaire, whom in my judgment Napoleon ran down too much. He brought out very forcibly all the faults and the want of local colour in *Zaïre*, *Alzire* and *Tancrède*. Of the tragedies of Racine, those he put first were *Bajazet*, *Mithridate* and *Britannicus*. But above all, he gave the palm to Corneille. And there we had no quarrel with him.

As soon as the meal was over, Napoleon said:

'Let's go and see the Guards.'

We all turned out. But by the end of the round, which was exhausting, if I remember rightly there was no one with him but M. de Caulaincourt, Junot, Rapp and myself.

Scarcely had we reached the line when Napoleon was recognised, and the men stood up at sight of him.

We had hardly gone fifty paces when a bit of wood across our path made him stumble. But luckily we caught hold of him in time, and he did not lose his balance. Then the grenadiers, of their own accord, took the straw on which they were lying, twisted it up to provide something like torches, which they set alight, and then walked in front of us to light the general, making the air ring with their shouts. This impulse was electric. All down the line torches were made, and each troop, as it were, took over escort duty from the one before. Then, as always happens at these moments of enthusiasm, what remained of the beds was soon ablaze. This demonstration was not without its risk, because of the cartridges. And so we kept on shouting to the men: 'Mind your pouches!' And luckily no mishap occurred.

IMPERIAL INTERVIEW

The Russians were in full flight. The Austrians were suing for peace. A hundred millions in gold (to start with) would find their way into Napoleon's personal treasury. Kingdoms would spring up.

The Emperor Francis had to bow to the demands put forward by Napoleon at the interview of which Thiard *was an observer.*

The mill had been sacked. Napoleon did not care for it. It was a beautiful day. He preferred to have the conference in the open, in a kind of bight formed either by the caprice of nature or by the working of a gravel-pit.

At that point the slope of the hill is very steep. Two light cavalry vedettes were posted there, and looked as though they were overhead. The sappers of the Guard lit a big fire, and, as it was thawing slightly, we ourselves carried off all the straw that was left in the mill to surround the bivouac, and lay down a path from the fire to the point of the roadway where the Emperor Francis II would be alighting.

On the Hungarian side the slope is much gentler. One can see a great stretch of the road. It was from that direction that the Emperor of Austria would appear. He was rather a long time coming. Napoleon even began to grow impatient, fearing that there might be some misunderstanding even yet. At last, we caught sight of several carriages and a large party of horse.

It was Francis II, escorted by a division of Kienmayer's hussars and one of Schwarzenberg's uhlans, and accompanied by several generals, including Prince John of Lichtenstein.

Instantly, the Guards beat the general salute. The trumpeters sounded the march. The spectacle was magnificent. What was to take place gave it a stamp of gravity which awoke in every mind a reverential and solemn feeling difficult to convey.

Napoleon advanced to the roadside, helped Francis II from his carriage and embraced him, saying something I did not catch. But he undoubtedly mentioned the English, for I heard the Emperor of Austria pronounce these words, very distinctly:

'The English are dealers in human flesh.'

Napoleon then conducted him to the fire, and remained alone with him, not with Marshal Berthier as well, as some accounts have it. So visibly was it his object to be alone with Francis II that, by a courteous gesture, he invited Prince John to withdraw. But, as far as we could judge by the dumb show, the Emperor of Austria seemed to be insisting that the prince should remain, and in fact the conference took place almost entirely between the Emperor and him.

When it was over, Napoleon escorted Francis II back to his carriage and took leave of him. Then, mounting his horse, he said to us:

'Gentlemen, we return to Paris. The peace is made.'

With that he galloped off again towards Austerlitz.

From Austerlitz to Wagram

(1805–1809)

The French require a prince to be active, enter-
prising and courageous, and above all (with
a smile) *to take them robbing abroad.*

NAPOLEON

THE EMPEROR AT PLAY

*Napoleon was never to be more glorious than on his return from Auster-
litz. His prestige was immense. He himself was radiant. Already it
would have been true to say, what was to be said shortly after: 'He
looked as though he were walking about in his halo.'*

*What had he in mind? Another war. But before starting a fresh
campaign, he allowed himself some diversion. The narrator is* Constant.

In the morning the Emperor called me and said:

'Constant, I've made up my mind to go to the Italian ambassador's ball this evening. During the day you will take ten complete costumes to the apartments he has made ready for me.'

I obeyed, and in the evening attended His Majesty to M. de
Marescalchi's. I dressed him as best I could in a black domino, and
applied myself to making him quite unrecognisable. All was
going fairly well, in spite of a good many remarks from the
Emperor on the absurdity of fancy-dress, the unbecoming effect
of a domino, etc. But when it came to changing his shoes, he
refused flatly, in spite of all I could say on the point. So he was
recognised as soon as he entered the ballroom. He went straight
up to a masque, his hands behind his back in the usual way. He
meant to broach an intrigue, and in reply to his first question he
was called 'sire'.

Then, disappointed, he turned brusquely away and came back
to me.

'You were right, Constant, I was recognised. Bring me ankle-
boots and another costume.'

I put on the boots and dressed him afresh, exhorting him to
keep his arms by his sides if he did not wish to be recognised at
first glance. His Majesty promised to follow what he called my
instructions from point to point. But he had scarcely appeared
in his new dress when he was accosted by a lady, who noticed the
hands that were still crossed behind his back:

'Sire, you are recognised.'

The Emperor at once let his arms drop, but it was too late,

and already everyone was respectfully falling back to make way for him.

He returned to his apartments once more and donned a third costume, assuring me that he would be very careful of his gestures, of his walk, and offering to bet that he would not be recognised.

Indeed this time he entered the ballroom as though it had been a barracks, pushing and jostling all around him, in spite of which he was again received with the murmur:

'Your Majesty is recognised.'

Fresh disappointment, fresh change of costume, fresh advice on my part, fresh assurances, and the same result, till at last His Majesty left the Embassy, convinced that he could not wear fancy-dress, and that the Emperor would show through any disguise whatever.

THE YOUNGER SET

He found his truest relaxation in children, and it was only with them that he showed a human side. Whoever—as Roustam *brings out—the children might be.*

One day, the Emperor was making his toilet. Little Napoleon (*son of Louis and Hortense*) is announced. He says to come in. He takes him in his arms. He kisses him often. He was between the two windows. He shows him the garden, and says:

'Whose garden is that?'

He replies:

'Uncle's!'

After that, he pulls his ears, saying:

'After me, it will be for you. I hope you will have a good estate!'

The Emperor was very fond of children. He would often ask after my son. One day I brought him down to the Emperor's bedroom. His Majesty was there. He said directly:

'So here you are, my fine fellow!'

He was four years old at the time, he called everyone *tu*, and as little shyness as usual at his age. The Emperor had him put in the window-recess and the child began straight away fingering his orders and asking about them.

The Emperor said:

'People only get things like these if they are good. Are *you* good?'

He immediately opens his eyes wide, and says:

'Just look in my eyes.'

'*They* say you're a famous rascal!'

I could not help being shocked at his saying *tu* and tried to make him a sign, but the Emperor noticed and made him turn his back, and the child went on prattling harder than ever. The Emperor asked:

'Can you say your prayers?'

'Yes,' said he, 'I say my prayers every day.'

The Emperor asked:

'What's your name?'

'My name is Achille Roustam. What's yours?'

I came up and I said: 'It's the Emperor!'

'Oh! Is it you that goes hunting with papa?'

His Majesty said to me:

'Doesn't he know me?'

'Sire, he has seen more often Your Majesty in a hunting coat; that's why he knows Your Majesty less in this one.'

The Emperor pulled his ears, rubbed his head. The child was delighted, and it seemed that he had still plenty to say to him. But His Majesty said:

'Now I must have breakfast. You shall come and see me again.'

Mme Durand, *the Empress's first lady in waiting, has a couple of stories:*

Napoleon was very fond of children. He enjoyed vexing them. One day when Hortense's two sons were at breakfast with him, little Prince Louis, aged three and a half, was eating a boiled egg. Napoleon got him to look away by drawing his attention to a plaything, and stole his egg. When the child saw it was gone, he picked up his knife and said to Napoleon:

'Give me back my egg, or I'll kill you.'

'What! You want to kill your uncle, you rogue?'

'I want my egg, or I'll kill you.'

Napoleon gave it back, saying:

'You'll be a fine blade.'

Another time, Princess Elisa's daughter, a little girl of five and very proud, was likewise breakfasting with Napoleon.

'Well, mademoiselle,' said he, looking very grave, 'this is a nice thing I hear. So you wet your bed last night?'

He was making it up.

The little princess stood up on her chair and said with an air of injured dignity:

'Uncle, if you can only talk nonsense I'm going away.'

Napoleon was much amused, but had great difficulty in getting her to sit down again.

MLLE DESPEAUX, MILLINER

To the torment of those about him, Napoleon was not always joking. On one distressing occasion he found a victim in Mlle Despeaux, then a celebrity of the fashion world. There have been many accounts of this incident, but Mlle Avrillon *was there at the time.*

Another day I witnessed a scene I should be tempted to call ridiculous, were it not for the respect I owe to the memory of Their Majesties. I shall describe it as it took place before my eyes. Then the reader may call it what he thinks fit.

The Empress was slightly unwell. One of the most famous milliners of the day, Mlle Despeaux, had come to offer her services to Her Majesty. She was waiting in the blue drawing-room leading into the bedroom, till she should be sent for.

Just then the Emperor was on his way to the Empress, and the first person to meet his sight as he entered the drawing-room, which he had to pass through, was Mlle Despeaux, armed with her bandboxes.

'Who are you?' he cried angrily.

When, trembling all over, she had given her name, he walked into the Empress's room like a madman. He strode about, he gesticulated, he shouted:

'Who sent for that woman? Who brought her here? I insist on knowing.'

Everyone begged pardon, of course without owning up.

However, the disclaimers of one and all only incensed the Emperor more and more. He was yelling like a maniac:

'I mean to know who is guilty. I will have you all put in prison!'

Now, when this frenzy burst out, the Empress was tied head and feet, that is to say, her coiffeur was dressing her hair and her legs were being bathed.

Maids and coiffeur all took to their heels, and I was left behind in the little dressing-room adjoining Her Majesty's room, with the door standing open. I confess that if I had been ruled by my first impulse I should have decamped as fast as the others. But thinking of the Empress's situation, I decided not to leave her alone, whatever might be the consequences. The Emperor saw me, but did not utter a word to me. After a few minutes he left the room, and the Empress had not been able to soothe him. For her part, she was trembling all over, and I found her with a contorted face.

Such was the scene at which I was present. And now for what came of it. Hardly had the Emperor got back to his study when he sent for the Duc de Rovigo [*Savary*], and ordered him to have Mlle Despeaux arrested by the constabulary and shut up in La Force prison. The duke did all that was humanly possible to prevent the Emperor from committing such an injustice, but his instances and entreaties were vain. The Emperor persisted in his determination, and there was nothing for it but to obey. Mlle Despeaux was arrested.

JOVIALITY AT THE COUNCIL-BOARD

Gaudin, *the minister of finance, gives us this view of Napoleon at a council of ministers, after Austerlitz.*

While Napoleon was detained in the heart of Germany by the famous campaign of Austerlitz, I had been thinking of extending to the various local Mints the new methods of manufacture which had been adopted in Paris, with great success. But to effect this scheme I needed a large amount of copper.

The army bulletins, reporting the enormous quantities of artillery taken from the enemy, inspired me with the idea of engrossing a modest share of this booty. On Napoleon's return, therefore, I lost no time in requesting him to hand over a score of field-guns.

M

'Twenty guns! And for what purpose? Have you a mind,' he added smiling, 'to go to war with me?'

'Oh, no indeed!' said I, 'it would not be a fair match. Only I should like to generalise the use of the new press which is working so well here, and whose merits Your Majesty is aware of. As Your Majesty knows, it is entirely of copper, and my budget can't support such an outlay. The whole problem would be solved if Your Majesty were to look favourably on my request.'

'But, minister, twenty guns! That's a lot!'

'I reckon twenty will be required. My idea,' I went on, 'is to call my new presses "Austerlitz presses", and put a band round them with the inscription: "Copper taken from the enemy at Austerlitz".'

'Ah,' said Napoleon in the most genial tone, 'you're laying a trap for my vanity. Well, you shall have your guns.'

THE NAPOLEONIC CIVIL SERVICE

This has been much praised and abused. The files preserved in record offices testify to delays and negligence out of keeping with the impatient character of the sovereign. The Duc de Broglie, who had an official post on the council of state, writes without passion of what he saw for himself.

Probably the want of favour with which I was long regarded gave me greater independence of judgment, and a more observant eye for what was passing around me. Not, however, that I was thrown by disappointment into a hostile attitude tending to produce a habit of denigration. On the contrary, I still admired the scope and power of the genius presiding over our destiny. I still regarded Napoleon as the unique, necessary man, as our sole guarantee against the recurrence of a revolution whose painful memories were always before me. But I did not shut my eyes to his faults, or to his misuse of power, or to the baneful advice of his flatterers, or to the excesses committed by agents of his authority.

My long service on the committee of appeal, the many claims reaching it, which I had had to study with care, yet sometimes without being able to secure the triumph of justice, had sufficiently enlightened me on the dangers of power as extensive as his. I shall give a few examples.

The Navy Office being in the hands of M. Decrès, he had been directed to see to the building and fitting out of the Boulogne flotilla. A Rouen contractor had undertaken to build flat-bottomed boats, and by the terms of his contract the price was to be paid him in thirds, on inspection of the work done. The first two payments had actually been made. But when the job was completely finished, the Navy could not be got to pay over the final third. Obviously the sole ground for this denial of justice was that the boats were useless, now that the scheme of invading England had been given up.

The unfortunate contractor, after applying and supplicating in vain, had recourse to the committee of appeal, whereupon the chief justice, as chairman, informed the Navy minister of the petition in the regular way, and asked for the documents filed in his department. As there was no answer to his repeated application, I, as recorder, was instructed to get them from the Navy Office myself.

I went to the head of the department. This was M. Jurier, a man of real ability and the most honourable character. Amazed by his confusion and the weakness of his excuses, I pressed the point. When he saw no further hope of eluding me:

'You shall judge for yourself,' said he, 'whether I can hand over a file like this.'

I then saw the contractor's letters accompanied by departmental reports, each more favourable than the last, but on which M. Decrès had thought it ruling enough to inscribe in the margin:

'He can f—— off!'

And to this fine sentiment he had punctiliously set his initials.

I acquainted the chief justice with this peculiar mode of vindicating decisions, and without further reference to the Navy Office, the committee pronounced in favour of the contractor. I then reported to the council of state, which confirmed the decision. But will it be believed—the order, which had to be signed by the Emperor, and which was sent to him in Germany, never came back. The minister, apprised of the committee's decision, which had been adopted by the council of state, found means to paralyse its effect, and the most odious bankruptcy became an accomplished fact.

What M. Decrès had done on the occasion I have described, M. Defermon also contrived to do more than once with decisions

taken by the council against his own findings and the judgment
of the finance committee, in which he held despotic sway.

Among the worst examples of abuse of this influence may be
cited the termination of the contract entered into with the
lessees of the Centre canal. It led the person chiefly concerned
to blow his brains out.

LESS AN ARCHITECT THAN A MECHANIC

*Towards an understanding of Napoleon at this period, we have the
study made of his person and bias by* Count Molé, *councillor of state,
minister, academician, peer of France, etc.*

*Napoleon had a strong liking for Molé. The Duc de Broglie explains
it thus:*

'*Napoleon was a great genius, he was the greatest of captains, but he
was likewise the greatest of talkers. According to connoisseurs who knew
him, when he wished to please nothing could compare with the charm,
variety and fecundity of his conversation on all subjects. To be sure
supreme rank did no harm, and endowed the merest trifles with value,
but there were some things very far from trifling.*

'*M. Molé was the first of listeners. He entered enchantingly into
one's idea, completed it if necessary, put in his timely word . . .*'

Napoleon's looks, from so close at hand, struck me beyond
anything I can convey. I have always believed in looks. His
matched his whole story. His head was magnificent and recalled
no other. Without putting much faith in the system of Gall,
which I had studied a little, I seemed nevertheless to distinguish
in the depth of his head, in the structure of his fine forehead,
in the setting of his eyes, in his well-moulded lips, in the droop of
his mouth at the corners, in the fine proportions of his face and
the regularity of his features, finally in his penetrating and veiled,
rather than mild, gaze, in his smile which was more disparaging
than cheerful, and rather derisive than ingratiating—I seemed,
once more, to distinguish all the powers that raise a man above
his fellows and fit him to dominate them, but none of the qualities or virtues that win affection or even regard in all ranks of life.

It might be more correct not to use the words fabric and
architect. At the peril of startling my readers, I shall say that

he was less an architect than a mechanic. Though a wonderful organiser, he always lacked the vast plan. There was not a wheel he could not install, not a detail beneath his care. Not a great thought, a great design that might not occur to him. But the aggregate, the proportions, the relations of the parts among themselves, the link or art which would have made them a unity, these not only escaped him, but he had no conception of them. He used all his powers, all the gifts he had received from heaven, with indefatigable energy, but he did not feel the absence of those he lacked.

In private, his one idea was to fathom the man he wished to know, to charm or astonish him. Above all he knew, better than anyone else has ever known, how to vary his manner, to alter his aspect, his glance, his countenance, according to the effect he wished to produce. To see him as nothing but an actor would be a denigration full of injustice, but to say that this astonishing mind scorned no detail of the stagecraft and histrionic business which, from Roscius to Talma, has shown its power, would be a mere statement of fact.

As he walked and talked, he was betraying some signs of fatigue. He stopped, leant on the billiard-table, began pushing the balls about with his hand and seemed on the verge of dropping asleep. He saw I observed this:

'It's remarkable,' said he, 'how the constitution is modified as one grows older, without any decline in strength or impairment of health. Our aptitudes change, and our plans should reflect the change. Once I would say to Montesquiou (his grand chamberlain) several times a day: "Montesquiou, bring me a glass of lemonade." Nowadays, what I ask for and feel I want is a cup of coffee or a glass of Madeira. Ah! believe me, Monsieur Molé, after thirty one begins to be less fit for soldiering. Alexander died before he knew he was going downhill.'

Pulling out his watch:

'It's late, let us join the Empress.'

Strange that though Napoleon's common sense amounted to genius, he never could see where the possible left off.

The more I saw of him, the more I observed him, the more firmly I was persuaded that, always under the sway of the moment, he thought of nothing but his own gratification, of magnifying himself and his power without limit and without rest. Irritated by the least obstacle, sacrificing everything to overcome it, and seeking only to establish at every juncture that nothing could resist his might and his will, when he had to choose between present and future he would choose the present, as being more certain and more subject to his control. In short, he was much less concerned to leave behind him a 'race', a dynasty, than a name which should have no equal and glory that could not be surpassed.

His dealings with Spain and with the head of Catholicism, even more inordinate than chimerical, had shown that he would not jib at any iniquity or abuse of strength to attain his object. But it was above all his Russian expedition and his notion of a continental blockade which demonstrated to every eye, even to the oldest comrades of his labours, that death alone could put an end to his undertakings and a curb on his ambition.

'The impossible,' he said to me one day, 'is a word of purely relative meaning. Every man has his "impossible", according to how much or little he can do. The impossible,' he added with a smile, 'is the ghost of the diffident and the refuge of the faint-hearted. On the lips of power, believe me, it is only a declaration of impotence.'

It was with this unbounded trust in his arm and his genius that, spreading through all the nations the sufferings and humiliation of conquest, he reduced them to despair.

PRUSSIA CONQUERED

In the autumn of 1806 it was Prussia's turn to be defeated. At Jena, by Napoleon; at Auerstädt, by Davout.

'*Auerstädt, a victory so distinct from that of Jena, though simultaneous,*' *wrote General the Comte de Ségur,* '*that eight or ten hours after Jena, Napoleon knew nothing of it.*

'*Yet it should excite no surprise that in his triumphal bulletin of the following day, he chose to merge that victory with his own.*

'*It was principally at Auerstädt, and by a single one of his lieutenants (Davout), that, though three times larger, the elite of the Prussian forces, with their most famous generals, their princes and their King himself, had just been laid low, while at Jena Napoleon, as strong as*

the enemy, turned out to have beaten only two lieutenants he had
separated from the rest.

'*The glory was too unequal for him to own up to it before the world,*
when glory was what he chiefly lived on.'

Here we come to one of the famous scenes of the epic: Napoleon's
clemency. The scene that took place—not the same as the legend—is
described by one of the chief actors, the Alsatian General Rapp.

Prince Hatzfeld had come to Potsdam as a delegate of the city
of Berlin, and had been well received. He sent a report of his
mission, if I remember rightly, to Count Hohenlohe, entering
into detail on the troops, guns and munitions in the capital,
or seen on his way. His letter was intercepted. Napoleon
handed it to me, with orders to have him arrested at once, and
send him to Marshal Davout's headquarters, a couple of leagues
off.

Berthier, Duroc, Caulaincourt and I tried in vain to calm
him. He refused to hear a word. M. de Hatzfeld was passing
on details, military information, which had nothing to do with
his mission. It was a clear case of espionage. Savary, who, as
commander of the gendarmes, usually dealt with affairs of this
kind, was on detached service. I was forced to deputise for
him. I ordered the prince's arrest, but instead of sending him
to the marshal I handed him over to the officer on guard at
the palace, whom I instructed to treat him with the greatest respect.

Caulaincourt and Duroc left the apartments.

Napoleon, alone with Berthier, told him to sit down and
write the order which would have the effect of placing M. de
Hatzfeld before a military court. The chief of staff attempted
some words of protest.

'Your Majesty cannot have a man shot who belongs to the
highest circles in Berlin, for such a small matter. The assumption
is impossible. You do not mean it.'

The Emperor's anger increased.

Berthier persisted. Napoleon lost patience. Berthier left the
room.

I was called in. I had overheard the scene that had been taking
place. I took good care not to venture the slightest comment. I
was on the rack. Apart from the unpleasantness of writing such

a harsh order, it had to be done as fast as speech, and I own I have
never had that gift. He dictated literally the following:

> *Our cousin Marshal Davout will appoint a military court com-*
> *posed of seven colonels of his army corps, of which he will be the*
> *president, in order to pass sentence on Prince Hatzfeld, convicted of*
> *treason and espionage.*
>
> *The sentence will be pronounced and executed before six o'clock this*
> *evening.*

It was about midday. Napoleon told me to dispatch this order
at once, along with Prince Hatzfeld's letter. I did nothing of the
kind. All the same I was shaking in my shoes. I was trembling
for the prince, I was trembling for myself, since instead of sending
him to headquarters I had left him in the palace.

Napoleon asked for his horses to pay a call on Prince and
Princess Ferdinand. When I went out to arrange this, I was told
that Princess Hatzfeld had fainted in the anteroom, that she
wished to speak to me. I went to her and did not conceal Napoleon's anger. I told her that we were riding out, and advised her
to get to Prince Ferdinand before us, so as to interest him in her
husband's fate. I do not know whether she appealed to him, but
she was in one of the corridors of his residence, and threw herself
weeping at the feet of the Emperor, to whom I gave her name.

She was pregnant.

Napoleon seemed affected by her situation, and told her to go
to the palace. At the same time, he instructed me to let Davout
know he was to defer the judgment. He thought M. de Hatzfeld
had gone.

Napoleon returned to the palace, where Mme de Hatzfeld was
waiting. He called her into the drawing-room, where I remained.

'Your husband,' he said kindly, 'has placed himself in an unfortunate position. By our laws he has deserved death. General
Rapp, give me his letter. There, read it, madam.'

She was trembling all over. Napoleon immediately took back
the letter, tore it up and threw it in the fire.

'Now I have no proof, madam, your husband is pardoned.'

He ordered me to have him back from headquarters at once. I
confessed that I had not sent him. He did not say anything. He
even looked pleased.

Berthier, Duroc and Caulaincourt behaved as usual in this
affair, I mean like good fellows, Berthier especially.

DAS IST GUT, DAS IST MISERABLE!

*On campaign as in Paris, Napoleon found time for women. In the
different capitals, he had his adventures—mostly rather commonplace.
But now and then they could be amusing. In this Prussian episode,
Constant is the narrator and go-between.*

In the course of a big review in Berlin, a young lady, accompanied by an aged woman, offered Napoleon a petition. On his
return to the palace, he looked through it and said:

'Constant, read this, it gives the address of the women who
presented it. You will go and find out who they are and what
they want.'

I read the petition, and saw that the young girl was begging
only the favour of a private interview with Napoleon.

Repairing to the address given, I found a damsel of fifteen or
sixteen, wonderfully handsome. Unluckily I perceived on speaking to her that she did not understand a word of French or
Italian. And at the thought of the 'interview' she was requesting,
I could not help laughing.

The mother, or the woman posing as such, talked French a
little, but with great difficulty. However, I succeeded in making
out that she was the widow of a Prussian officer, by whom she
had had this fair child.

'If the Emperor grants my daughter's request, I shall beg the
favour of being presented to H.M. the Emperor at the same time.'

I pointed out that as the audience had been solicited by her
daughter alone, it would hardly do for her to be present, and it
seemed she quite understood this necessity prescribed by
'etiquette'.

After our short interview, I returned to the palace and gave
Napoleon an account of my mission.

At ten o'clock in the evening I called for the two ladies in a
carriage and brought them back with me. I invited the mother
to wait in a small room while I took the young girl along to the
Emperor. Napoleon detained her, and I withdrew.

Though conversation was unlikely to be very interesting

between two people who could only communicate by signs, nevertheless it continued into the night.

Towards morning, Napoleon summoned me to ask for four thousand francs, and gave them himself to the young Prussian, who seemed very well pleased.

Then she rejoined her 'mother', who had not shown the faintest concern at the length of the interview. They got back into the carriage awaiting them, and I escorted them home.

Napoleon told me that he had failed to understand anything but *Das ist miserable, das ist gut*, and that for all the charm of a tête-à-tête with such a pretty woman, the interview had not been much to his taste.

IN EAST PRUSSIA

Having conquered the Prussians, Napoleon meant to conquer the Russians, and took the offensive. Here he was ill inspired. The long campaign before him was to be wound up by a spectacular peace, but France would get nothing out of it. Who would bear the cost? Prussia, where Napoleon was to increase the war tax. And who would have the last laugh? Russia, which was to wait and get its own back, with the whole-hearted support of the Prussian victims.

The campaign of 1806–1807 was atrocious. The French army nearly perished in mud. We will pass over these frightful scenes. Here is the day after Guttstadt, described by Norvins.

The day after the action at Guttstadt, in the morning, as the horse guards were pelting in the Emperor's wake at a fast trot, he turned abruptly off to the left and galloped his Arab horse up a large rounded hillock dominating the countryside. We followed him, and with us the galaxy of Mars's satellites.

It was then complete, that race of heroes of the age whom Napoleon had created marshals of his empire. Among them glittered the spoilt child of glory and Napoleon, the paladin Murat, in festal garb, covered with plumes, velvet, silk and laurels. He was in command of the cavalry.

On reaching the middle of a broad walk which crowned the eminence, the Emperor pulled up and jumped off his horse, saying:

'Berthier, my maps!'

Immediately the Master of the Horse beckoned the aide-de-camp in charge of the map-case, opened it and handed it to the chief of staff, who, bareheaded like himself, spread on the ground an immense map, on which the Emperor first knelt down, then propped himself on his hands, and finally stretched at full length, armed with a small pencil, with which he was marking it.

He remained in this attitude at least half an hour, completely silent. And in front of him, awaiting a sign or an order, stood the two great dignitaries, motionless, and still with their hats off, in spite of the burning sun of a Northern summer. The horse guards framed the picture, keeping a military eye on their sovereign.

I cannot say they

Copied his silence, as they stood around,

for I was there, a few paces behind the Emperor. Now General Guyot, commanding the light cavalry and gendarmes, in courteous response to a sign I had made him with a big bottle of old rum, had come and hanselled it, and then, after being induced to do the honours to his officers, brought it back with just, and only just, what was required for me to drink the Emperor's health aloud.

'Do be quiet, chatterboxes!' cried Napoleon without moving. For my toast had been repeated.

Then at last, to the great satisfaction of the Prince of Neuchâtel and the Duke of Vicenza, whose heads were burning, he got up again, turned towards us and began to laugh, showing his fine teeth, and thus tempering, like the Jupiter of Homer, the glory of his front.

He too, and rather better than Citizen Carnot, had been organising victory, studying the two theatres on which she was to descend on the wings of her eagle.

In a twinkling he was on horseback, off like a flash, and a huzza at the gallop, like an echo of his thought, brought us back on the road to battlefields.

BEFORE EYLAU

Napoleon's perplexity was increasing. He was at a distance from his corps, and without news. The mission on which he sent Krettly—*who tells the story—was not indeed of major importance, but it reflects his anxiety.*

Meanwhile, the Emperor had dispatched several officers to General Lannes, who had not come back. This gave him some uneasiness, and when we reached Landsberg he summoned General Corbineau, and asked for a very determined officer of his light horse.

That day I was with the Emperor on picket. He had seen me several times. But at that moment of grave concern, he did not think of me.

It is easy to understand that. We were only a week from the great battle of Eylau, and his brain was hard at work.

While General Corbineau was preparing to go and find the man he wanted, he too was searching his memory. Suddenly the thought of his old trumpet-major presented itself. He called the general back and said:

'I have it. Send me Lieutenant Krettly.'

I reported myself. He was writing. When he had finished, he raised his head.

'Ah! you're here.'

'Yes, sire.'

He folded his orders in silence, and handed them to me with an intent look.

'You are to go at once to the army corps commanded by Marshal Lannes. The way there is long and difficult. No matter. I must have an answer.'

'You shall have it, sire.'

So saying, I tucked his paper into the sleeve of my pelisse.

'What would you do if you were captured?' he asked with an air of great concern.

I guessed what was in his mind.

His eyes spoke.

'Sire, this order will never be read by an enemy. I give you my word for it.'

'Well, but what?'

'I should eat it.'

He clapped me on the shoulder with a look of gratification I was always disposed to share.

'Good,' said he, 'once you have eaten it you'll never forget it'—

yet all the same he repeated it aloud to fix it more deeply in my memory.

'Now, off with you. Use your wits, and you will come back.'

I believed his prophecy, for his words never misled the soldier.

A few days later, after being attacked, robbed and stripped, Krettly, who had retrieved nothing but a sabre, a busby and a pelisse, reported himself to Napoleon almost naked.

It was the 8th of February, 1807, a day of bloody memory.

'What do you want?'

Such was the Emperor's abrupt question when he saw me approaching at full gallop. He did not know me. His knitted and frowning brows betokened displeasure and anxiety.

'What do you want? Who are you?'

'Sire, your dispatch officer back from the 5th army corps.'

'Ah! . . . news at last!'

Who has not heard that 'ah!', so eloquent in the Emperor's mouth? His expression had already changed. And as I was pulling out the dispatches for him, he raised both hands to his brow, which was gradually clearing, and exclaimed in quite a loud voice, apparently oblivious of his surroundings:

'Oh! my head is much easier!'

One could see that. My arrival had worked a transformation. As he was reading I jumped off my horse, and when he had done he looked at me in amazement.

'What, in your skin?'

'Sire, I didn't make the whole journey like this; fifteen leagues or so is not too much for you.'

He smiled.

'Do you realise,' he added a moment later, 'that you're by no means unlike Robert, the brigand chief?'

And so saying, he took stock of me from head to foot. As for me, I was exclaiming inwardly at the liveliness of this astonishing genius, brimming with great matters, and passing like a flash from the deepest thought to the most childlike hilarity.

THE CHARNEL OF EYLAU

Hugo has immortalised it. Was it a victory? Was it a defeat? Neither; but during the night of that day of carnage (8th February) Napoleon learnt that the enemy was falling back. On the strength of which he dictated, on the 9th, a victory bulletin representing Eylau as a battle he had won the day before, at four in the afternoon!

Our first contrary witness is Pasquier, *councillor of state, minister, chancellor of the chamber of peers, baron, count, duke, etc.*

The outcome of the battle was so uncertain that on both sides, a retreat was ordered during the night. Marshal Davout, who was bivouacking with the most advanced corps, told a person who repeated it to me soon after, that just as he for his part was about to initiate the withdrawal, an officer arrived from the outposts to inform him that a very decided noise could be heard in the enemy bivouac.

He then went as far as possible towards the noise, and, on putting his ear to the ground, distinctly recognised a movement of guns and ammunition-waggons; and as the reverberation was growing fainter, he could have no doubt that the enemy was in full retreat.

When Napoleon was apprised of this, he at once ordered positions to be kept, and that was how the French army definitely retained the field.

And here is General de Saint-Chamans, *aide-de-camp to Marshal Soult.*

Up to daybreak on the 9th, we were still in doubt whether yesterday's butchery was not to start over again. Marshal Soult was on horseback at five in the morning, visiting his advanced posts to try for news of the enemy. As soon as objects could be made out, he saw that the Russian army had retired. On the ground where it had been fighting the day before, there remained only a few squadrons of Cossacks, watching our movements and apparently designed to cover the retreat of their army.

This Russian retreat gave us great pleasure. One would have had to be a complete savage not to desire an end to the bloody scenes of which we had been either actors or spectators for several days. The last two in particular had made a great impression, and the spirit of the French army was then far from being what it was in previous campaigns.

The marshal at once sent me to inform the Emperor that the enemy had retired. I made all speed, and found the Emperor in

a kind of small farmhouse, about half a league behind Eylau, on
the road we had covered two days before. All his guards were
bivouacked round this hovel. No one had yet entered the room
where he had passed the night, and I was told His Majesty was
asleep. I very much doubted it, for his position was anxious
enough to have kept him awake.

I went into a wretched kitchen, where I found the Emperor's
servants. (I mean the domestics, for the chamberlains, etc., were
lodged more nobly in the bivouac.) Some soup was being heated
for His Majesty. I desired a valet to announce that an aide-de-
camp of Marshal Soult was asking to see the Emperor, and as he
made some difficulty, I added that it was on urgent business.

He went into the Emperor's room. I remained near the door.
It was ajar, and when he had explained his errand I heard Napoleon tell him sharply to send me in.

I went straight into a dirty *Stube*. Two or three aides-de-camp,
among whom I seem to remember Caulaincourt and Lauriston,
were lying on a mattress in one corner. Napoleon, fully dressed
and with his boots on, was also lying on a mattress, by the stove.

He looked to me tired, uneasy and despondent.

'What news?' he asked sharply as I entered the room.

I replied in brief that Marshal Soult had sent me to report that
the enemy was retreating and to ask for orders.

By the way his countenance lit up, it was easy for me to judge
of the pleasure he felt at this news. The keen attention with which
he and his aides-de-camp had listened to my report showed me
that in this room, as in our bivouacs, there had been uneasiness as
to the results of the battle of Eylau, and that its inmates had been
fretting for intelligence of the movements of the enemy.

The Emperor's face became radiant. He ordered me to go
back to Marshal Soult and enjoin him to make no movement
without an order.

'Tell him,' he added, 'that I'm going to set Prince Murat with
all his cavalry at the Russians' heels.'

I lost no time in rejoining the marshal. As soon as he heard the
Emperor was coming, he made his corps take up arms, that is,
what was left of it.

It was pitiful to see all these regiments which, ten days ago, had
been so strong and so handsome, today collecting the fragments
of their three battalions to make up a half-battalion, with the

eagle in the centre. General Saint-Hilaire's infantry division,
which had still, on the day before battle, been seven thousand
strong, numbered less than two thousand the day after. Officers
and men looked cheerless and discontented. They were missing
the old comrades with whom, for ten years, they had been used
to conquer, and who had had that career of glory brought to an
end by Cossack and Tartar swords on the banks of the Pregel, or
by hunger and cold in the snows of Poland. Their political
science, less profound than Napoleon's, could not convince them
that this campaign was essential to the happiness of their country.

One regiment with the eagle loosened from its triumphal pike
by bullets and grapeshot had tied it on and secured it with black
ribbons. This regiment had also lost its colonel, and doubtless
wished to honour his memory by these signs of mourning. I
think it was the 43rd infantry regiment of the line. Its colonel,
killed on the previous day, was named Lemarois, and was a
brother of General Lemarois, the Emperor's aide-de-camp.

The Emperor came, attended by his staff and by sight-seeing
courtiers who, on learning that the enemy had retired, were
showing great eagerness to survey the battlefield. He inspected
it in detail. But on catching sight of these black ribbons, he displayed some resentment.

'I never wish,' he exclaimed, 'to see my standards in mourning.
We have lost a good many of our friends and of our brave comrades. But they died on the field of honour. Their fate is envi-
able.'

And he added some further bombast which made little impression. But the black ribbons that had offended his sight were
hastily removed.

When he walked down the line, among the shouts of 'Long
live the Emperor!' I heard many men shouting: 'Long live peace!'
Others: 'Long live peace and France!' Finally, there were some
shouting: 'Bread and peace!'

That battlefield was ghastly to view. I have never seen so many
dead collected in such a small space. Whole divisions, Russian
and French, had been hacked to pieces where they stood, and for
more than a quarter of a league there was nothing to be seen but
heaps of dead bodies. An enormous number of horses had been
killed as well, which enhanced the bloody effect of the picture.

THE CAMPAIGN GOES ON

Napoleon's propaganda falsehood was not designed simply to award him a victory; it was a question of restoring confidence to the French people, uneasy at the long absence and the silence of their head.

General Baron Paulin *shows Napoleon at work to convince even marshals and generals of his triumph.*

At last the day broke! It was the same scene, covered with debris, with dead and dying, but silent. The same sky, grey, dismal, cold. The French eyed each other. They doubted. They dared not believe in prognostics that spoke of disaster to the Russians. And they prepared to start over again. Batteries had been supplied afresh. Cartridges had been issued to every regiment.

Then an impressive spectacle met my gaze, when, to report on a mission he had given me, I doffed my hat and went up to General Chasseloup, who was next the Emperor.

Standing, with weariness in his face, but still with majestic countenance and lively eye, Napoleon was explaining to his marshals what the enemy would do, and how he would not dare to renew the conflict. The steadfastness, the firm attitude of his army had consummated the defeat of the Russians.

'When two armies have dealt each other enormous wounds all day long,' said he, 'the field has been won by the side which, armoured in constancy, refuses to quit it. That side is indubitably the stronger.'

Meanwhile, numerous and satisfying reports were coming in from all directions. 'Nothing to be seen.' 'No one stirring.' 'The enemy formations are moving off, veiled in mist.'

'Well! don't you see that yesterday the Russians came to the very end of their resources? They are retiring in defeat. They began their withdrawal at nightfall so as to be out of our reach by daylight,' exclaimed the Emperor.

And with that he dismissed each to his post.

All the marshals, uncovered, were awaiting this signal.

Among these stern-visaged men, Murat showed up in the foreground as a gallant knight without fear (later, he was not to be without reproach). He alone was smiling, in the rich and elegant Polish costume he had adopted for this campaign, during which

N

he cherished the dream of placing on his head the crown of the Jagellons and of Sobieski. The costly furs on his tunic of green velvet with gold brandenburgs, his embroidered and gleaming boots, his black hair streaming under the Polish cap with its white plume studded with gems, made a singular contrast to the uniforms of the other generals, tarnished by foul weather, and a two-day battle.

Close by, a few wretched planks had sheltered the Emperor through a night so replete with solemn thought. Two or three brands were still smoking which had warmed Napoleon.

The Emperor's toilet reflected the battle, much more than his lieutenant's. He was not shaved, though he had never before omitted this. His tabbed waistcoat, in one pocket of which was his gold snuff-box, his breeches, usually so irreproachable in their whiteness, proclaimed that he had been on horseback all through a long day, and had not gone to bed. His American boots, his silver spurs, normally so brilliant, were covered with mud. His fine doeskin gloves, blackened, said that the hand they clothed had been exerted convulsively, again and again, on the reins of several horses tired out in the struggle.

With the wonderful shrewdness which was peculiar to him, the Emperor had summed up the situation with astonishing accuracy. His persistence, the firmness of his attitude, had determined the Russian retreat.

IN PURSUIT OF A REAL VICTORY

Now that victory had been announced, it had to be won. Napoleon drove into East Prussia in pursuit of the enemy. At this moment de Gonneville, who had escaped from a perilous mission, saw him for the first time. For in the Grand Army, those who had never seen the Emperor were legion.

A few days after my return, the division of which we formed part was assembled for inspection by the Emperor, who had not reviewed it for two years.

I had never seen the Emperor, and I arrived on the parade-ground in keen excitement. At last, and for the first time, I was to have a close view of the author of the immortal campaigns of Italy and Egypt, the victor of Austerlitz!

The regiments, drawn up in a single line, waited for an hour. Then a group of horsemen appeared in the distance, and were soon close to us. At their head, fifty paces in advance of a brilliant staff, there came into view a man of the most martial figure and appearance. I thought this was the Emperor, but it was only Murat, Grand Duke of Berg, who, as commander-in-chief of the cavalry, had come to do the honours of the division.

He went by at the gallop, from left to right, then passed right down the line again at a walk, drew up on the left and waited.

The wait was not long. From the far side of the plain by which he had come, there soon emerged a very much larger group. First the mamelukes, covered with gold, their splendid horses, though mastered, capering as though in frenzy. Next came the aides-de-camp. And a hundred paces behind, the Emperor, followed by his immense staff. Bringing up the rear was the duty squadron of light horse.

The Emperor was far from cutting such a martial and terrible figure as the personage whom, in my ignorance, I had at first mistaken for him.

He wore a grey coat, extremely plain, and a little black-braided hat with no ornament but the cockade; the coat, unbuttoned, allowed a glimpse of a colonel's epaulettes on the undress uniform of the light cavalry, the only uniform which, from the beginning of the Empire, he ever wore in the field. He had white breeches and waistcoat, and riding-boots of soft leather. He was on a beautiful, light grey Arab horse.

He went down our line at a walk, towards the right. At the far end, he gave orders for us to form companies and dismount.

As he came to each regiment, the Emperor received its returns, which he passed on to the chief of staff, and then asked its colonel the following questions: 'What is your effective?—How many in hospital, in the cells, sick in quarters, or absent for any other reason?'

He repeated the same questions to the captains, and woe betide those whose memory or ignorance let them down. Harsh words, accompanied by looks which did not promise any imminent favours, gave them food for sad reflection.

When the Emperor reached my company, after questioning the captain, on whose left I was, he stopped in front of me and asked the colonel why the furniture of my horse was not standard. The colonel told him that I was just back from captivity, and had not yet been able to get the right furniture.

The Emperor did not like men to give themselves up, least of all cavalrymen, and he exclaimed, looking angrily at me:

'But your division has never yet faced the enemy!'

I was afraid to open my mouth, and the angry eyes fixing me so steadily gave me great discomfort. The colonel was beginning to explain what had happened when Lieutenant-General Espagne, who, on my return from captivity, had received me so ill, stepped forward and uttered the highest praise of my conduct on the occasion. During his account, the Emperor's face underwent a complete change, and when he had heard it all, he made me a gracious and deep bow.

We marched past by squadrons at the trot. On coming up to the Emperor, all raised their sabres and shouted: 'Long live the Emperor!' The shouts were tremendous, and the review seemed to have satisfied the person in whose honour it had been held.

On leaving our regiment, he said to Colonel d'Avenay:

'Colonel, at the next engagement, a cannon-ball or a general's stars!'

VICTORY AFTER ALL

At last the unhappy French managed to make their sacrifices useful to the policy of their chief. At Friedland (14th June, 1807), they scored a decisive victory over the Russians: which no one has recalled with greater enthusiasm than Norvins.

The march of the Emperor and his army was rapid, urged on by the terrific noise guiding us. The wind, which was from the north, brought, as it refreshed us, news of that great fight which would soon, at the voice of Napoleon, grow into a solemn battle. These echoes, interpreted and appraised by the wits and experience of the soldiers of the Guard, renewed their ardour, doubled their strength, to such a point, and this I shall always declare, did each one of them feel himself personally engaged in the cause of the great captain! All of them loved glory, and went running to meet the dangers that confer it. And so this great and heroic reserve of fifty thousand men, with Napoleon marching at its head, arrived before Friedland at five in the afternoon all in one mass, without leaving behind a single straggler.

This elect army had a wonderful esprit de corps. The idea was not to be first, but to be together. Valour was compact, indivisible. Such a memory can never die. With me it is forty years old, and today, at the end of my course, I testify that the honour of having made the campaign of 1807 in the Imperial Guard has remained the comfort of my old age. What a thing it was then to be French!

On reaching a modest plateau, the Emperor saw at once that the town of Friedland was in the centre of the Russian army, whose wings, while resting on it, projected each for about a league. Therefore, true to his invariable method of splitting the enemy forces so as to beat them separately, and moreover with the cardinal idea of taking from the Russians their one point of retreat, which was Friedland, Napoleon assigned its steeple as the focus of the attack.

It was in the middle of this great fight, while I was kneeling up on my saddle watching all its vicissitudes with devouring interest, that the Emperor, on foot and—I can see him now—lashing and smashing some tall weeds with his riding-whip, said to Marshal Berthier:

'What's the date?'

'The 14th of June, sire.'

'Marengo day, victory day!' returned the Emperor.

From my observation post, I saw Grouchy charge ten times with the dragoons. I also saw two magnificent regiments of Saxon cuirassiers, one red, the other white, burst like thunder through the Russian line and vanish into its rear ranks, to emerge victorious through the immense breach they had made with their great sabres. And so we joined rapturously in the huzzas with which the army saluted their gallantry.

And then I saw the last terrible scene of this great drama, in which seven or eight hundred field pieces made up the orchestra, and three hundred thousand combatants performed the dumbshow. Our infantry of the line of Ney's corps and Dupont's division went in for a bayonet attack on the Russian Imperial Guard—every man a colossus of the North—in the ravine encircling the town of Friedland, where, strongly placed, it was the final and redoubtable hope of the enemy's Grand Army.

It was the pigmies who beat the giants.

Two hours later, as we passed through this ravine, where our horses had blood up to their hocks, we saw, before entering the town of Friedland, all the bodies of the grenadiers of the Russian Guard still almost in line where they had fallen, and almost all with their wounds in the chest; that was as high as our soldiers could reach with the bayonet. Each of those brave men had defended and kept his station.

The battle had lasted six hours.

RETURN IN TRIUMPH

The Russians had been beaten. In a dainty pavilion on a raft moored in the middle of the Niemen, Napoleon and Alexander of Russia had met. Napoleon, conscious that he had been within an ace of ruin, was eager to treat. The Russian even succeeded in charming him. To such a degree that the campaign turned into a 'war for nothing', and all would be to do over again. But Napoleon was under the spell.

He returned to Paris bursting with pride. He had made his brothers kings. Joseph was King of Naples; Louis, King of Holland; Jerome, King of Westphalia. Murat would soon be a king; he was already a sovereign, since he was Grand Duke of Berg and Cleves. The sisters were on the same footing. Pauline was only Princess Borghese, but her husband could boast a prodigious fortune. Elisa was a sort of queen; sovereign of Tuscany, with the title of Grand Duchess.

Chancellor Pasquier describes him at this pinnacle of his reign.

With so many battles fought, so many victories won, so many obstacles overcome, and the triumphs of the diplomat added to those of the general, Napoleon left half Germany occupied by his troops, and retained the estuaries of the Weser, the Elbe and the Vistula. He re-entered his capital on the 27th of July. His absence had lasted fully six months; he had never yet been away so long.

This return was celebrated by public holidays, glittering with civil, military and religious display. Of these ceremonies, I particularly recall the *Te Deum* sung at Notre Dame. I attended it with the council of state, and being placed in the chancel, nearly opposite the throne, I was at pains to interpret the sensations revealed in the Emperor's countenance. It was obvious that he keenly appreciated the religious sanction hallowing, in the eyes of the people, his glory and his omnipotence. He valued it all the more because, till then, it had been completely lacking to all the works of the Revolution, because it distinguished him from all that had gone before him.

I do not think there was any stage in his career when he relished more fully, or at least with a more visible confidence, the favours of fortune. As a rule, in the midst of his greatest triumphs he affected an anxious air, as though to indicate that his great designs were not yet accomplished, and that it must not be supposed nothing was left to do. The observation I here set down was uniformly made by all who had dealings with him, and they never found him less accessible than at moments when some great stroke of fortune might have been expected to open his heart to the promptings of a more expansive benevolence.

In general, for those who had a favour to ask, it was better to approach him in some hour of difficulty than on one of his most brilliant days of triumph. Generosity was not the salient part of his character.

I seem to see him now, as he was that day in his garb of state, which, though slightly theatrical, was yet beautiful and noble. His features, always composed and grave, put one in mind of the cameos representing the Roman emperors. He was a small man, and yet his whole person, in that impressive ceremony, matched the role he had to sustain. The habit of command and the sense of his might increased his stature. A sword sparkling with gems hung at his side; the famous diamond known as the *Regent* formed the pommel of it. Its brilliance did not suffer one to forget that that sword was the heaviest and most triumphant the world had seen since those of Alexander and Caesar. I recall that M. Beugnot, who was sitting next me, made the remark. Both of us were then far from dreaming that less than seven years would suffice to break it.

WILL HE APPROPRIATE SPAIN?

The imperial display at an end, Napoleon turned his thoughts to fresh prizes. Which country should be next? Spain . . .?

Spain, which had been an ally of France for ten years, was ruled by an idiot king, Charles IV, his witless queen and her egregious and de-tested lover Godoy, to the ineffectual disgust of the son and heir. In

October, 1807, Napoleon concluded a secret treaty with Godoy for the partition of Portugal—incidentally, guaranteeing Charles IV's Spanish dominions. In pursuit of this 'healthful' aim (as the treaty expressed it) Junot led a French army into the peninsula. A stream of 'friendly' troops followed on, occupying a number of Spanish fortresses. The trio of rulers began to panic. Then, in March, 1808, the mob rose in Madrid, howling for Godoy's blood. Charles IV hastily abdicated in favour of his son, who was acclaimed with enthusiasm as Ferdinand VII. Having got over the fright, Charles demanded his throne back and denounced his son as a traitor. Both sides were angling for Napoleon's support.

So it was obviously his moment; but what should he do with it? Champagny records a discussion in which, as Foreign Minister, he took part.

Napoleon was at this time full of ideas on Spain, but they were not yet finally settled.

My appointment was too recent for me to aspire to advise him. But I remember a conversation which took place between him Prince Talleyrand and myself.

Napoleon set forth the condition of Spain: how impossible it was that, in its present state of anarchy, and considering the imbecility of the King, the ill repute of the Queen and the incapacity of the Prince of the Asturias, who had just struck a great blow without design and almost without knowing it, and would be unable to turn it to account, Spain should ever win through to a stable condition, a settled government, which, however, was necessary if this natural ally of France were to be of use: how it was to be feared that the English would profit by this anarchy to establish their influence, if not their sway in Europe: how he was therefore obliged to turn to the advantage of France, and indeed of Spain, an occurrence which might prove fatal to the latter kingdom.

'Two courses suggest themselves,' said he. 'Either to seize the whole of Spain and install a prince of my own blood, on the pretext of avenging the rebellion of a son against his father, of a subject against his king, or to appropriate and unite with France the northern provinces of Spain up to the Elbe [Ebro], by negotiating with Ferdinand VII and recognising him, on that condition, as King of Spain and the Indies.'

And he asked our views on this choice.

M. de Talleyrand gave it as his opinion that it was no use doing things by halves, that the one course would be as odious as the other, and would excite the same displeasure in Europe. That the cutting up of Spain would make it impossible to enjoy in peace an acquisition only to be preserved by a constant struggle, which would rather weaken than strengthen France.

My opinion was different. I was rather for an acquisition which would leave Spain a prince who seemed to be winning her affection: which, brought about by treaty, would have less of the stamp of usurpation and more resemblance to the common transactions of European diplomacy: which, less gigantic than what amounted to the confiscation of a kingdom, would be easier, exposed to fewer risks, and might be equally profitable.

Napoleon did not declare himself. But thenceforth, the acquisition of the whole of Spain was in his mind, and all his views were directed towards the execution of that grand design.

ON THE EVE OF THE GREAT BLUNDERS

Here he is, looking straight ahead, blind to the prodigious mistakes that lay before him—and a target for the eyes of distinguished strangers visiting Paris, like the Comte de Mérode-Westerloo.

About this time, Napoleon began the invasion of Rome and of Spain. Then I found an opportunity of seeing him close without being presented to him, which could not take place unless one were willing to serve him.

He was giving a state entertainment at the palace of the Tuileries. The auditorium presented the most brilliant appearance I had yet seen. From the orchestra to the door of the pit, there was nothing but gold and silk embroidery. All the boxes were full of ladies of the new regime, among whom one observed some from the old, and several sovereign princes of Germany and Italy. The Empress Josephine, sitting with the Queen of Holland in a box next to the Emperor's, was then in the last days of her grandeur.

Napoleon, alone in the imperial box, was stretched at full length in an armchair of crimson velvet trimmed with gold braid, his arms and legs crossed, now and then picking up the libretto of the Italian opera which was being performed before him.

Behind his chair stood the Grand Master of Ceremonies, Comte de Ségur, and the Grand Chamberlain, Comte de Montesquiou, both in red and gold uniform.

Napoleon frequently drew a snuff-box from his pocket and took a good deal of snuff, now and then speaking a few words to these gentlemen with a haughty air.

That day he looked ill-tempered and restless. I was sitting in a box opposite, but lower than his.

Needless to say, I took very little interest in the performance, and my eyes were always bent on Napoleon, whose postures and play of feature I still recall.

BREATH OF DECAY

Concord with the Church was short-lived. Pius VII would not embrace the Continental System; so Napoleon occupied the Papal states, took over the Papacy, and, on being excommunicated, carried the Pope off to prison.

By then the Spanish affair was wound up. Napoleon had invited— and in Ferdinand's case, decoyed—all those concerned to Bayonne, promising to smooth out their difficulties. Once they were in the trap, he said their best plan was to give him the throne; he would find an incumbent, and would also provide them with handsome pensions. After much bullying and wheedling, they gave in. Josephine, in 'the last days of her grandeur', came to help with the wheedling. Ferdinand, the last signatory, broke down under menacing allusions to the Duc d'Enghien. After which, Joseph Bonaparte was summoned from Naples and instructed that he was King of Spain.

At St Helena, Napoleon himself was to admit that he had 'gone about the Spanish affair very badly'—that the immorality was really too brazen.

The Duc de Broglie saw him going about it, in the literal sense.

This same period, at a time when I was staying in the country, witnessed the birth, prosecution and completion of that work of darkness which is still, in the official language of historians of the Empire, inoffensively termed the Bayonne settlement.

At Les Ormes we were in the way of news. No comings or goings could escape us.

I saw the Emperor passing, on his road to Bayonne. He stopped at Les Ormes to breakfast at the inn like a common

traveller. Already the young First Consul was gone, whom I had
seen for the first time striding nimbly through the Tuileries, his
right arm in Bourienne's and a little Turkish sabre under his left,
slim and easy, with olive complexion and untamed eye. Even
outwardly all was changed. His bust was short and thick, his
little legs fleshy, his complexion livid, his brow bald, his countenance affecting the Roman medal. I shall not say, like the serv-
ing-maid at our inn, that in all his doings he had a crown on his
head and a sceptre in his hand. For my part, I saw nothing of the
kind. But, as one of the crowd that thronged to watch him going
in and out, I did think everything about him smacked of the
Emperor, and the Emperor at his worst.

A few days later, I saw the Empress going by in great pomp,
got up like a picture wherever her person could not be seen, and
painted wherever it could be seen. A brilliant mob of ladies-in-
waiting, of the bedchamber and of the palace followed in her
train, and, also in her train, the cortège of readers who formed
our sultan's harem, helping him to put up a little longer with the
raddled old age of the superannuated sultana. Yet it would seem
that the bargain between the imperial spouses was not uncon-
ditional, for in another day or two we saw one of these odalisques
tearfully retracing her steps, and the curious learnt from the footman attending her that she had been dismissed for giving herself
airs.

At that time no one really understood the Spanish situation.
We were more or less ignorant of what was hatching at Bayonne,
and I am disposed to believe, for the credit of human nature, that
the Emperor himself was rather groping his way. He had
undoubtedly set the trap, but he may not have exactly foreseen
how much browbeating, baseness and perfidy would be required
to attain his end.

LADIES, FALL IN, EYES FRONT! . . .

*Wherever he might be, imperial majesty waived none of its rights. It
has been said that he had to have 'court everywhere'.*

*We see him now at Bordeaux, at the usual military reception of
ladies. Among them, the Marquise de La Tour du Pin—who, being
very shrewd, was to secure priceless favours from Napoleon, though a
royalist.*

My husband at once sent me a carriage, for there could be no hesitation. I had a number of gowns at Bordeaux. But there was no black one among them, and the court was in mourning. The drawing-room was to be at eight, and it was then five. Luckily, I noticed a grey silk one. I added some black ornaments. A good coiffeur put black ribbons in my hair. And I thought it all very becoming to a woman of thirty-eight who, be it said without vanity, did not look thirty.

We gathered in the large dining-hall of the palace. I knew hardly anyone at Bordeaux, except Mme de Couteneuil and Mme de Saluces, just those who were not present.

There were sixty or eighty women in the room. We were drawn up according to a list read aloud by a chamberlain, M. de Béarn. He reiterated that there was to be no changing of places on any pretext, or he should not be able to give our names correctly, and enjoined us to dress our line.

Hardly had this quasi-military manœuvre been completed when a loud voice announced:

'The Emperor!'

Which made my heart beat fast.

He began at one end, speaking to each lady in turn. As he drew near my place in the line, the chamberlain whispered to him. He fixed his eyes on me, smiling in the most gracious way, and when my turn came he said laughingly, in a familiar tone, scanning me from head to foot:

'Why, it seems you're not at all sorry for the death of the King of Denmark?'

'Not enough, sire, to give up the happiness of being presented to Your Majesty. I had no black gown.'

'Ah! that's an excellent reason,' he rejoined. 'And besides, you were in the country.'

Then addressing the woman next me:

'Your name, madam?'

She stammered. He did not catch it. I said:

'Montesquieu.'

'Ah, really!' he cried, 'that's a fine name to bear. I went to La Brède this morning to see Montesquieu's study.'

The poor woman, thinking she had hit on a bright idea, replied:

'He was a good citizen.'

The word citizen set the Emperor's teeth on edge. He darted at Mme de Montesquieu, with his eagle eyes, a look that might well have appalled her if she had understood it, and replied very brusquely:

'Not at all, he was a great man.'

Then he glanced at me with a shrug of the shoulders, as if to say: 'What a stupid woman!'

GOETHE BEFORE NAPOLEON

At Bayonne, Napoleon had started the Peninsular War, and made an immense breach for the 'English influence' he was trying to keep out. Indirectly, he had also given a powerful fillip to German nationalism.

This turn of events quickened his desire for a fresh hold on Alexander, who, though still an ally, was by now considerably estranged. He therefore set out for Germany, where the Emperors had a second meeting at Erfurt (27th September–14th October, 1808).

It was a round of display, ceremony and theatricals. Napoleon had brought along the Comédie Française, to play before 'a parterre of kings'. Nor did he omit to 'summon' Goethe during his breakfast hour. As he had really little to say to him, it was Daru, a distinguished civil servant and man of letters, who bore the brunt of the conversation.

Here Goethe is the speaker.

At about eleven in the morning (2nd October, 1808), I am summoned to the Emperor. A fat Polish chamberlain tells me to wait. The crowd melts away. Introduction to Savary and Talleyrand.

I am called into the Emperor's closet. Just then Daru presents himself and is admitted at once. So I am in doubt whether to go in. I am called again. I go in. The Emperor is breakfasting, seated at a large round table. On his right, a few steps from the table, Talleyrand is standing. On his left, and quite close to him, Daru, with whom he is discussing the taxes to be raised.

The Emperor beckons me to approach. I remain standing before him at a proper distance. After considering me attentively, he says:

'You are a man.'

I bow. He inquires:

'How old are you?'

'Sixty.'

'You are well preserved. You have written tragedies?'

I make the obligatory reply.

Here Daru begins to speak. In order to flatter the Germans and sweeten, up to a point, the harm he was forced to do them, he had studied their literature a little. Daru was very well up in Latin literature, he had even published an edition of Horace. He spoke of me as the most favourable Berlin critics might have done, at least I recognised their ideas and their way of thinking. He added that I had translated some French works, including Voltaire's *Mahomet*. The Emperor rejoined:

'That's not a good play.'

And he explained very circumstantially how ill it suited the conqueror of the world to draw such an unfavourable portrait of him.

He then turned the conversation to *Werther*, which he must have studied from end to end. After various remarks, all very just, he mentioned a passage and said:

'Why did you do that? It's against nature.'

And he developed this view with great lucidity, entering into many details. I listened serenely, and replied smiling with a gratified air:

'I doubt whether this charge has been made before. It strikes me as perfectly just, and I own the passage has something about it which is contrary to life.'

And I added these words:

'Perhaps some indulgence should be shown to the poet who uses a skilful artifice to produce certain effects he could hardly have reached by a simpler and more natural path.'

The Emperor appeared satisfied and returned to the subject of drama. He made far-reaching comments, like a man who had studied the tragic stage with the intentness of a criminal judge, and had felt keenly that the weakness of French drama lies in its deviation from truth and nature. While developing this theme, he took exception to dramas in which fate plays a large part.

'Those works belong to a dark age. Besides, what do they mean by their fate? Policy is fate.'

[*Here, Napoleon broke off the interview, addressing questions to Daru, Soult, etc. After some time, he remembered Goethe.*]

The Emperor got up, came towards me, and, by a kind of manœuvre, separated me from the other persons among whom I was standing. Turning his back on them, he addressed me in an undertone, asking whether I had children, whether I were married, and other things of personal interest to me. He also spoke of my relations with the reigning family. I replied in a completely natural voice. He seemed pleased, and translated my words into his own language, but with rather more precision and clearness than I could have done myself.

Here I ought to observe that I had been admiring, in the course of conversation, his varied way of expressing approval. He seldom listened impassively. He would shake his head with a thoughtful air, or he would say 'Yes!', or 'Good!' or other things.

Nor should I forget to recall that after having spoken, he would usually add:

'What does Monsieur Goet say?'

NAPOLEON BEFORE GOETHE

All the same, Goethe was a man who could understand Napoleon, far better than Napoleon was capable of understanding Goethe. (He was never to discuss the works of the great German writer throughout the seven years' leisure of his exile and captivity.) This is how Goethe, from a great height, spoke of him to Eckermann.

Goethe: My dear child, a name is no trifle. Did not Napoleon, for a great name, turn half the world upside down? . . . Great is the power of truth. The halo, the glamour with which journalists, historians and poets have invested Napoleon falls away before the dreadful reality of this book—the *Memoirs of Bourrienne.* . . . But the hero is not diminished. On the contrary, he is raised as he comes nearer truth.

Eckermann: His presence must have exerted a kind of fascination, to enable him to subjugate men in a twinkling, win them over and lead them.

Goethe: Beyond doubt his personality was of a superior order. But the essential point is that men felt sure of attaining their object in his company. That is why they became his followers, as they follow anyone who inspires a similar confidence. Do not actors grow fond of a manager from whom they expect good parts? That's an old story which is always repeating itself. Such is human nature, once and for all. No man works for his neighbour spontaneously. But if he thinks it is for himself, he is nothing loth. Napoleon was well acquainted with men, and knew how to turn their weaknesses to account.

THE IRRESISTIBLE FORCE AND THE IMMOVABLE OBSTACLE

But just as the Spanish game was lost in advance, so the Erfurt meeting was a speculation that failed. Napoleon got nothing from Alexander. Indeed their relations nearly suffered a premature death-blow.

Napoleon confided as much at the time to his Master of the Horse and ambassador to Russia, General Caulaincourt, *Duke of Vicenza, who has described the conversations between the emperors.*

They were, as I have already said, sometimes more than lively. At one such moment the Emperor Napoleon, unable to get what he wanted from the Emperor Alexander (it was a question of Austria), tried losing his temper; working himself up, he threw his hat or some other object on the floor and trampled on it. But the Emperor Alexander stood still (I should observe that the sovereigns, as they talked, were nearly always pacing the Emperor Napoleon's closet), eyed him with a smile, and said when he had calmed down a little, which was the work of a moment:

'You are a violent man, I am an obstinate one. Passion is therefore wasted on me. Let us talk, reason, or I am going.'

So saying, he made for the door, and would have acted on his words if the Emperor Napoleon had not advanced to stop him.

The conversation was resumed quietly, and the Emperor Napoleon gave way.

This incident repeated itself on the subject of Prussia, but less hotly, for, as the Emperor Napoleon told me several times, the Emperor Alexander was growing daily more headstrong in his resolves.

These details were related to me by Napoleon, who said:

'Your Emperor Alexander is as stubborn as a mule. He shams deaf when it doesn't suit him to hear.'

THE SCENTED VIRGIN OF MADRID

After a week at home, Napoleon set out for the Peninsula. Already it was high time. Spain was ablaze; Joseph had had to flee his 'capital' almost at sight. Worst of all, and a portent to all Europe—at Baylen about twenty thousand of the 'invincible' French, under the gallant General Dupont, had been cut off by the Spaniards and forced to lay down their arms.

But the patriots had no leadership. Napoleon, with a disciplined army and a numerical superiority of three to one, routed them again and again. For a short time, he led the life of a peaceful sovereign at Madrid and the royal residence of Chamartin. And at Chamartin, he had a somewhat comic adventure with a young Madrilene, brought to him by Constant.

At the grand theatre there was then a very pretty creature, fifteen or sixteen at most, with black hair, an eye full of fire and a bewitching bloom. She had contrived (or so it was said) to preserve her virtue from the perils to which it was exposed by her profession of actress. She had a noble spirit, a good heart, extraordinary vivacity of expression. She had everything, in short, she was adorable. . . .

So Napoleon heard one day from M. de Bausset, who had been to the theatre the night before and returned wonder-struck. M. de Bausset added that the young girl had lost her father and mother, that she lived with an old aunt, that this aunt (equally grasping and depraved) watched over her with peculiar care, affecting the strongest attachment to her, and everywhere exalting the charms and merits of her 'dear child', all in the hope that she would soon be able to found her fortune on the liberality of some rich and powerful protector.

Napoleon, on such an inviting portrait, having expressed the wish to see this beautiful actress, M. de Bausset sped to the aunt, with whom he was soon at one, and that evening the niece was at Chamartin, dazzlingly arrayed and scented with every scent imaginable.

Napoleon had an intense dislike of scent. Nor did he fail to show it when I entered his room with the poor girl, who had doubtless thought she would give Napoleon great pleasure by thus drenching herself with fragrance. But still, she was so pretty, so seductive, that as he looked at her, Napoleon felt his antipathy melt away.

o

I left the bedroom, and about two hours afterwards his bell went as though he would break the rope. I hurried in, and found only the young lady. Napoleon was in his dressing-room, with his head in his hands.

'Constant,' he exclaimed on seeing me, 'take that child away! Her perfumes are killing me! It's unbearable! Open all the windows, the doors . . . but above all, take her away! Hurry!'

It was a very late hour to dismiss a woman. However, the order admitted of no reply. So I went to acquaint the poor child with His Majesty's will.

She did not understand me at first, and I had to repeat several times:

'Mademoiselle, His Majesty desires you to withdraw . . .'

Then she began to cry, imploring me not to turn her out at such an hour. In vain I said that I should take every precaution, order a quiet, well-closed carriage—her entreaties and tears never stopped, though she found a little solace in the sight of a considerable present Napoleon had given me for her.

On my return, I found Napoleon still seated in his dressing-room, rubbing his temples with eau de cologne. He leant on me to regain his bed.

GO ON, PUT A BULLET IN HIM

But Napoleon did not stay long in Madrid. He had brought 300,000 men over the Pyrenees, and took it for granted that, while they went on to conquer the south of Spain, the small British army under Sir John Moore would retreat into Portugal. Instead, it suddenly turned up in his rear, threatening his communications with Bayonne. This heroic bid to draw off the pressure was a complete success. Napoleon shelved his plan of campaign, diverted the bulk of his forces, and gave chase in person. 'Put in your newspapers,' he wrote to Joseph, 'that 36,000 English are surrounded . . .'

On the march north, according to Geoffroy de Grandmaison, soldiers were shouting to the men around the Emperor: 'Go on, put a bullet in him!' Colonel de Gonneville heard that threat and many more.

The English army which had landed at La Corogne, under the command of General Hill [*sic*] was advancing on Madrid, threatening our communications with France and lending the Spanish rising moral support, besides what arose from an abundance of arms and ammunition placed at its disposal.

The Emperor having hurled himself in pursuit of this army with his Guards and Marshal Ney's army corps, we received orders to flank their column at a distance of two or three leagues, stopping every night as far as possible in line with the imperial headquarters, to which we would send every morning for orders on the operations of the day.

The English army set off in full retreat as soon as we marched on it. We crossed the mountains of Guadarrama in a frightful blizzard. The snow, driven by swirling winds, fell with furious violence, enveloped us and covered us in a thick layer which penetrated our cloaks. A number of men perished in this crossing, which took a whole day, and it was an incredible effort to get the artillery across.

As we were so painfully climbing the Guadarrama, we found ourselves on the flank of the infantry division commanded by General Lapisse, and, a few paces behind, the Emperor, who was on foot like ourselves, for no precaution had been taken in shoeing the horses, and they were continually falling down.

The soldiers of the Lapisse division were demonstrating aloud the most sinister attitude towards the Emperor's person, inciting one another to fire their muskets at him, and taunting each other with cowardice for not doing so. He heard it all quite as well as we did, and seemed to be taking no notice.

But Gonneville *also witnessed Napoleon's irritability.*

The Emperor was at the foot of the mountain, at the entrance to the defile. In another hundred paces he would have been under the fire of the first battery, which was covered by a breastwork flanked by sharp-shooters, and had in front two of the cuttings I have mentioned.

The Emperor ordered timber and plank bridges to be quickly laid over these cuttings. The sappers carried out his order, but with considerable losses.

He then ordered Colonel de Piré, aide-de-camp to the Prince of Neuchâtel, to go and see whether he could risk a cavalry charge on the first battery.

Piré set off at a gallop, was greeted by a fusillade, and, returning with a rather too startled air, told him out loud that the thing was impossible.

The word and the way it had been spoken goaded the Emperor to such fury that he lashed out with his riding-whip, and M. de Piré only avoided the blow by an abrupt retreat.

The Emperor ordered the chasseurs of the Guard to charge the first battery. They set off at a gallop in column of four, and dashed in with their invariable resolution. But the moment they were exposed, on rounding the part of the mountain which covered us, the gunfire and fusillade started again so briskly that they returned in great disorder, thus vindicating Colonel Piré's assertion.

NAPOLEON AND THE SURGEON

For a few days Napoleon fixed his headquarters at Valladolid. On 12th January, 1809, Baron Percy, surgeon-general of the Grand Army, waited on him at breakfast-time.

He was breakfasting with the prince (Berthier). I stationed myself opposite His Majesty, and here is our conversation:

'Good-morning, my dear Percy. How goes it?'

'Your Majesty does me too much honour. Your Majesty will allow me to congratulate him on his good health and on his appetite.'

'My appetite! That's in good order, and I am well. In general, we are all pretty well. But have we many sick here?'

'Sire, last night there were only a hundred and nineteen, and this morning there are nearly three hundred, but few are gravely affected.'

'You must have a great many leg and feet cases, chilblains, frostbitten hands.'

'That is so, sire. We also had plenty of dislocations and fractures crossing the sierra de Guadarrama, on account of the silver thaw. Most of them were from the artillery trains, because, as the soldiers had to support their mules and horses, when all four feet slipped at once the fall of the animal on the man necessarily entailed that mishap.'

'It must have. What did you do with those men?'

'I left some with surgeons at Villa-Castin, at Arevalo, at Medina

del Campo. On our march from Rio-Seco to Benavente we also
left some French sick and wounded in the villages, but on the way
back we collected them at the risk of being murdered, and there
again your surgeons imperilled their lives to rescue brave men for
Your Majesty.'

'Indeed, my surgeons are very good fellows. They're full of
courage, and I am much pleased with them.'

COMMENTARY ON CORNEILLE, OR THE BIG VALLADOLID SCENE

*Next day on parade, Napoleon caught sight of General Legendre, who
had been Dupont's chief of staff at Baylen.*

*His fury at the Baylen surrender, when he first heard of it, had
inspired one of those 'divagations' with which he was wont to hold up
and enthrall the council of state. Councillor Pelet writes:*

*'It was the first time that victory had deserted his standards, and that
his eagles had been brought low. The spell was broken. He indulged
the effusion of his grief to such a point that tears could be seen in his eyes,
and, after talking of the resources the general might have found in his
despair, he exclaimed: "Oh! how rightly, after saying:* He could have
died, *old Horatius goes on:* Or called a high despair to succour him.
*And how little they know the human heart, those who find fault with
Corneille and accuse him of having needlessly weakened, by this second
line, the effect of* He could have died." *It was curious to hear Corneille thus annotated by Napoleon.'*

*He was now to expand his commentary. As a matter of fact, he
himself was originally responsible for the surrender, by the way he had
hazarded Dupont and his men, short of everything and nearly dying of
hunger and thirst. And in any case, whatever might be thought of the
general, the chief of staff's conduct had been irreproachable. But it was
characteristic that Napoleon should vent his rage, not on Dupont, but on
the blameless Legendre. The big Valladolid scene is famous. No one
could recall it better than General Thiébault, of whom Napoleon had a
high opinion.*

On arriving at Valladolid shortly before noon, I attended the
parade, where the Emperor daily took the salute himself.

After the inspection, as he was returning to his place to direct
the march-past, he caught sight of General Legendre, who had

been chief of staff to Dupont's army corps, and whose presence at this review I for my part had thought calamitous.

Immediately, with a blasting look, he apostrophised him in these words:

'You are very bold to show me your face.'

In the most funereal silence, all eyes were turned on General Legendre, who, merely at this beginning, seemed already to have been struck by lightning. He replied, however, but so low that I could not hear a word, and hat in hand, in the humblest attitude, he endured the torture of all that was to follow this prelude. An appalling scene, which, on my return to quarters, I wrote down in a little notebook I still possess.

And in fact, his features convulsed, his eye terrible, his gestures threatening in the last degree and his voice ringing out so that the furthest officer, the furthest soldier present, might see and hear him, he at once began again, pacing up and down between General Legendre and the troops, halting unceasingly, now apostrophising him, now talking as though to himself, launching his broadsides at each of these comings and goings, but always with a terrible gaze, and signs of the most violent agitation:

'How can you go on showing yourself, when your shame is blazoned everywhere, when your dishonour is written on the foreheads of all the brave? Yes, you have been blushed for even in the depths of Russia, and France will blush far more hotly when, through the proceedings of the high court, she learns of your capitulation.

'And when has an armed force been known to capitulate on a battlefield? One capitulates in a fortress, when one has exhausted every resource, employed every means of resistance. When, with practicable breaches, one's misfortune has been honoured by three assaults sustained and repulsed. When there is no further means of holding out, no hope of relief. But on a field of battle, one fights, sir, and when instead of fighting one capitulates, one ought to be shot. . . . And where should we be, if army corps were to capitulate in the open? In open country, there are only two ways of succumbing: to die, or to be taken prisoner. But under a hail of rifle-butts! . . . War has its fortunes. One may be defeated. One may be taken prisoner. Tomorrow, I may be taken. . . . Francis I was taken. He was taken with honour. But if I am ever taken, it will be only under a hail of rifle-butts.'

Each of these sentences, emphatically pronounced, sometimes unconnected, never incoherent, laden with repetitions which in part I omit, but in general reducing the thought to its simplest expression, was cut off by pauses, very much in his style, and, in this situation, meant to ensure that his every word, clearly heard, clearly understood, should make its mark. . . . Now, the pause after these last words being rather more prolonged than the others, it gave rise to the following colloquy:

Legendre: We were facing more than twice our own numbers, and we had an equal force in our rear.

Napoleon: You should have done as Marshal Mortier did at Krems, where, with a handful of compact and serried men, he made his way through four lines of Russian troops. To deploy in such a case is to betray ignorance of all the rules of the art. In column you would have overturned those Spaniards. They were not a quarter as good as your troops.

Legendre: We had only conscripts.

Napoleon: Under good leaders, conscripts always make good soldiers.

Legendre: We wished to save the artillery.

Napoleon: It was not the artillery you wished to save, it was your waggons, that is to say the fruits of your pillaging. Whom do you expect to deceive? If you had not thought more of the tainted gold your waggons were carrying than of honour, you would have seen what duty demanded. But you had ceased to be either Frenchmen or generals, you were only thieves and traitors.

Legendre: We were only trying to preserve men for France.

Napoleon: France needs honour, she does not need men.

Legendre: The capitulation was not observed.

Napoleon: Would to heaven no part of it had been observed, that the Spaniards had given all of you your deserts, that I had received nothing, and above all that your capitulation had not been made public. . . . But you are surprised it was broken. . . . Did you not know that the English were masters of the sea? *

* *Here Napoleon was peculiarly disingenuous. Just as he had been primarily responsible for the misfortunes of Dupont's corps, so he was responsible for the non-fulfilment of the capitulation. Here it was provided that the 18,000 victims of this barbarous Napoleonic adventure should be repatriated by sea. The Spaniards kept their engagement and released the prisoners. The English humanely offered to transport them. But Napoleon decreed that these poor French conscripts should not be allowed to land in France.—J.S.*

. . . And what were your guarantees? . . . Did you even invoke the protection of an English consul? . . . No. It is unknown in history for 18,000 men, 18,000 Frenchmen, to pass under the yoke when they might have fought; for virgin arms to be surrendered, when the soldiers were more than willing to use them. But even if victory had been impossible, you had still your lives to sell. No one is a soldier unless he prefers death to ignominy. . . . A soldier must be able to die. . . . And what is death? Has it not always to be endured? A man who cannot die ought not to prostitute the dress and arms of the brave.'

I thought it was over. But suddenly he began again:

'And your hand did not wither as it gave the order to lay down arms? By what right did you snatch from all those brave men the arms they were bearing with honour? By what right did you paralyse their courage and their fidelity? Why make them parties to your dishonour? How could you employ the very force of discipline, the very powers I had given you, to hand over an army corps to the enemies of France? * So, in a subject, your capitulation was a crime; in a general, an absurdity; in a soldier, it was an act of cowardice; in a Frenchman, it was the first sacrilegious blow struck at the noblest of glories.

'And if, free from sordid interest, from disgraceful terror, you had fought instead of capitulating, if you had formed columns of attack instead of deploying, if you had kept your forces together instead of crumbling them, you could have beaten the Spaniards, you could have controlled our retreat. Madrid would not have been evacuated. The Spanish rising would not have been inflamed by an unparalleled success. England would not have an army in the Peninsula. And what a difference in all events and possibly in the fate of the world!'

Having uttered these last words, he turned his back on General Legendre, who forthwith left the parade, and, a few moments later, Valladolid.

* *Napoleon was abusing this 'force of discipline' to insult the innocent Legendre. The latter, on his return to Paris, went to ask the minister what would be his fate. 'But, general, you did not sign the capitulation,' said the minister, hinting at a new and brilliant appointment. 'That's true,' said Legendre, and taking the text of the capitulation, which was on the minister's desk, he added his signature.—J.S.*

BACK FROM THE PENINSULA

This was the swan-song of Napoleon's only Spanish campaign. He had missed his pounce on the English—but his face was dramatically saved by news from home. Austria was arming; Talleyrand and Fouché were laying their heads together. . . . It became necessary to hand over his troops and get back at once. However, he still thought he had settled matters in the Peninsula.

So it was in Paris that he heard of the fall of Saragossa to Marshal Lannes, after a terrible siege. The bearer of the message, General Baron Lejeune, *describes his reception by Napoleon.*

On the very night of the capitulation (21st February), I set off after dark, at full gallop, to rejoin my carriage at Bayonne. And fearing to be delayed by the escorts I should have taken, I braved the danger of travelling alone with a postilion through country where guerillas were opposing us to the knife.

Such of the enemy as our soldiers caught bearing arms were at once hanged on the olive trees by the roadside. One of these mutilated bodies, strung up to a branch and waving in the wind like a flag, barred my way in a sunken road I had to pass through. As I pushed it from my face, I had the curiosity to lift up this withered, but not disfigured body, which was that of a white-haired, grey-bearded peasant, still with all his clothes on, and I was much surprised to find these human remains weighing no more than a cardboard figure might have done.

I arrived without mishap at the Tuileries (27th February), where I was received by the Emperor.

I found him seated at a pedestal table with a pretty child of three on his lap; they were taking breakfast together with the same fork.

The Emperor congratulated me on bearing no further trace of the wound that was said to have disfigured me, and received with interest the latest details on the siege and surrender of Saragossa. The Emperor inquired after the marshal's health, the condition of the army, and expressed the most honourable regrets at the loss of his aide-de-camp, General Lacoste. He even instructed me to convey his sympathy to the widow, and to let her know that the Emperor would continue her in the enjoyment of the fifty thousand francs a year he had bestowed on her husband.

During our conversation, the Emperor kept on fondling this child, who was the eldest son of his brother Louis, King of Holland, the husband of Mlle Hortense de Beauharnais, daughter to the Empress Josephine.

The Emperor's very marked feeling for this little nephew, who was so pretty and engaging, led us to believe that he had chosen him to inherit the throne founded by his victories. At least the idea was then current in Paris.

After his very frugal meal, the Emperor, as he was wont, drank some coffee without sugar, and the child, who had stretched his pretty little arms to grasp the cup and drink some himself, was startled by the bitterness of the liquid and made a lively grimace as he pushed the cup away. The Emperor laughed, and I was struck by his comment:

'Ah! you've not been educated yet, since you can't dissemble.'

The Emperor promoted me colonel of engineers, and I took the oath according to the procedure then in use.

Great lustre was given to this oath-taking ceremony, so as to bind the officers of the army more closely to the head of the vast empire they had helped to found.

Turn about, the newly promoted were summoned into the throne-room, where the great officers of the crown were grouped round the Emperor.

At our entry, we made three bows, in which we had been instructed by M. Gardel, ballet-master of the Opera. This study greatly amused us, but as a rule it imparted very little of a courtier's suppleness to those of our number who were still rather uncouth soldiers, and republicans to boot. At last, when one had learnt to draw the right foot gracefully back while respectfully bending the head and shoulders, one arrived at the Tuileries, and advanced proudly into the throne-room, towards the noble and glorious company, there to take in the Emperor's presence the oath of loyalty to him, which was read out by the Duc de Bassano. Owing to the clumsiness with which certain of us performed this unwonted salute, the grave audience often had its work cut out to restrain a shout of laughter which would have impaired the dignity of the ceremony.

WHEN ONE IS AN ENGINEER ...

Engineer officers were not always so well received. And Bertrand—the same who was to accompany Napoleon to St Helena—repeated to the Duc de Broglie one of those cutting mots to which the Emperor was so much addicted.

At Fiume I made the acquaintance of General Bachelu, who was commandant of the town, and there I met General Bertrand again; he had come on the Emperor's orders, to examine the whole state of defence of the Illyrian provinces. It was in General Bachelu's study that he told me, with a blend of simplicity and shrewdness, the following story which has often recurred to my mind.

'I was,' he said, 'in a little town'—mentioning its name, which at the moment escapes me. 'The Emperor had directed me to examine the state of the place and the means of defence it offered. I pointed out that to get it on a sound footing, one would have to demolish a host of little dwellings with gardens round them, which were congesting the ditches and outer walls. I added that as the place was of small importance and the measure very severe, I thought it would be harsh to do this; and I was at pains to indicate other points where a little work would secure the only object it was reasonable to try for.

'The Emperor listened without interrupting, darting a stern look at me. When I asked for his orders, instead of replying he got up, and said:

'"When one is an engineer, one should be an engineer."

'Then he began walking rapidly up and down, pacing the room lengthwise, and repeating:

'"When one is an engineer, one should be an engineer. It's no use being an engineer, if one is not an engineer."

'Then, after pacing like this for about a quarter of an hour, he opened the door of his room, saying as he slammed it behind him:

'"And an engineer should be pitiless."

'He gave me no orders, and nothing was done.'

THE DEATH OF LANNES

Yet again, Napoleon was at war with Austria. This time a precarious and bloody victory was prefaced by two days of defeat with slaughter on the banks of the Danube.

Among the casualties of Essling was Marshal Lannes, Duke of Montebello. We owe the death-bed scene to Cadet de Gassicourt, *Napoleon's apothecary.*

The Duke of Montebello must have had dark presentiments as he rode off to the island of Lobau. I was with Dr Lannefranque when we met him on the Vienna bridge. The marshal was very fond of my colleague. He stopped, took his hand and said:

'No doubt you'll soon be coming to join us. We shall probably need you. Gentlemen, if I can trust to appearances there will be hot work today.'

'My lord duke,' said the doctor, 'it will add to your glory, and we and the whole army will rejoice.'

'Glory!' rejoined Montebello sharply, 'very expensive smoke! I would a hundred times rather. . . . Look, shall I be candid with you? We've been in too much of a hurry. . . . I don't like the idea of this engagement. But whatever its outcome, for me it will be the last battle.'

'How do you mean, general?'

'Goodbye, goodbye, gentlemen . . .'

And he galloped off.

'That last remark pains me,' said M. Lannefranque. 'Several times now the marshal has shown me this despondency and dissatisfaction. If he were not so genuinely fond of the Emperor he would have sent in his resignation. One can't suspect such a brave soldier of weakness. He's like many another, weary of his trade, and he's convinced this campaign will be fatal to him.'

. . . . .

The Emperor, on seeing Marshal Lannes carried off weltering in his blood, had the stretcher set down, flung himself on his knees, took the marshal in his arms, and said, bursting into tears:

'Montebello, do you know me?'

'Yes, sire, you're losing your best friend.'

'No, no, you will live!'

Then, turning to Larrey:

'You answer for his life, don't you?'

This affecting scene, worthy of the brush of Gérard, revived the courage of the unhappy wounded, who raised themselves on the sand with cries of: 'Long live the Emperor!'

.   .   .   .   .

Marshal Lannes's recovery was despaired of. He had endured with great strength and courage the amputation of his right thigh. But the cannon-ball had touched the left leg and broken the knee-cap. A second amputation might be required. The duke was in violent distress. A malignant fever had set in. The marshal had been lodged with a brewer at Ebersdorff, in an entresol over a stable. The house was surrounded by dead bodies of men and horses. The air in it was foul, the heat stifling. Yet it was the best that could be found.

The Emperor showed the tenderest concern for the patient. By his orders, the famous Franck had been summoned, along with MM Larrey, Yvan, Paulet and Lannefranque, who attended the marshal in turn. Napoleon had already been to see him twice.

At the last interview, the duke asked that everyone should withdraw into the next room, the door of which remained open.

On being left alone with the Emperor, he reminded him of all the services he had rendered, all the proofs of affection he had given him. Then, raising his voice:

'It is not,' said he, 'to urge the claims of my wife and children that I say these things. Since I am dying for you, I have no need to recommend them. You owe it to your own glory to protect them, and I am not afraid of changing your views by addressing to you the last reproaches of friendship. . . . You have just made a great blunder. It is costing you your best friend, but it will not correct you. Your insatiable ambition will be your ruin. You sacrifice without necessity, caution or regret those who serve you best. Your ingratitude estranges even those who admire you. There are now only flatterers around you. I see not one friend who dares to tell you the truth. You will be betrayed, you will be deserted. Make haste to finish this war; it is the wish of your generals; it must be that of your people. You will never be mightier, you may be far better loved! Forgive a dying man these truths; you are very dear to him . . .'

Finally, the marshal held out his hand, and the Emperor embraced him with tears, but made no reply.

BURYING THE HATCHET

One marshal was gone, three new ones (for the moment) were coming up. First, the brilliant but republican Macdonald. Napoleon had always slighted him; now, for his share in the hard-won battle of Wagram, he was awarded the baton and an embrace. And Berthier exclaimed: 'That's how good fellows make up!'
But let us hear Macdonald himself.

I was not slow to fall asleep. It did not last, for I was presently awakened by shouts of 'Long live the Emperor!', redoubling as he entered my camp.

I called for my horse, but it had been taken away. It was my only one, the others having been left far behind. As I could not walk, I was still lying on my straw when I heard someone asking for me. It was an orderly officer, M. Anatole de Montesquiou or his brother who was afterwards killed in Spain. The Emperor had sent him to fetch me. On hearing that I had no mount and could not walk, he offered me his horse, which I accepted.

I saw the Emperor surrounded by and congratulating my troops. He came up and cordially embraced me, saying:

'Let us be friends from now on.'

'Yes,' I replied, 'friends to the death.'

And I kept my word, not up to that point, indeed, but up to the abdication.

He added:

'You have behaved gallantly and done me the greatest services all through this campaign. It is on the field of your glory, where yesterday I owed you a great part of the day, that I create you marshal of France.'

He used that word (France) instead of the word empire.

'You deserved it long ago.'

'Sire,' I replied, 'since you are pleased with us, let the rewards be shared and spread through my army corps, beginning with Generals Lamarque, Broussier, etc., who seconded me so well.'

'Just as you please,' said he, 'I can refuse you nothing.'

With that he went away, greatly moved. So was I.

LET HIM BE SHOT!

Punishments were also being handed out—likewise with an eye to effect,
as the Marquis de Bonneval testifies.

Surgeon-major Mouton of the Guard was billeted on the
Princess of Lichtenstein.

Mouton, whose soldierly language was often far from choice,
wrote the princess a letter complaining of the sleeping arrangements, and that in terms which were really insolent, all but
indecent.

This letter fell into the hands of the Prince of Neuchâtel, who
took it to the Emperor. Napoleon's wrath knew no bounds!
He ordered the Prince of Neuchâtel to produce the culprit at the
following day's review, between four gendarmes.

The courtyard of Schönbrunn, much larger than that of Fontainebleau, has likewise a double flight of steps in front of the
palace.

The Guards having been massed in this courtyard, the culprit
was led in by his four gendarmes.

Then Napoleon showed himself on the perron, with a paper in
his hand. But instead of coming down four steps at a time, as he
usually did, he advanced deliberately, followed by the whole of
his brilliant staff, and still with the terrible paper in his hand.

Still with measured step, he approached the culprit, and flung
at him:

'Was it you that signed such filth?'

The wretched man hung his head by way of assent.

Then Napoleon, in ringing tones:

'Understand this, gentlemen, one kills men, but one never puts
them to shame. Let him be shot!'

The exhibition had been given, and General Dorsenne did not
have the unlucky doctor shot.

CHIVALRY IN VIENNA

Had the victory been decisive? Was Austria on her knees? Not exactly.
She had sued for peace. She had a new Foreign Secretary—Metternich.
And a month after Wagram, Metternich was writing to his emperor that
'From the day when peace is signed, we must confine our system to

*tacking and turning, and flattering . . . till the day of general deliver-
ance'.*

*But the peace was not to be signed for months.   Napoleon spent these
at Schönbrunn, with a variety of women to keep him amused.   Now and
then—as we learn from* Constant—*the adventure was an affecting one.*

Another day, Napoleon happened to observe a charming young
person.   It was one morning, in the neighbourhood of Schönbrunn.   Someone was instructed to call on this young lady and,
on Napoleon's behalf, invite her to wait on him at the palace the
evening after.

In this instance, Napoleon had great luck on his side.   The lustre
of such a famous name, the renown of his victories, had made a
deep impression on the girl's feelings, and inclined her to lend
a favourable ear to the proposal which was being made.   She consented therefore, and with alacrity, to call at the palace.

At the appointed hour, the same person went to fetch her.   I
received her at the palace, and ushered her into Napoleon's room.
She did not speak French, but had a thorough knowledge of
Italian.   Thus it was easy for Napoleon to talk with her.

He learned with amazement that this charming young lady
belonged to a most respectable Viennese family, and that her only
motive in coming to see him had been a desire to express her
admiration.   Napoleon respected the young girl's innocence, had
her escorted home, and gave orders that a marriage should be
arranged for her, making this easier and more brilliant by the
gift of a considerable dowry.

YOU ARE MAD, YOUNG MAN!

*And suddenly he was telling Champagny, his Foreign Minister: 'We
must make peace.'   He was giving him* carte blanche.   *'I leave it
entirely to you, but make peace.'   That very night (13th–14th October,
1809) the minister compromised and wound up the business, or rather
scrambled through it.   None too soon!*

*For there had just been an incident which might have terrible reper-
cussions.   General Rapp is the narrator.*

The peace was dragging out, the negotiations were making no
headway, Germany was still suffering.

A young man, led astray by blind love for his country, formed the design of ridding it of the person he regarded as the cause of its ills.

He presented himself at Schönbrunn on the 13th of October, as the troops were marching past. I was on duty. Napoleon was between me and the Prince of Neuchâtel. This young man, named Staps, approached the Emperor. Berthier, thinking he meant to offer a petition, stepped in front of him and told him to hand it to me. He replied that he wished to speak to Napoleon. He was told once more that if he had anything to communicate, he must apply to the aide-de-camp on duty. He fell back a few steps, repeating that he wished to speak to Napoleon himself. He advanced again, coming very close. I moved him back, and told him in German that he must withdraw. That if he had a request to make, it would be heard after the parade.

He kept his right hand thrust into a side pocket, under his great-coat. He was holding a paper, one end of which could be seen. He looked at me, and I was struck by his eyes. His determined air roused my suspicion. I called a gendarme officer who was present, and had him arrested and taken into the palace.

Everyone was intent on the parade. No one noticed.

Presently I was told that an enormous kitchen knife had been found on Staps. I informed Duroc. We both went to the place where he had been taken.

He was sitting on a bed on which he had laid out the portrait of a young woman, his pocket-book and a purse containing several old louis d'or. I asked him his name.

'I can tell no one but Napoleon.'

'What did you mean to do with this knife?'

'I can tell no one but Napoleon.'

'Were you going to attempt his life with it?'

'Yes, sir.'

'Why?'

'I can tell no one but him.'

I went to apprise the Emperor of this strange event. He told me to have the young man brought to his closet. I transmitted his orders and went back. He was with Bernadotte, Berthier, Savary and Duroc. Two gendarmes came in with Staps, his hands tied behind his back. He was composed. Napoleon's presence had not the slightest effect on him. He bowed, however, in a respectful way. The Emperor asked him whether he could speak

P

French. He replied confidently: 'Very little.' Napoleon instructed me to put the following questions in his name:

'Where do you come from?'

'Naumbourg.'

'What is your father?'

'A Protestant clergyman.'

'How old are you?'

'Eighteen.'

'What were you going to do with your knife?'

'Kill you.'

'You are mad, young man—you are an *illuminé*?'

'I am not mad. I don't know what an *illuminé* is.'

'Then you are sick?'

'I am not sick, I am in good health.'

'Why did you mean to kill me?'

'Because you are the bane of my country.'

'Have I done you any harm?'

'Me and all Germans.'

'Who sent you? Who is egging you to this crime?'

'No one. It was the deep-seated conviction that by killing you I should do the greatest service to my country and Europe which placed a weapon in my hand.'

'Is this the first time you have seen me?'

'I saw you at Erfurt, at the time of the interview.'

'Did you not mean to kill me at that time?'

'No, I thought you would not make war on Germany again. I was one of your greatest admirers.'

'How long have you been in Vienna?'

'Ten days.'

'Why have you waited so long to carry out your project?'

'I came to Schönbrunn a week ago, meaning to kill you, but the parade was just over. I deferred the execution of my plan till today.'

'You are mad, I tell you, or you are sick.'

'Neither.'

'Send for Corvisart.'

'What is Corvisart?'

'A doctor,' I answered.

'I don't need one.'

We awaited the doctor's coming in silence. Staps was impassive. Corvisart arrived. Napoleon told him to feel the young man's pulse. He did so.

'I am not sick, sir, am I?'

'The gentleman is in good health,' said the doctor, addressing the Emperor.

'I told you so,' put in Staps with a kind of satisfaction.

Napoleon, puzzled by so much confidence, began his questions again.

'You are an enthusiast, you will be the ruin of your family. I will spare your life, if you ask pardon for the crime you meant to commit, and for which you should be sorry.'

'I want no pardon. I am bitterly sorry to have failed.'

'The deuce! it seems a crime is nothing to you?'

'Killing you is not a crime, it is a duty.'

'What is this portrait they found on you?'

'That of a young lady I love.'

'Your adventure will be a grief to her!'

'It will be a great grief to her that I failed. She abhors you as much as I do.'

'Well, but if I pardon you, will you be grateful?'

'I shall kill you just the same.'

Napoleon was stupefied.

He ordered the prisoner to be taken away.

FIFTH STAGE

From Wagram to Moscow

(1809–1812)

*Europe is an old, rotten whore. I have 800,000
men. I shall do what I please with her.*

NAPOLEON

YOU'RE GRIPPING ME TOO TIGHT...

When he finally left Austria (in the latter half of October, 1809), it was to hunt and make love at Fontainebleau. Then suddenly he returned to the Tuileries, resolved to have his divorce and brave Josephine's resistance.

Why, at the close of 1809—ten years after Brumaire—did he make up his mind to a step from which he was still shrinking in 1804? He wanted an heir. (The little favourite nephew had died of croup.) For a long time Josephine had insisted that he was sterile. She circulated the mot: 'Bon-a-parte est bon-a-rien'. She said more indecent things than that. For instance, one night at Saint-Cloud Mme Duchâtel was in bed with Napoleon, and just as . . . in short, she burst out laughing. Astonishment of Napoleon. She explained: 'And the Empress says it was like piss!' Since then, he had had children here and there by his mistresses (in France, in Poland, in Austria). Therefore, he was bent on divorcing, and marrying a princess who would ensure him posterity. Josephine was sacrificed, and so we come to the painful scandal of 30th November, 1809, in which Bausset, *the prefect of the palace, acted a part.*

I had been on duty at the Tuileries since Monday, the 27th of November. That day, and on the Tuesday and Wednesday following, I could not fail to observe the Empress's ravaged looks, and Napoleon's constrained silence. If ever he broke the silence during dinner, it was to ask me a few brief questions, without listening to the answer. On those days dinner was over in ten minutes. The storm broke on Thursday, the 30th.

T.M. sat down to table. Josephine was wearing a large white hat tied under the chin, which partly concealed her face. Yet I thought I saw that she had been shedding tears, and that she could hardly restrain them even now. She gave me an impression of suffering and despair.

A dead silence prevailed through this meal. It was only for form's sake that they tasted the dishes offered them. Not a word was uttered, except when Napoleon asked me:

'What is the weather like?'

And with these words he left the table. Josephine slowly followed. Coffee was brought in, and Napoleon himself took his cup from the page on duty, making a sign that he wished to be alone.

I left the room in haste, but uneasy, agitated and given up to sad thoughts. I sat down in an armchair in the outer drawing-room, by the door of the Emperor's drawing-room. I was mechanically watching the staff as they removed the objects which had been used for T.M.'s dinner, when suddenly, from the Emperor's drawing-room, I heard piercing cries uttered by the Empress Josephine.

The usher, thinking she had been taken ill, was just about to open the door. I stopped him, remarking that the Emperor would call for help if he thought proper. I was standing near the door when Napoleon opened it himself, and on seeing me said quickly:

'Come in, Bausset, and shut the door.'

I went into the drawing-room, and saw the Empress stretched on the carpet, uttering heart-rending shrieks and moans.

'No, I shall never survive it,' the hapless woman was saying.

Napoleon said:

'Are you strong enough to pick Josephine up and carry her down the private staircase leading to her apartments, so that she may have the care and attention her state requires?'

I obeyed, and lifted the royal lady, whom I supposed to be in a fit of hysterics. With Napoleon's aid I took her up in my arms, and he himself, taking a candlestick from the table, lighted me and opened the door of the room, which led, by a dark passage, to the little staircase he had referred to.

On reaching the top of this stair, I pointed out to Napoleon that it was too narrow for me to get down without danger of falling.

He at once called the keeper of the portfolio, stationed day and night at one of the doors of his study, which opened on the head of the little staircase. Napoleon gave him the candlestick, of which we had little need, since these parts were already lighted. He ordered the man to go in front, and took Josephine's legs to enable me to descend more carefully. But my sword getting in the way, I thought we should all have fallen. Happily we got safely down, and deposited our precious burden on an ottoman in the bedchamber.

Napoleon made straight for the bellrope, and summoned the Empress's women.

When, in the drawing-room above, I picked up the Empress, her moans stopped. I thought she was in a swoon. But on becoming entangled with my sword halfway down the little staircase already mentioned, I was obliged to hold her closer, to avoid a fall which would have been baneful to the actors in this distressing scene, since our postures were not the result of an arrangement calculated at leisure.

I had the Empress in my arms, which were round her waist, her back was against my chest, and her head leaning on my right shoulder.

When she felt the efforts I was making to keep my balance, she said in a whisper:

'You're gripping me too tight.'

I then saw that I had nothing to fear for her health, and that she had not lost consciousness for a moment.

Throughout this scene, I had been thinking only of Josephine, whose condition grieved me. I had been unable to observe Napoleon. But when the Empress's women had reached her side, Napoleon went into a small room leading to the bedchamber. I followed him. His perturbation, his anxiety were extreme. In the disturbance of his mind, he acquainted me with the cause of all that had just taken place, and spoke the following words:

'The interest of France and of my dynasty has done violence to my heart. . . . Divorce has become a binding duty. . . . I am all the more distressed by the scene Josephine has just made, because it is three days since she must have learnt, from Hortense, of the unhappy obligation which condemns me to part from her. . . . I pity her with all my soul. I thought she was more strong-minded. . . . And I was not prepared for the outburst of her grief . . .'

Indeed, the violence of his feelings obliged him to make a long pause after every sentence, to get his breath. The words came with an effort, and incoherently. His voice was agitated, choked, and his eyes were filling with tears. He must have been really beside himself, to enter into so many details with one so remote by station from his counsels and confidence.

This whole scene did not last more than seven or eight minutes. Napoleon immediately sent for Corvisart, Queen Hortense,

Cambacérès, Fouché. And before going upstairs again, he looked
in to see Josephine's condition for himself, and found her quieter
and more resigned.

I followed him when he returned to his own apartments, and
I went back into the outer drawing-room, after picking up my
hat, which I had dropped on the carpet for greater freedom of
movement. To avoid comment of any sort, I said, before the
pages and ushers, that the Empress had had a most violent attack
of hysteria.

COURIER IN THE LION'S DEN

*Josephine made way. She went off with an income of three million in
gold, several châteaux, all her jewels, etc.*

*The quest for a new partner was ill-starred. In the end, after a definite
refusal from Russia, Napoleon fell back on Austria, which was ready
waiting, and applied for the hand of an arch-duchess: Marie-Louise.
Berthier was dispatched to Vienna to officiate in a marriage by proxy.
The Emperor of Austria, on his side, sent Napoleon a courier extraordinary, the* Prince de Clary-et-Aldringen (*Lolo to his intimates*),
who provided his family with a daily travel bulletin.

Wednesday, 21st March.—By eight in the morning I was at
Compiègne. I stop at the inn and put on my chocolate uniform
[*that of the* Landwehr] with white stockings, since the ambassador
had decided there was no objection to this, and besides, my red
uniform [*as a member of the Diet*] was not ready. Between ourselves, except for the distress to my vanity, which was rather
sharp, I was not sorry to appear in that coat. [*Because the* Landwehr
had done Napoleon a lot of damage in the campaign of 1809.]

I seek out Duroc. I am conducted into a huge drawing-room,
in which were chamberlains, red and silver, generals, blue and
gold, all of whom, greatly astonished to see a figure like mine in
this court sanctum, look at me like a cow at a new door. I own
it was a moment of cruel embarrassment. Finally, I am steered to
the quarters of this Grand Marshal Duroc, where he was supposed
to be and shortly turned up. He was extremely polite, and, after
a quarter of an hour's waiting, took me into a drawing-room
where I came face to face . . .

With Whom?

Here, if you like, all His titles . . .

I had prepared a little harangue, of a simple, manly and touching eloquence, beginning: 'The Emperor, my master, has commanded me, etc., etc.'

He cuts me short, taking my packet and questioning me on the journey.

'When did you start?'

'On the 13th, sire, two hours before the Empress.'

'Did you find the roads bad?'

And similar questions.

Then he says:

'I've had news of the Empress by *télégraphe*. Today she is . . . (*I forget where*). She will be here such a day.'

He asks after my Empress, and then:

'You are related to the Prince de Ligne?'

'He is my grandfather, sire.'

'How is he, the Prince de Ligne? His place near Vienna was a little the worse for us.'

'Yes, sire, a little.'

'I saw a Princess Clary at Vienna. Was that your mother?'

'Yes, sire.'

'What uniform is that?'

'Sire, it's one of the Bohemian volunteer corps.'

'Ah! the *Landwehr*!'

I had meant to dodge that word.

'Yes, sire.'

'You served in the last war?'

'I was in the army of Bohemia.'

'Have you been through other campaigns?'

'No, sire. I've only served in that war.'

'You will rest here. I shall see you again.'

He makes a little face, turns away, and before I had finished bowing he was reading my letters.

Back again in the outer drawing-room. I ask questions.

'The Emperor told me: *You will rest! I shall see you again.* What does that mean?'

'Why, sir, that you must stay at Compiègne till you're told to go away.'

Oh, dear! and I was expecting to go straight on and be in Paris for the ambassador's ball this evening!

'What have I to do?'

'Nothing, sir; you will join us in a drive.'

Then a tall general, dry and polite, says:

'Will you come and breakfast with us, sir?'

I asked someone else:

'Who is that general?'

'Savary.'

Phew!

'And the stout, bald one?'

'Davout.'

Ouch! These names give me goose-flesh!

After breakfast, a fresh bustle in the drawing-room. At last the carriages move off. The Emperor rides away into the woods. We follow. I was alone with M. Germain, chamberlain, and I forget whom. It was pretty cold. We drive for two hours without meeting the Emperor. Asking for him at every cross-road. Finally we return. He had been back a long time.

As this was the court's first day at Compiègne, and so far its installation was rudimentary, a fine disorder prevailed.

At six o'clock, dinner. I haven't much of an appetite yet. Evening pretty slow. At the end, M. de Nansouty, first or grand equerry, comes up to say:

'The Emperor informs you that you will join his hunting-party tomorrow, and permits you to order the hunt uniforms. For tomorrow, one of these gentlemen will lend you one. But you must try to have yours ready for the next occasion.'

I bow in reply.

'You have apartments in the château.'

Another bow.

We retire none too early, at half-past nine.

Napoleon's hunts were spectacular, and Napoleon the king of bad shots. The Prince de Clary soon found this out.

At nine o'clock this morning I was ready. The top half of the uniform fitted very well, but as I had neither riding-boots nor green riding-breeches, my costume was somewhat out of line. I had been offered a hat, but was so nervous that there might be a cockade on it that I preferred to wear my laced uniform hat.

Before the hunt, M. de Nansouty came and said:

'The Emperor grants you the (*I forget which*) *grandes* or *petites entrées* at his lever and coucher, and your name is added to the list.'

Which meant that I was to stay at Compiègne as long as he did. It was like a knell!

At ten o'clock we had breakfast without the Emperor, then we took our places. He in the first carriage, and we followed. Trim chariots going like the wind, trim horses, most of them grey, grooms in the English style, trimly turned out, and above all hussars in red breeches, known as guides, or it may have been chasseurs, made it a charming spectacle.

At the scene of the meet, another breakfast.

That was the only meal I shared with Napoleon. I found it the queerest sensation to be almost at his side, dressed like Savary, like Davout, like Duroc. I was pinching myself to try whether it could be me. Breakfast was the work of ten minutes. I was quietly drinking my coffee when, on looking up, I discovered I was the only one. I even thought I saw Napoleon exchange a smile with someone at the way the Austrian chamberlain took his time, and just as I was setting down my cup in a fright, every-one got up.

We get on horseback. The Emperor is off like a flash. It sur-prised me that all these gentlemen should take the liberty of not going after him. They stayed by the fire, in the hunting-box where we had breakfasted. Davout followed the hunt halfway, then went back to the château. Savary never left the Emperor; General de Nansouty, the captain of hunts, and M. d'Hannecourt, a huntsman-equerry, followed *ex officio*. Along with Roustam, and with me, who meant to preen myself on keeping up with Napoleon.

I was so busy making after him to keep him in sight, that once Savary said:

'Don't go so near the Emperor!'

Up to the first relay everything went very well. I was still close to him. But the moment he takes a fresh horse all is lost. He is, as one might expect, so well served, he is off again so fast, that one has no chance of keeping up. I roamed all over the forest. Now I ran into a groom, now into a stray general, now I saw the hunt going by in the distance, now walkers and sight-seers put me on the trail. In brief, I caught up with Napoleon only at the death of the stag. It was in the river, and was swimming. The Emperor had dismounted, so had everyone. I alone remained absent-mindedly in the saddle. As you see, I made plenty of solecisms!

Napoleon fired five times right into the middle of the hounds. It's incredible that he doesn't kill any. But he never gives that a thought. He missed three times, scored two hits, and at the second, on the stag's head, it vanished under the water.

'Well,' he asked me, 'have you ever seen such a fine hunt? Eh?' 'Never, sire.'

We mount again, and return to Compiègne at full gallop.

ENTER MARIE-LOUISE

At last Marie-Louise arrived, escorted by Caroline Bonaparte, wife of Murat and Queen of Naples. Napoleon had gone to meet his new Empress, and, in his impatience to have a son, had slept with her straight away, in advance of the usual ceremonies.

As Clary tells us, the reception arranged for them did not take place.

Yesterday morning we read and conned over ten folio pages of ceremonial against the arrival of the Empress. I return to my own room. At three o'clock I go down to the outer drawing-room to see what's happening. I am told:

'The Emperor, in a grey coat, has just got into a barouche with the King of Naples, and they're off to catch the Empress somewhere. They mean to hasten her journey and get her here this evening.'

So the camp is roused, and everyone in the field dressing up. These surprises are a joke that kings never weary of!

It was pouring wet.

All afternoon the carriages were ready to start, the drawing-room crowded with all the ladies, embellished and in full dress.

We spent the evening like that, waiting. At the slightest noise, at the smallest page opening the door, everyone was agog. Finally, about ten o'clock, a very muddy page came and said things were getting serious. We bestir ourselves. We cover the staircase. The kings and queens stood at the bottom. The courtyard of the château was illuminated. Bands everywhere, torches and to spare. An uproar is heard. A roll of drums. Here come marshals, generals, equerries, chamberlains, pages at the gallop, three or four coaches-and-six at full speed, finally a coach-and-eight carrying the sovereigns and the Queen of Naples. A band of wind instruments, fine though rather mournful, strikes up a greeting.

I saw the Empress jump quite nimbly from her coach, promptly embrace the whole family, and mount the staircase on the arm of her little husband. She and her ladies were wearing hooded cloaks, poppy-coloured or rather ox-blood, with narrow gold trimmings. Everyone thought her very well-looking, very tall, much better than they expected. As she has the advantage of Him by half a head, she did look quite striking. We lined up on each side, and the family disappeared into the private apartments.

After that we cooled our heels, and heaven knows it was tedious! Voices were hushed, the ladies were dying of sleep and at a loss what to do. We were still expecting the Empress to reappear. Not a sign.

It was, I think, half-past twelve or one in the morning when our ladies were informed they might go to bed, and they did not have to be told twice.

WHAT THE SERGEANT SAW

With the nation the 'Austrian' marriage was unpopular. In the army it was not generally approved. Sergeant Coignet, *one of the Old Guard, describes the ceremonies from his angle.*

If the Emperor was pleased with us, we were not pleased with him. It was rumoured in the Guards that he was divorcing his wife to take an Austrian princess, in payment of the expenses of the second war with the Emperor of Austria, and that he wanted a successor to the throne. That meant turning away the wife he had always had, taking a foreign woman who would bring about a general peace. The Emperor was holding big reviews to distract him from his troubles.

We were told that Prince Berthier was going to Vienna to take the princess our Emperor's portrait and ask for her hand, and that he was to be married to this princess before he brought her away, and that he was to sleep with her before presenting her to his sovereign. Knowing no better, I thought to myself: 'He's very lucky to be the first; I'd like to be in his shoes.' I made my captain laugh.

Everything was being got ready for this new Empress. On the 15th her whole family escorted her from Vienna, for a long way. She said she would miss her dog and her parrot. Orders were given directly, and it was a great surprise for her, on reaching Saint-Cloud, to find her cage, her birds, her beautiful dog who knew his mistress, and her parrot who called her by name.

Our first battalion was ordered to Saint-Cloud to await the Emperor. When the couriers arrived, we were put under arms. We saw that fine carriage drawn by eight horses, and the Emperor sitting by his bride.

How happy he looked!

They drove up Saint-Cloud at a slow walk and we had time to see all the fine carriages go by. They were married civilly at Saint-Cloud. Next day they set off to make their entry into the capital. We had orders to attend the big ceremony of the religious marriage, which was performed on the 5th of April in the chapel of the Louvre.

No one can imagine all the preparations. In the grand gallery of the Louvre, from the old Louvre to the chapel (this is an immense way), there were three rows of benches for the ladies and gentlemen to sit on. In the fourth row were fifty decorated non-commissioned officers, placed at intervals within iron rings (so that no one could jostle them). General Dorsenne was in command of us. When he had stationed us at our posts, he told the ladies that we were their cavaliers to see that they had refreshments. We must get acquainted. We had twenty-four on either side of us (forty-eight apiece), and we were to get what they asked for. In the thickness of the main wall, big recesses had been made to take ninety-six canteens with all the refreshments that could be desired. These little mobile cafés did a good trade.

This is what the ladies were wearing: gowns with a neckline down to the middle of their backs. And in front one could see half their chests, their bare shoulders, their naked arms. And necklaces! and bracelets! and earrings! Nothing but rubies, pearls and diamonds all over. That was where to see skins of every shade: greasy skins, mulatto skins, yellow skins and satin skins. The old ones had salt-cellars to hold their supplies of scent. I can say that I had never seen the fine ladies of Paris so close, half undressed. It's not a pretty sight.

The men were dressed in the French style. All alike: black coat, knee-breeches, diamond-cut steel buttons. All the extras cost them 1,800 francs. They could not appear at court without this costume. Hackney-cabs were forbidden that day. No one can imagine the throng of fine carriages around the Tuileries.

The great ceremony left the château for the old Louvre, and went up the great staircase of the Louvre on its way to the chapel of the Tuileries. How stately it was! Everyone was standing, in the most religious silence. The procession walked slowly. As soon as it had passed, General Dorsenne got us together, led us to the chapel and drew us up in a circle.

We saw the Emperor on the right, kneeling on a cushion with bees on it, and his wife kneeling beside him to receive the benediction. After placing the crown on his head and on his wife's, he got up and seated himself with her in an armchair. The Mass began.

The general signed to us to return to our posts, and there we saw the ceremony on its way back. The new Empress was handsome under that fine diadem. The wives of our marshals were carrying the tail of her gown, which dragged eight or ten paces along the floor. She must have been proud to have such ladies-in-waiting in her train. But one could say that she was a fine sultana, that the Emperor looked pleased, that his expression was gracious. That day, all was roses. But it must have been different at Malmaison [to which Josephine had retired].

All the Old Guard were under arms to guard the procession, and we were all properly sharp-set. Each of us received twenty-five sous and a litre of wine.

After the rejoicings the Emperor went off with Marie-Louise.

·　　·　　·　　·　　·

On the 1st of June they returned to Paris. The town offered them a fête and a most brilliant banquet in the Town Hall. I was detailed to command a piquet of twenty men inside, fronting that beautiful horse-shoe table, and my twenty grenadiers, arms at the order, before the feast all spread with gold and cold dishes. Around the horse-shoe, armchairs. The big one marking the Emperor's place was in the middle. The cortège was announced. The general came to post me and give me his instructions.

The master of ceremonies announced:

'The Emperor!'

Q

He appeared, followed by his wife and by five crowned heads. I gave the command to shoulder and present arms. Then I was commanded to return them to the order. I was in front of my party, opposite the Emperor. He sat down first, and motioned the others to take their places. When these crowned heads had sat down, the table was cleared, everything was taken away and vanished, the carvers were at work in an adjoining room. Behind each king or queen, three footmen at short intervals. The furthest off were in touch with the carvers and passed the plates, taking them with no more than an about turn. When the plate reached the one nearest the sovereign, the first footman would offer it, and if the sovereign shook his head, the plate would vanish. Immediately there was another instead. If the head kept still, the footman would set the plate before his master.

As the morsels were well cut up, everyone took his roll, broke it and bit into it, never using a knife, and with every mouthful he used a napkin to wipe his mouth. The napkin disappeared and the footman slid him another. And so on, so that behind every personage there was a heap of napkins that had only been once to his mouth.

Not a word was spoken. Each guest had a decanter of wine and water, and nobody filled his neighbour's glass. They bit into their bread and filled their own glasses as they liked. They accepted or refused with nods and headshakes. There was no talking allowed except when the sovereign lord spoke to his neighbour. This may be dignified, it's not cheerful.

The Emperor gets up. I give the order to shoulder and present arms, and they all go into a big drawing-room. I remained by the festal board. The general came and took me by the arm:

'Sergeant, come with us. I'm going to give you some of the Emperor's wine, and by the way, your twenty men shall have some as well. Stand there! I'll just tell your party to wait patiently, and they shall have a drink in their turn.'

Those two glasses of wine did me good, and my grenadiers each got half a litre. How pleased they were to have drunk some of the Emperor's wine!

KEEPING UP APPEARANCES

Here is a typical snapshot from the life of Napoleon, taken by the Duc
de Broglie, *then a minor official.*

These grave debates were not suspended by the Emperor's
faustissinae nuptiae. He could cope with everything. We moved
simultaneously from fête to fête, and from problem to problem.
As the inferiority of my position kept me at a distance from the
event these fêtes were designed to welcome, I attended them only
as a spectator. But being young, curious, launched in the official
world, I attended nearly all.

One morning, I think it was at Compiègne, the gallery was
thronged. Napoleon was passing through it, now with rolling
gait like a prince of the old stock, now with hasty and jerky
steps. Everyone was falling back to line his path. By a purely
casual conjunction of circumstances, I found myself willy-nilly
in the front row. He observed my modest uniform, among all
those ribbons and embroidered coats, came straight up to me
and asked my name. I gave it. He then, with a kindly smile,
said a few words to me on my stay in the Illyrian provinces, and
walked on, pleased, I assume, to have given a demonstration
of omniscience and ubiquity *in anima vili.* This was much admired.

BECAUSE THE SINGER WAS FLAT

*There was a concert at court. One of Napoleon's mistresses, the famous
Giuseppina Grassini, was singing. He doted on her voice. But that
evening she was flat.*

'Lolo' *gives us a view of the imperial box.*

The Empress was in pink and looked very well.

The Emperor was sleeping like a log. Never shall I forget his
face, his pale complexion, his closed eyes. It was the sleep of the
lion. It made a peculiar impression on me.

Now and then the Empress would say something, to wake him
up. He would make an agreeable and attentive face, answer her
and go back to sleep, which was not gallant. She even permitted
herself to smile at it with the Queen of Naples.

At last a fresh blunder of Grassini's drove him out of the hall. In the gallery he encountered a general from his brother Jerome's kingdom of Westphalia . . .

This scene was even worse than the one at Valladolid. General Morio died the following year. He was no coward; and Napoleon, to do him justice, was to regret keenly (but too late) the way he had treated him on this occasion, which is described by Norvins.

We left the Grand Marshal's house to attend the concert. It was the first time the Empress had appeared in public. She was dazzling in her youth, her attire and also her happiness.

The air of the concert hall was stifling. But—more fortunate than our companions the ladies of the palace—though obliged to stand, we had and took leave to sit down and refresh ourselves in the adjoining gallery.

Through the open door, the music came to us a little subdued, and thus more agreeable. But poor Grassini, whom I had seen and heard so beautiful and tuneful, ten years before, at the soirée given by M. de Talleyrand for the victor of Marengo, all of a sudden went so flat that the Emperor abruptly left the hall, rushed into the gallery, and halted only on seeing us all, according to custom, drawn up in line, motionless and mute.

I was next to the Westphalian Master of the Horse, Lieutenant-General Morio, a former minister of war, who had lately been commanding the Westphalian contingent in Spain, without much success.

The Emperor came to a dead stop in front of him, as though he had himself been struck by the thunderbolt he was going to hurl.

Here is what I can remember of that violent improvisation:

'What are you doing here?'

'I came with the King.'

'What are you?'

'Master of the Horse.'

'Master of the Horse, minister, general, lieutenant-general! Who gave you those stars? Where did you win stars? . . . You disgrace the epaulette. . . . Take off your epaulettes! . . . You are a coward!'

Morio nearly dropped dead.

The Emperor walked on to the end of the gallery. We were

aghast. From the other side there was a burst of song. Grassini had recovered herself. . . .

The Emperor returned on Morio and raged at him:

'Take off the uniform! . . . You disgrace it! You are a coward!' Then he went back to the concert.

According to custom, everyone had edged away from Morio, who seemed rooted to the spot. I did my duty, little as I cared for the man:

'Go at once,' I said, 'before the Emperor comes back. He might have you arrested, and then it would be a short step to trial.'

'I daren't move,' he replied.

'Give me your arm; we'll go together.'

And I saw him home.

'Quick,' I said, 'get into a chaise and be off to Paris, where we shall be tomorrow. The Emperor must know that you didn't spend the night at Compiègne, and I'll see to that.'

Morio went off . . .

Perhaps the only surviving witness of this horrible scene, I still ask myself what was Napoleon's nature, that he could pass so abruptly from the intoxication of love to that of wrath and fury. It was the nature of the volcano: Etna roars while covered with flowers.

WHY THIS CONTEMPT FOR MANKIND?

That was what General de Ricard wanted to know. As a young man at Marseilles, he could remember playing with nice little girls who were none other than the sisters of Napoleon Bonaparte.

Where did Napoleon get that contempt for mankind which, they say, never ceased to grow on him? To be sure he had about his person, in his entourage (and in his family—perhaps one may say: especially in his family), beings who really deserved contempt. But yet there were, in his time, steadfast characters and virtues, men he could neither tame by his caresses nor cow by his threats. Even among those who were devoted to his fortunes from admiration of his genius, there were men of honour and spirit. If he had ministers to whom he could take his fists, he had others who gave him 'an inkling that they would forget his station, if he forgot theirs' (the Duke of Gaeta).

Napoleon could not, *in petto*, despise such men. I believe rather that contempt for humanity was with Napoleon a matter of pose and policy. He wished to debase and corrupt men. Therefore it suited his ambition to think them base and corruptible.

Napoleon's genius remains incomparable. But alas, his heart! ... And it was by his heart that he judged mankind. What right had *he* to despise mankind who, to attain power, had taken Josephine almost from Barras's lap, and who went on to discard his Josephine for a Marie-Louise?

MASSÉNA MORTIFIED

Marshal Masséna, Duke of Rivoli, Prince of Essling, was one of the leading generals of the age. He had often gained the day for Napoleon, who owed him boundless gratitude.

Now, Napoleon was subject to epileptic fits; one of these caused him to be discovered in bed with the actress George, for at sight of it the unlucky girl raised the whole palace.

He had also disturbing fits of abstraction. At the time of the Austrian marriage he had one that stupefied his whole court, and Thiébault *records what Marshal Masséna got for trying—as on the battlefield—to come to the rescue.*

I felt obliged, before the Emperor should leave Compiègne, where he had betaken himself immediately after the marriage ceremonies, to make some show of zeal by going to pay my court to Their Majesties. And I spent three days there.

The second of them ended like this. I was in the card-room, the furthest of the apartments used as reception-rooms. The Empress was at cards. And while so many kings, archdukes, princes, foreigners of the highest rank, and so many illustrious Frenchmen followed the Emperor with their eyes and hung on his slightest movements, he himself was exchanging a few words with one, honouring another with a nod, going from one card-table to the next and greeting the ladies with remarks more pungent than gallant.

At the end of his circuit, finding himself by the door between this card-room and the adjoining salon, he passed through it. And at once an immense train hurried in his wake.

Rolling to and fro, he came to the middle of the room, stood still, crossed his arms over his chest, bent his gaze on the floor six feet ahead of him and became fixed.

The kings, Archduke Ferdinand, the Empress's uncle, and the other exalted persons who were following, also stopped. Some of them fell back. Others drew aside. All crowded together. And a pretty wide circle was formed, with the Emperor at its centre in a fixity copied by one and all, and a silence which nothing broke.

To start with, all had avoided even looking at each other. Gradually, eyes were raised, and each looked about him. A few moments more, and these glances became so interrogative in character that all seemed to be asking each other what this stage business was leading up to. A tacit inquiry, which, in the presence of so many and such foreigners, made every Frenchman uncomfortable.

And indeed, an abstraction so sudden, but equally bizarre and ill-timed, might for three or four minutes be set down to the Emperor's wish to concentrate on some important idea which had unexpectedly occurred to him.

But after five, six, seven, eight minutes there was no one who could make head or tail of it. However, it stood to reason that at a moment when a haughty and vainglorious master was pleased to make such a peculiar exhibition of himself, the thing to do was to do nothing.

Unhappily Marshal Masséna, who was in the front row, and behind whom I was standing, thought differently. Indeed I felt convinced that this man, who had such felicitous promptings and such an unerring glance on the field of battle, but who retained none of his advantages at court, thought he would be doing Napoleon a service by enabling him to put a natural end to this absurd scene—in its way the most ludicrous I have ever seen in my life.

He did not realise that if he provided a leader 'offended at his glory' with a chance of mortifying him, he would get him out of the scrape just as well, but by substituting cruelty for claptrap.

As a result, when not a soul budged or thought of budging, he left his place, entered the circle which an evil genius seemed to have drawn on purpose to lure him in quest of an affront, and then walked slowly up to the Emperor. . . .

Amazement and curiosity were depicted on every face. Mine could express nothing but dread. In any case, the suspense was brief. For no sooner had the marshal uttered a few words too low to be heard than, without raising or turning his eyes, without moving a muscle, the Emperor pronounced in a voice of thunder:

'Mind your own business!'

And the old marshal, who, in spite of his glory and his dignities, had just been humiliated before all Europe, instead of taking leave on the spot and hiding his shame in his own house, dumbly returned to his place and, to complete my discomfiture, returned to it backwards.

Never have I felt more mortified. Never was Napoleon the despot revealed to me in a more arrogant and impudent light. For this was an equally gratuitous and cruel insult to France in the person of one of her oldest and most illustrious defenders.

As for Napoleon, after awarding this prize for such great services, he continued his statue scene a few moments longer.

Then, as though emerging from a dream, he raised his head, uncrossed his arms, threw a scrutinising glance on all about him, turned without speaking to anyone, and went back into the card-room.

At a sign, the Empress threw down her cards and rose. All the games stopped and all got to their feet.

Passing Marie-Louise, he said to her in rather a sharp tone:

'Come, madam . . .'

And he walked on, while she followed three steps behind. As soon as he approached the door of the inner apartments, this door opened, and the moment the Empress had passed through, it closed on them. The time was not half-past nine.

PORTRAIT OF NAPOLEON IN 1810

Already he was very different from the Napoleon of 1805. His age was now forty-one. He had provided his secretary Méneval with a colleague, Fain, who was equally well paid, and to whom we owe the following picture.

In describing Napoleon's person, I refer to the time of his second marriage. This is not the Napoleon long familiar to M. de Bourrienne. It is not yet the Napoleon to be depicted later by the scribes of St Helena; it is the one I knew.

Let us begin like a police description: his height was five feet two inches. He was small, but well made. However, he was rather short in the neck and perhaps already too stout.

His fibre was soft and his lymph thick. There was never any colour in his complexion. His cheeks were a dull white, which gave him a full, pale face, but not with the pallor which denotes a sick person.

I never saw him unwell enough to take to his bed. Never, to use his own expression, did he feel his head or his stomach. I never knew him to have anything wrong except a discomfort of the bladder, which sometimes bothered him. I think the doctors ascribed this trouble to the after-effects of the herpes or rather scabies he had caught and neglected at the siege of Toulon.

His chestnut hair was cut short and worn flat on his head. He had a round head, a broad and high forehead, greyish-blue eyes with a mild expression, a well-shaped nose, a pleasingly cut mouth and fine teeth.

His sight was not of the best. He helped it out with a pair of opera-glasses he always carried.

He had a most fastidious sense of smell. I have seen him withdraw from more than one servant who had no idea of the secret aversion he had incurred.

When he was at work or preoccupied, the regularity of his features easily assumed a tinge of imposing sternness. But in the relaxation of intimacy his smile became very pleasant.

He seldom laughed. When he did, he shouted with laughter. But it was more for ironic effect than in hearty mirth.

I may add that no human face ever changed more promptly in response to varying states of mind. The very glance that had just been benign would suddenly dart lightning.

He has been accused wrongly of an immoderate addiction to coffee and snuff. He drank no more coffee than anyone else. He merely breathed his snuff. But he was constantly changing his snuff-box. The moment he had sniffed he would turn the box upside down and hand it to one of us, saying:

'Go and get me some snuff.'

This was one of our regular errands. On the chest of drawers in his bedroom we would find a row of snuff-boxes, prepared in advance to last out the renewals of the day. In private, this was his most frequent commission to his chamberlains. In council, I have seen more than one minister courting it as a favour.

What has been said of his over-indulgence in baths is better founded. He took them too often, and too hot. It seems likely that he had this bad habit to thank for the premature corpulence which his historical painters have not played down.

At least one cannot impute it to good cheer, for that man was certainly no lover of the table! He was abstemious, he lived frugally and ate fast, too fast for his whole circle. Moreover, nature had endowed him with a rather curious advantage, that of being powerless to exceed at table, even if he had chosen.

'If I went a fraction beyond my *draught*,' he used to say, 'my stomach would promptly return the surplus.'

When he was strolling in his garden, he liked to walk slightly bent, with his hands in his pockets, or swaying, with his hands behind his back.

He could sleep when and as he pleased. Whatever his need of sleep, three or four hours would be enough. I used to see him get up again without effort as soon as he woke in the night, set to work, and then go back to bed and immediately back to sleep.

In summer he liked to take a siesta. As a rule, he slept about seven hours in the twenty-four. But it was always in several spells, broken off at will night or day. During the evacuation of Leipzig he got two hours' untroubled sleep in an armchair; the blowing up of the bridge awoke him.

If he had been too long at ease, he would set himself some hard exercise. If, on the other hand, he had been through a period of overstrain, he condemned himself to twenty-four hours' compulsory rest. He called this 'restoring the balance'.

Fein's picture is not complete. We borrow the remaining touches from Mme Durand, *first lady to the Empress Marie-Louise.*

He was loud of speech, and when he was merry his bursts of laughter could be heard a great way off. He liked to sing, though he had a most untuneable voice and could never get a song right. He took great pleasure in singing:

Ah! c'en est fait, je me marie

or:

Si le roi m'avait donné Paris, sa grand'ville . . .

For the first three months after his marriage Napoleon was at the Empress's side day and night. The most urgent business could hardly tear him away for a few moments. He, who was passionately fond of work, who sometimes worked with his ministers for eight or ten hours on end without fatigue, who would tire out several secretaries in succession, was now summoning councils at which he did not appear till a couple of hours after they had met.

He gave very few private audiences, and he had to be reminded several times of those he could not avoid granting.

All were surprised at this alteration. The ministers were uttering cries of protest. Old courtiers watched, and said this state of things was too violent to last. The Empress alone had no doubts of the duration of a feeling which she returned and which was the source of her happiness.

A TRIP TO BELGIUM

Napoleon was eager to display his new wife to his subjects, to the people of his good towns. Here we find the imperial couple in Belgium, at Brussels, where the Marquise de La Tour du Pin was admitted to the 'august' table; for Napoleon, infatuated with blue blood (this weakness of his has been universally acknowledged), was now filling his antichambers with representatives of the old nobility.

This dinner-party is one of the most agreeable memories of my life. The diners, a party of eight, were seated as follows: the Emperor, on his right, the Queen of Westphalia, then Marshal Berthier, the King of Westphalia, the Empress, the Duc d'Ursel, Mme de Bouillé, finally myself, on the Emperor's left.

He talked to me, nearly the whole time, about the factories, the lace, the daily wage, the life of the lacemakers, and then of the public buildings, the antiquities, the charitable foundations, the beguine convent, the manners of the working class. Happily I was well up in all this.

We were not more than three-quarters of an hour at table. On our return to the drawing-room, Napoleon took a large cup of coffee and began talking again. First about the Empress's gown, which he liked. Then, breaking off, he asked me whether I was comfortably installed.

'Not badly,' I replied. 'In Your Majesty's suite.'

'Ah, really!' said he, 'well, it was expensive enough. It was that rogue —, M. de Pontécoulant's secretary, who had it fitted up. But half the cost went into his pocket, with all due deference to my brother,' he added, turning to the King of Westphalia, 'who has taken him into his service, for he likes rascals.'

And he shrugged his shoulders.

Jerome was making ready to answer, when he found that Napoleon had already broached quite a different topic.

He had leapt to the Duke of Burgundy [*Charles the Bold*] and Louis XI, and from there descended abruptly to Louis XIV, saying that it was only in his last years he had been truly great. On perceiving the interest with which I was listening, and, above all, that I understood him, he returned to Louis XI and expressed himself like this:

'I have my own view of *him*, and I'm well aware that it's not the common one.'

After a few words on the ignominies of Louis XV's reign, he pronounced the name of Louis XVI. Whereupon, pausing with a respectful, melancholy air, he said:

'That unhappy prince!'

Then he talked of other things, made game of his brother, who was receiving in Westphalia 'the sweepings of the French nation'. And heaven knows how many malicious jokes Jerome would have come in for, if at that moment someone had not said it was time to start for the ball.

M. d'Ursel and I flew to his carriage, and his horses took us at a gallop to the town hall. I went upstairs four steps at a time. An outfit was ready waiting for me. I put it on. And I was in the ballroom, after a complete change of dress, by the time Napoleon arrived.

He complimented me on my quickness, and asked whether I meant to dance. I told him no, since I was a woman of forty. At which he began to laugh, and said:

'So are plenty of others who dance, and who don't give away their age like that.'

The ball was a fine one. It continued after supper, at which the Empress's health was drunk, with the tacit thought that she might well have had her reasons for not dancing.

Napoleon and his young wife left the following morning. A

very ornate yacht conveyed them to the end of the Brussels canal, where they found carriages to take them to Antwerp.

As they went aboard, M. de La Tour du Pin caught sight of the Marquis de Trazegnies, commanding the guard of honour. Fearing that the Emperor would not invite him aboard the yacht, which could hold only a few people, he mentioned his name, adding:

'His ancestor was Constable under Saint Louis!'

These words worked like a charm; Napoleon immediately called the Marquis de Trazegnies and had a long chat with him.

Soon afterwards his wife was appointed a lady of the palace.

DINNER AT SAINT-CLOUD

Dining with Napoleon had become an almost prodigious honour. Even though at table he either said nothing or was ill-bred enough to go on talking business.

Countess Potocka, by dint of earnest entreaties, had procured the singular favour of an invitation. She had been unable to profit by it, and was heartbroken. Meeting Napoleon:

'I'm all the more heartbroken,' said she, 'because now I shall have nothing to tell my grandchildren when I'm an old woman.'

'Oh, but the chance is not lost, it will come again. How much longer are you staying?'

'A week, sire.'

'Well, it shall be for another time.'

The great day came. And there was nothing Mme Potocka failed to observe.

At half-past five I presented myself at the entrance gates of Saint-Cloud. As the sentry demurred at admitting my carriage into the courtyard, the chamberlain on duty kindly opened the way, and ushered me into the drawing-room.

There I found the Duchess of Montebello, who, in her capacity as lady of the palace, did the honours of it rather coldly, as though to enhance the confusion I felt at seeing no one of my acquaintance.

The Empress came in at six o'clock precisely, attended by her lady of the bedchamber, a 'ci-devant' whose name I always forget. She was said to be perfectly familiar with the ceremonial in use at the court of Louis XVI, a merit in great request at that time, on account of the young sovereign.

Marie-Louise was dressed very simply, in a white gown with a black ribbon round the hem. Princess Borghese arrived a moment later, along with the Emperor and the Duke of Wurtzburg, the Empress's uncle, who had escorted her to Paris. They were followed by M. de Montalivet, minister of the interior. That was all! There was no suite, and no pomp. It was to be a 'family dinner'.

After a few words to me, the Emperor rang the bell, and asked whether the carriages were at the door. On being told they were, he proposed a short drive in the park. He gave his arm to the Empress, and both stepped into an elegant barouche drawn, in the English style, by six magnificent bay horses, with three grooms in green-and-gold livery.

We followed in a pretty basket-shaped carriage, seating six and completely open. The Duke of Wurtzburg had rather a sheepish air, and spoke only a few words to Princess Borghese, of whom he was said to be enamoured. No one would have thought so.

The silence was broken only by lamentations and sighs from the three ladies, who, being hatless, were at the mercy of the dust and the sun.

We spent half an hour like this, driving all over the park, always at a fast trot.

I noticed that at the turnings, where we were obliged to slow down, people were standing with petitions in their hands, ready to throw them into the Emperor's barouche when he made a sign.

These drives were a fancy of the Emperor's; as in other cases, he did not see they lacked charm, and of course no one dared to mention it.

On our return, dinner was served, and the Emperor motioned Marie-Louise to take her uncle's arm and lead the way to the dining-room. He followed them. We also went in, except for the lady of the bedchamber and the Duchess of Montebello, who, to my great surprise, adjourned to another room, where a table of thirty covers was set for the great officers, and for the ladies on duty, with Grand Marshal Duroc to do the honours.

The Emperor's table was oblong. The Empress and her uncle, both silent figures, occupied one side. Napoleon, opposite, was between two empty places. Princess Borghese and I were at one end of the oblong, and M. de Montalivet at the other. The Emperor usually brought the minister with whom he had been working that morning to dine at his table, so as to go on talking of matters which, though less weighty, had some connection with the day's work.

It was the end of June, and broad daylight; the sun was flashing its beams through the treetops, but in spite of this brilliance the chandeliers were all alight and the windows open. This double lighting was far from pleasant. It was a peculiar whim. I am told that the Emperor invariably dined like that. A page stood behind his chair, holding a napkin. This page made a show of offering a plate, but Napoleon would not allow it; a butler performed that office.

The service of the meal was extremely rapid, and so noiseless that one might have thought it was in the hands of sylphs.

Napoleon ate little and very fast. The simplest dishes were those he preferred. Halfway through dinner he was offered a plate which did not belong to the course, with some peppered artichokes. He began to laugh, inviting us to share his 'modest' meal, and uttering a panegyric on this anchorite's dish. But as no one seemed inclined to try it, he had the plate set before him and ate it all!

The Empress, on the other hand, was engrossed by the dishes offered her, refused none, and seemed vexed at the speed with which they followed each other.

Towards the end of the meal Napoleon broke silence, and, addressing M. de Montalivet, asked for an account of the works begun at the palace of Versailles, which was now to be restored.

'I mean,' said he, 'to divert the Parisians in the old way. We must have the fountains playing every Sunday. But is it true that under Louis XVI that amusement cost a hundred thousand francs a time?'

When the minister said yes:

'That's a lot of money,' exclaimed Napoleon, 'for going to look at jets of water. Oh, well! if I deny the idlers of Paris that pleasure, when they value amusement more than anything, they won't have the sense to realise that it's in order to make better use of such a large sum.'

Speaking of the gardens of that royal residence and their immense size, he tried to recall the name of the celebrated Lenôtre, who laid them out.

By a singular chance, M. de Montalivet could not remember it, and they were both chafing to no purpose.

I ventured to whisper it to Princess Borghese, who repeated it aloud.

'Ah,' said Napoleon, 'that didn't come from *you*! I'll wager you never heard of Lenôtre's existence. He died before your time!'

Then he threw me a delightful glance.

Just as we were about to leave the table, the chamberlain came and informed the Emperor that the Viceroy of Italy was awaiting him in the garden. He started up, giving Marie-Louise no time to finish the ices, which vexed her so much that she could not resist complaining to her uncle.

On our return to the drawing-room, where the two ladies on duty already were, we found all the windows wide open. They looked out on the main avenue of the park.

Prince Eugène was walking up and down it in great excitement. As soon as Napoleon saw him, he went to meet him.

Judging by the warmth of their conversation, the subject must have been very serious. The Emperor was gesticulating like a true Corsican. The prince seemed to be trying to calm him down. One could easily see that Napoleon was not pleased. Bursts of voice were reaching us, but the wind carried away the sense.

Indoors, the silence was broken only by a few trite remarks M. de Montalivet felt obliged to make, so that he should not appear to be listening to the conversation taking place in the garden.

The Empress said not a word. Sitting by her uncle, who afforded her an example of the most perfect mumness, she looked vaguely out of the window, without the slightest concern for what was occurring in the park, where the discussion, livelier and livelier, still went on.

MUTINY IN THE FAMILY

All the kings Napoleon was setting up speedily lost ground with him. Not because most of them were sorry rulers, but because they forgot they were on the throne merely as governors or prefects appointed by the Emperor of the French, with the task of treating the natives as conquered and subject peoples. Often the outcries and sufferings of the countries they governed in Napoleon's interest alone would prompt these kings to

Napoleon in his study, 1810/12, by David engraved by Laugier

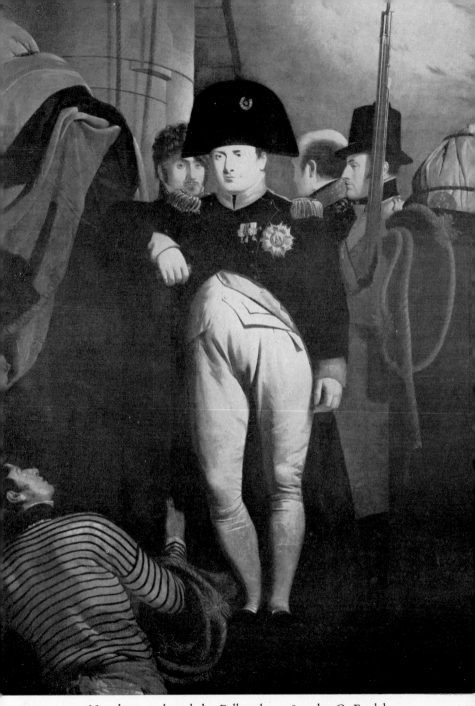

Napoleon on board the *Bellerophon*, 1815, by C. Eastlake

*fight back. And there would be an exchange of letters with Napoleon,
very painful to read. Or, when they were face to face, the most violent
quarrels. The minister Molé, who, as we know, enjoyed much of
Napoleon's confidence, paints this one from the life.*

I have never forgotten the scene I witnessed at the time when
he had in mind to unite Holland with France. One Sunday evening
I had gone to the Tuileries. The King and Queen of Naples, and
the King and Queen of Holland, who were still in Paris, had been
dining with him. As I approached the door of the drawing-room
where the imperial family were assembled, I heard Napoleon's
thundering voice. I went in. And here is the spectacle which
confronted me.

Amid the dazzle of a thousand candles, the blaze of diamonds
and other jewellery, men in uniform were drawn up in rows,
between which Napoleon was striding up and down. His features
were swollen and almost deformed by rage, his motions precipitate and uneven. His brother Louis was trying to keep up with
him, in spite of the paralytic affection which made it an effort for
him to walk. I went and stood by the King of Naples, who was
wearing the very brilliant uniform of his guards.

'Remember,' Napoleon was saying to the King of Holland, 'that
you are first of all, above all, a French prince. I placed you on the
throne of Holland merely to serve the interests of France, and to
second me in all I am doing for her.'

'You should have said so before appointing me to that crown.
I did not ask for it, anything but! I implored you to leave me in
the station of a French prince, which I owed to you, and which
was enough for my ambition. What you demand now would
mean ruin and disaster to a nation whose fate you have entrusted
to me, and whose welfare has become my first duty. To be sure
my heart is still French, but the day I have to sacrifice Holland to
your schemes, my reign will be over.'

At these last words Napoleon, more and more incensed, began
reproaching his brothers and sisters with their ingratitude and the
way they were setting up to be independent of the man who had
raised them from nothing.

*The Marquis de Bonneval, whose duties attached him to the palace,
had heard much worse. For instance, this tirade of Napoleon's against
the whole brood:*

R

Though not himself a man of exemplary morals, Napoleon was often ruffled by the scandalous conduct of most of the members of his family, and did not shrink from letting them know it.

One winter day there was no one in the room but his brothers and sisters and some officers of his household. Napoleon was gloomy. There was complete silence till dinner-time, which was itself short and silent. We returned to the drawing-room, the circle was formed.

Napoleon, as usual, stood warming the calves of his legs, with his hands crossed behind his back. He gazed at the ceiling. Jupiter's brow was dark. It was not long till the storm broke. As though talking to himself, he began:

'I don't believe any man in the world is more unfortunate in his family than I am. Suppose we sum up. Lucien is an ingrate. Joseph a Sardanapalus. Louis a paralytic. Jerome a scamp.'

Then, lowering his eyes and tracing a circle with his hand:

'As for you, ladies, you know what you are.'

As may be seen, the table was short, but complete.

THE KING OF ROME

At last Napoleon had a son. He gave this child the overweening title of King of Rome, that is, sovereign of the capital and dominions torn from the Pope, who was still languishing in his prison. Was this a good omen? And might not the imagination of contemporaries be struck, when they realised that the King of Rome was born (20th March, 1811) on the anniversary of the murder of the Duc d'Enghien (20th March, 1804)? Napoleon was superstitious; did it enter his mind? One may suppose not, for he was jubilant. His pride passed all human bounds. Every day (and quite seriously) he sent courtiers and ambassadors to bow down before the cradle and read long addresses to the baby. He could swallow anything. When the child was two and a half, he was to be shown a copy of verses as his son's work, and to remark: 'What good verse the King of Rome writes!'

Where propaganda was concerned, he had a brilliant assistant in Duroc, Grand Marshal of the palace. This appears from the narrative of our old friend Sergeant Coignet.

In 1811 rejoicings awaited us. On 20th March a courier came to the barracks to announce our Empress's delivery, and said we should be hearing the guns.

Everyone was on the alert. At the first reports from the Invalides we began silently counting. At the twenty-second and twenty-third everyone was jumping for joy. With one voice they shouted 'Long live the Emperor!'

The King of Rome was baptised on 9th June. We had entertainments and fireworks.

The darling child was always escorted by the governor of the palace when he went out for an airing with his handsome wet-nurse and a lady who carried him.

One day, when I was at the palace of Saint-Cloud, Marshal Duroc, who was escorting him, beckoned me to come up, and the dear child stretched out his little hands for my plume. I bent down, and he began tearing the feathers out. The marshal said:

'Let him.'

The child was bursting with glee, but it was all up with the plume. I felt rather sheepish. The marshal said:

'Let him have it; I'll see that you get another.'

The lady-in-waiting and the nurse laughed their heads off. The marshal said to the lady:

'Give the prince to this sergeant to carry.'

Heavens! I stretch out my arms to receive the precious burden. Everyone comes round me.

'Well,' said M. Duroc, 'is he heavy?'

'Yes, general.'

'Come, take a walk; you're strong enough to carry him!'

I took a little stroll on the terrace. The child was pulling my feathers out and taking no notice of me. His robes came down very low and I was afraid of stumbling. But I was happy to be carrying such a child. I gave him back to the lady, who thanked me, and the marshal said:

'Come to my room in an hour's time.'

So I present myself to the marshal, who gives me an order to select a fine new plume at the maker's.

'That's your only one?' said he.

'Yes, general.'

'I'll give you an order for two.'

'No, thank you, general.'

'Nonsense, man; you'll have one for Sundays!'

When I was back with my officers, they said:

'But your plume's gone.'

'The King of Rome took it from me.'

'That's a pretty story.'

'Look at this order from Marshal Duroc. Instead of one plume I'm to have two, and I carried the King of Rome in my arms for nearly a quarter of an hour. He tore up my plume.'

'Happy mortal,' they said. 'Such memories never fade away.'

GETTING RID OF A MINISTER

Napoleon never dismissed a minister in a personal interview. He would either write or send Cambacérès for his portfolio. The storm scenes never broke on the person concerned. At Valladolid it was Legendre who got the abuse intended for Dupont. At Compiègne, Morio got the abuse due to Jerome Bonaparte. Napoleon said nothing to Dupont or Jerome face to face. He was to say nothing to Pradt in 1812 on relieving him of his embassy. Nothing to Fouché, in a little while. And he said nothing to Champagny, whom he was now about to get rid of. How and why? Champagny gives his own version.

One fine morning, when I returned from a drive, I heard that M. Cambacérès was waiting in my drawing-room. I had no doubt of the object of his call. For some time I had been suspicious of Napoleon's intentions towards me. At a government council he had upbraided me for a letter I had written to Dantzig.

I had written that letter only by his orders. I told him so. And a very ill-timed exasperation prompted me to add that all I had ever done amiss was to carry out his orders too faithfully.

'Much obliged,' he replied, in a sombre, abstracted tone.

I had the impression of hearing my sentence, which did not upset me in the least, since I was not keen on my post. In the next few days it even surprised me that the sentence had not been carried out. Later on, M. Cambacérès told me the reason for this delay. He had called on a Monday evening to ask for my portfolio. He found me, either at dinner or just afterwards, with fifty persons as my guests. He felt this was not the moment to execute such a harsh order, and went away again without having fulfilled his mission. Napoleon highly approved his delicacy. He came back a few days later, but in the morning. It was a Wednesday, when the council met, and he called early enough to stop me from attending it.

I do not think my loss of favour was solely due to the little incident I have described. I was not in agreement with Napoleon on the subject of Russia, which was the great question of the moment. Recalling the Treaty of Vienna, he saw in me the spectator of a weakness he would have liked to disguise from himself.

I had had no part in the Spanish business, being unfit for anything like trickery or bad faith. I had made, I might almost say single-handed, the peace treaty of Vienna, which got him out of a difficult and even dangerous situation. Finally he dismissed me because he wanted to make war on Russia, which I might have hindered.

His return, after the most shocking disaster, justified the fears this project had raised in me. Before he left, I should have liked to remind him of what he had said one day, in one of those fits of moderation that were not common with him:

'I want to give up making war in person. I have little to gain and much to lose. It was all very well to imperil my fortune like that in its infancy, but at the present stage it is folly. But who can take my place in command of my armies?'

Then, passing his marshals and generals in review, he summed up one after another with energy and severity, and found none he could rely on. Some of them lacked talent, there were even some who lacked courage. Others made war for their own benefit instead of his.

'Didn't fat Soult try to set himself up as king of Portugal?'

'Well, then, sire, you should leave off making war!'

'Yes, but then how am I to maintain my army? And I must have an army.'

Such was the vice of his position. He had to preserve it by fighting, to attack in self-defence.

THE CROWNING BLUNDER

Napoleon, blinded by vainglory, had ceased to restrain himself. He was piling one mistake on another. But it was nothing to have decreed the murder of d'Enghien, the imprisonment of the Pope, the martyrdom of the Spaniards, the oppression of Europe. . . . He parted from Talleyrand, whom he could ill spare. Was that all? No, all that was nothing yet. But then he decided to take back Fouché's portfolio. . . . This time he was lost. Fouché, as we know, was the only statesman in France.

Single-handed, while Napoleon was away, he had saved Belgium and forced the English to re-embark. Now it turned out that he, and he alone, would be capable of making peace with England, likewise single-handed. At bottom Napoleon was afraid of him. He dreaded his political genius. He knew and used to observe that 'Fouché had wonderful parts'. One day in council he said to him:

'And so you make peace and war on your own account.'

Fouché, Duke of Otranto, minister of the general police, minister of the interior, with creatures in every assembly, in every department, in the army and on the bench—Fouché knew Napoleon better than he knew himself, and was no bad manipulator of 'perhaps the touchiest and most suspicious man that ever lived' (to use his own words).

He had an answer to everything.

One day he was urging Napoleon to take a strong line with the legislative body.

Fouché: If Louis XVI had done so, that poor prince would still be alive.

(A moment's silence. Napoleon stared at him open-mouthed. Then:)

Napoleon: Why, Duke of Otranto! I seem to remember that you were one of those who sent Louis XVI to the scaffold?

Fouché: Yes, sire, that was the first of the services I have been happy enough to do Your Majesty.

When Napoleon settled accounts with Fouché for his diplomatic feeler to England by withdrawing his portfolio, he was really settling his own fate.

'No doubt,' Fouché was to write, 'it would have been too hasty a prediction to recall the words of the prophet: "In forty days Nineveh will be destroyed." But I might safely have prophesied that in less than four years Napoleon's empire would cease to be.'

Pelet (de la Lozère), councillor of state and one of Fouché's chief police lieutenants (the other was Réal) has described Napoleon's relations with his minister.

Fouché's conversation had great charm for Napoleon, because he talked only of political surveillance, that is, of what related to the parties and to diplomatic and court intrigues, and never of the policing of streets and highways, in which neither took any interest. Fouché used to sign everything connected with this inferior branch without reading it.

He had a keen and audacious mind, concealing great depth

under a show of frivolity. He would jump from one topic to another as nimbly as a squirrel, never going far into any of them. This sprightliness, affected or natural, was his way of preserving secrecy.

His disposition would not suffer him to remain long in power, either under a free or under an absolute government. He had not frankness enough for the one, nor docility enough for the other.

At Napoleon's court he always retained the free manners of a *conventionnel*.

Napoleon declared that it went against the grain with him to restore the ministry of general police, that the intrigues of England forced him to do so, but that he would abolish it at the general peace. This ministry, in whatever hands it might be placed, seemed to him a power almost rivalling his own, which might be turned against him.

This suspicion led him to multiply bodies of counter-police. There was that of the palace, entrusted to the Grand Marshal; that of Paris, directed by the military governor, and the more extensive force of the inspector-general of gendarmerie; the gendarmes, distributed through every part of France, had to send off daily bulletins of what had been happening. The heads of these police forces worked directly with the Emperor.

Police Minister Fouché, in spite of the precautions taken against him, acquired the importance to be expected from his character and situation. He was the only man of influence under Napoleon. This influence, becoming too patent, led to his disgrace. Napoleon took umbrage at the service Fouché had done him by raising an army in his absence, to defend Antwerp against a surprise attack by the English.

'That means,' he said, 'that you could have raised it against me.'

Their breach was in the style of a lovers' quarrel. Napoleon asked for his letters back. Fouché pretended to have burnt them. Napoleon dictated an order *ab irato*, by which in future the papers of any minister giving up his office were to be placed under seal. He removed Fouché by appointing him governor of Rome.

'I have only two cities,' he said, 'Paris and Rome. I am giving you Rome. You ought to be satisfied.'

MÄDCHEN IN UNIFORM

Napoleon had founded schools for the daughters of members of the Legion of Honour, with a regime adapted by himself from that of his barracks.

Now and then he inspected them. Here we see him with the young ladies of Ecouen, whose superintendent was Mme Campan.

On 3rd June, 1811, Napoleon, accompanied by Marie-Louise and several magnates of his court, visited the foundation at Ecouen. After viewing the chapel and the refectories, he asked me to present the three most distinguished pupils.

'Sire,' I said, 'I cannot name three; I could name six.'

He spun round and made for the terrace-roof of the château, where, after seeing all the classes together, he repeated his request.

'Sire,' I replied again, 'I respectfully take leave to point out to Your Majesty that I should be doing an injustice to several pupils as forward as those I singled out.'

Berthier and others were telling me in an undertone:

'You'll ruin yourself by holding out against a man like that.'

Napoleon went all over the house, entered into the smallest details, and after questioning several of the pupils:

'Come, madam,' said he, 'I'm very pleased; name me your six pupils.'

I called them and presented them to him. And when he was about to drive off, he told me to send their names to Berthier.

On sending the list to the Prince of Neuchâtel, I added the names of four more pupils, and all ten obtained a pension of 300 francs.

In the three hours occupied by this visit, the Empress did not speak a word.

THE LOW COUNTRIES AGAIN

Louis Bonaparte had abdicated the throne of Holland. Then Napoleon simply annexed Holland to France. Once more he showed Marie-Louise about the North of the Empire. But the Emperor's prestige, observes the Comte de Mérode-Westerloo, *was greatly shaken.*

On Marie-Louise's arrival at Laeken, my mother was obliged to quit her retirement and attend the Empress's dinner-party.

And since to her other fears she added a fear of horses she was not used to, she had a bay horse dyed black to match one of her own.

The royal lady, then very young, and brought up, as is usual for an archduchess, in a very retired way, had as yet little self-possession or knowledge of the world. She seemed shy and awkward. She was seated on the right of the armchair awaiting the Emperor. My mother was on the left of this same chair. The Emperor was at Antwerp, but his arrival was expected at any moment, and my mother, placed so near him, was terribly apprehensive of his usual interrogatories on family details. She spent most of the dinner-party in dread of his coming. But he did not appear all that day.

Here I shall insert one or two circumstances I had forgotten when describing his stay in Brussels.

The year before, 1810, Mme de Ribaucourt made the ball an occasion for entreating the Emperor to let her only son stay at home; the boy was twelve or thirteen, and was to be taken away to La Flèche [*the military school near Anger*]. He gave his consent, providing he attended the lycée. When her petition had been granted, Mme de Ribaucourt fainted away. Happily, by then she was out of the Emperor's sight, or it might not have been granted after all, Napoleon professing an aversion to fainting-fits.

At the opening of this ball he said to the Empress:

'Go on, Louise, tomorrow you can write and tell your father how you danced with your worthy Belgians.'

On this tour she was received, as an archduchess, with great applause. The Emperor got very little. It had been heaped on him in 1803. But the captivity of the Pope, the threat to religion, the devastation of Spain and the odious abduction of its king, the total coercion of the press, the repeated conscriptions, the warrants, the banishments and the kidnappings of children had made a remarkable change.

People were gasping under that huge pressing-machine known as the French empire, and in its last five or six years they would have been very glad to hope for what M. Talleyrand, in 1813, called the beginning of the end.

MUSICIAN FOR A DAY

He was really a novelist heading for immense popularity—Paul de
Kock (1793–1871). But he wanted a good look at Napoleon, and this
is the way he came by it.

Everyone was still beaming in Paris, four months after the
birth of the King of Rome. They were beaming especially because they regarded this child as a pledge of peace. And as patriotic joy is infectious, I believe, like all other kinds, I, who till then
had never dreamed of looking the sun in the face—I repeat that
my one idea was to see Napoleon.

I had revealed this longing to Mengal, my violin teacher. One
evening in July, Mengal said to me:

'You want to see the Emperor? I can get you an opportunity.
The day after tomorrow there's to be a morning concert at the
Tuileries, in the Clock Court. I'm going to it, and you shall come
with me.'

'With you? On what pretext?'

'Why, as a violinist, to be sure! As you don't know the pieces
to be performed, you will merely pretend to play. I've told the
bandmaster, who is a friend of mine. He won't say anything.'

It was the 7th or 8th of July, 1811. Why was there a concert
that day in the Tuileries courtyard? I forget. Perhaps to cele-
brate the churching of Marie-Louise, which had been very long-
drawn, or the imperial baby's first tooth.

At any rate, while I made a show of scraping away at the fiddle,
it was given me to look my fill on the Emperor and even on the
Empress, for she appeared on the balcony at her husband's side.
Both were in full dress. Behind them crowded a host of princes,
of marshals, of great ladies flashing with gold and diamonds at
every seam.

Marie-Louise struck me as handsome, but I found Napoleon
yellow, obese, bloated, and with a head sunk too deep on his
shoulders. That was not the hero of my imagination. I was
expecting a god; I saw only a stout man.

He withdrew at the end of the concert after thanking *us* with a
gesture of which I had the vanity to assume a share! After all, if I
was not playing, neither was I being paid! I had gone out of my
way to see him; a civil acknowledgment was no more than proper.

NAPOLEON AND HIS TAILOR

Poumiès de la Siboutie, doctor and collector, also collected anecdotes from those who had been about Napoleon. For instance, Léger, the Emperor's tailor. And so we get a different view of Napoleon, which may be thought far more valuable than many statements by official personages.

To M. Durand, who long kept the door of the Emperor's closet, I owe some rather curious facts which I noted down.

Napoleon was very squeamish about pain. For a mere nothing, he would grumble and lament beyond all expression. In his military career, though he exposed himself a great deal, he met with no injury. The wound at Ratisbon, which has been so much talked of, did not even bleed; it was only a bruise, made by a spent bullet.

Furthermore, Napoleon was very superstitious, intractable in the matter of thirteen and Friday. Thus, the date of a coming journey had been fixed without reference to the day of the week. This turned out to be a Friday. When the Emperor was told, he put the date forward and left on Thursday.

Léger, formerly tailor to the Emperor and a neighbour of mine at Ville-d'Avray, has given me a number of details on the great man he dressed.

Up to 1810, Napoleon had as his tailor a certain Chevalier, who, though a good workman, dressed him very badly, because he was weak enough to give in to all the tasteless criticisms of his illustrious client.

In 1810, while Napoleon was at Compiègne awaiting Marie-Louise, one of his sisters (Princess Borghese, I think) said to him:

'Your clothes are badly made and very unbecoming. You persist in not wearing braces, and your breeches always seem to be on the point of falling down.'

'Well,' said the Emperor, 'what tailor do you recommend?'

'You should ask Constant's advice.'

Constant was summoned and suggested Léger, who worked for Murat, Prince Eugène, Joseph and Jerome Bonaparte, etc. A courier was sent to Léger, who appeared at Compiègne the following day. He made all Napoleon's clothes, while Napoleon, after his wont, made absurd suggestions. For instance, he wanted all his coats to have their skirts hooked up like those of Frederick.

'I will never consent to it,' said Léger; 'you would be ridiculous, and my reputation would be gone! The whole world has its eyes on Your Majesty, and if you were seen in the kind of uniform you require of me, your good name would suffer and it would be my fault. Even if you offered me the French empire, I would not consent to make such a uniform.'

The Emperor burst into a hearty laugh, and gave up his idea.

The day Marie-Louise was to make her entry into Paris, Léger went to Saint-Cloud very early in the morning, to take the Emperor his clothes and his embroidered mantle covered with bees. When Napoleon saw him, he said:

'Léger, will it be fine?'

'We shall have a wonderful day.'

'Good.'

And he ran to the window.

'All the same,' he said, 'it's very much overcast.'

'No matter, I guarantee that Your Majesty will have a fine day.'

'While I was trying on his clothes,' Léger ran on, 'he left me at least a dozen or fifteen times to go and study the weather.

'He was so thrifty with his clothes that one day he wanted me to sew a patch on a pair of hunting breeches. I flatly refused.

'He made a very bad customer. He had his own embroiderer, his own silk merchant. He argued personally over his bills, and on top of that he was always wasting my time.

'Once, about a coat, I went to Saint-Cloud fifteen days in succession. Either he was busy or he was asleep. For as he slept very little at night, he was apt to drop off during the day.

'I left off dressing him in 1813. My other customers were far more profitable. Murat, Prince Eugène, Borghese, Berthier used to spend on their personal wardrobe, not counting their households, from 40,000 to 60,000 francs. There were years when I made Murat, *for himself*, 100,000 francs' worth of coats, cloaks or uniforms. In those days my partner Michel and I often had a net profit of 400,000 francs a year.

'On the remonstrances of M. de Rémusat, Napoleon consented, in 1810, to increase his wardrobe. Till then he had been so niggardly that his wardrobe and linen, apart from embroidery, were not worth 2,000 francs. In winter I always made him half a dozen grey overcoats. In summer the same number of chasseur uniform coats, green, as may be seen in all his portraits. Every fortnight, a white kerseymere waistcoat and breeches. Those were his main expenses. And never a civilian coat.'

VAULTING AMBITION

The die was cast. Napoleon, with all Europe under his sway (in theory), had only Russia left to subdue. But this war, to which some flatterers encouraged him, was unpopular. Sensible men were crying Beware. And Fouché left his retirement to offer Napoleon a report on the disaster threatening him.

'Give it me; I'll read it. But I know already that the Russian war is no more to your taste than the Spanish war.'

'Sire, I don't think the latter is going so well that it would be safe to fight beyond the Pyrenees and beyond the Niemen at the same time. The wish and need to see Your Majesty's power consolidated for ever has emboldened me to submit a few remarks on the present crisis.'

'There is no crisis. This is merely a political war. You are no judge of my situation or of Europe as a whole. Since my marriage people have thought the lion was dozing. They'll see whether he's dozing. Spain will fall as soon as I have destroyed the English influence at St Petersburg. I needed eight hundred thousand men, and I have them. I am dragging all Europe with me, and nowadays Europe is only an old, rotten whore whom I shall treat as I please with eight hundred thousand men. Didn't you once tell me that for you the mark of genius was to think nothing impossible? Well, in six or eight months you will see what can be done by the most immense schemes combined with the vigour that can set things to work. I go more by the opinion of the army and the people than by yours, gentlemen; you are too rich, and are only trembling for me because you're in terror of a crash. Don't worry. Look on the Russian war as a war of common sense, for the real interests, tranquillity and security of all. Besides, can I help it if an excess of power is sweeping me on to the dictatorship of the world? Had you not a hand in it, you and plenty of others who are now finding fault with me, and would like to turn me into a King Log? My destiny is not fulfilled. I mean to finish what is only roughed out. We need a European code, a European court of appeal, the same currency, the same weights and measures, the same laws. I must make all the nations of Europe into the same nation, and Paris into the capital of the world. That, my lord duke, is the one ending that will do for me. Today you would not serve me well because you fancy everything is going to be unsettled again. But within a year you will be serving me with the same zeal and eagerness as in the days of Marengo and of Austerlitz. You will see something to beat all that. Take my word for it. Good-bye, my lord duke; don't set up as a victim or a malcontent, and put a little more faith in me.'

I withdrew aghast.

QUADRILLES UNDER A CLOUD

These were the last of the court quadrilles: 6th and 7th February, 1812. Napoleon had decided that his sisters Caroline and Pauline were to get up an evening-dress ball and his stepdaughter and sister-in-law Hortense a masked ball.

Now, Caroline and Pauline took it into their heads to present an allegory on the annexation of Rome. At the ball of 6th February Napoleon affected to be pleased, but the following day produced a lecture, of which we learn from Hortense.

On the day of the fête, the Tuileries theatre, in which it took place, had been turned into a ballroom. The Emperor was on a dais, between the Empress and me. The whole court and the distinguished foreigners filled the auditorium, and the boxes were allotted to the residents of Paris.

The two princesses were dazzling in their beauty and jewels. One of them [*Pauline*] representing Rome, and the other [*Caroline*] France. Their charming faces, their little helmets, their shields covered with diamonds and coloured jewels made a brilliant show. The other women, as naiads of the Tiber, as Hours, as Irises, were all handsome and graceful, but the chamberlains' and equerries' faces discovered as Stars, Zephyrs and Apollos excited mirth. And the dumb-show seemed out of keeping with the dignity of the persons and the scene of the performance.

After the quadrille the Empress and I opened the ball with a French country dance. All the usual dances followed.

Meanwhile the Emperor was going about speaking to everyone. He said not a word of the allegory. But the evening after, when I went to see him, and the Queen of Naples also looked in, he said to her rather testily:

'Where did you get the subject of your quadrille? There's no sense in it. Rome is obedient to France, but not content. What gave you the notion of representing her as happy and satisfied with her subjection? That's absurd flattery. Oh, I know you only wanted to look pretty and wear a fine costume, but you could have found other subjects without dragging politics into the dance.'

Then, turning to me:

'And you—have *you* been getting up some such twaddle? I don't like compliments. I give you notice.'

I hastened to say that my quadrille had nothing to do with politics or with him.

'Glad to hear it,' said he.

Then, realising the advantage he had given me over his sister, who, after all, had been trying to gratify him, or perhaps because he was in a scolding vein and was thinking what he might have to scold about, he went on, pacing up and down the room:

'Ah, these young women! They're harder to control than a regiment. And yet I am not a bear. I can be approached, consulted on what they would like to do. But no! The ladies never think twice about anything. And yet in our position nothing is immaterial.'

Then addressing me:

'And you? Who gave you the idea of dressing your son as a Polish lancer? Do you realise that you may have brought a war on me? Kurakin has been complaining already. They're already saying I intend to make your son King of Poland. Besides, what right have you to give him a captain's epaulettes? Those have to be got by fighting. You know I made him leave off his Dutch orders because I won't have a child, in France, wearing any decoration till he deserves it. My family must earn everything as I did, at the point of the sword. (*Softening.*) But if you need a soldier's coat to dress your son up, all right, then! give him the uniform of a red lancer of the Dutch Guard, and I'm being very indulgent in allowing you a second lieutenant's epaulette, which your son will earn, I hope, later on.'

All through this speech of the Emperor's I said nothing, for it was my mother who had ordered the Polish uniform as a New Year gift. The epaulettes were the tailor's doing, and the truth is that I had not given them a thought, nor had anyone else.

REWARDS AND VAGARIES

Before going off to this new war he multiplied rewards, cramming his marshals and generals with gold (some of them regularly received a million—three hundred of our millions—at the opening of every campaign), distributing titles, crosses, annuities. . . . But in his own way, which was deplored by all. Here are three authoritative critics: General Baron Thiébault, General Baron Pouget *and* Baron Mounier.

It was one of his greatest vices to be partial, often shamelessly partial, to men who had supplied every kind of reason for getting rid of them, while he hated independence to the point of repulsing those who, by their integrity and their virtues, denied him any of the holds which he regarded, quite wrongly, as guarantees of a blind and boundless devotion.

In the same way, favours and graces came to be scandalously allotted. And fools and scoundrels obtained from him decorations, titles of chevalier, even of baron (I will instance Lemière), and finally endowments, which he refused or did not give to men of outstanding merit who had reached the highest ranks.

A colonel was requesting the cross for his quartermaster.

'It's blood I want, and not ink,' replied Napoleon, who, soon afterwards, gave this cross for filth.

How many tales have gone round on his relations with the private soldier! Now these relations, so steady, so intelligent, so fruitful at the beginning, later evolve into the profligacy of power.

'Take that!' he says to a soldier, giving him a title and endowment.

'You can have twelve hundred francs a year,' he says to another. 'Drink them with your mates, and tell them to take pattern by you. As for you, you're invulnerable.'

Napoleon at St Helena, 1820, after a drawing by Captain Dodgin

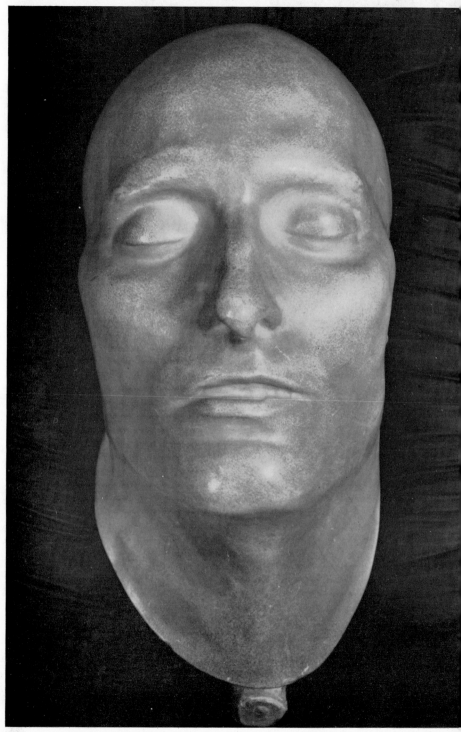

Napoleon's death mask, 1821, Lady Lever Art Gallery

At a review a sergeant steps forward to ask for the cross. The colonel wants the man to fall back, but Napoleon detains him with these words:

'What have you done to earn the cross?'

'Sire, I pulled up the palisades at the attack on Stralsund.'

'Is that true, colonel?'

'Yes, sire.'

'What else have you done?'

'I carried off a flag at such an engagement.'

'Is that true, colonel?'

'Yes, sire.'

'Well, then, why don't you want this man to have the cross?'

'Sire, he's a drunkard, a thief, a . . .'

'Pooh! blood washes out such things.'

And the cross was granted to this hero of a special stamp, who could not be long in disgracing it.

At another review Napoleon sees a soldier trying to catch his eye.

'Well, what is it you want?'

'A spree, sire.'

And the soldier is decorated.

And to balance these licentious favours, mere whims of omnipotence, one might give instances equally remote from fair dealing, but in the opposite direction.

A regimental adjutant, an excellent man, very devoted, punctual and faithful in the Emperor's service, but who from the nature of his duties had remained at the depot, is promoted colonel. In his delight, he thinks he should repair to the army and thank Napoleon. He presents himself, and receives this question:

'You were in the last engagement?'

'No, sire.'

'Then you were in such another?'

'No, sire.'

'At so-and-so, then?'

'I hadn't the honour.'

'And who f—— me a colonel like you? You haven't been anywhere.'

And the worthy man, who from the first question had lost

S

courage to say where he had been, was deprived of his rank, to which he had none the less every title.

On 4th May, 1809, the whole division was assembled. We were given notice that before leaving this bivouac, the Emperor would come and inspect us.

When His Majesty had dismounted, he asked me what sapper had dealt the first blow at the castle gate. I gave his name.

'Send for him.'

It was Hattin, their corporal.

'It was you that dealt the first blow at the castle gate?'

'Yes, sire.'

'You're a brave fellow, I award you the cross.'

'Send for your majors,' the Emperor told me.

When they were there His Majesty asked me who was the bravest officer in the regiment. This question, for which I was not prepared, rather took me aback.

'Well, did you hear what I said?'

'Yes, sire, but I know several who . . .'

'No rambling, answer me.'

I named Lieutenant Guyot of the light infantry. The Emperor looked at the majors and asked:

'Do you agree, gentlemen?'

'Yes, sire.'

'Send for that officer.'

He arrived in great agitation, not knowing why he was wanted.

'Your superiors have pointed you out as the bravest officer in the regiment. I create you baron, with an endowment of four thousand francs a year.'

The Emperor went on:

'Who is the bravest soldier in the regiment?'

This inquiry puzzled me even more than when I had been asked for the officer. One of the majors came to my rescue by saying:

'Colonel, what about Rifleman Bayonnette?'

I said yes, for it would not do to delay the answer.

'Bayonnette!' repeated the Emperor. 'You agree, gentlemen?'

'Yes, sire.'

'Send for him.'

He was much pleased by this surname, for he repeated it several times before the soldier appeared.

'You are the bravest soldier in the regiment,' said he. 'I name you chevalier of the Legion of Honour, and this title is accompanied by an endowment of fifteen hundred francs, which you will hand on to your children.'

What was the Emperor's object? Should it not have struck him that by putting questions of this kind so unexpectedly, and without permitting a moment's thought, he would expose himself to seeing his design miscarry?

I make these comments with no idea of censuring such a great man as Napoleon; he has never had a greater admirer, and I have been faithful to his memory all my life. But, I repeat, he may have failed of his purpose, and I allow the remark to stand.

After the battle of Eckmühl, when Napoleon had asked for the bravest captain, and the colonel had mentioned one, a little Gascon captain who had been a hairdresser in Paris burst from the ranks, exclaiming:

'That is not true. *I* am the bravest man in the regiment. No one would dare to deny it.'

Napoleon referred to the colonel, who stammered out:

'Why, yes; I hadn't time to compare, etc.'

And Napoleon granted him the favours which, but for his Gascon assurance, would have gone to another man.

NAPOLEON'S TREASURE

Napoleon's fortunes were at their peak, his personal treasure likewise. He would never be more powerful, he would never be richer. Though the figures supplied by Fouché *are necessarily approximate, they are undeniable and even, for certain 'items', short of the truth.*

Day by day, with a glee whose extravagance he had ceased to hide, he watched the increase of the enormous treasure buried in his vaults in the Pavillon Marsan. They were choked with it. This treasure already came to nearly five hundred million in specie. It was a residuum of the two milliards of coined money which had entered France through conquest. And so the lust of gold might one day have prevailed over the lust of battle in Napoleon's heart, if inexorable Nemesis had let him grow old.

In order to form an idea of the accumulation of riches inherent in the development of this man's power, add to the treasures hidden in the vaults of the Tuileries, forty millions' worth of furniture and four or five millions' worth of table-ware contained in the imperial residences: five hundred millions distributed to the army by way of endowments; finally the extraordinary estate, which came to more than seven hundred million, and which by its nature had no bounds, since it was composed of the assets 'which the Emperor, exercising the right of peace and war, acquired by conquest and treaty'; with a text so indefinite, nothing could escape him. Already the stock of this extraordinary estate was formed of whole provinces, of nations whose destiny was unfixed, and of the fruit of confiscations throughout the empire. There is no doubt that he would have come to absorb all the revenues and all public property that had escaped the other two creations of imperial estates and private estates. And indeed to put all France in fee and attach it to his estate by annual dues was one of Napoleon's favourite ideas.

What a magnificent regime of martial spoliation on the one hand, of gifts and prodigalities on the other! Where was it leading us? To shed all our blood for the sequestration of the whole world. And even so, there was little hope of sating the voracity of the favourites and familiars of an insatiable conqueror.

LAST EFFULGENCE OF THE REIGN

The Grand Army par excellence (800,000 men, 650,000 combatants) began its march towards Russia. Napoleon halted at Dresden, and then at Posen, to hold his court there. The last effulgence of the reign. . . . To the Poles he was still a liberator—in posse. He had been recruiting them since 1806. After Auerstädt he had turned ex-Prussian Poland into the 'Duchy of Warsaw'; after Wagram he had enlarged it at the expense of Austria. The restoration of the Kingdom of Poland was not exactly guaranteed—but it was hinted at, as the reward of 'zeal and efforts'. In other words, he wanted all the Polish blood he could get. Not that it would make a great difference. As he was to remark at St Helena: 'Poland and its resources were but poetry in the first months of 1812.'

In a few months he would be crossing Poland and Germany again, in the opposite direction, but as a fugitive. Here we see him at Posen, amid the illuminations and triumphal arches, as he appeared to society and to a Polish officer, Heinrich von Brandt.

On 29th May all the troops scattered around Posen, including those in formation, were abruptly recalled to the town, where the Emperor was expected. However, he did not arrive till nine o'clock the following evening, escorted by a French and Polish detachment of Guards. He was received as enthusiastically as in 1806. Nothing was to be seen but triumphal arches, illuminations, transparencies with mottoes proclaiming, in letters of fire, the wishes and the advance gratitude of a people too confident in the future. At the entrance to the suburbs a first triumphal arch had been erected with the inscription: *Heroi invincibili*. There the hero thus far invincible was welcomed and complimented by President Rose, head of the municipality, a personage no less pliant than grave, who has since complimented many another. I saw him again in 1831, addressing an equally eloquent harangue to the Prussian marshal Gneisenau.

At the top of the street leading to the Jesuit college, where the Emperor was to stay, one could read on a second triumphal arch: *Restauratori patriae*; on the gate of the college itself, in luminous characters: *Grati Poloni Imperatori magno*. The five big windows of the town hall were adorned with the city arms in transparency, quartered alternately by the initials of Napoleon and of Marie-Louise, the French eagle and the shield of the Grand Duchy of Warsaw. On the tower of the Cistercian church, which the Emperor could see from his windows, the illumination presented a gigantic laurel wreath over the motto: *Napoleoni magno Caesari et victori!*

A sky southern in its calm favoured the deceitful brilliance of this solemnity; an immense crowd thronged the streets, brighter than day in the universal illumination. The country people, who had flocked to share in the fête, were bivouacking in every square, especially in the one which was then called Napoleon Square, and which by the end of the following year was to be Frederick-William Square again! The old soldiers, the *grognards*, for we had a number in our own ranks, remained somewhat cool amid the general excitement. They maintained that this enthusiasm was partly factitious, stimulated by the authorities who wanted to 'throw dust in the Emperor's eyes'.

Next day we were reviewed, not by the Emperor but by Marshal Mortier. Though as yet only a third of our new recruits were fully clothed, he seemed pleased with their bearing, and agreeably surprised that so much had been done in so little time.

Napoleon suddenly arrived on horseback during the march-past. He looked anxious, preoccupied. He asked impatiently, out loud:

'Where is the prefect?'

When the prefect (Count Poninski) had come forward, the Emperor added, in the curt, grating voice of his bad days:

'These men look too young. I need men who can stand up to fatigue. When they're too young they only fill the hospitals . . .'

Since he was moving away as he talked, I heard no more.

An old University friend gave me details of the morning reception, which was held after Mass, in the old refectory of the college. It was attended by large numbers of the Polish nobility, in court dress. The Emperor's only greeting to them was:

'Gentlemen, I should have preferred to see you booted and spurred, the sabre by your side, like your ancestors at the approach of the Tartars and Cossacks. We are living in days when it is necessary to be armed from head to foot, with a hand on the sword-hilt.'

Several comic incidents enlivened this reception. Among the nobles who had come to greet the Emperor was a Count Szoldrcki, a great landowner and a magistrate in his district. He wore as his badge of office an enamelled plaque almost as big as a dinner-plate. The Emperor was misled by it (or pretended to be), and asked him point-blank how many workmen he employed in his 'china factory'. The poor count was quite overcome. The prefect hastened to say:

'Sire, it's Count Szoldrcki, the richest landowner in the country.'

'Ah! very good!' said the Emperor.

And he moved on.

A few moments later, when it was the ladies' turn, a Countess Mycielcka was presented to him—a young lady of eighteen, but looking much older, since she was unduly fat. So the Emperor took her for a woman who had been married some years, and asked in his usual way:

'How many children have you?'

'Sire . . . I haven't any.'

'You're divorced, then?'

'No, sire, I'm not married yet.'

'Ah! you shouldn't be too fussy, you have no time to waste!'

This remark made everyone smile, except of course the person addressed. Yet she must have thought it was good advice, for she married soon afterwards.

In short, this audience made an unfavourable impression on the Polish nobility, particularly on the women.

One of them, a great lady and a woman of parts, said at the time:

'He has not improved since the 26th of November, 1806!' (The day of his first visit to Posen.)

She thought that his abrupt manners, his cutting and haughty style, made a painful contrast to the gracious affability and kindliness of Prince Poniatowski. And to the objection that states are not founded by affability, she returned not without point that one can often make more conquests and see further with the heart than with the head.

A former chamberlain to King Stanislas, on being asked his opinion of Napoleon, is said to have summed it up in this Latin phrase: *Nec affabilis, nec amabilis, nec adibilis.* (Neither affable, nor agreeable, nor approachable.)

ON THE BANKS OF THE NIEMEN, OR THE HARE

The Grand Army had reached the Niemen. Napoleon was expected. Were they to cross the river? Sensible men would have liked Napoleon to stop there. But he had no such thought.

And yet he received a warning. . . . The authority for this detail and its effect is his Master of the Horse, General Caulaincourt.

Napoleon caught up the prince (Davout) at his headquarters a league from the Niemen and Kovno. Day was breaking. He went off at once to reconnoitre the banks of the river and the whole neighbourhood. He did not return till evening, when he dispatched orders for a couple of hours and then rode off again by moonlight to make a reconnaissance closer to the river and decide where to cross.

Everyone, without exception, was left some distance behind, so as not to attract the notice of any Russian vedettes across the river. Napoleon examined its banks in company with General Haxo of the Engineers. Even in the morning he had had to borrow a Polish officer's cloak, to be less conspicuous.

When the reconnaissance was over he rejoined his staff to make a fresh study of the different points which the troops might occupy. As we were galloping through the cornfields, a hare started up between the legs of Napoleon's horse, causing it to shy slightly.

Napoleon, who had a very bad seat on horseback, rolled on the ground, but got up again so quickly that he was on his feet before I arrived to help him.

He remounted his horse without a word. The ground being very soft, he was only slightly bruised on the lower part of the hip. It struck me at once that this was a bad omen, and I was certainly not the only one, for just then the Prince of Neuchâtel grasped my hand and said:

'We had far better not cross the Niemen. That fall is a bad sign.'

Napoleon, who had at first been completely silent and whose thoughts were probably no more cheerful than ours, presently affected to joke over his fall with the Prince of Neuchâtel and myself, but his ill-humour and black mood showed against his will.

At any other time he would have found fault with the horse for being so stupid, and also with the Master of Horse. At this juncture he affected serenity, and did all he could to banish the ideas he felt might occur to everyone, for one cannot help being superstitious on such great occasions and on the eve of such great events.

Everyone was talking of his fall and a number of the faces at headquarters were saying that Romans, who believed in augury, would not cross the Niemen.

Napoleon, ordinarily so gay, so full of eagerness at the moment when his troops were carrying out some great operation, remained all day very grave and absent.

CHARLES XII WAS GOING BY POLTAVA

He continued his advance, the Russians kindly giving him ground—a lot of ground. At Wilna he received an envoy of the Emperor of Russia, General Balachov. First he talked with him in private.

'*He was stalking about the room, and by certain signs of impatience that broke from him one could detect the ferment of his whole being. At*

*one point the ventilator of a window, which was not shut tight, came
open to admit puffs of fresh outside air. The Emperor pushed it roughly
back. But the woodwork was ill-fitting. After a moment the slender
hatch, yielding afresh to the wind, lifted and began tapping again. In
the state of his nerves, Napoleon could not endure that irritating noise.
With a violent gesture, he tore off the ventilator and flung it out. One
could hear it hitting the ground with a crash of broken glass.'*

Then he invited the Russian general to his table, along with Berthier,
Duroc, Bessières and Caulaincourt. Napoleon's insolent questions drew
down humiliating replies, of which we learn from the historian Albert
Vandal, *who had access to Balachov's manuscript notes.*

'Is it true that the Emperor Alexander used to visit Wilna every
day to take tea with one of its beauties?'

And turning to the chamberlain on duty, M. de Turenne, who
was standing behind his chair:

'What's her name, Turenne?'

'Sulistrovska, sire,' replied the chamberlain, whose duty it was
to be thoroughly informed on such matters.

'That's right, Sulistrovska.'

And Napoleon gave Balachov a look of inquiry.

'Sire, the Emperor Alexander is usually attentive to all women,
but at Wilna I saw him quite differently engaged.'

'Why not?' returned Napoleon. 'Even at headquarters it's
allowable.'

Then he talked of Russia, with a curiosity full of assurance, as
of a country he was soon to inspect and range far and wide.
Already the name of Moscow was on his lips:

'General, how many people have you in Moscow?'

'Three hundred thousand, sire.'

'And houses?'

'Ten thousand, sire.'

'And churches?'

'More than three hundred and forty.'

'Why so many?'

'Our people go a great deal.'

'Why is that?'

'They are a very religious people.'

'Bah! people are not religious nowadays.'

'I beg your pardon, sire, it varies. They may not be religious in Germany or Italy, but they are still religious in Spain and in Russia.'

The innuendo was biting and condign. Napoleon could not have been more wittily told that he would find Russia another Spain. This retort silenced him for a moment. Then, returning to the attack, lungeing out, he fixed his eyes on Balachov and asked:

'Which is the way to Moscow?'

The counter to this straight thrust did not come immediately. Balachov took his time, seemed to be considering. Then:

'Sire,' he replied, 'I find that rather a puzzling question. In Russia we say, as you do, that all roads lead to Rome. The way to Moscow is a matter of choice. Charles XII was going by Poltava.'

AT BORODINO

He had made on and on after the Russians, for the 'decisive battle'; but they had always slipped from his grasp. Meanwhile the Grand Army had been shrinking. But it still outnumbered the Russians when they turned at Borodino (7th September, 1812), for the battle Napoleon was to call after the neighbouring river Moskva, which flows through the capital.

The slaughter was not decisive. Napoleon was unwell. He did not set on the Guard. The French army lost about forty generals. What had been the matter? This is the Comte de Ségur's story.

At the battle of the Moskva, Napoleon is persistently re-presented as galloping several times into the fray. I aver that I never left his side all that day, and never saw him galloping for a moment. Since I must needs tell the whole story, I will add that the day before, when he was inspecting the future battlefield, it was observed that on dismounting he stood still for a long time, leaning his forehead on the wheel of a gun-carriage.

Further, I will add that during the night his aide-de-camp, Lauriston, from whom I learnt this, helped him to apply emollient poultices to his belly. It is equally certain that during the battle, when Caulaincourt had taken the main redoubt, and he felt obliged to go and judge for himself what remained to do, I saw him mount his horse slowly and with an effort.

We soon reached the conquered ground, which an occasional enemy ball or shell was still disputing. Napoleon, after studying the position, listening to his marshals and giving his orders, rode back to the tents slowly, as he had come.

General Comte Mathieu Dumas, *then commissary-general of the Grand Army, writes of Napoleon after the battle.*

About nine in the evening Comte Daru and I were summoned to Napoleon. His bivouac had been made in the square formed by his Guard, slightly to the rear of the redoubt. Supper had just been set before him. He was alone, and made us sit down on his right and left.

After inquiring what steps had been taken for the care of the wounded, and learning of the slight resources furnished by the monastery of Koloskoi, and by a small number of residences round about the village of Borodino, he talked of the end of the battle.

A moment later he fell asleep, and slept for about twenty minutes. Then, waking up all of a sudden, he went on:

'It will be thought surprising that I didn't throw in my reserves to achieve a greater effect. But I had to save them to strike a decisive blow in the great battle the enemy will offer us before Moscow. The success of the day was assured. I had to think of the success of the campaign, and that's why I'm keeping back my reserves.'

THE FIRE OF MOSCOW

The Russians went on giving ground. Napoleon exulted. He was himself again. He was before Moscow, and ordered a deputation of boyars to be rounded up to lay the keys of the city at his feet.

Alas! his generals ransacked Moscow in vain. No boyars! Nothing but beggars, and not many even of those. Napoleon was furious, crestfallen. What! the city had been abandoned?

Yet he lost no time in entering it, even without boyars, for he was in a hurry to send off some views of Moscow to Marie-Louise. (He instructed his chamberlain Turenne to go and buy them.) Then he took up his abode in the Kremlin.

One of his valets de chambre, Louis-Etienne Saint-Denis, nick-

named the Mameluke Ali, tells the story of Napoleon's first night in Moscow.

All was quiet in the palace of the tsars, all was silent, everyone was sound asleep, whatever his bed. In the middle of the night I woke up. It may have been midnight or one o'clock. I could hear nothing around me but the sound of sleep, breathings in and out. I opened my eyes, I rubbed them, found that the room was brightly lit. That seemed to me extraordinary. I got up. I made my way to a window to see where the light was coming from. What was my astonishment to see the town on fire, at least the southern and western sides, our windows facing the Moskva and the west.

It was awful to behold. Imagine a city, I should say as big as Paris, given up to the flames, and oneself on the towers of Notre-Dame by night watching it burn.

I woke up my companions, telling each of them to open his eyes. In a moment they all got to their feet and went to look through the windows at the immense fire that was consuming the town.

As it was urgent that the Emperor should know what was happening, Constant at once decided to go into His Majesty's room. The head valet came out again in a few moments, and as he had no orders for us, we all lay down again, having nothing better to do than wait for daylight. We did so impatiently.

What were Napoleon's thoughts as he contemplated the sublime, but most grievous spectacle of that sea of fire which was surrounding the Kremlin and turning it into an island? His generals, on seeing that the intendant's residence was only a heap of ashes and that the fire had just caught the bell-tower, earnestly entreated Napoleon to quit both the abode of the tsars and the ancient capital of their empire. At last he yielded to their pressing solicitations, but not without a great deal of argument.

When he had had breakfast he considered again, and about eleven or twelve o'clock he mounted his horse. Attended by his suite, he left the Kremlin and Moscow and made his way to Petrovskoi, a château a couple of leagues west of the city. The household baggage, that of the Guard, and the Guard itself followed on. But as the preparations for departure had taken some little time, we could not start off till quite late in the day.

It was with great difficulty that we got clear of the town, since the streets were choked with blazing timbers, with the debris of houses that had fallen in, and with flames barring the way. We had constantly to take a different route, or even turn back, to avoid being trapped. The wind also lent itself to this disaster. It was blowing hard, and eddying so as to blow up great clouds of dust, which blinded the men and horses. What made the obstruction still worse was a crowd of soldiers of all arms, carrying away on their backs, on horses and on local carts all manner of provisions and booty, which they had managed to lift from stores, shops, houses and cellars. This whole scene offered a picture of the greatest confusion.

I SHALL DIE IN MY BED . . .

Soon it was judged that Napoleon might safely reoccupy the Kremlin. So he returned to it and stayed a whole month, till 19th October, 1812. A month too long, which completed his ruin.

Every evening he got an usher to set candles in his window, and the soldiers exclaimed: 'Look, the Emperor never sleeps day or night. He's always at work!'

At St Helena, Napoleon was to describe himself as a kind of oracle. In Moscow—with a brutality startling to Saint-Denis—he foretold his end.

I think it was next day that the Emperor, the Guard, the household, the baggage, all moved back into the Kremlin. The stillness of destruction reigned in the town. All that had been timber was ashes. What was brick had largely collapsed. The churches, built wholly of brick, had been respected by the fire. Everywhere the debris were still smoking, giving off the most unbearable reek. It was estimated that two-thirds of all the houses had been destroyed.

We found the Kremlin and the palace just as they had been when we went away. Probably a guard had been left there.

Napoleon remained in this abode during our whole stay in Moscow, which continued for the space of thirty-nine days. My memory has retained this figure, I scarcely know why, for as a rule, in process of time, everything fades out or becomes extremely hazy.

I remember that one fine morning, when we got up, there was snow on the ground. It was about an inch deep. But it did not lie very long.

Almost every day at the Kremlin, Prince Eugène ate with the Emperor. The Prince of Neuchâtel always shared His Majesty's meals.

One day at breakfast Napoleon was conversing with Grand Marshal Duroc, and the subject of their discussion was the finest death. Napoleon said he thought the finest way to die was on the field of battle, struck down by a cannon-ball. That for his part, he expected no such luck:

'I shall die,' said he, 'in my bed, like a damned *coglione*.'

SIXTH STAGE

From Moscow to Fontainebleau

(1812–1814)

My dear fellow, if the Cossacks reach the gates of Paris, it's the end of empire and emperor.

NAPOLEON

A WRAITH AND A REVENANT

At last he woke from his long dream that the Russians would be coming to 'sue for peace', and saw himself beaten. More thoroughly than in Egypt of old, he had been imprisoned by his conquest. He was prisoner to the void, prisoner to the cold, and his troops were dying of hunger. Of the 800,000 men who had formed the Grand Army three months before, he had less than 100,000 left.

Between Moscow and France was Europe, all of it hostile. And this Europe had to be crossed.

The order to retreat was finally given. But the total strength melted from day to day. The crossing of the Beresina cost 12,000 prisoners, besides those who were killed, those who were wounded and abandoned, those who were drowned ...

The retreat went on, but not fast enough for Napoleon, who had suddenly learnt of a coup d'état *in France. The republican General Malet had made an attempt to deprive him of his throne. Whereupon, as usual, he prepared to throw everything to the winds and race for Paris. But that he should leave the remnants of his hapless army behind in Russia would be incomprehensible to the vulgar.*

So he resolved to decamp in secret. Only the staff were to be informed, and that they might accept his going without fuss, he distributed bounties. The most notable of these personages covered with embroidery from head to foot received 30,000 gold francs apiece, the less pampered 6,000 francs (also in gold). And attended by Caulaincourt, Duroc, Lefebvre-Desnouettes, an interpreter (Vonsovitch) and the mameluke Roustam, Napoleon took himself off ...

Here we find him in Warsaw, where he sends Caulaincourt for the French ambassador.

And who was this ambassador? An ecclesiastic, the Abbé de Pradt. *To speed up the mobilisation and training of Polish troops and make the necessary requisitions, Napoleon had sent his chaplain to Warsaw.*

The abbé, if not a good purveyor of battlefields, was a writer of talent; and this account of his interview with Napoleon on 10th December, 1812 (confirmed by Caulaincourt), is a masterpiece in its vein.

I had just had a dispatch from the Duke of Bassano [*Maret*] to announce the impending arrival of the diplomatic corps, which had spent the summer at Vilna. I was in the middle of a reply, pointing out the objections to its residence in an open town in face of the enemy, when the doors of my suite opened to admit a tall man leaning on one of my secretaries as he walked.

'Hurry up, come with me,' said this wraith.

His head was swathed in black taffeta. His face seemed to have got lost in the depths of the fur in which he was sunk. His step was weighed down by a double rampart of fur boots. It was a kind of ghost scene. I got up, I approached, and, catching a glimpse of his profile, I recognised him and said:

'Oh, it's you, Caulaincourt! Where is the Emperor?'

'At the Hôtel d'Angleterre. He's waiting for you.'

'Why are you not staying at the palace?'

'He doesn't wish to be recognised.'

'Have you everything you need?'

'Send us some burgundy and some malaga.'

'The cellar, the house, all is yours. And where are you going like this?'

'To Paris.'

'And the army?'

'All gone,' said he, casting his eyes up to heaven.

'And your victory at the Beresina, and the Duke of Bassano's six thousand prisoners?'

'We got across. . . . Several hundred escaped. . . . There's more to do than look after them.'

Then, taking him by the arm, I said:

'My lord duke, it's time to bethink ourselves, and for all the Emperor's real servants to unite in letting him know the truth.'

'What a mess!' he replied. 'At least, I have the knowledge of having said as much. Come, let's go, the Emperor's waiting.'

I dashed into the courtyard, into the street. I reached the Hôtel d'Angleterre. There was a Polish gendarme on guard outside. Mine host scrutinised me, hesitated a moment, and allowed me to cross his threshold. In the yard I saw the body of a small carriage mounted on a sleigh made of four bits of pine. It was half smashed. A couple of open sleighs were being used to carry General Lefebvre-Desnouettes and another officer, the mameluke Roustam and a manservant. That was all that remained of so much pomp and splendour. I thought of the winding-sheet carried before the great Saladin and his train.

The door of a small, low room opened mysteriously. A brief parley took place. Roustam recognised me and let me in. Dinner was being got ready. The Duke of Vicenza went in to the Emperor, announced me, showed me in and left me alone with him.

He was in a small, low parlour, icy cold, the shutters half closed to protect his incognito. A slatternly Polish servant-girl was breathless with puffing at a fire of green wood, which was defying her efforts and, with a great deal of noise, shedding more moisture on the corners of the fireplace than warmth on the room. The degradation of human greatness is a spectacle that has never appealed to me. I was passing without transition from the scenes at Dresden to this halt at a wretched inn. I had not seen the Emperor again since. A crowd of I know not what new and painful feelings rose up together in my heart.

The Emperor, after his wont, was pacing the room. He had walked from the Praga bridge to the Hôtel d'Angleterre. I found him wrapped in a superb fur-lined cloak of green cloth, with magnificent gold brandenburgs. On his head was a sort of fur-lined hood, and his leather boots had furs over them.

'Ah, it's the ambassador!' he said, laughing.

I accosted him hastily, and in the tone of voice which feeling alone can inspire, and alone may excuse from subject to sovereign. I said:

'You are in good health. I have been very anxious about you. But here you are at last. . . . How glad I am to see you!'

All this was spoken with a rapidity and intonation which should have told him what was passing within me. The unhappy man did not notice. A moment later, as I helped him to get rid of his pelisse:

'How are things in this country?'

Then, falling back into my role and resuming the decorum from which I had strayed only on an impulse very excusable in the circumstances, I gave him, with all the caution necessary to be observed with all sovereigns, but especially with a prince of his temper, a picture of the present state of the Duchy. It was not brilliant. Only that morning I had had the report of an engagement on the Boug, in which two battalions of new recruits had flung away their arms at the second volley, together with notice that of the 1,200 horses of these same troops, 400 were lost for want of care on the part of these raw soldiers. Further, that 5,000

Russians with artillery were marching on Zamosk. I told him so. I spoke of the ruined finances of the Duchy and of the Poles. He resisted this idea, and asked sharply:

'Why, who ruined them?'

'What they have done these six years,' I replied, 'last year's scarcity, and the Continental System, which is depriving them of all trade.'

At these words his eye kindled.

'Where are the Russians?'

I told him. He had not known.

'And the Austrians?'

I told him.

'I've heard nothing of them for a fortnight. And General Reynier?'

As before. I talked of all the Duchy had done towards the maintenance of the army. He knew nothing of it. I talked of the Polish army.

'I've seen nobody during the campaign,' he retorted.

I explained why and how, through the dispersal of the Polish forces, an army of 82,000 men had become almost invisible.

'What do the Poles want?'

'To be Prussian, if they can't be Polish.'

'And why not Russian?' (looking annoyed).

I explained the grounds of their attachment to the Prussian regime. He had no idea of them. I was all the more familiar with them since, the evening before, several ministers of the Duchy had sat a long time with me after dinner, and decided to fall back on Prussian rule as a plank in their shipwreck.

'You must raise 10,000 Polish Cossacks. They'll only need a lance and a horse. That will stop the Russians.'

I disputed this idea, which seemed to me to unite all possible grounds for condemnation. He persisted in it.

I complained of some French agents. And when I told him how awkward it was to employ men abroad who had neither decency nor capacity:

'And where are there men of capacity?'

Soon afterwards he dismissed me, saying that after his dinner I was to bring Count Stanislas Potocki and the finance minister, whom I had named as the two most influential members of the council.

This interview had lasted about a quarter of an hour.

The Emperor had kept on walking jerkily about, as always in my experience. Now and then he assumed an air of deep abstraction; such is his habit.

We waited on him towards three o'clock. He had just finished dinner.

'How long have I been in Warsaw? . . . A week. . . . Well, no, a couple of hours,' he said, laughing.

Without any preparation or preamble.

'From the sublime to the ridiculous there's only a step. How do you do, Monsieur Stanislas, and you, Mr finance minister?'

When these gentlemen had repeatedly expressed their gratification at finding him safe and sound after so many dangers:

'Dangers! not the slightest. Unrest is my lifeblood. The more plagues, the more I flourish. Only do-nothing kings grow fat in palaces. I fatten on horseback and in camp. From the sublime to the ridiculous there's only a step.'

It was clear that he saw himself dogged by the hisses of all Europe, which to him is the supreme torture.

'I find you're in a great fright here.'

'Because we know nothing except from rumour.'

'Bah! the army is superb. I have 120,000 men. I've always beaten the Russians. They daren't face us. They're not the men of Friedland and Eylau. They'll be held at Vilna. I'm going for 300,000 men. The Russians will be emboldened by success. I'll fight them two or three times on the Oder, and in six months I'll be back on the Niemen. I weigh more on my throne than at the head of my army. To be sure, I regret to leave it. But I must keep an eye on Austria and Prussia. And on my throne, I weigh more than at the head of my army. All this is nothing. It's an accident. It's due to the climate. The enemy had no hand in it. I've beaten him everywhere. They meant to cut me off at the Beresina. I snapped my fingers at that fool of an admiral (*he could never pronounce his name*). I had good troops and artillery. The position was superb. 1,500 fathoms of marsh, a stream . . .'

This recurred twice. He added a great deal about firmly-tempered minds, feeble minds, almost everything to be found in the 29th bulletin. Then he went on:

'I've seen a lot worse. At Marengo I was beaten till six in the evening. Next day I was master of Italy. At Essling I was master

of Austria. That archduke thought he had stopped me. He published some nonsense or other. By then my army had advanced
a league and a half. I had not done him the honour of making
dispositions, and it's known what that means with me. I can't
stop the Danube from rising sixteen feet in a night. Ah! but for
that, the Austrian monarchy was finished. But it was written in
the stars that I should marry an archduchess.'

This was said with a great show of gaiety.

'The same in Russia, I can't stop it freezing. Every morning
they come and tell me I've lost 10,000 horses during the night.
Well, good-bye, then!'

This recurred five or six times.

'Our Norman horses are less hardy than Russians. They can't
stand more than nine degrees of frost. The same with the men.
Go and look at the Bavarians. Not one left. . . . It may be said
that I stayed in Moscow too long. Possibly. But it was fine.
Winter came earlier than usual. I was awaiting peace there. On
the 5th of October I sent Lauriston to discuss it. I thought of
going to Petersburg. I had time. . . . To South Russia. . . . To
spend the winter at Smolensk. . . . They'll be held at Vilna. I left
the King of Naples there. Ah! ah! it's a great political scene.
Nothing venture nothing have. From the sublime to the ridiculous there's only a step. The Russians have revealed themselves.
The Emperor Alexander is beloved. They have clouds of Cossacks. That nation is something! The Crown peasants love their
government. The nobility is mounted. I was advised to emanci-
pate the slaves. I wouldn't hear of it. They would have butchered
without stopping. It would have been horrible. I was making
regular war on the Emperor Alexander. But for that matter, who
would ever have expected such a stroke as the burning of Moscow? Now they're putting it down to us. But it was their doing
all right. It was worthy of Rome. I had a lot of Frenchmen with
me. Ah! they're good subjects. They'll see me again.'

Then he threw himself into all manner of divagations on the
levying of this corps of Cossacks, who, according to him, were to
stop the Russian army before which 300,000 Frenchmen had just
melted away. In vain the ministers dwelt on the state of their
country; he would not give up his point.

Till then I had thought it right to leave them a clear field. I
did not venture to join in the conversation till he was being asked

to compassionate the distress of the Duchy. He conceded, as a loan, a sum of 2 or 3 million in Piedmontese copper coin, which had been in Warsaw for three months, and 3 or 4 million in notes out of the taxes from Courland. It was I who drew up the order for the minister of the treasury.

He announced the impending arrival of the diplomatic corps.

'They're spies,' said he. 'I didn't want them at my headquarters. They were sent. They're all spies pure and simple, and do nothing but send off bulletins to their courts.'

The conversation went on like this for nearly three hours. The fire had gone out. We were all shivering. The Emperor, who kept himself warm by talking, was unconscious of the fact. To the suggestion that he should go through Silesia, he had replied: 'Ah! ah! Prussia.'

At last, after repeating two or three times more 'From the sublime to the ridiculous there's only a step', after asking whether he had been recognised and saying it was all one to him, after giving the ministers fresh assurance of his protection and exhorting them to take courage, he stated his wish to leave.

I assured him once more that in the course of the embassy, nothing relating to his service had been forgotten. The ministers and I offered, in the most respectfully affectionate terms, our good wishes for the preservation of his health, for the success of his journey.

'My health has never been better. If I had the devil, I should thrive on it.'

Such were his last words.

With that he stepped into the humble sleigh that was carrying Caesar and his fortunes, and disappeared.

A severe jolt nearly overturned it as it passed through the gate.

PRATTLE IN A SLEIGH

Between Warsaw and Paris, they had to run for it. Caulaincourt travelled under his own name. Napoleon passed as Caulaincourt's secretary.

For days and days on end, by sleigh or by chaise, they drove on side by side, and Napoleon never stopped chattering except to ask questions, eat, drink and sleep. Caulaincourt recorded all this chat in his memoirs, one of the chief sources of Napoleonic history.

'I'm longing, Caulaincourt, for Europe to be at peace, so that I can rest and indulge my good-nature. Every year we'll spend four months travelling about the country. I shall go by easy stages, with my own horses. I shall see what the cottages of fair France are like inside. I want to inspect the departments that are short of communications, to make canals and roads, to help trade, encourage industry. There's a vast amount to be done in France, departments that are still virgin ground.'

To my great regret, this conversation was broken off by our arrival, before daybreak, at Posen, at the Hotel de Saxe. The Emperor's first words were:

'Give me my mail-bags.'

The postmaster, in obedience to my orders, had kept the two that were passing through. Such was the Emperor's eagerness that he would have ripped up the portmanteaux if he had had a knife handy. My fingers, numb with cold, were not quick enough to suit him in adjusting the code numbers of the combination lock. At last, I handed him the Empress's letter, and that of Mme de Montesquiou, enclosing the bulletin on the King of Rome. This was the first news from France since Vilna.

So it may be guessed how eagerly he read the dispatches of the arch-chancellor and the different ministers. I could not tear off the covers fast enough for his impatience. He skimmed rather than read the sheets, so as to get an idea of everything.

Having completed this review, he re-read the dispatches that had struck him as most important. He did me the honour of reading me the Empress's letters, and those of Mme de Montesquiou, and asked:

'Don't you think I have a good wife?'

He was anxious to get into Saxony. The thought of crossing Prussia was disagreeable to him, and led to the following conversation:

'If we were arrested, Caulaincourt, what would they do to us? Do you think I should be recognised, that they know I'm here? You're well liked in Germany, Caulaincourt. You speak the language. You used to protect the postmasters and take all my gendarmes to safeguard them. They wouldn't allow you to be arrested and ill-treated.'

'I should hardly think they remember a protection that was not stopping them from being pillaged.'

'Pooh! they suffered for twenty-four hours, but you got the horses back for them. Berthier was for ever telling me of your applications. Have you been in Silesia?'

'With Your Majesty.'

'Then you're not known here?'

'No, sire.'

'I didn't reach Glogau till the gates were shut. Unless the general's servants or the courier gossiped in front of the postilion, it can't be known that I am in Prussia.'

'No, to be sure, and no one has any idea that the Emperor himself is jogging along so modestly in this seedy chaise. As for the Master of Horse, he's not important enough for the Prussians to compromise themselves by abducting him. Your Majesty's journey has been so speedy that no one on the road has heard of it yet. For a surprise attack on us, there would have to be some sort of concert. A vindictive and resolute man can soon get three or four others to back him up.'

'If the Prussians were to stop us, what would they do to us?'

'If it were a concerted scheme, not knowing what to do with us, they would kill us. So we must defend ourselves to the last. We may have a good chance. There are four of us.'

'Well, but if you are taken alive, what will they do with you, my lord Duke of Vicenza?' asked the Emperor jestingly.

'If I am taken it will be on my secretary's account. Then it will be a bad look-out for me.'

'If they stop us,' returned the Emperor quickly, 'we shall be made prisoners of war like Francis I. Prussia will ask for her millions back and demand some more as well.'

'If they were to venture the stroke, we shouldn't get off as cheaply as that, sire!'

'I believe you're right. They're too much afraid of me. They'll want to keep me!'

'Very likely.'

'For fear of my escaping, or of terrible reprisals to set me free, the Prussians would hand me over to the English.'

'They might!'

'Can you imagine, Caulaincourt, how you would look in an iron cage in the Tower of London?'

'If I were sharing Your Majesty's fate, sire, I shouldn't complain!'

'It's not a question of complaining, but of something that may happen at any moment, and of the figure you would make in that cage, shut up like a wretched negro being exposed to the flies, after coating him with honey,' returned the Emperor, shouting with laughter.

And for a quarter of an hour he went on laughing at that comical idea and that figure in the cage.

I have never known the Emperor laugh so heartily, and his mirth proved so catching that it was a long time before we could utter a word without giving a fresh impetus to our good-humour. The Emperor also had the very reassuring thought that it was too soon for them to be aware of his departure, much less of the state of the army, and that the Prussians, in view of our supposed strength, and with their own troops in the middle of ours, would not dare to make any move against him, even though they got notice.

'But a secret murder, an ambuscade would be easy,' said the Emperor.

He had this idea so much on his mind that he asked me whether our pistols were in good order, and made sure those on his side were within reach.

This conversation led the Emperor to talk of various incidents in his life. He found pleasure in harking back to some circumstances of his early years, to his successes at the military school, to his family, of no great estate, yet occupying a distinguished position in Corsica, to a number of love-affairs, to the preference a number of society women had given him over some of his comrades, then more prominent than himself. . . .

He was fond of talking of his successes with women. Altogether, if that great and wonderful whole had its weak spot, it was vanity of the past, as though so much glory and such genius required antecedents.

Certain rather broad expressions he sometimes used were, I believe, one of the habits he had acquired in camp in the early years of the Revolution.

Generally speaking, he had a low opinion of mankind. He seldom praised anyone, even those who had done most, unless at moments when he wanted them to do even more.

Want of tact, want of courtesy and consideration affronted him, though his early training was not remarkable from this point of view, and though, being always in a political role, he felt it by no means incumbent on him to display the qualities he demanded from others. He would complain bitterly in private conversation. Altogether, he was fond of complaining of those about him, even of the Prince of Neuchâtel [*Berthier*], of Duroc, of the ministers, of the heads of departments, as though he had been ill served.

There are few people of whom the Emperor did not talk to me, from his wife and the sovereigns of Europe to the most obscure individuals. I therefore had frequent opportunities of observing that nothing escaped him. He had no more benevolence in private life than in political matters. His interpretations were all derogatory. Since he was always the emperor, he believed others were playing a part with him. And so his first impulse, his first impression, was invariably of distrust. It was the work of a moment. He would come round at once, but one had to expect that his first thought would be at least bitter, if not actually insulting.

The chivalrous side of the French character, its urbanity, the gracious and kindly tone affected by princes, even with ministers whose discharge they have just signed—the Emperor had nothing of this.

He often told tales.

He was in such a hurry to recount his successes that one might have thought his only reason for seeking them was to make them known. On those occasions the Empress (Josephine) was his first confidante. Woe to the beauty who had surrendered, if she were not a Medici Venus, for no detail escaped his critical faculty and the pleasure he took in exercising it with a number of persons, before whom he liked to display his triumphs. The Empress had all the details of the conquest of Mme —— that very evening. The day after their first rendezvous, the Emperor gave them to me as well, omitting nothing calculated to flatter or shock the vanity of the fair one.

HOME TO THE TUILERIES

On the 18th of December, 1812, a quarter before midnight, Napoleon at last reached the Tuileries. He was not expected, to be sure. But there was also a great change in his appearance. As we learn from Caulaincourt's narrative, he had some difficulty in getting in.

The postilion, still at full gallop, drove through the triumphal arch without being told and before the vedettes could stop him.

'That's a good omen,' said the Emperor.

He alighted safe and sound at the middle gateway, just as the clock was striking a quarter to midnight. I had unbuttoned my greatcoat so as to show the braid on my uniform. The sentries, taking us for officers with dispatches, let us pass, and we reached the doors of the gallery opening on the garden. The hall porter, who had been going to bed, came in his shirt, with a candle in his hand, to see who was knocking.

Our looks struck him as so outlandish that he summoned his wife. I had to give my name several times before I could convince them and induce them to let us in. It was not without a struggle and much rubbing of the eyes that he and his wife, who was holding the candle under my nose, contrived to recognise me. The woman opened the door, while her husband went for one of the footmen on duty.

The Empress had only just gone to bed. I asked to be taken to her women's apartments, on the pretext that I had news of the Emperor, who was following me, as we had arranged.

Throughout these colloquies, the hall porter and the servants were eyeing the Emperor from head to foot. One of them exclaimed:

'It's the Emperor!'

Their joy is impossible to conceive. They could not contain themselves.

The two women on duty with the Empress came out of her rooms just as I was entering theirs. They must have been as disagreeably struck by my fortnight's beard, my costume, my fur boots as the hall porter had been, for if I had not mentioned my good news of the Emperor they would have fled the ghost they thought was before them.

At last the Emperor's name reassured them and helped them to know me again. One of them announced me to the Empress.

Meanwhile the Emperor, who could hardly conceal his impatience, put an end to my embassy by going into the Empress's suite, with the words:

'Goodnight, Caulaincourt. You need rest yourself.'

EMBROIDERY, FEATHERS, DIAMONDS ...

... This was the Emperor. Within forty-eight hours, Napoleon had resumed his performance. Among those awaiting him was the adoring and enormously rich Saxon countess, Charlotte von Kielmannsegge.

Sunday, 20th December.—Though we knew there was to be no assembly at the Tuileries after Mass, of course everyone who had the entree made a point of going there, to testify their respectful joy to the Emperor and to see him.

He looked tired and anxious. He was wearing a costume embroidered in red, a bonnet set off with feathers and diamonds. The gentlemen of his suite were similarly attired. The Empress was in a court dress edged with sable. The bodice and sleeves were trimmed with diamond-studded embroidery. She looked cheerful, indeed, but one could tell that she was suffering. And everyone went away sad at heart.

21st December.—In the evening the Emperor did not join the Empress's circle. She talked of her happiness and ours, but was silent on the events of the day.

Friday, 1st January.—The Empress and her suite, composed of forty ladies of the palace, attended Mass at the Tuileries. By Their Majesties' side was Queen Hortense.

Though the Emperor has put on flesh, he looks ill and seems to have aged. He was wearing his tunic, embroidered with scarlet velvet, a bonnet with feathers and all his orders in diamonds. His character is revealed by the way he torments his bonnet, folding and crushing it nervously and roughly between his fingers. But the object, docile to his passion, yields only to revert without apparent injury to its former shape.

After Mass the Emperor held his drawing-room. The sovereign passed by several ladies of higher rank than myself, and came amicably up to me. I made him a curtsey, to which, with a slightly roguish air, he returned an equally deep bow, accompanied by the droll smile of his gracious moments.

'Good-day, Mme de Kielmannsegge,' he began.

'Yes, sire, a fine and good day, which gives Your Majesty back to us.'

But scarcely had I uttered these words when his face clouded, and he replied:

'For your own part, yes, I know you were sorry for me. We suffered a great deal.'

'So did we, sire, for you were far away, and we wished you here.'

'This evening you will wait on the Empress. You shall tell me your news and I'll tell you mine.'

Then, ignoring my neighbours, he mingled with the circle of gentlemen.

THE ARMY IS NO MORE! . . .

In these tragically famous words Berthier announced to Napoleon the end of the Russian campaign. In all, 4,000 came back from it (officers, non-commissioned officers and men). The Guard, though privileged, had melted away.

In January, 1813, Napoleon reviewed it at Trianon. One of the survivors was the young Baron de Bourgoing, *later a senator, ambassador and peer of France.*

That day Napoleon was reviewing what remained of his Guard, the old and the young. When he came up to my regiment, he stopped.

It was one of those that had suffered most. The colonel, a few officers and non-commissioned officers and a little drummer—these were the surviving cadres of a regiment of fifteen hundred men. We had left at Posen about twenty privates and corporals. The rest had perished in Russia or were prisoners there. Let me add, to avoid exaggeration, that luckily not all these absent figures were gone for ever. All whom fortune had detained in Germany and in Russia, we might hope to meet again.

The Emperor was very affectionate in his manner to us. He spoke to several officers, smiling his most gracious smile. As he passed me, he asked my age.

'Twenty-one, sire.'

'That was the age of the whole regiment,' said Colonel Hennequin, 'and it was the young men who suffered most.'

The Emperor's countenance darkened for the space of a lightning-flash. He seemed to be giving a thought to all those young conscripts, who had just sunk beneath unparalleled sufferings. This impression soon faded. He regained all his serenity. Apparently he had made up his mind to encourage us rather than revive memories which were painful to him as to all the loyal.

Just then, like so many of my comrades, I had an ambitious idea and the courage to express it.

'Sire,' I said to the Emperor, 'I have just been through the Russian campaign. I feel equal to commanding a company, and request the rank of captain.'

'Granted,' said the Emperor. 'Take his name.'

Already a general who was with him had entered me in a little red morocco notebook which I can still see, and which, for me, had opened like the book of destiny. But as the general was writing, my colonel said rather crossly:

'Sire, he's only been a lieutenant three months.'

'What!' exclaimed the Emperor, smiling. 'Stairs are not meant to be taken four steps at once!'

Then he added:

'Come, my friend, you need another campaign to make a captain of you.'

'They're all like that,' muttered the general, crossing out my name, 'they're never satisfied.'

Then the book of destiny closed, and in fact I did not become a captain till six months later, at the end of the campaign of this same year, 1813.

TO PLEASE THE MARQUISE

The end was drawing near. The empire existed only in name. Revolts and conspiracies were multiplying. The kings of the Bonaparte family were about to be swept from their thrones. Napoleon had not a horse left, therefore no cavalry. He had to enroll children. . . . Molé, though young and an ardent supporter of the regime, was cast down:

'*I had seen Napoleon reviewing, on the Carrousel, long files of conscripts whom the Moniteur was next day to call "splendid men", and whose extreme youth and air of frailty had inspired the crowd surrounding them with deep compassion.*

'*I spent a long time walking about the Tuileries gardens, reflecting on what I had just seen, and presently on a situation which was becoming acute, and whose perilous end could not be far off.*'

At this moment, when it was vital that he should be everywhere, see everything, toil without respite, one is amazed to find Napoleon sacrificing

an hour of his time and revising a transfer of prefects, for the gratifica-
tion of a marquise whose husband had just been moved, and who was
worrying about the effect on her daughter's marriage prospects. Mme de
La Tour du Pin *betook herself to Versailles and sent in a note, and he*
suspended all other business to receive her.

The door opened. The usher beckoned me to come in. Then
the door was shut behind me. I found myself in the presence of
Napoleon. He came towards me, and said in quite a gracious
manner:

'Madam, I fear you're greatly displeased with me.'

I bent my head in assent, and the conversation began. After all
these years, and having lost my written account of this long
audience, which lasted fifty-nine minutes by the clock, I cannot
remember every detail of the interview. In brief, Napoleon tried
to convince me that he had been right in what he had done. Then
I described to him in few words the state of society in Brussels,
the esteem my husband had acquired there, in contrast to all
former prefects. . . .

All this came out rapidly, and, being encouraged by gracious
airs of approval, I wound up by informing the Emperor that my
daughter was to be married to one of the greatest nobles in
Brussels. Here he interrupted, laying his beautiful hand on my
arm, and saying:

'I hope this won't break off the marriage, and if so, you ought
not to regret it.'

Then, as he walked up and down the large room with me following at his side, he spoke these words. (It may have been the
only time he ever uttered them in his life, and to me was reserved
the privilege of hearing them):

'It was wrong of me. But what's to be done?'

I rejoined:

'Your Majesty can set it right.'

Then he passed his hand over his forehead, and said:

'Ah, there's a piece of work on the prefectures. The minister of
the interior is coming this evening.'

And, after running through the names of four or five departments:

'There's Amiens. Would that suit you?'

I replied without hesitation:

'Perfectly, sire.'

'In that case, it's done. You may go and tell Montalivet.'

And with the charming smile which has been so much talked of:

'Have you forgiven me now?'

I replied in my best manner:

'I need Your Majesty's forgiveness as well, for having spoken so freely.'

'Oh, you were very right!'

I made my curtsey, and he came to the door to open it himself.

GONE IS THE TIME WHEN ALL WAS GAY!

The number of Napoleon's supporters was shrinking. The nation had been indignant at the 29th bulletin, announcing the destruction of the Grand Army, and concluding cynically with these words: 'His Majesty's health has never been better.'

Nowadays, when he went to the theatre, there was no applause but that of the cheering squad from police headquarters. But these licensed claqueurs were silent on an evening which old Dupin, a playwright as prolific as Scribe, described to Ludovic Halévy.

It should be said that next day the piece in question was banned.

I had always a lively taste for old Dupin's conversation. He retained a very vivid, very precise impression of all the little dramatic and literary events of the first twenty years of the century.

One evening I was sitting next him in the stalls of the Opéra Comique. The piece was the *Talking Picture*.

'Ah!' said he, 'I saw a very curious performance of the *Talking Picture*. The Emperor was at the performance. It was soon after his return from Russia. There was Columbine, beginning her song:

> *Ah! you were what you are no more,*
> *You were not what you are today,*
> *And you had then a conquering way,*
> *Had then a way you have no more.*
> *Gone is the time when all was gay!*
> *That time is gone and will return no more.*

U

'And Columbine resumed five or six times, with vocalisations and flourishes: *Gone is the time when all was gay! That time is gone, it will return no more! . . .*

'Dead silence in the house.

'No one dared to look straight at the Emperor. But everyone was giving him furtive or sidelong glances.

'*He* sat quiet, impassive, not moving, not seeming to hear.

'No one dared to clap, and the singer, thunderstruck as she caught the meaning of this great silence, began trembling in every limb, and stammered rather than sang the last repetition of her aria.'

Old Dupin had not, incidentally, a very favourable memory of the Emperor. For instance, I said one day:

'But you've seen Napoleon oftener and plainer than we have Louis-Philippe.'

'Seen Napoleon. . . . More than a hundred times.'

'He was handsome, wasn't he? Very handsome . . .'

'Napoleon handsome! He was a little fat, vulgar-looking man.'

'. . . TILL THE DAY OF GENERAL DELIVERANCE'

In the course of 1813, 350,000—600,000—1,300,000 adolescents were given a musket, and marched off in Napoleon's wake. By the beginning of the following year, there would be nothing left of them.

Yet with these conscripts, who received the name of 'Marie-Louise', he was able to give Europe a fright. Prussia, to his surprise, had at last been racked into mutiny and an alliance with Alexander. Their forces were defeated at Lützen and Bautzen, but not crushingly. (At Bautzen, the Emperor lost Duroc—struck down by a cannon-ball.) Then, on 4th June, 1813, a two months' armistice was concluded. Napoleon's real aim was to build up his shattered cavalry for a final blow: his avowed aim was a general peace congress, to be held in Prague. It was a mistake, however; just then the allies were in difficulties he knew nothing about. Austria was to profit by the lull (and the mistake) to impose her armed mediation—the term itself shows how Napoleon had come down in the world—and then prepare her own entry into the struggle.

It is at this juncture (26th June, 1813) that we have the historic meeting with Metternich.

'I should find it difficult,' wrote the latter, 'to convey the painful

*uneasiness expressed in the faces of those courtiers, and those generals
bedizened with gold, who were gathered in the Emperor's apartments.
The Prince of Neuchâtel (Berthier) said to me in an undertone: "Don't
forget that Europe needs peace, France especially, that is all she wants."* '

The interview—reported by Metternich himself—lasted for eight
hours.

Napoleon was waiting for me, standing in the middle of his
closet, his sword by his side, his hat under his arm. He came towards me with affected composure, and inquired after the Emperor's health. Soon his face darkened, and, placing himself in
front of me, he addressed me in these terms:

'So you want war. Good. You shall have it. I've destroyed
the Prussian army at Lützen. I've beaten the Russians at Bautzen.
You want your turn. I engage to meet you in Vienna. Men are
incorrigible. The lessons of experience are wasted on them. Three
times I've replaced the Emperor Francis on his throne. I promised
to remain at peace with him as long as I lived. I married his daughter. I said to myself at the time: "You're doing a stupid thing!"
But it's done. I am sorry for it now.'

This preamble made me even more conscious of the strength
of my position. At this crucial moment I looked on myself as
representing the whole community of Europe. Dare I say it?
Napoleon seemed to me petty.

'Peace and war,' I replied, 'are in Your Majesty's hands. The
Emperor my master has duties to perform which throw all other
considerations into the shade. The fate of Europe, its future and
yours, all this depends on you alone. Between the aspirations of
Europe and your wishes, there is a chasm. The world needs peace.
To ensure this peace, you must either withdraw to the boundaries
which are compatible with the tranquillity of all, or succumb in
the conflict. Today you may still conclude peace. Tomorrow it
might be too late. The Emperor, my master, permits nothing to
guide his conduct but the voice of conscience. It is your turn,
sire, to consult yours.'

'Well, what am I expected to do?' asked Napoleon brusquely.
'To disgrace myself? Never! I am ready to die, but I will not
give up an inch of territory. Your sovereigns, born on the throne,
can be beaten twenty times and still return to their capitals. *I*
can't, because I'm an upstart soldier. My rule will not survive the

day when I cease to be strong, and consequently to be feared. I made a great blunder in overlooking what has cost me an army, the finest that was ever seen. I can fight men, but not the elements. It was the cold that defeated and ruined me. In one night I lost thirty thousand horses. I lost everything but honour, and the sense of what I owe to a brave nation which, after these unparalleled reverses, has given me fresh proofs of its loyalty and its conviction that I alone can rule it. I've made up the losses of last year. Look at my army after the battles I have just won. I'll parade it before you.'

'And it's just the army,' I returned, 'that wishes for peace.'

'No, it's not the army,' Napoleon sharply interrupted me, 'it's my generals who want peace. I have no generals now. The cold of Moscow demoralised them. I saw the bravest cry like children. They were physically and morally shattered. A fortnight ago I could still have made peace. Today I can't. I have won two battles. I shall not make peace.'

'In all that Your Majesty has just said to me,' I remarked, 'I see a further proof that Europe and Your Majesty cannot come to an understanding. Your peace treaties have never been more than suspensions of arms. Reverses and successes alike urge you on to war. We have reached the point when Europe and you are about to throw down the gauntlet to each other. You will both take it up, you and Europe. But it is not Europe that will succumb in the conflict.'

'Do you think you can overthrow me by coalition?' rejoined Napoleon. 'Well, how many allies are you? Four, five, six, twenty? The more numerous you are, the less I shall worry. I accept the challenge. But I can assure you,' he continued with a forced laugh, 'that in October next we shall meet in Vienna. Then we shall see what has become of your friends, the Russians and the Prussians. Are you relying on Germany? Look what she did in 1809. If you declare yourselves neutral, and if you observe your neutrality, then I'll consent to negotiate at Prague. Do you want an armed neutrality? Very well! Station three hundred thousand men in Bohemia, and let the Emperor give me his word not to make war before the end of the negotiations. That's all I ask.'

'The Emperor,' I replied, 'has offered the powers his mediation, not neutrality. Russia and Prussia have accepted his mediation. It is for you to declare yourself this very day. Either you will accept the proposal I have just made, and we'll fix a time for the duration of the talks. Or you will refuse, and the Emperor, my master, will hold himself unfettered in his decisions and attitude. We have no time to waste. The army must live. In a few days there will be two hundred and fifty thousand men in Bohemia; they can stay there in quarters for a few weeks, but not for months on end.'

Here Napoleon interrupted me for the second time to embark on a long digression on the possible strength of our army. By his reckoning we could only concentrate sixty-five thousand men in Bohemia at the utmost. He based this on the normal population of the empire, on an estimate of our losses in men in the recent wars, on our system of conscription, etc. I showed great surprise at the incorrectness of his intelligence, when it would have been so easy for him to obtain more exact, more reliable data.

'I will engage,' I declared, 'to draw up the complete roster of your battalions; can Your Majesty be less well informed on the strength of the Austrian army?'

'My information is good,' returned Napoleon. 'I have very circumstantial reports on the state of your forces. But I know better than anyone how much weight can be given to intelligence of that kind. My calculations are based on mathematical data. That's why they are reliable. When all is said, one never has more than one can have.'

Napoleon took me into his study and showed me the rosters of our army, as he received them from day to day. He checked them with great care and, so to speak, regiment by regiment. Our debate on this subject lasted more than an hour.

Back in his reception room, he said no more of the political question, and I might have thought he was trying to distract me from the object of my mission if I had not learnt from past experience that these studied omissions were a habit with him. He talked of his operations in Russia as a whole, and dwelt in long and minute detail on the period of his last return to France. All he said of this made it clear to me that his uniform purpose was to convey that his defeat in 1812 should be ascribed solely to the weather, and that his prestige in France had never been greater than as a result of these same events.

'It was a severe trial,' he said, 'but I have come through it perfectly.'

After listening for more than half an hour, I interrupted with the remark that in what he had just told me, I saw a striking proof of the necessity for putting an end to these constant vicissitudes.

'Fortune,' I added, 'may betray you as it did in 1812. At a normal time armies form only a small part of the population. Today it's the whole nation you are calling to arms. Is not your existing army a generation drawn in advance? I've seen your soldiers. They are children. Your Majesty is convinced of being absolutely essential to the country. But do you not need the country in your turn? And when this army of adolescents you are calling up has disappeared, what will you do?'

At these words Napoleon lost his temper. He turned pale, and his features contracted.

'You are not a soldier,' he said roughly, 'and you don't know what goes on in a soldier's mind. I grew up on battlefields, and a man like me cares little for the lives of a million men.'

(Here I dare not repeat the much coarser expression Napoleon used.)

As he said, or rather shouted these words, he flung into a corner of the room the hat which, till then, had been in his hand. I remained still, leaning on a console between the two windows; and deeply affected by what I had just heard, I said to him:

'Why address yourself to me? Why make such an announcement within four walls? Let us throw open the doors, and may your voice be heard from one end of France to the other! The cause I represent will not be the loser.'

Then Napoleon contained himself, and in a quieter tone spoke these words, no less remarkable than his last:

'The French can't complain of me. To spare them, I've sacrificed the Germans and Poles. I lost three hundred thousand men in the Russian campaign, but of that number only thirty thousand were French.'

'You forget, sire,' I exclaimed, 'that you are speaking to a German.'

Napoleon again started pacing the room with me. The second time round he picked up his hat. Meanwhile he came back to the subject of his marriage.

'Yes,' he said, 'I was doing a very foolish thing when I married an arch-duchess of Austria.'

'Since Your Majesty wishes for my opinion,' I rejoined, 'I will say very frankly that Napoleon *the Conqueror* was making a mistake.'

'So the Emperor Francis means to dethrone his daughter?'

'The Emperor,' I replied, 'has no thought but his duties, and he will perform them. Whatever fortune may have in store for his daughter, the Emperor Francis is above all a sovereign, and will always study the interest of his peoples before all else.'

'Yes,' Napoleon interrupted, 'you don't surprise me. Everything confirms me in the view that I made an unforgivable blunder. By marrying an arch-duchess I meant to unite the present and the past, Gothic prejudices and the institutions of my century. I was mistaken, and today I feel the whole extent of my error. It may cost me my throne, but I shall bury the world beneath my ruins.'

The interview had drawn out till half-past eight in the evening. Already it was pitch dark. No one had dared to enter the closet. Not a moment's silence interrupted these sharp debates. On six different occasions my words had all the force of a declaration of war. I am not, of course, proposing to set down all Napoleon said to me throughout this long interview. I have dwelt only on the outstanding points, those that had a direct bearing on the object of my mission. A score of times we had been very far afield. To those who knew Napoleon and have talked business with him, this will be no surprise.

When Napoleon dismissed me, his tone of voice had become quiet and friendly. I could no longer distinguish his features. He accompanied me to the door of the outer drawing-room. Laying his hand on the door-knob, he said to me:

'We shall meet again, I trust.'

'At your orders, sire,' I replied, 'but I have no hope of achieving the aim of my mission.'

'Well,' returned Napoleon, clapping me on the shoulder, 'do you know what will happen? You will not make war on me.'

'You are lost, sire!' I burst out. 'I had a presentiment of it when I came. Going away, I'm sure of it.'

In the anterooms I found the same generals I had seen on my arrival. They thronged about me, trying to read in my face the impression I was taking away from this interview which had lasted nearly nine hours. I did not stop, and do not believe I gratified their curiosity.

Berthier saw me to my carriage. He seized a moment when no one could overhear us to ask whether I was satisfied with the Emperor.

'Yes,' I replied. 'He told me everything I wanted to know. It's all up with him.'

AND WITH A WAVE OF THE HAND . . .

During the armistice Napoleon was residing at the Palazzo Marcolini in Dresden. That was where the scene with Metternich had taken place. Here is another scene, at the luncheon-table, recorded by Charlotte Kielmannsegge.

At one o'clock on the 17th of July I returned to the Palazzo Marcolini. Napoleon immediately sat down to luncheon, with the Prince of Neuchâtel, the Duke of Bassano, Marshal Oudinot and myself. He discussed with these gentlemen the advantages and drawbacks of prolonging the armistice and the war. All three were of opinion that the sooner peace was concluded the better, even if it meant giving up the Rhine frontier.

Napoleon showed great annoyance at this view, and declared himself ready for every sacrifice to attain peace, but not on these conditions.

The Emperor also talked of the Russian campaign, on which he expatiated at length, never failing, when the town of Kaluga was in question, to call it Caligula. Finally, returning to his initial subject of conversation, he said to Marshal Oudinot:

'Well then, it's agreed, we make war?'

'Oh, yes, sire, we make war; in other words a bad thing.'

At that Napoleon seized the latch of the door, by which he was standing, opened it, and with a wave of the hand signalled the marshal to leave the room. The latter bowed, smiled and withdrew. MM. de Neuchâtel and de Bassano, who were in rather heated conversation by the window, did not appear to notice this scene. But it struck me with an astonishment mingled with terror.

I hurried home, intending to go straight to the marshal's for news. But on entering my own room, I found him sitting peacefully on the sofa, playing with my little girl. When he saw me, he began to laugh, and said:

'You mustn't worry about this little affair. It's quite usual. But the Emperor needs me, and I'm sure that before ten o'clock tomorrow morning he'll send for me. If not I shall come and take coffee with you. But don't expect me.'

A WEEK AT MAINZ

The armistice was extended. At Prague, the 'peace talks' began. But they were only a farce. Europe was ready to treat, Napoleon refused all concessions. Less than four months before his death, he was to say again: 'The fact is that I never intended peace at Prague.'

Therefore it would soon be time to renew the struggle. But before that he spent a week at Mainz (the last week of July, 1813). There he was joined by Marie-Louise and the court. He summoned the minister Beugnot to work with him—and, as we shall see, it is a pity this chronicler was not his daily companion for a decade.

I am inclined to think that after the engagements of Lützen and Bautzen, the Emperor meant to turn the ensuing armistice to account by opening negotiations. He repaired to Mainz with a small suite, and sent for the Empress. I was ordered to proceed there from Düsseldorf.

I found the Emperor's mind as firm and alert as ever, but he no longer conversed with the same freedom, and obviously felt he had a part to play.

The very first day he made me a recital of his forces of all arms. On throwing into the account some statement which might be apt to strain my credulity, he would look hard at me to read in my bearing the effect of what he had said. Thus, when he told me that the King of Denmark was providing him with 40,000 horses, with which he would soon have the most formidable cavalry in Europe, I must, really quite against my will, have given some sign of impatience, from which he took it that I had no great faith in his formidable cavalry.

This incensed him.

'You are,' he said, 'one of those learned know-alls who dogmatise without rhyme or reason. You repeat after Frederick that it takes seven years to make a good trooper. And *I* say that with good cadres one can turn out cavalry regiments as fast as any. One puts men on horseback and they stay there. That's the whole secret.'

The conversation passed on to the new levies which had just

been ordered by Austria and Bavaria. I ventured to observe that they were very large, and expressed some doubts on the policy of these two powers. The Emperor combated my doubts, but was not at all annoyed by them. Only I judged, from the concatenation of his ideas and the fluency of expression, that he had already thought of this and was repeating to me what he had said more than once to himself.

'I don't know,' he added, 'what can ail those powers, Austria especially, to be levying troops on such an absurd scale. At that rate there's no reason to stop, and if I do likewise there will be only women left in Europe to till the soil. I have an army as good as ever, and of more than 400,000 men. That's enough to restore my position in the north. I shan't take it into my head to double it, though nothing would be easier.'

I left it at that, and showed every sign of acquiescence in what the Emperor wished me to believe. When he considered me well posted on the ground I was meant to occupy, he asked for details on the grand duchy [of Hesse]. I gave them, disguising the weak points, but without greatly colouring the remainder.

'I'm not satisfied with your troops. You spend a lot of my money on their equipment, and they desert from night to morning.'

I besought the Emperor to take note that the men from the grand duchy who deserted were not soldiers, but peasants who had been hurried off to the corps three days after their arrival at Düsseldorf.

'You keep on saying the same thing. Just look at the guards of honour.'

'I was wrong, sire, I beg Your Majesty's pardon, but Your Majesty can't compare the elite of French youth fighting by your side with German yokels who have nothing of the soldier but his coat.'

'We'll discuss it tomorrow more at length. I'll see you at ten o'clock.'

HANDLING NAPOLEON'S LETTERS

Next day the Emperor harked back to the affairs of the grand duchy.

'I must have troops, and above all steady troops. Go about it as you please. We're past the time for being fussy.'

The Emperor dictated letters to me for two or three hours on end, and a sufficiency of decrees for the care of drawing them up to run away with the whole night.

The Emperor, striding about his closet, dictated at great speed. He would pause a little over the first word of the sentence, but as soon as he had it, the rest came out in one spurt.

On my first day of writing to his dictation I could not keep up, struggle as I might, and all I had produced was an inchoate scribble in which I feared everyone, including myself, would be at sea. M. Fain asked me whether the gist of each letter was clear in my mind. I said it was.

'In that case,' he replied, 'all is well. That's all you need. It would be hopeless to try to write as fast as the Emperor dictates, and set down on paper the exact words he used. For he goes too quickly, and won't consent to pause, much less to repeat anything. One must stick to what can be done, grasp the subject of the letter, and retain the order in which the ideas came out. If the Emperor has used any of the figures of speech he's fond of and which are the hallmark of his style, don't leave them out. Then, in the fair copy, condense the structure of the sentence and be sparing of words. In this way you'll have met the Emperor's wishes, and besides he's easy and confiding with his secretaries, for he doesn't re-read.'

I followed this good advice, and sure enough, next morning when I presented the letters for signature, the Emperor did not trouble to re-read them. He merely said it was a violation of etiquette to have left all that margin in my fair copies. I had left a sixth of an inch at most, but that was far too much; there ought to be none at all.

The Emperor sincerely thought that the forms peculiar to a sovereign's letters were quite unknown to me, and that I was edified by all he had the kindness to teach me on the point. I took care not to shake him in this additional advantage he was assuming over me, while reflecting, however, that I was well up in such things, and had already had occasion to apply my small wits to them while *he* was still hidden in military schools or beneath a second lieutenant's uniform.

That day, after dictating a number of letters and a few rulings on business all connected with the grand duchy, the Emperor handed me the rather bulky file of a question relating to the town of Hanau, and ordered me to go into it immediately.

HANDLING NAPOLEON

On leaving the palace I sought out the prefect of Mainz, to secure his recognition of me as an associate, by the Emperor's orders, in the study of the Hanau question. M. Jean-Bon-Saint-André was anything but touchy; he seemed delighted, and said two of us would not be too many to combat the extravagant ideas state councillor Jollivet had been trying to put into the Emperor's head on the rights of the sovereign of Hanau.

I had had a glimpse of M. Jean-Bon-Saint-André when he was sitting in the Convention. He had been one of the most vigorous members of the revolutionary government, and he was one of those men with whom one could have business dealings, but never confidential relations. I own I was brought round to him a little by the report he had drawn up on this Hanau question. He had put into it not only all his conscience, to borrow an expression of the Emperor's, but also a first-rate lucidity and logic. I congratulated him, and declared there was nothing for me to do but approve it afresh in the presence of the Emperor.

'You mustn't do that,' said he, 'if you feel the slightest interest in the town of Hanau, or rather in the triumph of justice. The Emperor would infer, either that you haven't really looked into it or that we're as thick as thieves. We'd better agree on some points of dispute which we'll go at hammer and tongs, to fix his attention and give him the opportunity of saying to himself, and perhaps to us: "You poor fish! What would become of you if I were not there to show you the right track and keep you in it?"'

I thought the advice piquant enough to be worth taking. The difficulty was to find any points in Jean-Bon-Saint-André's report that I could attack with a show of advantage, and, must I confess it? he introduced a few blots into that excellent piece of work to give me the amusement of pointing them out.

The day came which had been appointed for discussing the Hanau question before the Emperor, in the government council. Jean-Bon began his report, as we had arranged. I attacked it on two points, trying to make good the opinion of state councillor Jollivet, which was contrary to the prefect's. The Emperor summed the question up with his wonted lucidity, and gave such weight to my objections that I came to think they were genuine.

But after laying down what he called the rigour of the law, he relaxed it in favour of the town of Hanau, and granted pretty much what had been requested.

THE FATE OF THE WORLD DEPENDS ON A KICK

That day the prefect and I had been invited to dine with the Emperor. It was nearly five when the council came to an end, and to pass the time till dinner, the Emperor proposed a sail on the Rhine, with the idea of trying out an elegant little boat he had just received as a tribute from the Prince of Nassau.

We descended from the palace of the Teutonic Order to the river-bank, where the Prince of Nassau was awaiting the Emperor.

Without actually inviting Jean-Bon and myself to accompany him, he had expressed himself in such a way as to sanction it. We followed in his train, and went aboard with the rest. The Emperor was escorted by two aides-de-camp and an adjutant from the palace. Then came the Prince of Nassau with a kind of naval officer who was in command of the expedition, Jean-Bon, myself, and finally the indispensable mameluke.

The Emperor's suite were occupying one end of the boat. We occupied the other. He himself remained in the middle with the Prince of Nassau, who was showing off the magnificent vineyards crowning the right bank of the Rhine, with the castle of Biberich spread out in their midst. The Emperor seemed wholly pre-occupied with this view, which he was dissecting, spy-glass in hand. He wanted particulars on the castle of Biberich, and the prince was giving them with a servile complaisance which would soon have had its day.

Jean-Bon and I were keeping as great a distance from the Emperor as the length of the boat would admit. But it was not such as to prevent one from hearing what might be said on either side.

While the Emperor, standing on one edge and leaning over the water, seemed to be fixed in contemplation, Jean-Bon said to me, and not under his breath:

'What a strange posture! The fate of the world depends on a kick or no kick.'

I shuddered in every limb, and could only find strength to reply:

'For heaven's sake! do be quiet!'

The man ignored both my terror and my entreaty, and continued:

'Don't worry, determined men are rare.'

I wheeled about to protect myself from this dialogue, and for the rest of the excursion there was no chance of resuming it.

We stepped ashore. The Emperor's retinue followed him to the palace. Going up the great staircase, I was next to Jean-Bon, while the Emperor was seven or eight steps ahead. Distance emboldened me, and I said to my companion:

'Do you realise what a fright you gave me?'

'To be sure I do. I only wonder your legs haven't refused their office. But let me tell you that we'll be shedding tears of blood because today's outing was not his last.'

'You're a madman!'

'And you a fool, with all due deference to Your Excellency.'

We reached the outer drawing-room. Dispatches had just come in. At that time they were of such gravity that not a moment was lost in opening them. The Emperor had gone into his closet to read them, and dinner was being kept back. The drawing-room was thronged with chamberlains, aides-de-camp, orderly officers, secretaries, distinguished from one another by costumes of varying splendour and refined elegance . . .

AN APRICOT FOR THE MINISTER

We were notified that the Emperor was ready to dine, and we entered the dining-room.

The Emperor came in almost at once. His brow was heavily overclouded, and so lost in meditation that he took only a mechanical share in what was passing around him. He sat down, however, and ate very little. Two or three times he addressed the Prince of Nassau on trifling subjects, without listening to the answer, so that they might have been playing a game of inconsequences. He asked the prefect whether it was not time he saw to the paving of Mainz, which was execrable. The Empress contrived to put in a few words, and did so most unassumingly. His replies were none the less brusque, and into the bargain em-

braced some unflattering remarks on the Emperor of Austria.
For my part, I obtained only a fleeting moment of His Majesty's
attention. At dessert he had a bowl of apricots in front of him,
and was pleased to send me one.

The Emperor went to his own rooms almost immediately after
dinner, after ordering me to come and work next day as usual.

OF MALICE AFORETHOUGHT

I entered the closet at ten o'clock. The Emperor dictated very
short rulings on five or six pieces of business, giving me the
grounds for them in brief. And he ordered me to draft them for
his signature the same day.

He was walking rather briskly about the room, and I remained
standing, awaiting his leave to sit down. He motioned me to do
so when I was to begin writing.

I made straight for his armchair, which had nothing about it
to warn me off. The Emperor was, if not shocked, at least greatly
astonished, and enjoined me rather sharply to find myself a seat
and leave his alone. I obeyed most promptly. Work went on.

The Emperor needed a paper which was likely to be on the
table where I was working. It took me some time to find it, and
having done so, I sprang from my new place to present it to him.
The Emperor read it, and its contents gave him occasion to ask
me a question, to which I replied while walking about in step
with him. Thence a discussion lasting two or three minutes, after
which he made me a sign to go and write.

I don't know what the deuce I was thinking of that day; I went
straight back to the Emperor's armchair, and began writing as
calmly as though I had been somewhere else. The Emperor gave
me time to finish the sentence, and then said, in a tone which had
lost all its severity:

'So you're taking my place of malice aforethought? You've
chosen a bad time.'

This last remark astonished me strangely and emboldened me
a little. That day, the Emperor and I were in a strange position. I
could not help inferring, from the nature of the business he was
giving first place, and from the expressions that escaped him in
his anxiety, that he had received bad political news of which he
did not wish to speak. And he himself must have noticed, from

my manner and my replies, that I was aware of this news and dared not mention it.

We were years away from the time when he was going to have a more formidable army than ever, when the King of Denmark was supplying 40,000 horses for his cavalry, etc., etc. And yet, only five days had elapsed between the day he had held this language to me and the one when it was escaping him that 'the time would be ill-chosen' to take his seat.

But between the two speeches the Emperor had heard of the defection of Bavaria and the more than doubtful preparations of Austria. When two persons in this frame of mind converse at any length, the talk will almost invariably tend to base itself on their secret understanding, without any need to own up to it.

THE PACKS OF FOOLS

Thus when, at the end of that day's work, the Emperor mentioned the plots that would be hatched in the rear of his army, and the need for keeping a check on them, I replied that it was only the county of La Mark I felt afraid of, and that was why I had been so strongly against imposing a tobacco monopoly during the war, reserving the right to come back to it in peace-time.

'It was,' I added, 'only a slight concession. There are crucial moments when the public opinion of a district has to be considered.'

'I understand you,' returned the Emperor, throwing me a sharp look. 'You advise concessions, consideration, and above all a great respect for public opinion. Those are the big words of the school you belong to.'

'Sire, I don't belong to any school but the Emperor's.'

'That's a phrase and nothing more. You're one of the ideologues, like Regnault, Roederer, like Louis, like Fontaines. . . . Fontanes, no, that's wrong; he belongs to another pack of fools. You suppose I can't see what's in your mind through the veils you wrap round it? You're one of those that are sighing at the bottom of their hearts for freedom of the press, freedom of debate, who believe in the omnipotence of public opinion. Well, now you shall hear my last word!'

Then, laying his right hand on the hilt of his sword, he went on:

'As long as this hangs by my side—and may it hang there a long time yet!—you shall have none of the liberties you're sighing for, not even, Monsieur Beugnot, that of making one of your fine speeches from the rostrum.'

'But, sire, I wonder what enemy can have deformed me like this in Your Majesty's mind.'

'No one. But I know you, better than you know yourself. This evening you will bring your work back to the closet.'

OUR GLORIOUS MASTER'S FAVOURITE GAME

In the evening I received the usual countersign:

'Tomorrow at ten o'clock, and don't leave the house without saying where you're to be found.'

I returned next day at ten o'clock. The Emperor was busy with his secretaries, and sent word that I was to come back at four in the afternoon. It was a Sunday, and I had an invitation to dine with M. Jean-Bon-Saint-André. I arrived at two o'clock. I knew this was the dinner-hour, but I asked the master of the house to arrange things so that I could be at the palace of the Teutonic Order at half-past three, to await the Emperor's orders.

'The Emperor won't be here,' said Jean-Bon, 'at the time he appointed you. He's leaving, if he's not already on the highroad. Why, where have you been that you don't know that?'

I maintained my point. I insisted that Jean-Bon was misinformed. I produced my evidence to the contrary.

'Well,' was his reply, 'you've been hoaxed. It's our glorious master's favourite game. But I tell you again that he's leaving; you must try to get over it. And very likely we've seen the last of him.'

As he was finishing his sentence, enter a chamberlain who had been running, and who panted out:

'Gentlemen, I have the honour of informing you that the Emperor is about to leave.'

'And I,' returned Jean-Bon-Saint-André, 'have the honour of replying that the prefect is about to dine.'

NAPOLEON IN THE FIELD

On 11th August, 1813, the truce was over and Austria in turn declared war.

This campaign against the new-born Army of Europe opened with a victory for Napoleon at Dresden, stultified by the loss of five battles on the periphery; it was soon to culminate in the total disaster of Leipzig, cutting the French armies off from France.

Up to this point, curiously enough, no eye-witness has offered us a view of 'Napoleon in the field'. And the only collection of notes on this subject comes from a Saxon, attached to Napoleon's staff during the campaign of 1813, General Baron Odeleben.

All that was happening at headquarters came without a moment's warning, and yet everyone had to be ready at once to perform his task. Unexpected moments of rest, unforeseen departures, changes of appointed times, and often of roads and stopping-places as well, followed each other unceasingly. Even when the Master of Horse had some hint of them, the execution was left to the last moment, and all the others had to cudgel their brains to guess what would come next.

Very often the march would be held up for several hours, or even half a day, and to the last word Napoleon dictated in his closet was appended a curt order:

'The carriage! to horse!'

With that all who had to attend him would be in motion, as though struck by an electric shock.

Not till then was it announced which way we were going.

The Master of Horse or, if he were on detached service, an equerry rode on the right hand of the coach. General Guyot or the officer next him in rank was on the left. The aides-de-camp on duty, the equerries, the orderly officers, the pages, a few led horses for Napoleon and Berthier, Roustam, the keeper of the portfolio, and another outrider at Caulaincourt's disposal, were directly behind Bonaparte's carriage.

This whole throng was followed by an escort of twenty-four mounted chasseurs with an officer in command.

This grouping, settled once and for all, was obligatory, and was uniformly maintained with the greatest exactness. Not all the officers who were required or permitted to follow in his train

dared to overtake the escort. Only those of high rank had leave
to ride either behind or alongside the carriage.

Thus the cohort swept on like a thunderstorm, at a fast trot, by
day or by night, for several leagues at a stretch, and those who
had to follow this whirlwind through the night were rather hard
put to it. Where the road was narrow all would be charging
each other, so to speak, with brutal zeal. Those who were best
off were the two orderly officers in front of the carriage, and two
chasseurs who were still further ahead. All the rest were in peril
of breaking their necks or their legs. The servants leading Napoleon's horses thought they were leading the convoy. The keeper
of the portfolio, the orderly officers and the pages had the same
pretension. And indeed each became an important man when
Bonaparte called for him. Thus the whole troop went crowding,
scurrying, jostling each other in the heat of the day, in dust and
fog, and in the darkness of night.

When Napoleon stopped, the saddle-horses had to do likewise,
and four chasseurs from the head of the escort dismounted, fixed
their bayonets to the end of their carbines, presented arms, and
posted themselves round him in a square. It was the same when a
call of nature forced him to alight from his horse or carriage, or
when he stopped for a walk round, to observe the enemy. Then
the square was larger and kept pace with his movements, but
loosely, so that he had a clear space and could observe in all directions. If the objects were distant, the page on duty would come
forward with the spy-glass, which Bonaparte propped on his
shoulder or on that of Caulaincourt.

When Napoleon was obliged by circumstances, either in the
early morning or the evening, to spend some time in the open, the
chasseurs made him a good fire. This fire was always fed with an
extraordinary amount of wood; great chunks of wood and, whenever possible, whole beams were set ablaze, by way of a signal
marking the spot where Bonaparte might be found.

Berthier was his companion there, as at table. He rarely had
any other. Everyone kept at a certain distance, forming a semi-
circle, or they would show the same eagerness to draw near the
marshals' fire so as to be admitted to their table.

Napoleon would walk about musing by himself, or chatting
with Berthier, as he awaited the sound of gunfire or other signals
from his generals. When he was growing bored he took snuff, or

amused himself by flicking pebbles here and there with his feet, or pushing wood up to the fire. He was incapable of doing nothing.

Though a bad rider, he would often commit himself unreservedly to the skill of his horses, which were usually small and mean-looking. Very often he ventured into the narrowest, the swampiest of bridle-paths, and on deplorable and dangerous roads, through flood-water.

The Master of Horse, who, by virtue of his office, was his immediate forerunner, spent most of the time looking for the more practicable places. He himself once remarked very ingenuously that he had learnt a great deal, but had never been able to familiarise himself with the horse. Nor was his physique adapted to this exercise. At the gallop he would let himself slump in the saddle, usually managing the reins with his right hand, while all the upper part of his body, with the motion of the horse, was jerked sideways or forward, and the left arm hung carelessly down. If the horse chanced to put a foot wrong, he immediately lost his balance.

It was Napoleon's habit to study the field of battle in detail after the engagement, whenever the weather made it possible. He seemed to be scanning the position that had been occupied by the enemy as a means of learning about his forces and probing his designs.

When Napoleon went over the battlefield, the French dead had usually been buried and the wounded of that nation removed. It was known for a fact that he found the sight of his losses very disagreeable.

By an unbridled impetuosity, he often gave even his generals cause to make him pretty rough answers. One day he began upbraiding General Sebastiani, affirming that his cavalry had done less than that of General Latour-Maubourg, which had captured so many flags and guns, and had made so many prisoners, and concluding with these terrible words:

'F——! do as much yourself! Your men are riff-raff, not soldiers.'

'Sire, my men are not riff-raff,' retorted Sebastiani in a dry and firm voice; and he pointed out that considering the state they were in and all the privations they were suffering, his troops could not have done more.

The Duke of Taranto (Macdonald) backed this up, and between

them they were able to silence him, while Caulaincourt, to avoid
a scandal, had desired all those present to fall back.

At Muglitz near Pirna, Napoleon, giving way to a fit of spleen,
struck one of his generals in the face.

This tendency to inordinate rage was well known, and yet I
have heard some high-ranking officers say of him:

'Believe me, he's not ill-natured.'

When he had been dispensing some favour, his guards com-
monly looked for some very hot affair. The most certain pre-
ludes were harangues to the men and the delivery of the eagle to
the battalions. If his hopes had been deceived, or if, despite these
preambles, no bloody scene had taken place, which happened
with several battles he had meant to fight, owing to the skilfully
calculated retreat of the allies, then Napoleon's fury burst out. He
was annoyed that these theatrical farces had missed their aim.

On more than one occasion Napoleon's words affected the
troops like witchcraft.

At the end of the campaign misery and privation lost him the
hearts of the rank and file, who preferred facing death on the
battlefield to enduring hunger. Yet a part of the Young Guard
went on raising their customary shouts, and even when fortune
had forsaken him, at the time when he was beaten and forced to
leave Saxony, these shouts were reiterated with incredible vehe-
mence, as though to comfort him in adversity. At the time of the
forced marches, which went on and on without victuals, in the
neighbourhood of Dresden, Bautzen and Pirna, the huzzas of this
same corps had only a feeble ring, and a number of men could be
heard saying:

'Nobody will shout!'

His travelling-coach was so arranged that he could sleep in it
and stretch out on cushions. Between the seat he occupied and
that of Berthier there was some difference, so that his travelling
companion could not lie down.

Dressed in uniform, his head done up in a parti-coloured
handkerchief, he could sleep on the road as though he had been in
bed. Inside his carriage were a quantity of locked drawers, containing the news from Paris, reports as yet unopened, and books.
Opposite Napoleon was a list of the relay stations, and a big
lantern hung up at the back of the carriage lit the inside, while
four more lanterns shed their light on the road.

The cushions, which Roustam arranged, were deftly packed up in the carriage, and under the magazine a number of spare candles were stowed away. Roustam sat on the box by himself, and there were six heavy Limousin horses, driven by two coachmen, to draw the coach, which was plain, green, seating two, and well sprung.

IN THE DEPTHS

Three days of battle (16th, 17th, 18th October, 1813). This was Leipzig, Napoleon's destruction. And what escaped from the battle safe and sound would not escape from Germany alive. A fresh disaster took place, after the battle of Leipzig, at the crossing of the Elster, where an order was misconstrued, and a bridge blown up before the rearguard and stragglers could pass.

Marshal Macdonald *wept at this scene; perhaps he was in tears when he wrote of it.*

There was still firing on the other side of the Elster. Suddenly it died away. Our ill-starred troops were crowding down to the river. Whole companies were plunging in and being swept away, cries of distress burst out on the other bank. The soldiers caught sight of me. In spite of the shouting and uproar, I distinctly heard these words: 'Monsieur le maréchal, save your soldiers! save your children!' And I could do nothing for them! Shaken in turn by rage, anger, fury, I was in tears!

Powerless to give these unfortunates any help, I quitted the place of anguish. Some who had seen me fall into the river thought I was drowned. The report of my death spread rapidly. The Emperor asked to see me. But I was so indignant that I refused to go. However, I was begged, I was urged so warmly, for the very sake of the army and of France, to give advice, for fear of new follies, that at last I gave way.

There were a good many people with Napoleon. He was sitting at a table with a map spread out on it, leaning his head on one hand.

With tears I gave an account of what had happened. Even long after, I had that ghastly picture in my mind's eye, and those cries: 'Monsieur le maréchal, save your children! save your soldiers!' to this day make my heart swell for the unfortunates I can still see plunging into the waves, preferring this certain chance of death to that of massacre or captivity!

Napoleon listened without interrupting me. The hearers were variously moved, in attitudes masking their grief. I concluded by saying that the army's losses in men and material were enormous, and that if we were to save the remnant and get back to the Rhine there was not a moment to lose. We were then at Markranstadt; I had covered three leagues on foot in my wet clothes, I was very tired. Napoleon observed this, and said frigidly:

'Go and get some rest.'

I went away indignant at this callousness, for he offered neither cheer nor help.

Next day (20th October) I met Marshal Augereau.

'Does the bugger know what he's doing?' he returned. 'Haven't you noticed it yet? Couldn't you see, in these last events and the catastrophe that followed, that he'd lost his head? The coward, he was deserting us, sacrificing us all . . .'

THE HERO AND THE VALET

After Leipzig, Saint-Denis had gone looking for his master. He reached the house where he assumed Napoleon to have found shelter.

I did not find a single person to speak to. I entered one room, then a second. I was just going into a third when in the fourth room, opposite the door, I caught sight of the Emperor sitting in one of his folding chairs. His legs stretched out on a paltry common chair, his hands clasped on his belly, his head hanging, his eyes closed, he seemed to be dozing, or rather to be absorbed in the deepest thought.

This posture of the Emperor's wrung my heart and brought tears to my eyes. Never had I seen him in such a state of prostration. I withdrew cautiously and returned to the front room, so as to prevent any stranger from intruding on him, for there was not a single sentry at his door.

YOU NEED A HUNDRED THOUSAND . . .

Mainz saw him again, no longer in regal state, but overwhelmed by events and yet determined to hope in spite of them. But his army was gone. Beugnot describes a visit he paid, by order of Napoleon, to Macdonald's headquarters six leagues from Aix-la-Chapelle.

'Would you like,' asked Macdonald, 'to review my army? It won't take long. The personnel is composed of my own person, which you already see, and that of my chief of staff, General Grundler, who will shortly appear, and as for material, so far it consists of four straw-bottomed chairs and a deal table.'

He added: 'The danger is extreme and the time for bombast is over.'

But Napoleon went on building on illusions. Marshal Marmont describes the forlorn struggle to bring him round. The marshal was right in thinking an immediate settlement would pay. As a matter of fact, the allies were just about to offer Napoleon highly favourable terms; these were not to remain open long, and were never to be repeated.

Napoleon was at Mainz till the 7th of November.

I spent nearly all my time with him. Gloomy and silent, he was pinning all his hopes to delay and indulging the idea that the enemy would not attempt a winter campaign against us. He reckoned that with six months to dispose of, he should be able to form a new army large enough to dispute with success the sacred territory (which was his name for French soil).

And indeed in Old France levies were still proving easy to call up.

These could be distinguished in the campaign, first by ignorance of the very rudiments of their trade, and secondly by their clothing. For as there had only been time for them to receive a greatcoat, a police cap, shoes, a cartridge-pouch and a musket, they were never in uniform.

They could also be distinguished by a quiet and sublime courage, seemingly inborn. I shall give a few instances in their place.

Napoleon agreed, when we were alone, that his position was awkward, and then invariably, at the end of each conversation, wound up by hoping. When several of us were with him, his language of trust in the future was more haughty and decided; ours was always the same, based on the profound conviction of being on the eve of a catastrophe.

When I say we, I am speaking of myself, Berthier, the Duke of Vicenza [*Caulaincourt*] and a few other generals whom the Emperor admitted informally of an evening. We were trying, at all costs, to induce him to make peace.

The Emperor had possession of many fortresses, in Germany

and Poland. The enemy had sustained great losses. France might really make common cause with Napoleon when she saw her freedom and honour threatened. These considerations must be powerful in the eyes of the sovereigns. It was therefore possible, and it is in fact true, that they were not unwilling to end the struggle. And so we were in favour of snatching at the first chance to negotiate in good faith and make peace without delay. But Napoleon did not enter into this reasoning, and seemed, at least from his public utterances, to be cherishing the most idle hopes.

One evening, about the 4th or 5th of November, we were discussing what the enemy was likely to do. I said he would move a large part of his forces up the Rhine, violate Swiss territory and cross the Rhine at Bâle.

'And then what?' said the Emperor impatiently.

'He will march on Paris!' I replied.

'That's a hare-brained scheme,' returned the Emperor.

'No, sire; for what is to prevent him from getting there?'

With that Napoleon began to rail and grumble at the lack of zeal he found nowadays in his army commanders, and he had certainly picked the wrong man, for that unflagging zeal, that sacred fire, as he called it, never ceased to actuate me till the catastrophe was complete.

Total silence on the part of his hearers endorsed what I had been saying. The Emperor, meaning to bespeak one voice by flattery, suddenly turned to Drouot. Tapping him on the chest, he said:

'What I need is a hundred men like this!'

Drouot, a sensible and an honest man, rejected this compliment with admirable tact and with that austere countenance which lends a peculiar weight to his words. He replied:

'No, sire, you are mistaken. You need a hundred thousand.'

Holland, already in revolt, was obliging General Molitor, who commanded there with only a small force, to evacuate it. Louis Bonaparte, the former King of Holland, wrote to the Emperor suggesting that he should go back to that country, so as to exert in Napoleon's favour the influence he believed himself to retain. Napoleon at once told me of this letter, and added:

'I'd rather return Holland to the Prince of Orange than send my brother back there!'

I FOUND HIM SO LOW-SPIRITED, SO WORN OUT

Napoleon re-entered the capital on 10th November, 1813, and up to 25th January, 1814, he was toiling to form a new army. He demanded another 500,000 men. The Senate voted, but the legislative body was beginning to raise its voice in protest: 'For the last two years, we've been harvesting men three times a year.' (Napoleon promptly dissolved it.)

Why would he not make peace? It was being urged by those who loved him to adoration. Among them, the ultra-devoted Lavallette.

The Emperor returned to Paris once more, on the 10th or 11th of November. So deeply were all the French attached to him that one heard nothing on all sides but cries of grief. And if insults were uttered, no one should be taxed with them but the emigrés, who had a glimpse of his fall and the return of the Bourbons.

His stay in Paris lasted about six weeks. I think I have already said in these memoirs that he used to come back to me in misfortune. I ought not to be vain of it. My attachment to his person was a duty. My shunning of ambition and intrigue was a natural bent.

On my arrival he ordered me to come every evening to the bathroom next to his bedchamber. Every evening he took me into his room, where he warmed himself undressed before the fire. We chatted. (I can find no other word for that hour-long conversation before he went to sleep.)

In the early days I found him so low-spirited, so worn out, that it frightened me. I called on his secretary [*Fain*], who was a friend of mine. To him I confided my apprehension that that strong head was slightly enfeebled.

'Never fear,' said he. 'He's just the same. But all you see in the evening is a man crushed by fatigue. He goes to bed at eleven, but he gets up at three in the morning, and from then till night there isn't a moment when he's not working. It can't go on, or it will be the death of him, and of me before him.'

Our conversations turned chiefly on the state of France. I told him, with a candour whose guilelessness alone could excuse its bluntness, that France was tired to death, that it was impossible she should much longer endure the intolerable burden weighing down on her, and that she would slip her yoke and surrender, after a sorry custom, to novelty, her favourite goddess.

Above all I talked of the Bourbons, who would come into the reversion of his royalty if he succumbed to fortune. At the word Bourbons he became pensive, and threw himself on his bed without a word. But a few minutes later, on approaching the bed to find out whether I might withdraw, I could see he was fast asleep.

I ENTRUST TO YOU MY WIFE AND MY SON!

The armies of Europe, in their turn, were invading France. Napoleon hastened to form a council of regency. His brother Joseph, ousted from the throne of Spain, was to assist Marie-Louise, together with Cambacérès (minister of war), Savary (minister of police), etc.

He also hastened to form a national guard which would defend Paris, the throne, the Empress, the King of Rome. On 23rd January he received its officers (many of whom could not ride), and he was careful, when showing them his little boy, not to talk of 'majesty'. He fell back on simple words: 'I entrust to you my wife and my son!' He was cheered.

Pichon, an opponent of the regime, gives this view of the demonstration:

One of the most memorable displays of that spirit of romantic violence occurred on the 23rd of January, when the officers of the Parisian national guard were presented to him at the Tuileries. We know how extravagantly the official tongues of the press cried up this scene and the effect of the speeches he made there. What an instance it was of that habit of dissimulation, of imposing on oneself and on others, which has been the mark of Parisian circles in recent years. Granted the initial resolve to think well of everything and to renounce all judgment and reflection, it was only natural for a scene of that kind to be rated as it was at the time. Tears were seen to flow (the cupidity which lies at the root of sycophancy can be as tearful as fondness), and there was in fact cheering.

Tears and cheers were, to a thinking onlooker, the effect of either meanness or terror run mad. For me, it was the live pageant of a meeting of the Roman senate under Tiberius.

I knew Napoleon well. I am familiar enough with the progress of his tyranny. But I had never seen with my own eyes anything calculated to bring home to the mind such a conclusive certainty of the future that hung over us.

The harangue he addressed to us struck me as that of a mame-luke chief to his men. A voice strong but undignified, with an accent patently ultramontane; a countenance animated rather by fury than noble feeling; a speech dictated by frenzy, pronounced or rather mangled by rage; the intent to astonish and deceive rather than to persuade and convince; a constant appeal to the national vanity, and nothing directed to its welfare or happiness; the style of a desperado inciting his gang to make a noble end, rather than that of a calm and magnanimously devoted leader heartening a nation: there you have the substance and form of that famous monologue.

Lavallette—as zealous for Napoleon as Pichon was hostile to him—drew almost the same conclusion. At any rate, he was not taken in by what he had seen and heard.

The shouts of 'Long live the Emperor!' were so hearty and unanimous that I too was excited by them, and thought for a few moments that a feeling expressed with such enthusiasm might produce something great.

Reflection brought me round again to the melancholy truths with which I was imbued.

I saw the Emperor again that evening. He spoke of the morning's excitement. I gave him my whole opinion. That this frame of mind was very well during the campaign, if the war did not come near Paris. But it ought not to be tested by the approach of the enemy.

He smiled and said, pulling my ear, after his wont:

'So now you have no illusions, my Roman friend.'

'No, sire,' I replied. 'But I have hopes of this campaign. And a brilliant victory will be better than this morning's enthusiasm.'

'Ah,' he said as he lay down, 'we have to win it!'

I spent that night in the Tuileries.

At four in the morning he set out.

He seemed cheerful, resolute, and in perfect health.

I had always seen him like that when he was going away, and the temper in which I found him restored some of my confidence.

PASSEZ VITE, IL VA TOMBER!

For more than a decade Napoleon had been keeping ten thousand British civilians captive on French soil. Here an anonymous 'Détenu' describes life in Paris during the campaign of 1814—the 'campaign of France'.

Notwithstanding the exertions of government to 'Nationalise the war', the greatest indifference was evidently felt by the middle and lower classes, now that their vanity was no longer gratified by conquest for themselves and insult to others. Every artifice was resorted to by the Police to arouse the slaves of its power from this apathy; one of these was the attempting to recall to the minds of the populace (what they had been for years labouring to destroy) the energy they had manifested at the beginning of the Republic. Towards effecting this, they had that celebrated, but long-proscribed air, the Marseillois hymn, set on the street barrel-organs, and songs in praise of the Emperor adapted to it, which were sung in the streets. The attempt made in these songs to preserve the imperial dignity, and at the same time combine the revolutionary slang, was most ludicrous.

During the twelve years of my residence in France I never had heard this piece of music, and only once (in 1803) had heard 'Ça ira', which was in passing an obscure wine shop near the Place de Grève.

About the beginning of January someone in conversation with Talleyrand said he could not comprehend what was going on, alluding to the confusion which it was then known reigned in every branch of the government. Talleyrand replied, '*C'est le commencement de la fin.*'

A paper was stuck at the base of the column which supported the statue of Napoleon in the Place Vendôme; on it was written:

'*Passez vite, il va tomber!*'

BACK ON THE VISTULA!

This two months' campaign was distinguished by the rapidity of Napoleon's movements, and by a series of victories less dazzling than Austerlitz, but more thrilling. That of Champaubert (near Epernay), won by Marmont's troops, made the Emperor drunk with joy, and, as Marmont could bitterly observe, blinded him afresh.

Immediately on Napoleon's arrival at Vitry, I went to see him.
The *Moniteur* had announced the formation of a camp at Châlons.
I spoke of the reinforcements he was doubtless bringing us. He
replied:

'None. There was not a man at Châlons.'

'But what are you going to fight with?'

'We're going to try our luck with what we have. Fortune may
be favourable!'

It was enough to make one think one was dreaming.

On the 10th of February I passed through the defile of Saint-
Gond and marched on the enemy occupying Bayes.

I attacked immediately.

The Russians showed a bold front and fought with courage.
They had a large number of field-guns, but no cavalry. Bayes was
carried. Their main body, drawn up before Champaubert, was
overborne and began to retire.

Assuming that it would make for Vertus, I had the cavalry
posted on my right and brought it up behind the village of
Champaubert, which the head of the retreating column was just
reaching. With its dislodgement from the main artery, in difficult
and wooded country, a steady movement was succeeded by
disorder and chaos.

All was taken or destroyed, except for seven or eight hundred
men who made their way to Vertus in small groups. Fifteen
pieces of ordnance fell into our hands. We took more than four
thousand prisoners, including General Olsufiev, commanding
this corps.

Our troops showed great gallantry. Conscripts who had
arrived the day before went into the line and behaved, as regards courage, like old soldiers. Oh, what heroism there is in the
blood of France! I cannot deny myself the pleasure of quoting
two such conscripts, whose words depict at once the spirit of
these young men, and the kind of instruments it was our lot to
employ.

Two conscripts were with the sharpshooters. They had been
ordered out when their turn came. I was there myself. I noticed
one who took the whistling of the bullets quite calmly, yet was
not using his musket. I asked:

'Why are you not firing?'

He replied ingenuously:

'I could fire as well as the next if I had anyone to load my musket.'

Such was the poor boy's ignorance of his calling.

Another, more astute and perceiving that he was useless, went up to his lieutenant and said:

'Sir, you've been at this job a long time. You take the musket and fire, and I'll give you cartridges.'

The lieutenant accepted this proposal, and the conscript, exposed to a murderous fire, showed no alarm throughout the whole action.

After settling my troops at Etoges, I returned myself to Champaubert, which Napoleon had made his headquarters. I had sent General Olsufiev on ahead.

I found Napoleon at table, along with Olsufiev, the Prince of Neuchâtel and Marshal Ney. I sat down. There were five of us. The Russian general did not know a word of French. So Napoleon's speech to us was not for his ears.

The Emperor was mad with joy. Yet this success of ours, however glorious for the Sixth Corps with its small numbers, could have no great weight in the balance of our destiny; nevertheless, here is the thought it suggested to Napoleon:

'On what does the fate of empires hang!' said he. 'If we can beat Sacken tomorrow as we did Olsufiev today, the enemy will recross the Rhine quicker than he came, and I'll be back on the Vistula.'

And so at Champaubert his imagination was still taking in all Europe. He saw his hearers grimacing, and said, to wipe out the ill effect of these words:

'And then I'll make peace on the natural frontiers of the Rhine.'

As if he would!

And yet this man, so full of illusions, so irrational, had still the eye of genius when his passions were not at work! His insight was deep and keen, his brain the most fertile that ever was. I have often known him uncanny in his prediction and judgment of events. And then judgment would disappear in action, when passion declared on the other side. Then he was no longer himself.

I shall give a fresh instance of it at this juncture.

Before he left Paris, M. Mollien, minister of the treasury, had said to him:

'As you are opening the campaign with such slight resources, there is some reason to fear that the enemy may reach the heart of France, and the Cossacks obstruct communications with Paris. Would it not be proper to remove the treasury to the Loire, so as to ensure its functioning?'

The Emperor replied in these exact words, clapping him on the shoulder, which was a way of his:

'My dear fellow, if the Cossacks reach the gates of Paris, it's the end of empire and emperor.'

SILENCE, YOUNG MAN!

Napoleon's new 'harvest' of conscripts had been secured by promise to make peace. The generals fought the campaign because he could show that it was being accompanied by negotiations – at the congress of Châtillon-sur-Seine, to which he sent Caulaincourt as his representative. But he refused to give him carte-blanche, and his instructions were such as to make agreement impossible.

His staff soon woke up to the fact. When Rumigny was being sent on a mission to Caulaincourt, marshals and generals urged him to implore the negotiator to 'make peace at any price'. General Belliard, deputy chief of staff, made this appeal:

'You are going to Châtillon? I beg you to tell the Duke of Vicenza that he's our last hope. Tell him we have no longer an army. You've seen our troops—Well, tell him we have only 89,000 left. The Emperor may try exaggerating his strength, but assure the Duke of Vicenza that the truth is what I have told you. No one can know it better than I do.'

Rumigny soon returned from Châtillon and asked Napoleon for formal instructions enabling Caulaincourt to treat. He also conveyed a private warning from Metternich, that the Emperor had 'violent personal enemies' in the other cabinets ('especially the English minister, Lord Castlereagh'), who would turn his shilly-shallying to account.

The young man described his reception to a friend of his, the Chevalier de Cussy, who has passed it on.

On his return to Napoleon, M. de Rumigny repeated the verbal message entrusted to him by the Duke of Vicenza, and then told of his conversation with Metternich.

Napoleon listened carefully, but without a word in reply. He sent for a secretary, and, clasping his hands behind his back, dictated fresh instructions for M. de Caulaincourt. But these instructions, like all that had gone before, were indefinite, and did not give him the explicit powers he required to sign an honourable peace.

M. de Rumigny, deeply persuaded that he was bound, in the Emperor's own interest, to voice the attitude of his chief, twice ventured to interrupt Napoleon by pointing out 'this was not what the Duke of Vicenza asked for'.

Napoleon, looking at him without anger, went on dictating.

At last, carried away by his devotion, M. de Rumigny burst out:

'Sire, even though I should incur Your Majesty's displeasure, as a loyal and devoted subject I must say that with instructions like these it will be impossible for the Duke of Vicenza to forward the negotiations as he could wish. Time is short. The foreign powers are aiming at Your Majesty's self. They are still restrained by a vestige of decency. But they want only an excuse to wrest the sceptre from Your Majesty.'

At this the Duke of Bassano [*Maret*], who was present at the scene, said to M. de Rumigny:

'Silence, young man! His Imperial Majesty knows what he is about.'

'Yes, my lord duke, I dare say, but I am speaking as a loyal subject. What is it to me, as far as my private interest is concerned, what comes of all this? I have a father to take me in, a pillow where I can lay my head. But the Emperor, my lord duke, the Emperor—I tell you again, it's not only his power they are aiming at, but his person.'

'Very well, young man,' returned the Duke of Bassano. 'It is a noble heart that prompts you to talk so. The feelings you express are generous. But all this is troublesome to the Emperor. Come with me.'

And taking M. de Rumigny by the arm, he led him out of the room.

All this time Napoleon, while giving no sign of impatience, said not a word.

When the instructions were completed—not as the Duke of Vicenza would have wished—M. de Rumigny left for Châtillon. The rest is known.

Y

PARIS CAPITULATES

While he thought he was 'finessing' at Châtillon, and destroying his opponents one by one, they kept him amused with part of their forces, and led the bulk of them straight to Paris, which surrendered.

Marie-Louise, the King of Rome, Joseph Bonaparte, the ministers ran away.

Napoleon had fallen back on Fontainebleau, and it was General Belliard *who brought him the terrible news.*

When the convention for the evacuation of Paris had been signed, I was ordered to make for Fontainebleau with all the horse under my command. The army would follow me. I stopped at the Cour de France to get my bearings and spend the night.

Just then I ran into an imperial courier, who was coming from Fontainebleau and announced that His Majesty was close behind. Napoleon drove up. He was disturbed by this troop movement. Stopping the carriage, he asked:

'Who is there?'

'General Belliard, sire,' said the courier.

I was at the carriage door. He had it opened, jumped out and led me down the highroad.

'Well, Belliard, what's this? Why are you here with your cavalry? Where's the enemy?'

'At the gates of Paris, sire.'

'And the army?'

'Following me.'

'And who is defending Paris?'

'It's evacuated. The enemy is to enter at nine o'clock tomorrow morning. The national guard is on duty at the gates.'

'And my wife, and my son—what's become of them? Where's Mortier? Where's Marmont?'

'The Empress, your son and the whole court left the day before yesterday for Rambouillet. Marshals Mortier and Marmont must still be in Paris winding up the arrangements.'

Napoleon had to be told with the rapidity of lightning all that had happened to us. I acquainted him with the positions of our little army and those of the enemy during the battle, and with all the sublime efforts of a handful of Frenchmen on that memorable day. Napoleon was attended by Prince Berthier and the Duke of Vicenza.

'Well, you hear what Belliard says, gentlemen! Come, I'm going to Paris. Let's get on. Caulaincourt, have my carriage brought up.'

We were already a good way along the road. I pointed out to His Majesty that he could not go to Paris now, there were no troops left there.

'I shall find the national guard. The troops will rejoin me. We'll be gaining time. Things may be put right.'

'But I repeat, Your Majesty cannot go to Paris. According to the agreement, the national guard was to keep the gates and the foreigners were not to make their entry till tomorrow. But it would not be surprising if they had infringed it and if Your Majesty found Russian or Prussian posts at the gates, or on the ramparts, or even inside the town.'

'No matter, I'm going there. My carriage. . . . You go on with your cavalry.'

'But, sire, Your Majesty would lay yourself open to having Paris taken and sacked. I tell Your Majesty once again, the enemy, more than a hundred and twenty thousand strong, is before the gates and has occupied all the positions. Besides, I left in virtue of a convention and I cannot re-enter Paris.'

'What convention is this? Who made it? Who's been giving orders? What have they done with my wife and son? What's Joseph doing? Where's the minister of war?'

'I don't know the convention, sire. The Duke of Treviso [*Mortier*] sent me word of its existence, and that I was to make for Fontainebleau. I heard it had been arranged by Marshals Mortier and Marmont. We've had no orders all day. Each marshal, keeping his own position, was acting for himself and defending the approaches of Paris. I don't know what's happened to Prince Joseph and the minister of war. I had the honour of telling Your Majesty that the Empress, the King of Rome and the court had left for Rambouillet.'

'But why send them out of Paris?'

'I know nothing of that, sire, except that it was said to be on Your Majesty's orders.'

'I must go to Paris. When I'm not there they only make fools of themselves.'

Prince Berthier and M. de Caulaincourt joined me in dissuading Napoleon. Napoleon kept asking for his carriage. M. de Caulaincourt said it was coming, and it did not appear. Napoleon continued working himself up, walking and asking questions.

'Come, I see they've all lost their heads. Joseph is a *coglione* and Clarke a dolt, or a traitor.'

Napoleon kept on walking, and already we were almost a league from the post-house. Then, after Prince Berthier, M. de Caulaincourt and I had renewed our protests to the Emperor, he made up his mind to return to the Cour de France. He ate supper there, and afterwards left for Fontainebleau.

When we reached the post-house, and the light, I scrutinised Napoleon's countenance, which I had been unable to see in the dark as we walked along. There was no change in it whatever, and one could not detect what must have been his sensations at all he had just heard.

He was very tired.

THE ABDICATION

Still he had no idea of throwing up the sponge. But in Paris, he had been formally deposed by the politicians; and at Fontainebleau, after hearing the views of their officers and men, the marshals were about to demand his abdication.

Some generals feared Napoleon would have them shot for it.

'Times have changed,' said Macdonald. 'He wouldn't dare, especially as the army is with us.'

Here Macdonald is the narrator.

As soon as we had been announced, the Duke of Reggio (Oudinot) and I were shown into the closet, where we found the Emperor with the Dukes of Bassano (Maret) and Vicenza (Caulaincourt), the Prince of the Moskova (Ney), the Prince of Neuchâtel (Berthier), Marshal Lefebvre, and others I have forgotten.

Here began the scene that was to change so many lives.

Napoleon came up to me:

'Good day, Duke of Taranto, how goes it?'

'Wretchedly,' said I. 'So many unhappy events! To yield

without glory! To have done nothing to save Paris! We are all overwhelmed, mortified!'

'It's a great misfortune, that's true,' he replied. 'And what are your men saying?'

'That you are summoning us to march on the capital. They share our grief, and I have come to inform you in their name that they cannot expose it to the fate of Moscow. We think we have done enough, given proofs enough of our will to save France from the disasters now hanging over her, to dispense us from risking a worse than unequal bid which would be the end of everything. The troops are starving to death in the heart of their own country, and greatly reduced by the disastrous events of this campaign, by privations, sickness, and, I must add, by discouragement. Since the occupation of the capital a large number of men have been going home. The others can't live off the forest of Fontainebleau. If they advance, they will be entering open country with our meagre, exhausted cavalry, with teams that are used up, very little ammunition, not enough for an engagement, no means of replacing it. And if, as is probable, we fail, the remains of us will be wiped out and all France will be at the enemy's mercy. He has still a respect for us, let us maintain our attitude. In any case, our minds are made up, and whatever decision may be taken, we are resolved to have done. For my part, I give you notice that my sword shall never be drawn on Frenchmen or stained with French blood. Whatever may be decided, this unhappy war is enough, without kindling civil war.'

'Oh, no,' said Napoleon, 'there's no idea of marching on Paris.'

I should have expected him to explode! On the contrary, the tone of his reply was quiet and friendly. He repeated:

'It's true, the taking of Paris is a great misfortune.'

'Do you know,' I asked, 'what is going on there?'

'They say the allies won't treat with me in future.'

'Is that all you know?'

'Yes.'

'Well, then, look at this letter!'

I handed him the letter from Beurnonville.

'You'll see exactly what measures are being taken, since the writer is a member of the provisional government.'

'Can it be read publicly?'

'Yes, for it already has been. You will see by the cover that it's not intended for me alone; the Duke of Ragusa (Marmont) sent it me by an aide-de-camp, open.'

Napoleon gave it to the Duke of Bassano, who read it aloud. When he had finished, Napoleon took it back and returned it to me, thanking me for this mark of confidence.

'You should never have doubted it,' said I.

'That's true, I was wrong. You're a good fellow, a man of honour.'

'Enough of compliments, never mind that,' said I. 'The thing is to take a decision. Public opinion is making strides. There's no time to lose.'

Then, addressing all those present:

'Well, gentlemen!' said he, 'since this is the case, I'll abdicate. I meant to make France happy. I have not succeeded. Events have turned against me. I don't want to increase our misfortunes. But if I abdicate, what will you do? Will you have the King of Rome as my successor and the Empress as regent?'

We agreed with one voice.

'First of all,' he added, 'an armistice must be arranged, and I'm going to send commissioners to Paris. To fulfil this important charge I nominate Marshals the Prince of the Moskova and the Duke of Ragusa (Ney and Marmont), and the Duke of Vicenza (Caulaincourt). Do these choices suit you?'

We replied in the affirmative.

He drafted the act of abdication, the wording of which was altered two or three times.

'Gentlemen, you may now withdraw. I'm going to draw up instructions for the commissioners, but I forbid them to demand anything personal to myself.'

Then, throwing himself on a sofa and slapping his thigh, he added in an off-hand way:

'Nonsense, gentlemen, let's drop this and march tomorrow, we'll beat them!'

I repeated in brief what I had just told him about the condition of the army.

'No,' we added, 'we've had enough. And don't forget that with every hour that goes by the commissioners will be less likely to succeed in their task.'

He left it at that.

SEVENTH STAGE

From Fontainebleau to Waterloo

(1814–1815)

I will never take and never have taken a step to evade death.   NAPOLEON

I AM A DEAD MAN

He was nothing now. What aberration had persuaded him and his marshals that he would be allowed to name his successor, and that successor a three-year-old Bonaparte? Was he not 'deposed'?

Indeed it was precisely the monarchical regime he had set up which made it possible to restore the Bourbons. Napoleon was succeeded on the throne by Louis XVIII, brother to Louis XVI.

However, the allied powers, and Louis XVIII himself, granted him an unexpected retreat, a kingdom in the Mediterranean: Elba. Foreign commissioners (Köller for Austria, Schuvalov for Russia, Waldburg-Truchsess for Prussia, Campbell for England) were appointed to escort him there. He gauged the depth of his fall and reiterated: 'I am a dead man.'

The Emperor of Austria had offered to let his daughter go with him. Napoleon thought this very kind. He wished to spare his wife the sight of a France where he reigned no longer. So she went away, taking their little boy. He was never to see them again.

(At this point, two minor satellites—and sources of information—likewise disappear. The 'faithful mameluke' was to attend the Emperor with his wife and children. Napoleon gave him leave of absence to arrange this. He did not come back, but merely sent word that it was not convenient. Simultaneously, Constant took himself off without notice, and with a sum of 5,000 francs.)

On the 17th of April, 1814, in the very palace of Fontainebleau where he had kept the Pope a prisoner (and in solitary confinement), Napoleon attended Mass, so as to appear before the commissioners of the powers as a sovereign and make an impression on them. Judging by Campbell's report, it did not come off.

On the following morning (17th April) the other Commissioners and myself assembled at breakfast, in company with Generals Bertrand, Drouot, Lefebvre-Desnouettes, and Flahault, three or four other Generals of the Guards, and some junior aides-de-camp. As soon as the meal was finished, Count Flahault informed us individually, that the Emperor was then in the chapel, attending Mass, and that immediately afterwards he wished to have separate interviews with each of us. General Köller passed out of the gallery, and saw him at his devotions. He described him as appearing in the most perturbed and distressed state of mind—sometimes rubbing his forehead with his hands, then stuffing part of his fingers into his mouth, and gnawing the ends of them in the most agitated and excited manner.

It was a strange feeling that came over me, when the aide-de-camp, after announcing my name, retired shutting the door, and I found myself closeted with that extraordinary man, whose name had been for so many years the touchstone of my professional and national feelings, and whose appearance had been presented to my imagination in every form that exaggeration and caricature could render impressive. I saw before me a short active-looking man, who was rapidly pacing the length of his apartment, like some wild animal in his cell. He was dressed in an old green uniform with gold epaulets, blue pantaloons, and red topboots, unshaven, uncombed, with the fallen particles of snuff scattered profusely upon his upper lip and breast.

Upon his becoming aware of my presence, he turned quickly towards me, and saluted me with a courteous smile, evidently endeavouring to conceal his anxiety and agitation by an assumed placidity of manner.

INTO EXILE

Elba was a gilded exile, but exile it was. Napoleon threatened not to go. Idle talk, for he knew that force would be used and that it would make him ridiculous. Within a few days he had realised that his wife was lost to him. He accused his father-in-law of urging divorce, quite unjustly, for in opposition to Metternich, who was really urging it, Francis II was to keep his foot down. It is undeniable, however, that the Pope would regard the marriage as null, since Napoleon had gone through a religious marriage with Josephine on the eve of the coronation. Thus he remained her husband, the Church (like Napoleon himself) declining to recognise divorce.

At last, on 20th April, 1814, Napoleon brought himself to leave Fontainebleau. The Prussian commissioner, Waldburg-Truchsess, has left the fullest account of this painful journey.

It was eleven o'clock, and M. de Bussy, aide-de-camp to the Emperor, came from the grand marshal to inform him that all was ready for the start.

'Does the grand marshal not know me? Since when have I been obliged to go by his watch? I shall start when I please and possibly not at all.'

Colonel Bussy left the room, and Napoleon paced up and down it, talking incessantly of the wrongs that were being done him. He accused the Emperor of Austria of having no religion and of labouring to get his daughter divorced, whereas his duty was to maintain a good understanding among his children. He also complained of the Emperor of Russia for his want of delicacy, said it was entirely his fault that the Empress had not kept the regency, and described his visits to Rambouillet as very ill-timed, accusing the Emperor Alexander and the King of Prussia of going there to deride his misfortune.

General Köller strove to convince him that the only motive of the two sovereigns had been to show their regard for the Empress, but Napoleon would relinquish none of his grievances against the King of Prussia, and betrayed his hate of him at every turn.

He dismissed General Köller and sent for Colonel Campbell. With him he talked a great deal of his plan for putting himself under the protection of the English.

Then he granted very brief audiences to General Schuvalov and to me. He spoke only of indifferent matters, and at noon he went down into the courtyard of the palace, where the grenadiers of his Guard were lined up.

He was at once surrounded by all the officers and men. He made them a speech of such dignity and warmth that all present were affected. Then he clasped General Petit in his arms, kissed the imperial eagle, and said in a broken voice:

'Farewell, my children! My good wishes will always attend you. Do not forget me.'

General Drouot took the lead, in a closed carriage for four. Directly behind was Napoleon's carriage. Then General Köller. Next to him, General Schuvalov. Then Colonel Campbell. And last, myself. Each of us in his own barouche. I was followed by an aide-de-camp of General Schuvalov. And eight of Napoleon's carriages, with his whole suite, wound up our procession.

He was greeted everywhere with shouts of 'Long live the Emperor', and we had much to endure from the insults addressed to us by the crowd.

It is noteworthy that Napoleon always apologised to General

Köller for the rudeness of the crowd, while he heard with malicious glee, and took pleasure in repeating, the gibes directed at the King of Prussia's commissioner.

He was escorted as far as Briare by his Guard.

The shouts of 'Long live the Emperor' left off as soon as the French troops had quitted us.

At Moulins we saw the first white cockades, and the inhabitants received us with cheers of 'Long live the allies!'

Colonel Campbell set out from Lyons in advance, to look for an English frigate at Toulon or Marseilles which might carry Napoleon to his island, as he had requested.

In Lyons, which we passed through at about eleven in the evening, a few groups collected shouting 'Long live Napoleon!'

AUGEREAU, THE VICTOR OF CASTIGLIONE

As Sir Neil Campbell had gone on ahead, he was the first to encounter Marshal Augereau, Duke of Castiglione.

'*When I informed him that Napoleon was close behind, the marshal seemed slightly disconcerted, as he had thought Napoleon would take the other route, through Grenoble. He accused Napoleon of causing bloodshed from personal ambition and vanity.*

'"*He didn't even finish,*" *he added,* "*as he ought to have done, and as many people were expecting. He's a coward. I always thought so. He ought to have marched on a battery and got himself killed. If I meet Napoleon*" (*he said further*), "*I shall let him know what I think.*"'

He was just about to meet Napoleon, and Waldburg-Truchsess *records the incident.*

On the 24th of April, about noon, we met Marshal Augereau near Valence. Napoleon and the marshal alighted. Napoleon doffed his hat and held out his arms to Augereau, who embraced him, but did not bow.

'Where are you off to?' said Napoleon, taking him by the arm. 'You're going to court?'

Augereau replied that just then he was going to Lyons. They walked along together for nearly a quarter of an hour, on the Valence road. I have had the upshot of this conversation on good authority. Napoleon upbraided the marshal with his conduct towards him, and said:

'That proclamation of yours is very silly. Why the abuse of me? You should simply have said: "The nation having declared its wish for a new sovereign, the army's duty is to comply with it. Long live the King! Long live Louis XVIII!"'

Augereau then started calling Bonaparte *tu* as well, and upbraided him bitterly, in turn, with his insatiable ambition, to which he had sacrificed everything, even the good of all France. This talk being wearisome to Napoleon, he turned abruptly towards the marshal, embraced him, took off his hat and flung himself into his carriage.

Augereau kept his hands behind his back and his cap on his head, and merely, when Napoleon was again seated in the carriage, waved him a contemptuous farewell. As he turned away he bowed very courteously to the commissioners.

Napoleon, with his unfailing devotion to truth, said to General Köller an hour later:

'I have this moment heard of Augereau's infamous proclamation. If I had known of it when I met him, I should have given him a good dressing-down.'

At Valence we found French troops of Augereau's corps, who had mounted the white cockade, and who nevertheless rendered Napoleon all the honours due to his rank. The soldiers plainly revealed their displeasure when they saw us following him. But that was his last triumph, for he heard no vivats all the rest of the way.

On the 25th of April we reached Orange. We were greeted with shouts of 'Long live the King! Long live Louis XVIII!'

Thus far Napoleon had been in very good spirits, often jesting at his own situation. For instance, one day he said to the commissioners, after recalling with great frankness all the stages he had passed through in his career, from the age of twenty-five:

'After all, I've lost nothing. For I began the game with a six-franc piece in my pocket and I've come out of it very rich.'

DOWN WITH THE TYRANT, THE RASCAL!

The evidence of Waldburg-Truchsess *can be accepted without reserve, since it is confirmed in every detail by numerous statements from the most varied observers, and by Napoleon himself.*

On the same day, in the morning, Napoleon found, a little
· before Avignon, at the place where we were to change horses, a
large crowd which was on the look-out for him, and welcomed
us with shouts of 'Long live the King! Long live the allies!
Down with Nicholas! [*contemptuous nickname for Napoleon*] Down
with the tyrant, the rascal, the wicked knave! . . .'

These were only a few of the insults belched forth by the
multitude.

We did our utmost to put an end to this scene and break up the
throng which was hurling itself at his carriage. We could not
prevail on these furies to leave off reviling the man who, they said,
had made them so wretched, and whose sole desire was to add
to their misery. At last, under our remonstrances, they gave way
and, with what they thought great forbearance, restricted themselves to shouting 'Long live the allies, our liberators, the generous
Emperor of Russia and the good king Frederick-William!'

They even tried to make Napoleon's coachman shout 'Long
live the King!' He refused, and one of these men, who was
armed, drew a sabre on him. Luckily he was prevented from
striking. As the horses had then been put to, they were driven off
at a gallop, so fast that we were within a league of Avignon when
we caught Napoleon up.

At every place we passed through he was received in the same
way.

At Orgon, a little village where we changed horses, the frenzy
of the crowd was at its height. Before the very inn where he was
to stop they had erected a gallows on which hung a dummy in
French uniform, covered with blood, and with a placard on its
chest bearing the inscription: 'This, sooner or later, will be the
tyrant's end.'

They were hanging on to Napoleon's carriage, trying to get a
sight of him and hurl the most violent abuse in his face.

Napoleon was doing his best to hide behind General Bertrand.
He was pale and discomposed, and spoke not a word.

By dint of holding forth to the crowd, we managed to get him
out of this tight corner.

Count Schuvalov, from beside Buonaparte's carriage, haran-
gued the populace in these terms:

'Are you not ashamed to insult a defenceless wretch? He is
humbled enough by the sorry plight he has been reduced to, he

who fancied he could dictate to the world and who now sees himself at the mercy of your generosity! Leave him to himself. Look at him. You can see that contempt is the only weapon you ought to use on this man, who is dangerous no longer. It would be beneath the French nation to take any other revenge!'

The crowd cheered this speech, and Buonaparte, seeing the effect it was having, made Count Schuvalov signs of approval and afterwards thanked him for the service.

NAPOLEON IN DISGUISE

A quarter of a league beyond Orgon he felt it absolutely necessary to disguise himself. He put on a seedy blue overcoat and a round hat with a white cockade, and mounted a post-horse to gallop in front of his carriage, hoping he would pass for a courier.

As we were unable to keep up, we reached Saint-Canat long after him. Being unaware of the means he had taken to elude the crowd, we thought him in the greatest danger, for we saw his carriage beset by furious people who were trying to get the doors open. Luckily they were well secured: which saved General Bertrand's life.

It was the pertinacity of the women that astonished us most. They implored us to hand him over, saying:

'He so richly deserves it for all he has done to us, and to you, too, that we're asking no more than is right.'

Half a league from Saint-Canat we overtook Napoleon's carriage, which soon afterwards turned off at a poor inn on the main road, known as 'La Calade'. We followed it. And it was there we first heard of the disguise he had resorted to, and of how he had reached the inn under cover of this outlandish rig. He had been attended only by a single courier. His suite, from general to cook's boy, were adorned with white cockades, of which they seemed to have laid in a stock in advance.

His valet-de-chambre, coming out to meet us, desired us to let Napoleon pose as Colonel Campbell, since it was by that name he had announced himself to the landlady. We promised to comply with his wish, and I was the first to enter a kind of private room, where I was impressed to find the quondam sovereign of the world sunk in thought, with his head in his hands.

I did not recognise him at first, and came closer. He started up on hearing my tread, and I could see his face bathed in tears. He signed to me to say nothing, made me sit down by him, and, as long as the landlady was in the room, talked of indifferent things. But when she went out he resumed his former attitude. I thought it proper to leave him alone. However, he sent asking us to come into his room now and then, to keep his presence from being suspected.

We apprised him that Colonel Campbell was known to have passed through this very spot the day before, on his way to Toulon. He immediately decided to take the name of 'Lord Burghersh'.

We sat down to table, but as it was not his own cooks who had made the dinner, he could not bring himself to touch anything, for fear of being poisoned.

Nevertheless, on seeing us eat heartily, he was ashamed to reveal the terrors agitating him, and helped himself to everything he was offered. He made a show of tasting it, but sent the dishes away untouched. Sometimes he would throw what he had accepted under the table to make us think he had eaten it. His dinner was made up of a little bread and a bottle of wine which came from his carriage, and which he even shared with us.

He talked a great deal and was strikingly friendly. When we were alone and the landlady, who waited on us, had left the room, he disclosed to us how much he feared for his life. He was convinced that the French government had taken steps to have him kidnapped or murdered in this place.

A thousand different plans for escape were going through his head. He was also pondering how he could outwit the people of Aix, for he had been warned that there was a very large crowd awaiting him at the post-house. He therefore intimated that he thought the best plan would be to go back as far as Lyons, and then proceed to embark for Italy by another route.

We could in no case have agreed to this scheme, and we tried to persuade him to go straight to Toulon, or to Fréjus by way of Digne. We strove to convince him that it was impossible the French government should have these treacherous designs against him, and that the populace, in spite of the indecencies it was giving way to, would not commit a crime of that sort.

In order to talk us round, and prove what good cause, in his judgment, he had for his fears, he told us what had passed between him and the landlady, who had not recognised him.

'Well,' she had asked, 'did you meet Buonaparte?'

'No,' he had replied.

'I'm curious,' she went on, 'to see whether he'll get away. I can't help thinking the people will murder him. And there's no denying he richly deserves it, the scoundrel! Do tell me—they're going to ship him off to his island?'

'Yes, of course.'

'They'll drown him, won't they?'

'I should hope so!' returned Napoleon.

'So you see,' he added, 'the danger I'm in.'

And again he started wearying us with his anxieties and hesitations. He even asked us to try whether we could find a secret door he might slip out of, and whether the window, which he had shuttered on his arrival, was too high for him to escape by jumping from it.

The window was barred on the outside, and I threw him into the utmost perplexity by imparting this discovery. At the slightest noise he would start and change colour.

After dinner we left him to his thoughts, and on going into his room from time to time, agreeably to the wish he had expressed, we always found him in tears.

A NEW DISGUISE

Napoleon had not reached the end of his calvary, and in his terror of the people, especially of women demanding the sons, fathers, brothers, husbands who were rotting in every corner of Europe, he was about to change his get-up.

The new one would startle his sister Pauline when he met her at Le Luc, and she would refuse to kiss him till he changed into his accustomed uniform.

This last part of Waldburg-Truchsess's *story, like the rest, is wholly authentic. The narrative of the Prussian commissioner was published in 1815, and a copy was to find its way to St Helena. General Gourgaud was to read it with indignation. 'I can't believe it . . .' He was to ask Bertrand: 'Tell me, is it true?'—'It's true.'*

A great many people had collected in this inn. Most of them had come from Aix, on a suspicion that it was the Emperor Napoleon's presence which was keeping us here. We tried to

z

make them believe he had gone on ahead. But they refused to credit what they were told. They assured us that they did not mean to hurt him, only to have a look at him and see how he was bearing misfortune. That at most they would upbraid him a little face to face, or that they would tell him the truth, which he had so rarely heard.

We did all we could to divert them from this purpose, and succeeded in quieting them. Then General Schuvalov's aide-de-camp came and told us that the mob outside in the street had nearly all gone away. Napoleon decided to leave at midnight.

With exaggerated caution, he adopted yet other means of passing unrecognised.

He constrained General Schuvalov's aide-de-camp, by his importunities, to put on the blue greatcoat and round hat in which he had arrived at the inn, apparently so that in case of need the aide-de-camp might be insulted or even murdered instead of him. (As no harm befell the aide-de-camp who took over Buonaparte's role, it is clear enough that the danger to Napoleon was at an end, and that his disguise was quite uncalled for. In fact it served only to make him ridiculous and contemptible.)

Buonaparte, who now intended to pose as an Austrian colonel, put on General Köller's uniform, decorated himself with the general's order of St Theresa, set my travelling cap on his head, and wrapped himself in General Schuvalov's cloak.

After the commissioners of the powers had thus fitted him out, the carriages were brought to the door. But before going down we rehearsed, in our room, what was to be the order of our going.

General Drouot opened the procession. Next came the counterfeit emperor (General Schuvalov's aide-de-camp), then General Köller, Napoleon, General Schuvalov and myself, who had the honour to form part of the rear-guard, with Napoleon's suite following on.

In this manner we passed through the gaping crowd, who were trying with might and main to detect among us the person they called their 'tyrant'.

Schuvalov's aide-de-camp (Major Oleviev) took Napoleon's seat in his carriage, and Napoleon set off with General Köller in his barouche.

A party of gendarmes dispatched to Aix by order of the mayor broke up the crowd which was trying to surround us, and our journey went on most peacefully.

A detail I should wish to omit, but which as an historian I have no right to pass over, is that our familiarity with Napoleon, while we were constantly with him in the same room, made us aware that he was suffering from an amorous complaint. He made so little secret of it that he would apply the needful remedies in our presence. And on questioning his doctor [*Foureau de Beauregard*], we learnt that he had contracted it on his last journey to Paris.

Everywhere we found gatherings who received us with the heartiest shouts of 'Long live the King!' They also bawled abuse of Napoleon. But nothing alarming was attempted.

And yet Napoleon could not make himself easy. He stayed on in the Austrian general's barouche, and he ordered the coachman to smoke, hoping such a liberty would disguise his presence. He even asked General Köller to sing, and on the general's replying that he could not sing, Buonaparte told him to whistle.

And thus he pursued his way, huddled in one corner of the barouche, pretending to be asleep, lulled by the sweet music of the general and censed by the coachman's smoke.

NAPOLEON, KING OF ELBA

A mockery, to be sure, but that was his title. And indeed in his ten months there he behaved as a king. He had a court, with a grand marshal of the palace (Bertrand), chamberlains, etc., and nearly as many servants as at the Tuileries. His mother and Pauline shared his state, surrounded by a bevy of ladies-in-waiting, most of them Napoleon's mistresses.

He had a little army and a staff, a flotilla and ordnance. He received tourists, and other mistresses who had come expressly from France (Walevska, Theologos); he gave audiences, dinners and balls.

French and foreign observers have left many documents on Napoleon's life in Elba, reports of talk with the beaten conqueror. The fullest is that of Pons (de l'Hérault), director of mines on the island. Pons was a republican. Napoleon set about his conquest. As we shall see, he succeeded pretty well.

Napoleon's residence on the island of Elba had four very distinct periods, and I define them. The period of stability, the period of uncertainty, the period of plans, the period of execution. The first two were the most protracted.

Napoleon arrived at Elba disgusted with greatness and desirous of tranquillity. No doubt in such a man as the Emperor that disgust and that desire could not be lasting, but they were genuine at the time. His building, his purchases, his treaties could be prompted only by the anticipation of lasting tenure, and a view to ephemeral tenure would be consistent only with a state of complete unreason. Napoleon was not the man to exhaust his treasury to surround himself with a momentary splendour.

In private life he was less addicted to cutting remarks than in public life. Indeed he made use of private life to redress the injuries of public life. Yet it was not easy for him to play the good-natured man; his habit of absolute power did not lend itself to bonhomie. Nevertheless, there were circumstances when only the good-natured man could be seen. For instance, it was only the good-natured man who appeared on small occasions, when he could regard himself as being in private, and then there was nothing to mark the emperor, who stood entirely aside. I enjoyed this honourable distinction four times, once to eat oysters, throughout which meal the Emperor was inexpressibly merry. This was his gayest moment.

Amid his great qualities Napoleon had one idiosyncrasy of the small-minded which surprises me even now. Napoleon was too fond of learning the vulgar details of private life, the tittle-tattle in different cliques, what so-and-so said, what such another was doing, and he was not always free from touchiness on trumpery matters.

Everything in his nature bowed to the force of his will. Both morally and physically he appeared only what he chose to appear. One knew nothing about him, least of all when fancying one knew something. He, on the other hand, never missed any thought of which he was the object, for it was he who called up these thoughts, and he gave them whatever direction would be most useful to him.

Napoleon's evening receptions were of a very homely character. The Emperor passed the time in chat; there was a card-table for his guests. The play was extremely modest. But each of these almost patriarchal soirées had a remarkable feature, the most remarkable of all those that gave a clue to Napoleon's disposition. Napoleon had his faults, prejudices, whims. Among his faults,

Napoleon had one whose untoward nature, frequently recurring, always gave offence, and beyond doubt made him the enemies who were inexorably bent on his ruin. Napoleon was not irascible, even when indignant, but in the heat of a first impulse he said things which were cruelly wounding, and which never ceased to bleed.

Napoleon was often unconscious of having wounded, and when the fact that he had dealt a wound was brought home to him, he would at once try to heal it. He did not always succeed. Nevertheless, the fullness of his goodwill was manifest. This goodwill showed itself more particularly at the soirées. These were not regular. Nor, but for some privileged exceptions, could one go uninvited.

When Napoleon had had some argument, when he had let fly with insulting gibes, the victim was invariably bidden to the soirée, and he was the most favoured guest.

Napoleon usually retired at nine o'clock. When the clock struck nine he went up to the piano and tapped out with his forefinger the following notes: *do do sol sol la la sol fa fa mi mi re re do*.

And when this imperial concert was at an end, Napoleon would go up to the person he had quarrelled with and lay a friendly hand on his shoulder. He would say affectionately:

'Well, now we've done as lovers do, fallen out! But lovers make up, and afterwards they love all the more. Goodbye, good night, no ill feeling!'

And Napoleon would withdraw with such an eloquent air of satisfaction that all were touched by it.

Napoleon wore no mask. He showed himself just as he was. He could not go off to bed on bad terms with anyone. Bad terms weighed on him like a nightmare.

ON THE BRINK

Napoleon was bored. He was longing for a turn of events that would allow him to reappear on the great stage of Europe. Now, in France the restored Bourbons were facing difficulties: a diminished France, an empty treasury, immense war taxes. Louis XVIII and his government had no choice but to disband the cadres of Napoleon's army, as a burden on the exchequer. These aristocrats of war were not prepared to find other employment, and started agitating against the regime.

Napoleon got wind of this. Then his former minister Maret, Duke of Bassano (of whom Talleyrand used to say: 'There's no one stupider than M. Maret, unless it's the Duke of Bassano')—Maret sent an emissary, Fleury de Chaboulon, to suggest his return to France. An act of stupendous folly, well worthy of Maret, and which Napoleon was to endorse.

While Fleury was repeating Maret's message, Napoleon 'strode up and down, violently agitated, and gesticulating'. Finally he said:

'I could be in France in two days, if the nation were to recall me. . . . Do you think I ought to go back?'

As he spoke these words, Napoleon averted his eyes, and I could easily see that he attached more importance to the question than he wished to reveal, and that he was awaiting my answer with anxiety.

'Sire, I dare not decide such a question of myself, but . . .'

(*Abruptly.*)

'That's not what I'm asking you. Answer yes or no.'

'Well, yes, sire.'

(*With emotion.*)

'You think so?'

'Yes, sire, I am convinced, like the Duke of Bassano, that the people and the army would welcome you as a liberator and embrace your cause with enthusiasm.'

(*In an anxious, disturbed manner.*)

'So Maret advises me to come back?'

'We foresaw that Your Majesty would question me on that point, and here are his exact words:

'"You will tell the Emperor that I dare not take it on myself to decide such an important question, but that he may regard it as a positive and incontestable fact that the present government has ruined itself in the eyes of the people and the army, that disaffection is at the highest pitch, and that the regime is not expected to hold out for long against the general censure. You will add that the Emperor has become the object of the regrets and wishes of the army and the nation. After that the Emperor will decide, in his wisdom, what he has to do."'

Napoleon became pensive, was silent, and after a long pondering said to me:

'I will think it over. You are to stay here. Come at eleven o'clock tomorrow.'

NAPOLEON AT GRENOBLE

On 26th February, 1815, on board the Inconstant *(a gift from Louis XVIII), and escorted by the other units of his flotilla, Napoleon left Elba. On 1st March he landed in the Gulf of Juan with his little force. He took a different route from the one which had nearly been fatal to him the year before. There were few or no troops to oppose him. Many generals refused to take part in the adventure, but several joined him, and brought over their men. Besides, he was distributing a great deal of money.*

On 7th March he had reached Grenoble. 'As far as Grenoble,' he was to say, 'I was only an adventurer. At Grenoble I was a prince.'

*During his stay at Grenoble he had a secretary with an illustrious name—*Champollion, *brother to the egyptologist. The name, because it included half his own (*lion*), took Napoleon's fancy. As for Champollion himself, we owe him the best work to be published on 'the flight of the eagle' (Napoleon's march from the Gulf of Juan to Paris) and the 'hundred days'.*

Very early on the following day, 8th March, I went with part of my family to the terrace of the public gardens, in order to get a sight of Napoleon when he showed himself at a casement overlooking these gardens.

On my return home (it was about nine o'clock) I learnt that an officer of artillery had already called twice to ask for me on the Emperor's behalf and invite me to wait on him immediately. Before I could recover from the surprise, or the misgiving, occasioned me by this news, the same officer presented himself a third time and delivered his errand to me in person, though he could not explain the object of it. I told him I should comply with the instructions I was being given.

I immediately left the house, but for the town hall, so as to consult the mayor on what was happening and get his advice. And there I was informed that, Napoleon having applied to the mayor himself for someone to help with his desk-work and correspondence, the latter had mentioned me, and the Emperor, writing down my address, had said:

'It's a good omen, he has half of my name.'

I at once betook myself to the place appointed. I was announced and promptly shown in. The dark room serving as a lobby was congested with people.

A very unpretentious door opened, showing me a room which was not less so, forming an oblong from the door to the casement. The chimney-piece was on the left. It was adorned with a plaster bust of Napoleon, and I immediately recollected that, a few months before, I had lent someone the original bust in bronze of which this was a copy. It was a work by the sculptor Chaudet, belonging to the municipal library, and at the Restoration it had been put away in a cupboard, from which I had temporarily extracted it with no notion of what was to take place.

A writing-table stood near the fireplace. Opposite this was a sofa. The Emperor was seated on it, but lengthwise, facing the door and with his back to the window, his left leg stretched on the sofa and his right foot resting on the floor.

He got up, came towards me, and in that picturesque, penetrating voice, here and there slightly charged with foreign intonations and accent, addressed to me, with much else, the following words, which I have not forgotten:

'I am very glad to see you. You were described to me as a person respected in this town, and of moderate principles. That's the kind of man I mean to have about me in future. We must explain to the people why I have come back. But for me you were in for a republican revolution. The Bourbons did not know France, and today I am quite convinced that her destiny can only be fulfilled under the guidance of a liberal government.'

The review of the Grenoble national guard was appointed to take place on the morning of Wednesday the 9th, a market day, in the main square.

The Emperor made his appearance on foot.

As soon as he had been acclaimed by the troops, and by the citizens who were packing the square and the windows of every house, the band immediately struck up the old republican song: *Veillons au salut de l'empire, veillons au maintien de nos droits.*

This air at once caught the Emperor's attention, and, turning his head towards the musicians, he said graciously:

'Very good, very good.'

When the review was over, the Emperor walked back amid the cheers of the crowd, and it is a fact that on this walk through the streets a charcoal-burner who had got up on a corner-post shouted to Napoleon as he went by:

'Is it you that's our emperor?'

'Yes, my friend,' said the Emperor.

'Well, then, put it there!'

And the Emperor put it there, in the hand of the charcoal-burner. And the crowd applauded with stupendous enthusiasm.

IT'S YOU! IT'S YOU AT LAST!

From Grenoble to Paris, Napoleon went on advancing. Marshal Ney, who had been dispatched with troops to intercept the 'usurper', and had sworn to Louis XVIII that he would 'bring Buonaparte back in an iron cage', lost no time in betraying the King to Napoleon's profit.

Louis XVIII, badly advised, thought fit to give place and flee the country, when (we have Napoleon's own word for it) a single musket-shot would have been enough to unleash civil war and bring the adventure to an end. But no shot was fired, and Napoleon's military clients rushed to the Tuileries.

There, on 20th March, 1815, he was welcomed by the devoted Lavallette, *who had already compromised himself, and who, like Ney, was to be condemned to death after Waterloo. (Lavallette, however, was to escape in conventionally romantic style, by changing clothes with his wife on the eve of execution.)*

For the moment he was delirious with joy.

After providing for the whole service as I thought best, in the Emperor's interest, I repaired to the Tuileries.

Five or six officers on half-pay were strolling in the vast court-yard, embracing each other, rejoicing that Napoleon was coming back.

In the apartments the Emperor's two sisters-in-law, the Queen of Spain and the Queen of Holland, were awaiting him with deep emotion. They were soon joined by their ladies and those of the Empress. Everywhere fleurs-de-lis had expelled the bees. However, on inspecting the immense carpet covering the throne-room in which they were, one of them observed that one of the lilies seemed to be loose. She tore it off, and presently the bee could be seen. The ladies all set to work, and in less than half an hour, to peals of laughter from the whole bevy, the carpet again became imperial.

Meanwhile the hours went by. Paris was quiet. Those who lived at a distance from the Tuileries kept their distance. Each kept to his own house. The King's going, the Emperor's coming were an enormous event, and one so strange that the fourteen centuries of the monarchy had offered nothing so extraordinary. And yet indifference seemed to rule every mind.

Was the event above the compass of vulgar souls? Or was it the common sense of the people, which declared it was not well for them that these two monarchs should come to grips, and that they could expect nothing from it but pain and sacrifice?

But it was not the same in country places. Officers arriving from Fontainebleau ahead of the Emperor told us it was very difficult to move along the road. Solid masses of peasants were lining it on both sides, or rather had taken possession of it. Enthusiasm was at its height.

There was no knowing what time he would arrive.

It was to be hoped that he would pass unrecognised, for in all this delirium and confusion the hand of an assassin might be able to reach him.

But he had chosen to fling himself, with the Duke of Vicenza, into a seedy cabriolet, and at last, at nine o'clock in the evening, this vehicle stopped before the entrance nearest the gateway on the Quai du Louvre.

Scarcely had he alighted when a shout of 'Long live the Emperor!', but a roof-splitting, a tremendous shout, made itself heard.

It was that of the half-pay officers, packed, jammed together in the entrance-hall and crowding the staircase to the top.

The Emperor was in his famous grey overcoat. I advanced towards him, and the Duke of Vicenza called out to me:

'For heaven's sake, get in front of him, so that he can move!'

He began to climb the staircase.

I went before him, backwards, one step ahead, gazing on him with deep excitement, my eyes suffused with tears, and repeating in my delirium:

'What! it's you! it's you! it's you at last!'

As for him, he went slowly up, his eyes closed, his hands stretched out in front of him, like a blind man, expressing his happiness only by a smile.

HE CAME LIKE A THIEF . . .

Lavallette's account is that of a bonapartist, and shows us only the interior of the Tuileries, with its people attached to Napoleon from interest. (For no one can fail to observe that these same people, in 1814, had not lifted a finger to save him or to save his throne.)

Around the Tuileries was Paris, and the Duc de Broglie, in company with Augustin Thierry (the famous historian), also witnessed Napoleon's arrival. This impression is very different.

Together we often wandered about the streets, squares and public places, mingling with the crowd, and listening to what was said. All was glum, quiet, indifferent. At bottom, regret was absent, hope was absent, but not uneasiness.

'My dear fellow,' said Napoleon to Mollien a few days later, 'they have let me come as they let the others go.'

The day that followed the going of the man they were letting go, and saw the coming of the man they were letting come, turned out even drearier than the day before. Paris was lugubrious, public squares deserted, cafés and places of assembly half closed. The passers-by avoided each other. In the streets one met hardly anyone but belated soldiery, officers on the spree and men in their cups, shouting, singing the *Marseillaise*, the rowdy's everlasting refrain, and offering all comers, in jeering tones and all but at the point of the sword, tricolour cockades.

At nightfall we had the curtain-raiser. We saw Saint-Didier, former prefect of the palace, at the head of the imperial domestic staff, footmen, butlers, cooks, scullions, each of whom had unearthed his livery, taking triumphal possession of the disordered apartments, of beds that were still unmade, of chafing-dishes that were still smoking, and chasing what was left of the royal staff with brooms and spits.

After dark the master came. He came like a thief, in the New Testament expression, which was never more to the point. He climbed the great staircase of the Tuileries, borne up on the arms of his generals, of his former ministers, of all the past and present servants of his fortune, in whose faces, nevertheless, one could read as much anxiety as joy.

WHAT? . . . ME, AMBITIOUS?

By the morning of the next day, 21st March, rapture had died down. Night had led the majority into painful reflections. Napoleon tried bluffing. He reiterated that he had done with war, that the powers were glad of his return, that he was going to make treaties with them. But his old ministers saw through this, and did not all consent to take back their portfolios. Several marshals (among them Augereau and Macdonald) had stuck to Louis XVIII. The generals were in two minds.

General Rapp, the defender of Dantzig, the blunt, outspoken Alsatian, needed a lot of coaxing to present himself to Napoleon.

Napoleon: So there you are, General Rapp! You've taken your time. Where have you been?

Rapp: At Ecouen, sire, where I left my troops at the disposal of the minister for war.

Napoleon: Did you really mean to fight against me?

Rapp: Yes, sire.

Napoleon: The devil!

Rapp: There was no choice.

Napoleon (with animation): F——! I knew you were in front of me. If there had been fighting, I'd have sought you out on the battlefield. I'd have shown you Medusa's head. Would you have dared to fire on me?

Rapp: To be sure. My duty . . .

Napoleon: That's the limit. But the men wouldn't have obeyed you. *Their* attachment had lasted longer. Anyhow, if you had fired a single shot, your Alsatian peasants would have stoned you to death.

Rapp: You will admit, sire, that the situation was a painful one. You abdicate, you go away, you urge us to serve the King, you come back again. . . . It is beyond even the power of memories to delude us.

Napoleon: How so? What do you mean? Do you suppose I came back without alliances, without agreements? . . . Besides, my system is changed. No more war, no more conquests. I mean to reign in peace, and to make my subjects happy.

Rapp: So you say. But already your anterooms are filled with the time-servers who always humoured your bent for arms.

Napoleon: Fiddlesticks! Experience. . . . Did you often go to the Tuileries?

Rapp: Now and then, sire.

Napoleon: How did those people treat you?

Rapp: I have nothing to complain of.

Napoleon: It seems you were well received by the King on your return from Russia?

Rapp: Extremely well, sire.

Napoleon: I dare say. Wheedled to start with, then shown the door. That's what was coming to all of you. For, after all, you were not their men. It was impossible you should suit them. It takes other claims, other rights to please them.

Rapp: The King has relieved France of the allies.

Napoleon: All right, but at what a cost! And his promises—have they been kept? It was that, it was the insolence of the nobles and the priests that made me leave Elba. I might have returned with three million peasants who were flocking to complain and offer their services. But I was sure I should meet with no resistance before Paris. It's very lucky for the Bourbons that I came back. But for me they'd have wound up with an appalling revolution.

Have you seen Châteaubriand's pamphlet, which doesn't even allow me courage on the battlefield? I think you've seen me in action sometimes? Am I a coward?

Rapp: I shared the indignation felt by all honest men, at a charge as unjust as it is ignoble.

Napoleon: Have you seen anything of the Duc d'Orléans?

Rapp: I only met him once.

Napoleon: That's the one with a sense of conduct and tact! The others have bad friends, bad advisers. They don't like me. They're going to be more furious than ever. And well they may. I got here without striking a blow. Now they'll be denouncing my ambition with a vengeance. That's the everlasting reproach. It's all they can find to say.

Rapp: They're not the only ones to accuse you of ambition.

Napoleon: What—me ambitious! Would a man with ambition be as fat as this?

(He was slapping his belly with both hands.)

Rapp: Your Majesty is joking.

THE DEATH OF BERTHIER

He himself was beginning to question the outcome of his adventure. Everything was lacking. His wife and son, whatever he might say to Rapp and others, would not be coming back. At the Foreign Office he needed a spokesman able to hold his own with Europe; he therefore made advances to Talleyrand, promising him millions on millions. . . . But Talleyrand, knowing him to be a doomed man, declined with a sneer.

He needed an outstanding chief of staff (for he would soon be fighting again), and the one who had been part author of all his victories died suddenly and obscurely.

(Napoleon had written to Berthier from Elba, angling for his support. Berthier did not answer; nor did he warn Louis XVIII. When Napoleon came back, he retired to Bamberg. There he saw Russian troops marching by on their way to France, and threw himself from a window.)

Napoleon had disparaged Berthier in the past. How he reacted to his death, we learn from General Thiébault.

I was at the Elysée on the evening of the day Napoleon heard this news. No one was better at hiding or showing his feelings. But he seemed to have lost his power of dissimulation.

Indeed, I never saw him so melancholy. He did not stir from a little room leading to the one in which we were received, and he spent, alone with Count Boulay de la Meurthe, a full hour, throughout which his face was drawn, his attitude sombre, his speech more laconic than usual. His haughty head drooped in spite of him, there was something fateful in his glance, and his gestures were all the more eloquent of grief because his slightest movements had something convulsive about them.

WE ARE LOST . . .

All the way through France, from the Gulf of Juan to Paris, Napoleon had been strewing demagogic promises. He had been vowing that he would not make war again. He would reduce the taxes. He would give the country a liberal constitution. His despotic system had run its course . . .

On reaching Paris he took it all back. Fouché (whom he had been quick to send for, without whom he would not have had a politician by his side, and who was to seal his fate)—Fouché urged him in vain to keep his promises.

Lucien Bonaparte, who had come hurrying to make it up with his brother, was likewise disheartened. He said to Fouché: 'We are lost. Napoleon ought to be killed to save France and his family.' 'I think so too,' replied Fouché, 'but you'll have to see to it yourself.'

The one concession Napoleon would grant 'his' people—his 'subjects', he went so far as to call them—was to be entitled an 'additional act' (i.e. additional to the Constitutions of the Empire). This Additional Act was received by the country with discontent or indignation, and drove Napoleon's collaborators to despair.

What Fouché writes on the subject is repeated in almost the same terms in nearly all contemporary memoirs.

Napoleon found himself perplexed in a maze of affairs, each more serious than the other, while at the same time his spirits were entirely absorbed by the thought of coping with the armaments of Europe. He would have liked to turn France into a camp and towns into arsenals. The soldiers were his own, but the citizens were still divided. Moreover, it was only with trembling that he put the instruments of the revolution to work, by sanctioning the return of popular clubs and the formation of civic confederacies, which made him fear that he had exhumed anarchy, after all his boasts of having dethroned it. And what solicitude, what misgivings, what constraint he displayed at every turn, in order to curb these associations which were so risky to handle!

This affectation of popularity had shielded him in public opinion up to the moment when he published his act in addition to the constitutions of the empire. Napoleon regarded these as the title-deeds of his crown, and by repealing them he would have thought he was starting a new reign. He, who could only date from actual possession, chose rather to take absurd pattern by Louis XVIII, who reckoned in ages on the basis of legitimacy.

Instead of granting the national constitution he had promised, he thought it enough to modify the political acts and senatus-consults governing the empire. He restored the confiscation of property, in the teeth of nearly all his advisers. Finally, at a council held on this subject, he insisted on withholding his constitution from public debate and presenting it as an additional act.

I strongly opposed his view, as did Decrès, Caulaincourt and nearly all the members present. Despite our efforts, he persisted in reducing all his concessions to this crude outline. The word 'additional' disillusioned the friends of liberty. They saw in it the perpetuation, clumsily disguised, of the principal institutions created in favour of absolute power.

From that moment Napoleon was seen only as an incurable despot. For my part, I regarded him as a madman bound hand and foot and delivered up to the mercy of Europe.

EMBROIDERED SHOES WITH ROSETTES . . .

His last great parade, the ceremony of the 'Field of May', called after the general assemblies of Charlemagne's Frankish empire, was delayed till the 1st of June. Napoleon made a speech and held a review. Signs of discontent increased. General Thiébault *explains his.*

Having to make a speech at this Field of May (or of death), Napoleon instructed I forget whom to draft it for him. And this draft, worded so as to work up the patriotic feelings of the nation, displeased him in that it was to have met his views. He therefore summoned his aide-de-camp Bernard, and, avoiding anything explicit, merely said to him:

'Read this speech; it's no good, and you will do it again.'

Bernard did it again, making it more liberal than before. Certainly nothing could be worthier, but nothing could be more fatuous. Accordingly, Napoleon had scarcely run through this demagogic amplification when the sheet on which it was written had been crushed in his fist, and he had flung it in the fire and turned his back on the said Bernard. For how deliver an almost revolutionary speech in the costume in which Napoleon had resolved to appear? The contrast would have been as strange as, in their incongruity with the circumstances, his speech, his articles and that same costume were shocking.

Never has an orator shown more adroitness in substituting thrilling phrases for positive concessions, and referring everything to a future in which he still expected to be once more lord of all. Never was an actor at more pains to depict imperial majesty in all its splendour, but never did Napoleon choose a worse time to exchange his war costume, his grey overcoat, his old sword, his little hat and his boots, for white silk stockings, embroidered shoes with rosettes, a stage sword, a coat, a sash, a cloak dazzling with embroidery, and the crown of a Roman emperor.

This pomp, seeming to intimate that he was finished as a man of war, distressed me, and many besides me.

Barely, in the days of prosperity, could all this appear to suit him, for such disguises never disguise anything.

What was greatest in him was still the old General Bonaparte, and the only vanity of dress he could safely indulge was to outdo himself in haughty simplicity.

As Emperor, all he stood for was a concession France had made only with reluctance, which continental Europe had accepted only with rage and disdain, which England had not ceased to oppose; while as a general he depended only on his sword, to which he owed everything, and he was certain of inspiring an enthusiasm which deified him.

Therefore I repeat: on the 31st of May, on the 1st of June, 1815, it was a question of war and not of pomp, since it was a question of results and not of illusions, and we were dumbfounded to see Napoleon rig himself out in garments which, as all were reflecting, might be stripped from him on the morrow.

FACES WERE GRAVE AND SOMBRE
Another sketch of this scene, by Dr Poumiès de La Siboutie.

As an elector of Maine-et-Loire, I had a ticket for the Field of May which was held on the Field of Mars. There were three or four hundred of us, occupying two wooden pavilions with their backs to the Field of Mars, and facing the Clock House of the military school, with which they were linked by a dais for the Emperor, his family and the great officers.

Most of the electors were old patriots of '89, still full of energy. Faces were grave and sombre, like the situation in which we found ourselves. The act additional to the constitutions of the empire had alienated many hearts from Napoleon. It was being freely censured out loud. In short, this gathering struck me as unfavourable to the Emperor.

He was a long time coming. On his appearance, everyone stood up. Shouts of 'Long live France, long live the nation!' drowned the sparse and timid cries of 'Long live the Emperor!'

His countenance darkened. Everyone observed how changed he was. He had grown fat, his plump and full face was without freshness, but still agreeable and commanding.

The speech drawn up by Carrion-Nisas on behalf of the electors was pronounced by Dubois d'Angers, in a clear and ringing voice. Napoleon said only a few words in reply.

Thereupon he left the dais and made his way to the Field of Mars to review the numerous troops and hand over the colours. He was welcomed with acclamation and frantic cheering. As the Field of Mars was behind us, we heard everything without seeing anything or knowing exactly what was going forward. We had been advised not to leave our places.

After this review, which lasted an hour and a half or more, Napoleon again passed in front of us. There was life in his face, pride in his eye. He bowed to us with a haughty air. It was easy to see that the welcome of the electors and that of the troops had affected him very differently.

The enthusiasm which had greeted Napoleon on his arrival was no longer the same. History will tell us why. For my part, I am reporting what I saw for myself.

MORITURI TE SALUTANT!

We are at the zenith of this hundred days' reign. So it is not surprising that all contemporaries should have laid stress on this historic moment. The Duc de Broglie's view rounds off those of Thiébault and Poumiès.

On the 1st of June I attended the Field of May. It took place on the Field of Mars. I attended it at a distance, not caring for crowds, still less for pomps. 'There are,' said Chamfort, 'three things I hate both literally and figuratively: noise, wind and smoke.' I agree with Chamfort.

I saw the imperial squad go by, in full gala dress—waving plumes, cocked hats, short Spanish cloaks, white satin pantaloons, shoes with rosettes and so on. This masquerade, in the shadow of such a crisis, with France on the brink of being invaded and carved up, owing to and for love of these fine gentlemen—this masquerade, I say, filled me with as much indignation as contempt.

I saw the Guard and several line regiments go by, with martial air, proud step and anxious brows, like men ready for a game at double or quits. As they marched past the Emperor, their eyes were glittering with an ardent and sombre fire. One seemed to see *Morituri te salutant* hovering on their lips, and the frantic cheers which were being drawn from them by order marred the effect without dispelling it.

In the Emperor's speech there was loftiness, to be sure, brilliance, majesty. But even so, it smacked far too much of the theatrical hero, the upstart of glory. Why should he have perched himself up on stilts to take a high tone, and opened a big mouth to recall big things? And was this the moment in any case—when France, reduced by one invasion to her old boundaries, was struggling under the threat of a second, from which it seemed only a miracle could save her? How much worthier of admiration and of respect had been the simple words of William III, cutting the dykes of Holland in face of Louis XIV's armies, in face of Turenne, of Condé, of Vauban, and replying to those who scoffed at his preparations:

'One can always die in the last ditch.'

William III conquered neither Italy nor Egypt. He won neither the battle of Marengo nor the battle of Austerlitz. But he did not abandon his country twice over to the foreigner. He did not, thrice in two years, immolate five hundred thousand men to his insane pride. He would have died in the last ditch of Waterloo. The world would not have seen him acting the Themistocles, begging asylum at the court of the Great King.

THE LAST MASS

Since 20th March he had never stopped calling up, forming regiments. Already his army corps were on their way to the Belgian frontier. He too would be setting off, on Monday, 12th June, at four in the morning, to attack the English and the Prussians.

On Sunday, the 11th (Thiébault is mistaken in calling it the 10th) he gave his last audiences and, for the last time, heard Mass at the Tuileries.

The time required for the troops that had attended the Field of May to reach their destination would expire on the 10th of June, and there was every sign that Napoleon would be off at once.

Now, as the 10th happened to be a Sunday, I attended the last Mass he heard at the Tuileries, the last audience he was to give there.

The throng was considerable, anxiety general. Yet everyone was trying to put a good face on it, while achieving only a show of that false confidence which, expressed in banalities, inspires none. I do not mean to say they had no hope, but still less had they easy minds.

Napoleon, who had so often played at double or quits of his own accord, was this time being driven back on it by necessity. The sovereign arbiter of so many fates, the man who, with a look, a gesture, a word, overturned life or made it happy or magnificent, might have come to the point when he would have nowhere to lay his head.

Hoping to escape from my trying presentiments and find in this man himself the grounds for confidence which seemed to elude me and which he alone could still furnish, recalling the physical distress in which I had seen him on the day he heard of Berthier's death, and trying to hearten myself against such memories, I never stopped gazing at him. And my eyes dwelt on him with the more avidity, and I might add pain, because the longer I looked, the less I could find him as he had been in his strength and greatness.

Never has the impression I felt at the sight of him, at the moment when fate was about to decide between the world and him—never has that impression left my mind.

His glance, so formidable of old in its searching quality, had lost its power and even its steadiness. His face, which I had so often seen as though beaming with grace or moulded in bronze, had lost all expression and all appearance of strength. His contracted mouth retained none of its old magic. Even his head had no longer the carriage that marked the overlord of the world, and his gait was as awkward as his bearing and gestures were uncertain.

Everything about him seemed distorted, blighted. The usual pallor of his skin had given place to a very decided greenish hue, which startled me.

What had become of the victor of Italy twice docile to his arms, of Austria twice conquered, of Egypt where he seated himself *de facto* on the throne of Sesostris, of Prussia which he had needed only one battle to destroy, of Russia which its climate alone could save?

And what a difference between the days we were living through and those I remember! Days when the meanest soldier thrilled at his sight, as at the sound of his voice, when his lightest words were passed round with enthusiasm and had the ring of prophecy, and when, after exalting the career of arms by his Ossianic eloquence, he dared to say: 'Soon I shall reappear at your head and it will be seen that you are of the race of heroes.'

Where were the days when it was his boast that he could afford a hundred thousand men and a hundred millions a year? A horrible calculation, at least as regards the men, and one which may have been his ruin, from the day the receipts no longer matched the expenditure!

Napoleon's history is summed up in this: as his fortunes grow, he gains in ambition what he loses in foresight and capacity, therefore in real strength.

WATERLOO, THE PANIC

On 14th June he was at Avesnes, issuing a proclamation to the troops: 'Today is the anniversary of Marengo and Friedland. . . .' He made small account of his adversaries, English and Prussian. 'Madmen! A moment's good fortune has blinded them. The oppression and humiliation of the French people is beyond their power! If they enter France, they will find their graves there.'

On the 16th he attacked the Prussians and beat them, but not decisively. On the 18th he attacked the English, and he was already in difficulties when, instead of Grouchy coming to his relief, the Prussians unexpectedly returned, causing the defeat and rout of Napoleon's army— here described by Fleury de Chaboulon, *the messenger of whom we had a glimpse at Elba, and who was with Napoleon as a secretary.*

The Emperor, satisfied, was repeating joyfully:
'They're ours! I've got them!'
And Marshal Soult and all the generals likewise regarded victory as assured.
Meanwhile our cavalry, worn out by considerable losses and unequal fights endlessly renewed, was beginning to lose heart and give way. The issue of the battle seemed to be growing

dubious. It was time to strike a great blow by a desperate attack.

The Emperor did not waver.

Orders were immediately given to Count Reille to gather all his forces and hurl himself on the enemy's right, while Napoleon in person would make a frontal attack with his reserves. The Emperor was already marshalling his Guard in column of attack when he heard that our cavalry had just been forced to abandon part of the heights of Mont-Saint-Jean. He at once ordered Marshal Ney to take four battalions of the Middle Guard and make all speed to the fatal plateau, to support the cuirassiers who still occupied it.

The bold front of the Guard and the harangues of Napoleon fired every mind; the cavalry and some battalions which had been drawn into its retreat faced the enemy with shouts of 'Long live the Emperor!'

At that moment a burst of rifle-fire was heard.

'There's Grouchy!' cried the Emperor. 'Victory is ours.'

Labédoyère flew to tell the army this joyful news. He broke through the enemy to the head of our columns:

'Marshal Grouchy is here, the Guards are being thrown in! Courage! Courage! The English are lost.'

Just then Ziethen's thirty thousand Prussians, who had been taken for Grouchy's army, carried the village of La Haie by main force, driving us before them. Our cavalry, our infantry, already shaken by the defeat of the Middle Guard, were afraid of being cut off and retired headlong. The English cavalry, taking advantage of the confusion caused by this sudden retreat, made a way through our ranks and brought their disorder and discouragement to a climax. The other troops on the right, who had already all they could do to withstand the Prussian attacks, and had been short of ammunition for more than an hour, on seeing some squadrons in chaos and men of the Guard stampeding, thought all was lost and abandoned their position. This contagious impulse spread to the left in a flash, and the whole army, which had so gallantly carried the best positions of the enemy, became as eager to give them up as it had been zealous in seizing them.

The English army, which had been advancing as we fell back, the Prussians, who had not ceased to pursue us, swooped with one accord on our scattered battalions; darkness increased the turmoil and panic; and soon the whole army was only a chaotic mass, which the English and the Prussians overcame without effort and slaughtered without pity.

The Emperor, witness to this appalling defection, could scarcely believe his eyes.

Two or three hundred fugitives of all arms were rounded up to escort the Emperor. Along with General Bertrand, he got into a barouche and drove off. It was thus that Charles XII fled before his conquerors after the battle of Poltava.

EIGHTH STAGE

From Waterloo to the End

(1815–1821)

Admiral Malcolm: *Yet you can no longer be treated as a sovereign.*
Bonaparte: *And why not? Let them leave me these honours as an amusement.*

*Beaten, he deserted his troops and raced off to Paris. Always the same
story.*

*Reaching the Elysée on the morning of 21st June, he blamed everyone
for the loss of the battle. He demanded a bath. Those about him were
stupefied. 'Don't stay here an hour,' they told him. 'Go at once. Go
back to the head of your army.' No, he was not interested. His interest
was in the throne, and he thought that by staying in Paris he could keep
it. But he was now at a discount, and in barely twenty-four hours
Fouché 'threw him overboard'.*

*On being requested to leave Paris forthwith, he announced that he
would go to America, and meanwhile put in several days at Malmaison.
He received a few of the faithful (very few), and a succession of mistresses (one of whom was bent on accompanying him, dressed as a man).
And he made haste to realise a lump sum, with the complicity of his
treasurer Peyrusse whom he called Peyrousse. Among other operations,
he extracted from the Treasury three millions in gold to which he was
not entitled. But one of these transactions, set down by Peyrusse in his
'Memorial', gave him a bad moment.*

The Emperor went to Malmaison and declared his intention of
proceeding to America. M. Otto left for England, with instructions to apply to the English ministry for a safe-conduct.

While awaiting him, Napoleon received us at Malmaison. I
laid before him all my accounts and the state of my funds.

The army of Waterloo, flung back on Paris, was concentrating
there. Napoleon offered the provisional government to take command of the troops, promising to lay down his power when he
had expelled the enemy. But the government replied to this offer
by placing the frigate *Justice* at Napoleon's disposal, and strongly
insisting that, for his own safety, he should leave France.

I saw Napoleon. I found him in his closet, reading the gazettes.

'Well, Peyrousse, will you come with us?'

I did not hesitate to reply that the care of handing over my
duties and discharging myself of the great responsibility with
which I was burdened would not permit me to accompany him

at present. But that as he was not going to the ends of the earth, he might rely on my zeal and devotion.

Napoleon was good enough to admit my reasons, and gave me his directions with regard to the funds which were still at Rome. I was to have them paid out at once and remit them to M. Laffitte the banker.

Napoleon was the owner of some 15,150 franc scrip, in the name of Napoleon Buonaparte. He ordered me to sell it. I observed that a power of attorney would be required for this transfer, and that I would have it drawn up by his notary.

The Emperor angrily repelled my suggestion.

'Write: *Baron Peyrusse, my treasurer, sell my 15,150 franc scrip and remit me the value. Wherewith, I pray God, etc.*'

I did not think proper to insist.

In the certainty of a refusal, I had the power of attorney drawn up, and repaired to Malmaison with M. Noel, the notary. I sent in my name to His Majesty. I acquainted him with my lack of success at the transfer office. He then ordered me to apply to his notary.

'I have anticipated Your Majesty's will,' said I, 'and the notary is in the outer drawing-room.'

M. Noel was brought in, and took out the power of attorney, which I offered to Napoleon.

On reading: 'In the presence of us and his colleague, Napoleon Buonaparte . . .' he turned sharply towards us.

His silence was eloquent.

The Emperor took the pen and signed Napoleon.

I did myself the further violence of pointing out to His Majesty that the scrip carried the name of Buonaparte.

He scrawled his name, and gave me back the paper with head averted.

I COME, LIKE THEMISTOCLES . . .

At last, on 29th June, 1815, he brought himself, under pressure, to leave Malmaison, along with a company of the 'faithful', some of whom he had practically never seen before (Las Cases, Montholon), while others (Bertrand, Gourgaud, Savary, Lallemand), had the immediate prospect of being shot if they remained in France. He got to Rochefort on 3rd July, and spent a few more days shilly-shallying. What course should he take?

The truth was that he had no choice. He had lost three weeks since the abdication, and these three weeks had been turned to account by the English, who were blockading the coast. Napoleon was trapped.

For he had known for several months that the English were resolved to transport him to St Helena, and for a few weeks that the Prussians meant him to share the fate of the Duc d'Enghien: a post and twelve bullets.

So he affected to throw himself on the hospitality of the English by a voluntary surrender, and composed a personal letter to the Prince Regent:

'Your Royal Highness: Exposed to the factions dividing my country and to the enmity of the greatest powers of Europe, I have concluded my political career, and I am going [sic], like Themistocles, to seat myself on the hearth [sic] of the British people. I place myself under the protection of their laws, which I claim from Your Royal Highness as the most powerful, the most constant, and the most generous of my enemies.'

In the main, this artful dodge of Napoleon's was rather severely judged, even by his old partisans and collaborators. The minister Molé wrote: 'Bonaparte was trying to blind himself to the weakness of his decision by the heroic tone of this letter. One cannot imagine that he thought anything would come of it.'

On 14th July Gourgaud and Las Cases showed it to the captain of the Bellerophon—a cruiser with a symbolic name, which formed part of the blockading fleet under Admiral Hotham. Captain Maitland then promised to convey Napoleon to England, adding explicitly that he could make no promise as to his reception, and that 'he would be entirely at the disposal of the Prince Regent.' Las Cases knew English, so there was no mistake. And Napoleon embarked from the French brig Epervier the day after.

Maitland was to be sorry he had not asked for a written acknowledgment of his statement. But it was no small thing to have the 'monster' on board his ship, and he recorded the episode in detail.

On coming on board the *Bellerophon*, he was received without any of the honours generally paid to persons of high rank; the guard was drawn out on the break of the poop, but did not present arms. His Majesty's Government had merely given directions, in the event of his being captured, for his being removed into any one of his Majesty's ships that might fall in with him; but no instructions had been given as to the light in which he was to be viewed. As it is not customary, however, on board a British ship of war, to pay any such honours before the colours are hoisted at eight o'clock in the morning, or after sunset, I made the early hour an excuse for withholding them upon this occasion.

Buonaparte's dress was an olive-coloured great-coat over a green uniform, with scarlet cape and cuffs, green lapels turned back and edged with scarlet, skirts hooked back with bugle horns embroidered in gold, plain sugar-loaf buttons and gold epaulettes; being the uniform of the Chasseur à Cheval of the Imperial Guard. He wore the star or grand cross of the Legion of Honour, and the small cross of that order; the Iron Crown; and the Union, appended to the button-hole of his left lapel. He had on a small cocked hat, with a tri-coloured cockade; plain gold-hilted sword, military boots, and white waistcoat and breeches. The following day he appeared in shoes, with gold buckles, and silk stockings— the dress he always wore afterwards, while with me.

On leaving the *Epervier*, he was cheered by her ship's company as long as the boat was within hearing; and Mr Mott informed me that most of the officers and men had tears in their eyes.

General Bertrand came first up the ship's side, and said to me: 'The Emperor is in the boat.'

He then ascended, and, when he came on the quarter-deck, pulled off his hat, and, addressing me in a firm tone of voice, said:

'I am come to throw myself on the protection of your Prince and laws.'

When I showed him into the cabin, he looked round and said: '*Une belle chambre.*—This is a handsome cabin.'

I answered:

'Such as it is, sir, it is at your service while you remain on board the ship I command.'

He then looked at a portrait that was hanging up, and said: '*Qui est cette jeune personne?*—Who is that young lady?'

'My wife,' I replied.

'*Ah! elle est très jeune et très jolie.*—Ah! she is both young and pretty.'

He then asked what countrywoman she was, begged to know if I had any children, and put a number of questions respecting my country, and the service I had seen. He next requested I would send for the officers and introduce them to him: which was done according to their rank. He asked several questions of each, as to

the place of his birth, the situation he held in the ship, the length
of time he had served, and the actions he had been in. He then
expressed a desire to go round the ship; but, as the men had not
done cleaning, I told him it was customary to clean the lower
decks immediately after their breakfast, that they were then so
employed, and, if he would defer visiting the ship until they had
finished, he would see her to more advantage.

At this time I proposed to him to allow me to address him in
English, as I had heard he understood that language, and I had
considerable difficulty in expressing myself in French.

He replied in French: 'The thing is impossible; I hardly understand a word of your language.'

PASSENGER ON THE BELLEROPHON

The Bellerophon *weighed anchor on 16th July. She reached Plymouth
on the 22nd, went on to Torbay, and returned to anchor at Plymouth on
the 26th. Napoleon, as we learn from* Maitland, *was continuously
affable.*

Dinner was served about five o'clock upon Buonaparte's plate.
This was arranged by his Maître d'Hôtel, whom I had told to
regulate everything in the manner most likely to be agreeable to
his master.

When dinner was announced, Buonaparte, viewing himself as
a Royal personage, which he continued to do while on board the
Bellerophon, and which, under the circumstances, I considered it
would have been both ungracious and uncalled for in me to have
disputed, led the way into the dining-room. He seated himself in
the centre at one side of the table, requesting Sir Henry Hotham
to sit at his right hand, and Madame Bertrand on his left. For that
day I sat as usual at the head of the table, but on the following day,
and every other, whilst Buonaparte remained on board, I sat by
his request at his right hand, and General Bertrand took the top.
Two of the ward-room officers dined daily at the table, by invitation from Buonaparte, conveyed through Count Bertrand.

He conversed a great deal, and showed no depression of spirits:
among other things, he asked me where I was born. I told him, in
Scotland.

'Have you any property there?' said he.

'No, I am a younger brother, and they do not bestow much on people of that description in Scotland.'

'Is your elder brother a Lord?'

'No, Lord Lauderdale is the head of our family.'

'Ah! you are a relation of Lord Lauderdale's! he is an acquaintance of mine, he was sent Ambassador from your King to me, when Mr Fox was Prime Minister: had Mr Fox lived, it never would have come to this, but his death put an end to all hopes of peace. *Milord Lauderdale est un bon garçon*': adding, 'I think you resemble him a little, though he is dark and you are fair.'

When dinner was over, a cup of strong coffee was handed round; he then rose and went into the after-cabin, asking the Admiral and all the party to accompany him, the ladies among the rest. This was the only time I ever saw them in the apartment in which he slept.

After some conversation he said, in a cheerful and playful way, that he would show us his camp bed; and sent for Marchand, his premier valet-de-chambre, who received his order, and soon returned with two small packages in leather cases; one of which contained the bedstead, which was composed of steel, and, when packed up, was not above two feet long and eighteen inches in circumference; the other contained the mattress and curtains, the latter of green silk. In three minutes the whole was put together, and formed a very elegant small bed, about thirty inches wide.

He then went out, and walked the quarter-deck for some time, and retired to his cabin about half-past seven o'clock. Soon after, when the Admiral was going to return to his ship, he proposed to Bertrand to take leave of him. He went into the cabin, but returned immediately with an apology, saying he was undressed, and going to bed.

On the 20th of July, early in the morning, we spoke the *Swiftsure*, on her way from England to reinforce me in the blockade of Rochefort. The astonishment of Captain Webley can scarcely be conceived, when, on his entering the ship, I said:

'Well, I have got him.'

'Got him! got whom?'

'Why, Buonaparte; the man that has been keeping all Europe in a ferment these last twenty years.'

'Is it possible?' said he. 'Well, you are a lucky fellow.'

During the 21st and 22nd of July we exchanged signals with two or three other of our ships, which I took care to explain were on the look-out for my guest; and he seemed by this time pretty well convinced that an attempt to elude our cruisers would have been fruitless. On the latter day the *Prometheus* showed her number, while we were at dinner: when Buonaparte expressed a wish to know whether the ships at Brest had hoisted the white flag or not. I sent for the officer of the watch, and desired him to ask the question by semaphore. In a few minutes he returned, with an answer in the affirmative. Buonaparte made no remark upon this information; but asked, with apparent indifference, how the question and answer had been conveyed; and when I explained it to him, he approved highly of the usefulness of the invention.

During meals he always entered very freely and familiarly into conversation with those about him, addressing himself frequently to Las Cases and me; asking many questions about the manners, customs and laws of the English; often repeating the observation he had made on first coming on board, that he must gain all the information possible on those subjects, and conform himself to them, as he should probably end his life among that people. Monsieur Las Cases, it appears, had emigrated from France early in the revolution, and remained in England until the peace of Amiens.

Sunday, the 23rd of July, we passed very near to Ushant: the day was fine, and Buonaparte remained upon deck a great part of the morning. He cast many a melancholy look at the coast of France, but made few observations on it. He asked several questions about the coast of England: whether it was safe to approach; its distance and the part we were likely to make. About eight in the evening the high land of Dartmoor was discovered, when I went into the cabin and told him of it: I found him in a flannel dressing-gown, nearly undressed, and preparing to go to bed. He put on his great-coat, came out upon deck, and remained some time looking at the land; asking its distance from Torbay, and the probable time of our arrival there.

At daybreak of the 24th of July we were close off Dartmouth. Count Bertrand went into the cabin and informed Buonaparte of it, who came upon deck about half-past four, and remained on the poop until the ship anchored in Torbay. He talked with admiration of the boldness of the coast, saying:

B B

'You have in that respect a great advantage over France, which is surrounded by rocks and dangers.'

On opening Torbay he was much struck with the beauty of the scenery, and exclaimed:

'What a beautiful country! it very much resembles the bay of Porto Ferrajo, in Elba.'

· *NO ASYLUM?*

At Torbay and Plymouth, Napoleon received the English papers and had them translated to him. (Mme Bertrand also knew English; she was an Irishman's daughter.) Up to this point the 'faithful' had been entertaining very rosy ideas; and Maitland was shortly to be accused of beguiling them. ('It did not, however,' he observes, 'require my assistance to raise the hopes of those about Buonaparte . . . as one of his followers, on the passage home, asked me if I thought the Prince Regent would confer the Order of the Garter upon him.') But now reality started to break in.

Napoleon and all his attendants were very anxious to see as many newspapers as possible, but particularly the *Courier*, which they considered the Ministerial paper, and most likely to contain the intentions of Government respecting them. They received little encouragement from any of them, but least of all from those which are supposed to take the Ministerial side in politics, as they not only contained a great deal that was personally offensive, but stated, in very plain terms, that none of the party would be allowed to land in England, and that St Helena was the probable place of their ultimate destination.

Buonaparte himself always affected to consider this as a mere newspaper report, though I believe it gave him a good deal of uneasiness. His followers received it with much irritation and impatience, frequently endeavouring to convince me that our Government could have no right to dispose of them in that way, and talking to me as if I had been one of his Majesty's Ministers, and had influence in determining on their future destination.

I WILL NOT GO TO ST HELENA! . . .

On 31st July Admiral Keith came to give him official notice of his relegation to St Helena. He protested, stormed; he demanded the rights of a British citizen; he announced that he was not a prisoner but a passenger on the Bellerophon, *that Maitland had deliberately ensnared him, that St Helena would kill him in three months. 'I will not go to St Helena. I prefer to redden the* Bellerophon *with my blood.' This he said more than ten times.*

(But to Maitland he said in private: 'I have no complaint against you; your conduct to me has been that of a man of honour.')

Many of his intending companions now changed their minds. Mme Bertrand made a scene with her husband, who had agreed to share his captivity. She made another with Napoleon, then threw herself into the sea. Bertrand caught her by one leg, and Savary shouted: 'Let go of her, just let go of her!'

Savary and Lallemand were not permitted to accompany General Buonaparte. Those permitted were: Bertrand and his wife, Montholon and his wife, Gourgaud, and Las Cases and his son, besides a large number of servants—Marchand, Saint-Denis, etc.

And on the 7th of August, Napoleon removed from the Bellerophon *to the* Northumberland (*Captain Ross*).

We have an account of the parting scene, as it appeared to a romantic young midshipman, George Home.

The 7th came; it was a dull, cloudy, sunless day, and every countenance was overcast with gloom. We had not seen the Emperor for a week, and we were all anxious to observe the change that the horrible tidings of his destination had made upon him. Lord Keith, Admiral Cockburn, and Captain Ross came on board about eleven o'clock; and it was intimated to Napoleon, that they were ready to conduct him on board the *Northumberland*. A general's guard of marines was drawn up on the quarter-deck, to receive him as he came out of the cabin; while part of his suite, and we officers, were ranged about, anxiously awaiting the appearance of the future exile of St Helena.

Napoleon was long in attending to the intimation of the Admiral's; and upon Cockburn's becoming impatient, and remarking to old Lord Keith that he should be put in mind, Keith replied:

'No, no, much greater men than either you or I have waited longer for him before now; let him take his time, let him take his time.'

At length Napoleon appeared, but oh, how sadly changed from the time we had last seen him on deck. Though quite plain, he was scrupulously cleanly in his person and dress, but that had been forgot, his clothes were ill put on, his beard unshaved, and his countenance pale and haggard. There was a want of firmness in his gait; his brow was overcast, and his whole visage bespoke the deepest melancholy; and it needed but a glance to convince the most careless observer that Napoleon considered himself a doomed man. In this trying hour, however, he lost not his courtesy or presence of mind; instinctively he raised his hat to the guard of marines, when they presented arms as he passed, slightly inclined his head, and even smiled to us officers as he passed through us, returned the salute of the admirals with calm dignity, and, walking up to Captain Maitland, addressed him with great eagerness for nearly ten minutes.

How distinct is every feature, every trait, every line of that majestic countenance in my mind's eye at this moment, now that two-and-twenty years have passed away; but who could witness such a scene and ever forget it? The Romans said that a 'great man struggling with adversity was a sight that the gods looked on with pleasure'. Here, indeed, was adversity, and here was true greatness struggling against it; but to a mere mortal it was a heart-rending sight. The ship's deck looked like a place of execution, and we only wanted the headsman, his block and his axe, to complete the scene.

The purport of his speech to Captain Maitland was thanking *him*, his officers, and ship's company, for the polite attention he had received while on board of the *Bellerophon*, which he should ever hold in kind remembrance. Something more he would have said after the first pause, and a feeling of deep emotion laboured in his face, and swelled his breast, he looked earnestly in Maitland's face for a moment, as if he was about to renew his speech, but utterance seemed denied; and, slightly moving his hat in salutation, he turned to Savary and Lallemand, who were not allowed to accompany him to St Helena, and spoke to them for a few minutes.

What a horrid gloom overhung the ship: had his execution

been about to take place there could not have prevailed a more
dead silence, so much so, that had a pin fallen from one of the
tops on the deck, I am convinced it would have been heard; and
to anyone who has known the general buzz of one of our seventy-
fours, even at the quietest hour, it is a proof how deeply the attention of every man on board must have been riveted.

Before leaving the ship he turned to us on the quarter-deck,
once more waved his hand in token of adieu, took hold of the
man-ropes, and walked down the side, taking his seat in the
Northumberland's barge between Lord Keith and Admiral Cockburn.

AT THE BRIARS WITH BETSY BALCOMBE

*In those days it was a long voyage to St Helena, and Napoleon, who
had gone aboard the* Northumberland *on 7th August, did not land at
Jamestown till 17th October.*

*This long passage was marked only by the squabbling of the prisoner's
French companions, which it amused him to foster, and in which the
bone of contention was a look, a word, a smile from the man who still
required his suite to address him as 'Majesty'.*

*Admiral Cockburn was on board, and it was he who set about in-
stalling Napoleon at St Helena. But as the house designed for him was
not yet ready, he was to spend his first seven weeks at the Briars, with a
Mr and Mrs Balcombe. Now the Balcombes had children, one of them
a girl of fourteen. Betsy Balcombe took a good many liberties with
Napoleon, and twenty-five years later, as Mrs Abell, was proud to tell
the tale.*

The party arrived at the gate, and there being no carriage-road,
they all dismounted, excepting the Emperor, who was now fully
visible. He retained his seat and rode up the avenue, his horse's
feet cutting up the turf on our pretty lawn. Sir George Cockburn
walked on one side of his horse, and General Bertrand on the
other. How vividly I recollect my feelings of dread, mingled
with admiration, as I now first looked upon him whom I had
learned to fear so much.

Napoleon's position on horseback, by adding height to his
figure, supplied all that was wanting to make me think him the
most majestic person I had ever seen. His dress was green, and

covered with orders, and his saddle and housings were of crimson velvet richly embroidered with gold. He alighted at our house, and we all moved to the entrance to receive him. Sir George Cockburn introduced us to him.

On a nearer approach Napoleon, contrasting, as his shorter figure did, with the noble height and aristocratic bearing of Sir George Cockburn, lost something of the dignity which had so much struck me on first seeing him. He was deadly pale, and I thought his features, though cold and immovable and somewhat stern, were exceedingly beautiful. He seated himself on one of our cottage chairs, and after scanning our little apartment with his eagle glance, he complimented mamma on the pretty situation of the Briars. When once he began to speak, his fascinating smile and kind manner removed every vestige of the fear with which I had hitherto regarded him.

His teeth were even, but rather dark, and I afterwards found that this arose from his constant habit of eating liquorice, of which he always kept a supply in his waistcoat pocket.

Some chairs were brought out at his request, upon the lawn, and seating himself on one, he desired me to take another, which I did with a beating heart. He then said:

'You speak French?'

I replied that I did, and he asked me who had taught me. I informed him, and he put several questions to me about my studies, and more particularly concerning geography. He inquired the capitals of the different countries of Europe.

'What is the capital of France?'

'Paris.'

'Of Italy?'

'Rome.'

'Of Russia?'

'Petersburg now,' I replied, 'Moscow formerly.'

On my saying this, he turned abruptly round, and, fixing his piercing eyes full in my face, he demanded sternly:

'Qui l'a brûlé?'

When I saw the expression of his eye, and heard his changed voice, all my former terror of him returned, and I was unable to utter a syllable.

I had often heard the burning of Moscow talked of, and had been present at discussions as to whether the French or the

Russians were the authors of that dreadful conflagration; I therefore feared to offend him by alluding to it. He repeated the
question, and I stammered:

'I do not know, sir.'

'*Oui, oui,*' he replied, laughing violently. '*Vous savez très bien,
c'est moi qui l'a brûlé.*' [*Sic.*]

On seeing him laugh, I gained a little courage, and said:

'I believe, sir, the Russians burnt it to get rid of the
French.'

He again laughed and seemed pleased to find that I knew anything about the matter.

Shortly after his arrival, a little girl, Miss Legg, the daughter of
a friend, came to visit us at the Briars. The poor child had heard
such terrific stories of Bonaparte, that when I told her he was coming up the lawn, she clung to me in an agony of terror. Forgetting
my own former fears, I was cruel enough to run out and tell
Napoleon of the child's fright, begging him to come into the
house. He walked up to her, and, brushing up his hair with his
hand, shook his head, making horrible faces, and giving a sort
of savage howl. The little girl screamed so violently that mamma
was afraid she would go into hysterics, and took her out of the
room.

Napoleon laughed a good deal at the idea of his being such a
bugbear, and would hardly believe me when I told him that I had
stood in the same dismay of him.

I never met with anyone who bore childish liberties so well as
Napoleon. He seemed to enter into every sort of mirth or fun
with the glee of a child, and though I have often tried his patience
severely, I never knew him lose his temper or fall back upon his
rank or age.

My brothers were at this time quite children, and Napoleon
used to allow them to sit on his knee and amuse themselves by
playing with his orders, etc. More than once he has desired me to
cut them off to please them.

One day Alexander took up a pack of cards, on which was the
usual figure of the Great Mogul. The child held it up to Napoleon, saying:

'See, Bony, this is you.'

He did not understand what my brother meant by calling him

Bony. I explained that it was an abbreviation—the short for Bonaparte, but Las Cases interpreted the word literally, and said it meant a bony person.

Napoleon laughed and said, '*Je ne suis pas osseux*', which he certainly never could have been, even in his thinnest days. His hand was the fattest and prettiest in the world; his knuckles dimpled like those of a baby, his fingers tapered and beautifully formed, and his nails perfect. I have often admired its symmetry, and once told him it did not look large and strong enough to wield a sword.

Napoleon then produced from a richly embossed case the most magnificent sword I ever beheld. The sheath was composed of an entire piece of most splendidly marked tortoise-shell, thickly studded with golden bees. The handle, not unlike a fleur-de-lys in shape, was of exquisitely wrought gold. It was indeed the most costly and elegant weapon I had ever seen.

I requested Napoleon to allow me to examine it more closely; and then a circumstance which had occurred in the morning, in which I had been much piqued at the Emperor's conduct, flashed across me. The temptation was irresistible, and I determined to punish him for what he had done. I drew the blade out quickly from the scabbard, and began to flourish it over his head, making passes at him, the Emperor retreating, until at last I fairly pinned him up in the corner; I kept telling him all the time that he had better say his prayers, for I was going to kill him. My exulting cries at last brought my sister to Napoleon's assistance. She scolded me violently, and said she would inform my father if I did not instantly desist; but I only laughed at her, and maintained my post, keeping the Emperor at bay until my arm dropped from sheer exhaustion.

When I resigned my sword, Napoleon took hold of my ear, which had been bored only the day before, and pinched it, giving me great pain. I called out, and he then took hold of my nose, which he pulled heartily, but quite in fun; his good humour never left him during the whole scene.

The Emperor usually played cards every evening. He said: 'Now we will go down to the cottage and play whist.'

We all walked down together. Our little whist table was soon formed, but the cards did not run smoothly, and Napoleon desired Las Cases to seat himself at a side table and deal them until they dealt easily.

While the grand chamberlain was thus employed, Napoleon asked me what my *robe de bal* was to be. I must mention that on my father's refusal to allow me to go to the ball, which was to be given by Sir George Cockburn, I had implored the Emperor's intercession for me. He most kindly asked my father to let me go, and his request, of course, was instantly acceded to. I now ran upstairs to bring my dress down to him. It was the first ball dress I had ever possessed, and I was not a little proud of it. He said it was very pretty; and the cards being now ready I placed it on the sofa and sat down to play.

Napoleon and my sister were partners, and Las Cases fell to my lot. We had always hitherto played for sugar-plums, but tonight Napoleon said:

'Mademoiselle Betsee, I will bet you a napoleon on the game.'

I had had a pagoda presented to me, which made up the sum of all my worldly riches, and I said I would bet him that against his napoleon. The Emperor agreed to this, and we commenced playing.

He seemed determined to terminate this day of *espièglerie* as he had begun it. Peeping under his cards as they were dealt to him, he endeavoured whenever he got an important one, to draw off my attention, and then slyly held it up for my sister to see. I soon discovered this, and calling him to order, told him he was cheating, and that if he continued to do so I would not play. At last he revoked intentionally, and at the end of the game tried to mix the cards together to prevent his being discovered, but I started up, and, seizing hold of his hands, I pointed out to him and the others what he had done.

He laughed until the tears ran out of his eyes, and declared he had played fair, but that I had cheated, and should pay him the pagoda; and when I persisted that he had revoked, he said I was *méchante* and a cheat; and catching up my ball dress from off the sofa, he ran out of the room with it, and up to the pavilion, leaving me in terror lest he should crush and spoil all my pretty roses.

I instantly set off in chase of him, but he was too quick, and darting through the marquee, he reached the inner room and locked himself in. I then commenced a series of the most pathetic

remonstrances and entreaties, both in English and French, to persuade him to restore me my frock, but in vain; he was inexorable,
and I had the mortification of hearing him laugh at what I thought
the most touching of my appeals. I was obliged to return without
it. He afterwards sent down word he intended to keep it, and that
I might make up my mind not to go to the ball. I lay awake half
the night, and at last cried myself to sleep.

FIRST INTERVIEW WITH HUDSON LOWE

*On 10th December, 1815, Napoleon moved into Longwood, his last
residence, where he was to live exactly as at the Tuileries. The same
etiquette, the same slavery. General Count Bertrand performed, without
a smile, the stately duties of grand marshal of the palace. He insisted that
the handful of exiled French, his companions, should address him as
'Monsieur le grand maréchal', etc. The Count de Montholon was His
Majesty's aide-de-camp, his finance minister, his minister of external
and internal affairs, and his prefect of the palace (for he had the same
functions as Bausset of old). General Gourgaud remained the Emperor's
chief orderly officer. He deputised for the Master of Horse and was in
charge of the stables (men, horses, carriages). Count Las Cases filled
the double office of chamberlain and principal secretary.*

*As for the women, Countess Bertrand and Countess de Montholon,
they were rivals for the limelight. The haughty Albine de Montholon
(twice repudiated for adultery before her union with Montholon) acted
the Montespan and was to give Napoleon a daughter. The husband was
complaisant. He was to get several million francs by it.*

The domestic staff also had its hierarchy and etiquette.

*Thus Napoleon was himself again, and had adopted an attitude irre-
concilable with his situation. To the allied powers, who had spared his
life while making it impossible for him to do any further harm, he was
once more General Buonaparte. He on his side expected the world to
salute him as emperor and his keepers to call him 'Imperial and Royal
Majesty'. The English smiled. The struggle was to continue till his
last hour.*

*But if he could not get his own way, he could at any rate make their
lives a burden and blacken their characters. The chief target of this
campaign was to be the new Governor, Sir Hudson Lowe. In the
following scene he presents himself—and is treated—as an unknown
quantity.*

But—'*You have no idea,*' wrote Colonel Bingham of the 53rd (*who had made the voyage with Napoleon, and seen his rudeness to Cockburn afterwards*), '*of the dirty little intrigues of himself and his set: if Sir H. Lowe has firmness enough not to give way to them, he will in a short time treat him in the same manner*' (*as he had done Cockburn*).

Had my first interview with him at four o'clock in the afternoon; was accompanied to his house by Rear-Admiral Sir George Cockburn. General Bertrand received us in his dining-room, serving as an ante-chamber, and instantly afterwards ushered me into an inner room, where I found him standing, having his hat in his hand.

Not addressing me when I came in, but apparently waiting for me to speak to him, I broke silence by saying:

'I am come, sir, to present my respects to you.'

'You speak French, sir, I perceive; but you also speak Italian. You once commanded a regiment of Corsicans.'

I replied, the language was alike to me.

'We will speak, then, in Italian,' he said; and immediately commenced in that language a conversation which lasted about half an hour, the purport of which was principally as follows: He first asked me where I had served—how I liked the Corsicans—

'They carry the stiletto: are they not a bad people?' looking at me very significantly for an answer. My reply was:

'They do not carry the stiletto, having abandoned that custom in our service; they always conducted themselves with propriety. I was very well satisfied with them.'

He asked me if I had not been in Egypt with them; and, on my replying in the affirmative, entered into a long discussion respecting that country.

'Menou was a weak man. If Kléber had been there, you would have been all made prisoners.'

He then passed in review all our operations in that country, with which he seemed as well acquainted as if he had himself been there; blamed Abercromby for not landing sooner, or, if he could not land sooner, not proceeding to another point; Moore, with his 6,000 men, should have been all destroyed; they had shown themselves good generals, however, and merited success from their boldness and valour.

The subject of Egypt was again resumed. It was the most

important geographical point in the world, and had always been considered so. He had reconnoitred the line of the canal across the Isthmus of Suez; he had calculated the expense of it at ten or twelve millions of livres—'Half a million sterling,' he said, to make me understand more clearly the probable cost of it: that, a powerful colony being established there, it would have been impossible for us to have preserved our empire in India. He then fell again to rallying at Menou; and concluded with the following remark, which he pronounced in a very serious manner:

'In war, the game is always with him who commits the fewest faults.'

It struck me as if he was reproaching himself with some great error.

He then asked me some further questions regarding myself—whether I was not married?—if I had not become so shortly before my leaving England?—how I liked St Helena?

I replied, I had not been a sufficient time here to form a judgment upon it.

'Ah! you have your wife; you are well off!'

After a short pause he asked how many years I had been in the service.

'Twenty-eight,' I replied.

'I am, therefore, an older soldier than you,' he said.

'Of which history will make mention in a very different manner,' I answered.

He smiled, but said nothing. I proceeded immediately afterwards to take my leave, asking permission to present to him two officers of my suite, Lieutenant-Colonel Sir Thomas Reade and Major Gorrequer, who had accompanied me, to which he assented. He spoke little to them, but, as we were going away, turned to me and said:

'You are settling your affairs with the Catholics, I see; it is well done. The Pope has made concessions, and smoothed the way to you.'

Thus the interview terminated.

YOU MAKE ME SMILE, SIR!

On 18th August, 1816, Lowe had a fifth and last interview with Napoleon. In between, the situation had been getting worse. All the *attentions of the Governor and the English government had been thrown away. After Napoleon's death, when Montholon and an English officer of Lowe's staff met again in France, Montholon was to say: 'My dear fellow, an angel from heaven could not have pleased us as Governor of St Helena.'*

Such was the policy of the exile. In the days of his grandeur he had allowed only 15,000 francs a year for the total maintenance of the Pope and cardinals he had under lock and key. The English were spending millions on him, serving him with staggering quantities of victuals, choice wines, champagne . . . 'Seventeen bottles of wine, eighty-eight pounds of meat and nine chickens a day,' noted Gourgaud; and he said to Napoleon: 'It's giving them a handle against us!'

But the victor of Austerlitz did not intend to be fair. He would embark on interminable polemics over a saucepan that needed resilvering, and go on and on about the iniquities of the English Cabinet, which was trying to poison him with verdigris. His companions took pattern, and made it their business to insult the English.

And the upshot was that after the scene he describes here (a report confirmed by Admiral Malcolm in every detail), Sir Hudson Lowe was never to see Napoleon again.

Having called at Longwood in company with Sir Pulteney Malcolm, we found General Bonaparte was walking in his garden. He went off immediately as he saw us; but having inquired for Count Montholon, and sent a message by him to say we were there, Bonaparte returned to the garden, and the Admiral and myself joined him.

He spoke solely to the Admiral, in which I made no attempt to interrupt him, but, profiting by the first interval of silence, I commenced and addressed him as follows: That I was sorry to be under the necessity of saying anything which tended to incommode him, but I was placed under such peculiar circumstances, from the conduct towards me of General Bertrand, that it became a matter of indispensable necessity I should make known the details of it to him.

[*Sir Hudson Lowe related to him what had occurred, and described Count Bertrand's rude demeanour and offensive expressions. He then observed to Napoleon:*]

'It was obvious, after this, I could have no further communication with General Bertrand, and I thought it proper to call and

acquaint him of it; that, whatever might have been General
Bertrand's personal feelings towards me, I called upon him by the
desire of the person whom he acknowledged as his Emperor to
speak of *his* business; that it was a failure of respect to him as well
as to me; that I wished in consequence to learn with whom it was
his desire I should in future communicate on questions of such
nature in regard to his affairs.'

General Bonaparte made no reply for so considerable a space
of time that I thought he did not mean to speak at all; but finally,
in a hollow, angry tone of voice, commenced a string of remarks
to the following purport, addressing himself entirely to the
Admiral:

'General Bertrand is a man who has commanded armies, and *he*
treats him as if he were a corporal; he is a man well known
throughout Europe, and *he* had no right to insult him. *He* treats
us all as if we were deserters from the Royal Corsican or some
Italian regiment; he has insulted Marshal Bertrand and he deserved what the marshal said to him.'

I repeated what I had said in a former conversation—that
General Bertrand had first insulted me; that in the conversation
which had passed nothing could be more temperate and moderate
than my language to him, as could be testified by my military
secretary, who was present at the interview; that I had said nothing which, in tone or manner, could justify the reply he gave
to me.

He recommenced his reproaches of my having written insulting
letters to General Bertrand, and provoked him to say to me what
he did.

I again referred to his having first written an insulting one to
me; that he had said I rendered his (Bonaparte's) situation
affreuse; had accused me of *abus de pouvoir et injustice*. I then
added:

'I am a subject of a free government. Every kind of despotism
and tyranny I hold in abhorrence, and I will repel every accusation
of my conduct in this respect as a calumny against him whom it
is impossible to attack with the arms of truth.'

He stopped a little on my making this observation, but soon
resumed, addressing himself to the Admiral, and with language
more bitter than before.

'There are two kinds of people,' he said, 'employed by Govern-

ments—those whom they honour, and those whom they dishonour; he is one of the latter; the situation they have given him
is that of an executioner.'

I answered:

'I perfectly understand this kind of manœuvre—endeavour to
brand with infamy, if one cannot attack with other arms. I am
perfectly indifferent to all this. I did not seek my present employment; but, it being offered to me, I considered it a sacred duty to
accept it.'

'Then,' said he, 'if the order were given you to assassinate me,
you would accept it.'

'No, sir.'

He again proceeded (to the Admiral), and said I had rendered
his situation forty times worse than it was before my arrival; that,
though he had some disputes with Sir George Cockburn, he
always treated him in a different manner; that they were content
with each other, but that I did not know how to conduct myself
towards men of honour; that I had put General Bertrand under
arrest in his own house; and had taken away from him the permission to give passes to Longwood.

The Admiral said it was Sir George Cockburn who had done
this. Bonaparte replied:

'No, sir; *he* told you so, but it is not true.'

The Admiral again told him it was not me, but Sir George
Cockburn had told him so.

Bonaparte then said he could not even write a *billet de galanterie*
to my Lady Malcolm without my seeing it; that he could not
now have a woman come to see him without my permission; and
that he could not see the Lieutenant-Colonel and the officers of
the 53rd.

I interrupted him here by saying he had refused to see the
Lieutenant-Colonel and the officers of the 66th Regiment.

If they wanted to see him, he answered, why did they not apply
to the 'Grand Maréchal'?

I had mentioned it to General Bertrand, I observed.

'But the Lieutenant-Colonel ought to have spoken to him, and
not to you.'

He again broke out into invectives on my mode of treatment;
said I had no feeling; that the soldiers of the 53rd looked upon
him with compassion, and wept when they passed him.

Continuing, he said to the Admiral:

'He kept back a book which had been sent me by a Member of Parliament, and then boasted of it.'

'How boasted of it?' I exclaimed, struck with the falsehood of the assertion.

'Yes, sir' (interrupting me), 'you boasted of it to the Governor of the island of Bourbon; he told me so.'

[*Colonel Keating, who is alluded to, 'denied in the strongest terms that he had made any such communication to Napoleon'.*]

He again addressed himself to the Admiral; accused me of having published the contents of a letter he had received from his mother.

The Admiral defended me; said he knew I never published the contents of any private letters received from his family. I replied, it was not me that had done so; it must have been his own people that did it; that everything was misrepresented to him.

'You have *bad people about you*, sir,' I said.

The Admiral shortly afterwards repeated a similar remark, saying:

'You have bad people around you.'

He appeared to me struck at both our observations in this respect, and made no attempt to reply, but went on again in his strain of invective, general and personal; told me, as he had done once before:

'You are a Lieutenant-General, but you perform your duty as if you were a sentinel; there is no dealing with you; you are a most intractable man. If you are afraid that I should escape, why do you not bind me?'

I answered, I merely executed my instructions; that, if my conduct was disapproved of, I might be readily removed.

'Your instructions are the same as Sir George Cockburn's,' he replied, 'he told me they were the same.'

He said he was to be treated as a prisoner of war; that the Ministers had no right to treat him in any other way than as prescribed by the Act of Parliament; that the nation was disposed to treat him well, but Ministers acted otherwise; accused me of being a mere instrument of the blind hatred of Lord Bathurst. I remarked:

'Lord Bathurst, sir, does not know what blind hatred is.'

He talked about our calling him General; said he was 'Empereur'; that when England and Europe should be no more, and no such name known as Lord Bathurst, he would still be Emperor. He told me he always went out of the way to avoid me, and had twice pretended to be in the bath that he might not see me. He attacked me about the note which had been sent back to Count Bertrand, saying:

'You had no right to put him under arrest; you never commanded armies; you were nothing but the scribe of an Etat-Major. I had imagined I should be well among the English, but you are not an Englishman.'

He was continuing in this strain, when I interrupted him with saying:

'You make me smile, sir.'

'How smile, sir?' he replied, at the same time turning round with surprise at the remark, and, looking at me, added:

'I say what I think.'

'Yes, sir,' I answered, with a tone indicative of the sentiment I felt, and looking at him, 'you force me to *smile*; your misconception of my character and the rudeness of your manners excite my *pity*. I wish you good day.'

And I left him (evidently a good deal embarrassed) without any other salutation.

The Admiral quitted him immediately afterwards with a salute of the hat.

AUSTRIAN COMMENTARY

Each of the powers was kept informed of Napoleon's life and doings on St Helena by a resident Commissioner. Here we quote from the reports Sturmer dispatched to Metternich. (Those of the other Commissioners come to much the same.)

It should be said that Napoleon's 'enclosure', in which he could move unaccompanied by a British officer, was about twelve miles round. Further, he was to tell Gourgaud that 'if he had the whole island for exercise he would not go out'.

I shall now speak of Bonaparte himself.

His mental state is rather unequal. Usually he is out of temper, but his body shows no effect of these vexations of mind. He is still in good health and threatens to live long. As yet no one can be sure whether he is resigned to his fate or is nursing hopes.

C C

He is said to have been reckoning a great deal on the opposition, in England, to take him from St Helena. And it is a fact that he continues to protest at his detention, and has himself treated as emperor at Longwood. Bertrand, Montholon, Las Cases, Gourgaud and his whole suite pay him, as of old, the greatest honours.

He receives foreigners who ask to see him, but he gives neither meals nor soirées and never leaves his enclosure. He feels the presence of an English officer, who has to accompany him, as a burden and affliction. For the same reason, he avoids the posts and sentries on his outings.

He gets up at noon, breakfasts, occupies himself indoors until three o'clock, at four admits persons who are announced, often goes out walking or in a carriage and six, rarely on horseback, dines at eight, remains at table only three-quarters of an hour, plays his game of *reversis*, goes to bed, and repeatedly gets up to work in the night.

He is writing his history with the aid of the *Moniteur*, and is also learning English.

His conversation would be interesting if one had a chance to hear it, for with management he lets himself go, but he has no regular society but his French and seldom confides in the English.

General Lowe treats him with all possible consideration and even lends himself, in a way, to his craze for playing the emperor. In spite of this, he does not like him and has seen him only two or three times.

He seems to have a slight preference for Admiral Malcolm, who acts the good fellow to perfection and will not swerve, any more than the other, from the course laid down for him.

13th December, 1816.—Bonaparte continues to enjoy perfect health. He eats a great deal, is getting visibly fatter, and takes no exercise. He has given up riding or driving out, and one has only an occasional glimpse of him, strolling in front of his house.

Bonaparte seldom talks of the Moscow campaign. One day he said to Admiral Cockburn:

'For my glory, I ought to have died at Moscow. My generals would be getting the blame for the calamities of that war.'

When his doctor, O'Meara, told him that Marshal Ney had been shot, Bonaparte replied:

'Shot? His trial was before the house of peers. I wonder he was not beheaded.'

Then, after a moment's reflection:

'He was brave, but he betrayed me at Fontainebleau.'

31st December, 1816.—Bonaparte has been suffering from attacks of dizziness, along with a touch of fever. On the doctor ordering eau de Cologne mixed with fresh water to be poured over his head, the servants went about it so clumsily that he got his eyes filled. This caused him such agony that he was yelling murder and assassination, raging, storming, swearing and lashing out at all who had come near him. The result was an inflammation of the eyes, from which he was in pain for several days.

His doctor, O'Meara, told me he had implored him to change his way of life, and either take more exercise or not eat so much.

28th January, 1817.—Bonaparte is well. He lives more retired than ever and is now almost invisible. Report has it that he is beginning to treat his French with more kindliness and affection. He sees them oftener and is trying to increase their attachment to him. The inference drawn is that Las Cases was a malcontent and that Bonaparte fears to be completely deserted. It is now Mme de Montholon who writes to his dictation, and takes the place of a secretary. He is still engaged on the history of his life, which he is narrating in the third person, like Caesar.

ILL OR NOT ILL?

It was another item of Napoleon's policy to find fault with the climate, and ascribe to it a variety of diseases from which he declared himself to be suffering. The evidence of the English and French who were breathing the same air as Napoleon and survived to publish their memoirs, the works of qualified doctors, everything goes to show that the climate of St Helena was (and remains) good, agreeable, almost Mediterranean.

Napoleon ordered Pauline to be told: 'He is dying untended on this hideous rock. His last agonies are frightful.' With much of the same kind, for other correspondents.

In reality, from 1815 to 1821, he commanded as many doctors as he could wish (O'Meara, Baxter, Verling, Stokoe, Arnott, etc., and Antommarchi). But, once again, it was his policy to melt all hearts to his situation, and for pity's sake (he had come to that!) get himself removed to Europe.

On the question of Napoleon's health throughout this period, we may believe Saint-Denis, who was with him, so to speak, day and night.

The Emperor had long since announced, and frequently used to say, that death would be coming sooner than we thought to put an end to his sufferings; and neither he nor anyone else gave any credit to these prophetic words, which, however, were to be fulfilled a few years later.

What led us to dismiss the idea was that his physique in no way suggested a sick man. He had not lost weight, he had a good appetite and was often in good spirits.

The only notable thing that ever ailed him at St Helena was a kind of catarrh, and he had been subject to it before 1814. He caught cold very easily, and the attacks were usually most violent. When he had a cold, it was astonishing the quantity of humour he discharged from his nose and mouth.

Besides this ailment, which was merely transitory, he had another amounting only to discomfort, which he talked of feeling in his body and which now and then gave him a dull pain; he thought his liver must be affected.

We took it that he was claiming to be ill so as to impose on the Governor and the English ministry, and induce the latter to give orders for him to be removed to another country or set at liberty.

NAPOLEON AT WORK

His great concern was : 'What will history say? What will posterity say?' He had misgivings and fears.

So he resolved to compose his legend. Hence the 'Memorial', designed to present him, not as he had been (the 'Memorial', from a historical point of view, is a tissue of humbug), but as he wished coming generations to see him. He set Las Cases, Gourgaud, Montholon, Bertrand to work, and had them all taking dictation. Not only of his history, but of pamphlets as well, for he remained an inveterate pamphleteer, and the expostulations of the company could not stop him.

His generals and chamberlains being too few to cover the ground, he made secretaries of his valets: Marchand, Saint-Denis, etc. It was no sinecure, as Saint-Denis rapidly found out. But thanks to him, we have a view of Napoleon in his study at St Helena.

Napoleon wrote fast enough, but he had not patience to write. The first few lines were tolerably well written, but those that followed would be illegible. One had to be very familiar with the shape of his letters, his notations and the way they were joined in order to make him out. And even the cleverest could only divine these hieroglyphs after long pondering.

To read Napoleon's hand-writing one needed sharp eyes and a good memory, because, for one thing, he sometimes wrote very small, and besides that, some words were spelt differently in different places.

What made the difficulty still worse was that the Emperor usually wrote in a very curtailed way, often leaving out the letters required, or putting in some that were uncalled for.

Indeed, he was nearly always baffled himself. Many a time, when I came and asked what he had written here, the reply would be:

'Why, can't you read, then, fathead?'

'No, sire.'

'But it's as plain as print! Look at it!'

'Sire, I've been looking with all my eyes, and I still don't know what Your Majesty has put here.'

Napoleon would look as well. But he would find himself no wiser than I. After vainly puzzling for a minute or two, he would say:

'Sit down there and write.'

And he would begin dictating a few sentences or a paragraph to replace the part that had illegible words in it.

He had finally given up ink and pens in favour of pencils. He had a good supply ready on his desk, which enabled him to write faster and saved the time spent in dipping into the ink. If he imagined that what he had to write would take more pencils than he possessed, he would keep someone by him to sharpen them as they wore down, and even so he often found himself writing with the wood.

The Emperor was for ever correcting all that had been done. He was for ever telling one to delete words, sentences, entire lines, even a whole quarter of a page. One was always having to add, alter, strike out. There would be corrections on corrections, even in the fair copies, which he regarded as work finished and complete. He would say on this point:

'Well, what of it? Rousseau made seven drafts of his *Nouvelle Héloise*!'

He worked only by fits and starts. He did not like fagging away for months on one subject. His imagination prompted him to keep changing, and for that reason all he undertook was apt to stay in the rough. His ideas, so to speak, were only flung down on paper, and in order to complete and develop them, he was awaiting materials.

Napoleon was in such a hurry when something was to be done that he gave one no chance to do it properly.

READING

He wrote, and he read. . . . Often he would wake a valet up in the night to read to him. In society, with his court, the evening had probably been spent in reading aloud. Every day, Gourgaud's journal has notes like this: 'In the evening, we are reading Cinna. Ah, how fine it is! . . . We are reading Horace. A noble work. Those are men!'

(It will be seen that Napoleon's taste was static. In after-years Montholon was to tell Lord Holland that they got rather too much of the same thing—and also that—'Napoleon slept himself when read to, but was very observant and jealous if others slept while he read. He watched his audience vigilantly, and "Mme Montholon, vous dormez" was a frequent ejaculation in the course of reading.')*

After the reading he would criticise or admire. But who (besides Corneille) were his chosen authors? We are told by Saint-Denis.

Napoleon was prodigiously fond of reading. He would often take up the Greek and Roman historians, especially Plutarch. No one was so well able to appreciate that excellent writer. He often glanced through Rollin. The history of the Middle Ages, modern history and special histories engaged him only in passing. He had no sacred books but the Bible. He was fond of re-reading chapters that had been read to him on the ruins of the ancient cities of Syria. They recalled to him the manners of the inhabitants of those regions and the patriarchal life of the desert. It was, he said, a faithful picture of what he had seen with his own eyes.

Whenever he read Homer, it was with fresh admiration. No one, to his mind, had excelled this author in the sense of true beauty, true grandeur. So he frequently took him up, and re-read him from the first page to the last. The drama had great charm for the Emperor. The Corneilles, the Racines, the Voltaires often had an act or two of their plays read aloud. Corneille, in spite of his faults, was preferred to the others. He always chose what was on a level with himself, Napoleon.

Now and then he would ask for a comedy, one he had seen performed, and occasionally some piece of poetry.

He also enjoyed reading some passages of Voltaire's *Essai sur les moeurs et l'esprit des nations*, and some articles from the *Dictionnaire philosophique*, by the same author.

Novels served to relax his mind and relieve the gravity of his usual occupations. *Gil Blas*, *Don Quixote* and a few others were favourites. Those of Mmes de Staël, Genlis, Cottin, Souza, etc., he would sometimes pick up again.

He had almost constantly before his eyes all works dealing with the military art and the campaigns of the great captains. One author, Polybius, whom he had long wished for, he received only towards the end, and at that time he had almost given up work.

If he opened a scientific book, it was by chance. Works of that kind were only for reference.

When the Emperor had his hands on a book that interested him, he did not let go till he had a thorough knowledge of it. 'He read with his thumb,' in the Abbé de Pradt's expression. And yet nothing of the contents escaped him, and he had mastered it so well that, long afterwards, he could analyse it in great detail, and even quote, practically word for word, the passages he had found most striking.

When he heard of something unfamiliar or unknown to him, he immediately sent for all the books in his library which might refer to it. He did not confine himself to a superficial knowledge, but went as deep into the subject as he could. That was his way of gaining enlightenment and furnishing his mind.

When boxes of books came in, the Emperor gave himself no rest till they had been opened. The volumes were handed to him in turn. He looked through them cursorily, and placed on a table those he guessed to have something in them. The others he tossed aside one by one in a heap, to be examined later. The books he had picked out were taken into his closet and laid on the table by his sofa. A few mornings would be agreeably occupied by the new publications.

IN THE STEPS OF LE NÔTRE

The faithful were fewer now. Las Cases had gone first; the details are enigmatic, but there is no doubt Montholon and Gourgaud had been persecuting him. After that, Gourgaud challenged Montholon to a duel; Napoleon put a stop to it, and he left in a huff.

O'Meara was gone too. He was a British officer, lately surgeon of the Bellerophon, whom Napoleon had suborned and who turned out to be smuggling his correspondence.

However, one day a party of travellers arrived from Europe, sent to the exile by his mother, his uncle Fesch and his sister Pauline. These were compatriots: Antommarchi (a doctor) and Buonavita and Vignali (priests).

Antommarchi remonstrated with Napoleon on his choice of life; nowadays he would not go out, would not dress or shave, and spent his time behind closed shutters, when he could have been making excursions of 18 or 20 kilometres. No wonder he was constipated!

The newcomer succeeded in rousing him, and induced him to take up gardening as an occupation. Soon he was mad for it, and had set everyone to work, including Chinese servants supplied by the English.

Here again we quote Saint-Denis, as the most faithful and human source.

Never had Longwood been so sprightly as in this gardening period. The activity seemed to have brought us to life again. Before that we had been in a kind of stupor.

Napoleon had never felt better since he came to St Helena. And so he was always in a good humour.

He used to get up about five or half-past, chafing till the sentries were withdrawn and he could go into the garden. He would have his windows opened and go down to walk in the grove, chatting with the valet on duty.

The moment the sun appeared on the horizon, he would have everyone called. When I was not on duty, he would summon me by throwing a few clods of earth at the window-panes of my room, which looked out on the grove.

'Ali! Ali! wake up!'

Then, singing:

> *Your sleep will be more tranquil*
> *Once you are back at home!*

And so on.

Meanwhile I would open the window.

'Come along, lazy-bones!' he would cry on perceiving me; 'don't you see the sun?'

Another time, he would call more simply:

'Ali! Ali! Oh! Oh! Allah! it's getting light.'

Marchand had his turn as well, but less frequently, because the Emperor was not so often on that side of the house.

'Marchand! Mam'zelle Marchand!' he would call out to him, 'it's getting light, get up!'

When Marchand came out, he would look at him, and ask banteringly:

'Have you had your sleep out? Were you roused from your slumbers? You'll be ill all day with getting up so early.'

Then in his ordinary tone:

'Come along, take this pick, this spade, make me a hole for such and such a tree.'

While Marchand was digging the hole, Napoleon would walk on, and seeing a tree that had just been planted:

'Marchand, bring some water here for this tree.'

And a moment later:

'Go and get my foot-rule, my measuring-stick.'

Coming up to another man:

'Go and tell Archambault to bring some manure, and tell the Chinese to cut some turf. There's none left.'

Etc., etc.

Then passing on to me, as I was shovelling earth into a wheel-barrow:

'What, you've not done moving that earth!'

'No, sire, and yet I've not been playing.'

'By the way, rascal, have you done the chapter I gave you yesterday?'

'No, sire.'

'You preferred to sleep, eh?'

'But, sire, Your Majesty only gave it me last night.'

'Try to finish it today. I have another for you.'

The Emperor would go on to Pierron, who was laying a piece of turf.

'Why, haven't you got that wall done? . . . Have you plenty of turf for it?'

'Yes, sire.'

Then, coming back my way:

'What time did I wake you up last night?'

'It was two o'clock, sire.'

A little later:

'Is Montholon awake?'

'I don't know, sire.'

'Go and see. But mind you don't wake him. Let him sleep.'

Then, going up to Noverraz, who was digging:

'Come now, *hard*! (*With emphasis.*) Why, lazy-bones, what have you been doing all morning?'

'Yesterday Your Majesty said I was to get the bath tarred. As there were no volunteers, I've done it myself . . .'

'Sire, here is M. de Montholon.'

'Ah! good day, Montholon.'

M. de Montholon, with a respectful bow:

'How is Your Majesty?'

'Pretty well. Did they disturb you just now?'

'No, sire, I was getting up.'

'Has Your Excellency any news for me? They say a vessel has been sighted.'

'I don't know, sire. I haven't spoken to anyone yet.'

'Take my field-glass. Go and have a look.'

M. de Montholon would return in a few minutes and tell the Emperor what he had seen.

Well, they would fall into conversation. Napoleon would be strolling about, now and then coming back to his workmen. That was how he passed the time till breakfast.

When he began to feel hungry, he would ask the time. And if he heard it was nearly ten o'clock, he would order his meal to be served. Very often it would be served in his own room. Then the Emperor would leave his workmen and sit down to table. Those who had to wait on him dropped their tools, and went off to wash their faces and hands and attend on him. M. de Montholon, as I have already said, ate with the Emperor, and if the grand marshal were there, he would be invited.

[*The Bertrands lived in a separate house.*]

After breakfast the Emperor would return to his workmen, and stay with them till noon—or only till eleven, if the sun were too powerful. He would say on leaving them:

'Go and have your meal. That's enough for today. It's too hot.'

The outcome of the gardens was, for the Emperor, to have given his people something to do, to have amused himself, to have walks around him and near his house where he could feel at home, and to have shut out the guards, who, before that, were under his windows.

As for produce, there was none, except now and then a small salad on his table, a few beans or peas and a bunch of small radishes. Peaches were the only fruit, and it was not Napoleon who ate them.

When he saw something from the garden on his table, he would say:

'Well, there! we haven't lost all our labour. Our gardens are feeding us.'

Alack! we would reply inwardly, if we had nothing to eat but what comes out of the garden, our bodies would do for lanterns.

We could not help smiling.

'What! are you laughing, rascal?' said Napoleon, fixing one of his attendants.

And he would be laughing himself.

THE LAST CAMPAIGN

Of the two ladies of Napoleon's 'court' at St Helena, the Countess de Montholon had long been his mistress. But one morning she went off, loaded with bills of exchange, bonds, jewels, etc.

A few months later Napoleon conceived a passion for Countess Bertrand. This fancy rose to an extraordinary pitch as he drew near his end. Now, he could think of nothing better than to enlist Dr Antommarchi as intermediary between himself and la grande Fanny, as Mme Bertrand was called.

Antommarchi refused. Napoleon then insisted that he should give up attending the countess, who was unwell. The doctor again refused. Napoleon's rage knew no bounds. He shrieked that Antommarchi was the countess's lover, hence his refusal, etc. . . .

Our authority for this act of the drama is none other than the husband, General Count Bertrand—a thick-witted sapper, who noted all the sayings and doings of his master with unexampled piety, and, in spite of everything, persisted in his idolatry.

At nine o'clock he dismisses the doctor. At ten o'clock he sends for him. He is called for at Mme Bertrand's.

He waits on the Emperor, who does not receive him, but, at two in the morning, sends for him and makes a scene with him for two hours:

'The grand marshal should appoint him head valet to his wife. Antommarchi is a great rogue, a great gallows-bird, a great scoundrel. He has a valet's *cazzo*.'

Then he summons Noverraz to bring him a cup of tea, and repeats in French all that he has been saying in Italian about the grand . . .

He tells the doctor that he can take himself off with Buonavita. He replies that it shall be just as the Emperor pleases, that he has no cause to reproach himself. Napoleon caresses him and claps him on the shoulder.

At midday the doctor calls on Mme Bertrand. He is quite out of countenance. He warns the grand marshal to expect a scene. The grand marshal waits on Napoleon at the usual time. He is asleep. The grand marshal returns at three o'clock. He has removed to his drawing-room and is still asleep.

The grand marshal laughs heartily all evening, at: 'He has a valet's *cazzo*.'

This is irresistibly droll. Only truths can wound. Mme Bertrand thinks nothing of Napoleon's abuse.

29th January.—After waiting some time, the grand marshal is admitted to Napoleon.

'Antommarchi is a dunce. He's not to be trusted. He repeats what he's heard. That's against the first law of his profession. He works Mme Bertrand up. If I had asked him: "How is *le grand comte?*", he would pass that on, and call him *le grand coglione* or something quite different.'

9th April.—At half-past seven Antommarchi waits on Napoleon, who flies into a great rage with him.

'He should be here by six in the morning. He spends his whole time with Mme Bertrand.'

Napoleon sends for the grand marshal, who arrives at a quarter to eight. He repeats what he has been saying. He adds that the doctor thinks of nothing but his sluts.

'Well, let him spend his whole time with his sluts! Let him f—— them fore and aft and by the mouth and ears! But kindly relieve me of that man, who is a blockhead, an ignoramus, a fop, a sneak. Kindly get Arnott to attend me in future. Arrange it with Montholon. I won't see Antommarchi again.'

This scene takes place before Marchand and Antommarchi.

Napoleon repeats five or six times that Mme Bertrand is a slut.

21st April.—Napoleon once told Antommarchi that the grand marshal ought to have prostituted his wife. That he owed it to him to persuade her, if she was perverse about it. That, however, there was this to be said for the grand marshal, he always approved the Emperor, never complained. . . . He wanted Antommarchi to act as Mercury and induce Mme Bertrand to become his mistress.

'But how can I do that? What would the grand marshal think of me?'

The doctor arrived here full of esteem and respect for the grand marshal and his wife. The very next day he was being told that the grand marshal was a numskull, that he was of no use to the Emperor, that he had come here not from attachment but to avoid the fate of Labédoyère and Ney. That to be sure his wife had rather a pretty figure and was pleasing, but that she was an abandoned woman who went into the ditches with all the English officers passing her house. That she was the vilest of women.

Antommarchi was stupefied by all he heard. He could not form a high idea of Napoleon's morals.

26th April.—Napoleon says to Montholon:

'I'm vexed with her (Mme Bertrand) for not becoming my mistress. And I mean to teach her a lesson. If you had been her lover, I should have treated you as a corsair, instead of heaping gifts on you as I do. . . . As for Antommarchi, I shall never forgive him for attending a woman who had refused to be my mistress, and encouraging her in it.'

THIS WAS THE GREAT NAPOLEON: PITIFUL, HUMBLE

After the brighter period in which he not only took up gardening but started riding again, Napoleon had become a sick man in earnest. And the end was now very near. This was the 3rd of May, 1821. He had only two days left; and thanks to Bertrand, we can follow them hour by hour.

The other witnesses were to cook up equally stagy and mendacious descriptions of these last days. Bertrand simply jotted down everything he had managed to see and hear.

A few days earlier Napoleon had drawn up his will and the codicils attached to it. Antommarchi had been supplemented by an English physician, Arnott. (It was Arnott who finally diagnosed cancer of the stomach.) Vignali was making ready to pray, before an altar on which were sacred vessels mentioned in the will, and one day to be pledged at the Parisian pawn-office by the 'faithful'.

Napoleon lay down on his right side, which he had rarely done since his illness, nearly always lying on his left side, with his face to the wall. In this position the slanting light from the casement showed me a profile thinner and more wasted than I had yet seen it.

His deafness had increased, since yesterday, to an extraordinary degree. One had to speak very loud, and he was yelling himself, which was something new to me, though he had always in my experience, or at least for many years, been rather hard of hearing.

The doctors have come in. They insist—it was five o'clock—on Napoleon's taking an enema.

'Well, I'll take it this evening. Marchand, get it ready.'

Marchand brings the syringe.

'But I can't take it before these gentlemen.'

The grand marshal leads Dr Arnott away. Antommarchi stays behind, with Montholon and Marchand. Napoleon places himself on the syringe. His head swims. He falls on his bed. They propose to give the enema.

'Do you take me for a *coglione*, for a woman?'

They insist . . .

About two o'clock the grand marshal being in front of him, he had asked Montholon:

'Do you know whether Bertrand signed the codicils?'

'Yes, sire.'

He could not see the grand marshal, though he was staring at him.

In the morning he had asked twenty times whether he might have some coffee.

'No, sire.'

'Will the doctors let me have a spoonful?'

'No, sire, not just yet. The stomach is too much inflamed. You might vomit a little sooner.'

He has vomited perhaps eight or nine times during the day.

How many thoughts on so great a change! Tears came into my eyes as I watched this man, who was so terrible, who gave his commands so proudly, so absolutely, pleading for a spoonful of coffee, begging leave and obeying like a child, asking again and being refused, harking back and never succeeding, never resenting it. At other times in his illness he used to scout his doctors and their advice and do as he pleased. Now he had the docility of a child. This was the great Napoleon: pitiful, humble.

ON THE EVE

All the French were gathered around Napoleon's bed or at his door. Sir Hudson Lowe, who had sent Arnott, offered two more doctors. And Bertrand was still noting down every word, every sign, every sigh.

4th May.—At half-past eleven, stool. From midnight to three o'clock, quiet sleep. From three to five, hiccup. At half-past six, stool. The Emperor's clothes changed. Voice clearer, pulse stronger, less rapid. At eight o'clock, very feeble. . . . Avoid false hopes. At a quarter to eleven:

'Well, Bertrand, my friend.'

At midday, fresh stool. Changed. He revives. Jelly. At a quarter to two, he looks at everyone. Seven or eight fainting-fits in succession on the stool. Recovers immediately.

At two o'clock, eyes all around, several times. At half-past two:

'Madame Bertrand, oh!'

Looks full of commiseration. At a quarter to three, two fainting-fits five minutes apart. Stool. The Emperor, often, on this and the previous day, crosses his hands on his chest, with fingers interlaced.

About a quarter past four the Governor told General Montholon that he was obliged to go to Plantation House; that he wished to know how Napoleon did.

Montholon said he was very ill and had little hope.

THE 5TH OF MAY, *1821*

It was the end. Napoleon was passing from the world. He was less than fifty-two. He had been ten years an emperor and seven years an exile or prisoner. Up to that time, every year of his life, from Toulon onwards, had been partly occupied by a war. And his last words were: 'At the head of the army!'

What was he thinking of? His return from Waterloo? The urgent advice of his friends: 'Go at once! Go back to the head of your army'? Possibly—since for six years, day after day, he had kept on brooding over his lost empire, Waterloo. . . .

To his son the King of Rome (it was only in passing that he spoke of his other children), he always referred as 'the little King', 'the King'. Never by his Christian name, François. In the hour of death he was thinking of this child, and asked again and again: 'What is my son's name?'

5th May.—From midnight to one o'clock, the same hiccup, but louder.

From one o'clock to three, drank oftener. First he raised his hand, then turned his head to stop drinking.

At three o'clock, rather loud hiccup. Groan seeming to come from a distance.

From three to half-past four, a few hiccups, subdued moans then groaning. He yawns. Would seem to be in great pain. Said a few words which were inaudible, and: *'falling back'*, or, certainly: *'at the head of the army'*.

From half-past four to five, great weakness, moans. The doctor has him raised slightly on his pillow. Napoleon no longer opens his eyes. He seems weaker than last night. Now only a dead body.

At six o'clock, the doctor (Antommarchi) having tapped Napoleon's belly with his finger, it rang like a drum: it seemed distended and already lifeless.

The doctor intimated that the last moment was at hand. The grand marshal and Mme Bertrand were warned.

From six to half-past, very quiet, breathing easy. During this half-hour, the head slightly turned to the left, the eyes open and fixed on Count Bertrand's waistcoat, but owing to its position, rather than from interest.

Napoleon seems to see nothing. A veil over the eyes.

At half-past six he straightened his head, staring at the bed-foot, his eyes open, fixed and veiled.

Till eight o'clock, a little quiet sleep, sometimes with sighs every quarter of an hour.

At eight o'clock, a few groans, or rather a few hollow sounds, seeming to be formed in the lower abdomen and whistle as they pass through the windpipe. They seem rather to be produced by an instrument than to be a groan. A tear came out of the left eye, at the corner next to the ear. Bertrand wiped it away. Arnott wondered at Napoleon's lasting so long.

From six o'clock in the morning, very quiet, motionless.

Sixteen persons present, twelve of them French, Mme Bertrand, with two women, Ali, Noverraz, Napoleon Bertrand, at seven o'clock.

At half-past seven he fell into a swoon.

From eleven to noon, Arnott applied two mustard plasters to the feet, and Antommarchi two blisters, one on the chest, the second on the calf. Several times the doctor (Antommarchi) felt for the pulse in the neck.

At half-past two Dr Arnott had a hot-water bottle placed on the stomach.

At forty-nine minutes past five Napoleon breathed his last.

VALEDICTION

We take the final words from Count Molé, *who had not only worked under Napoleon but, as 'the first of listeners', heard a great deal of his mind.*

He pronounced his summing-up, not on the death of Napoleon but after his relegation to St Helena.

Will he ever leave it? Or, as everything leads one to suppose, will he there depart a life of which the beginning augured so much greatness, of which the middle brought forth so many wonders, and of which the end displayed only the shabbiness peculiar to that of adventurers?

Let us conclude what relates to him with a last reflection, which will serve to account for these three stages of his career.

The beginning was full of greatness because, to launch himself from obscurity to the summit of glory and of power, he had recourse only to what was heroic and vast in him, his will and his intellect.

The middle abounded in wonders because, with the aid of absolute power, he could give his genius full scope.

The end was shabby because he had a hard heart and a small soul, and only the soul and heart make a hero in adversity.

THE REPUBLICAN CALENDAR

The Republican Calendar was reckoned from Sept. 22nd, 1792 (Year I), and discarded after Dec. 31st, 1805 (Year XIV). Roughly, it had 12 months of 30 days each, plus 5 (in leap years 6) 'complementary days', or 'sansculottides', at the end of the year. The nomenclature was as follows:—*Vendémiaire* (Sept. 22–Oct. 21), *Brumaire* (Oct. 22–Nov. 20), *Frimaire* (Nov. 21-Dec. 20) *Nivôse* (Dec. 21–Jan. 19), *Pluviôse* (Jan. 20–Feb. 18), *Ventôse* (Feb. 19–Mar. 20), *Germinal* (Mar. 21–April 19), *Floréal* (April 20–May 19), *Prairial* (May 20–June 18), *Messidor* (June 19–July 18), *Thermidor* (July 19–Aug. 17), *Fructidor* (Aug. 18–Sept. 16).

SOME NAPOLEONIC DATES

Born	1769
Siege of Toulon	1793
Marriage and command in Italy	1796
Egyptian expedition	1798
Coup d'etat and Consulate	1799
Marengo	1800
Peace of Amiens	1802
Emperor	1804
Austerlitz	1805
Jena	1806
Friedland: Treaty of Tilsit	1807
'Bayonne Settlement'	1808
Wagram and Divorce	1809
Marriage with Marie-Louise	1810
Retreat from Moscow	1812
Vittoria: Leipzig	1813
Abdication and Elba	1814
Hundred Days and Waterloo	1815
Died	1821

INDEX OF SOURCES

ABRANTÈS, Duchesse de. *Mémoires.* (Brussels 1838.)

ARNAULT. *Souvenirs d'un Sexagénaire.* (Paris 1833.)

AVRILLON, Mlle. *Mémoires de Mlle Avrillon, première femme de chambre de l'impératrice.* (Paris, Garnier, s. d.)

BAILLEUL, J.-Ch. *Examen critique des considérations de Mme la baronne de Staël, etc.* (Paris 1822.)

BALCOMBE, Betsy (Mrs Abell). *Recollections of the Emperor Napoleon at St Helena.* (1844.)

BARRAS, Paul. *Mémoires de Barras, membre du Directoire.* (Paris 1895.)

BAUSSET. *Mémoires anecdotiques.*

BEAUREGARD, Costa de. *Un homme d'autrefois: souvenirs recueillis par son arrière-petit-fils.* (Paris 1891.)

BELLIARD, General. *Mémoires du comte Belliard, écrits par lui-même.* (Paris 1842.)

BERTRAND, General Count. *Journal du général Bertrand, grand maréchal du palais. Cahiers de Sainte-Hélène.* (Paris 1949.)

BESNARD, F.-Y. *Souvenirs d'un nonagénaire.* (Paris 1880.)

BEUGNOT. *Mémoires du comte Beugnot.* (Paris 1889.)

BONAPARTE, Lucien. Th. Iung, *Lucien Bonaparte et ses mémoires, 1775–1840.* (Paris 1882.)

BONNEVAL, Marquis de. *Mémoires anecdotiques.* (Paris 1900.)

BOURGOING, Baron de. *Souvenirs militaires.* (Paris 1897.)

BOURRIENNE, Louis de. *Mémoires sur Napoléon, etc.* (Paris, Garnier, s.d.)

BRANDT, Heinrich von. Baron Ernouf, *Souvenirs d'un officier polonais* (H. v. B.). (Paris 1877.)

BROGLIE, Duc de. *Souvenirs (1786–1870) du feu duc de Broglie.* (Paris 1886.)

CAMPAN, Mme. *Lettres inédites,* in 'Toute l'Histoire de Napoléon', No. 4.

CAMPBELL, Sir Neil. *Napoleon at Fontainebleau and Elba.* (1869)

CARRION-NISAS. *Journal* (Mss, Institut de France).

CAULAINCOURT, General de. *Mémoires.* (Paris 1933.)

CHAMPAGNY. *Souvenirs.* (Paris 1846.)

CHAMPOLLION. *L'Egypte et les Cent Jours.* Mémoires et Documents inédits, par M. Champollion-Figeac. (Paris 1844.)

CHAPTAL. *Mes Souvenirs sur Napoleon.* (Paris 1893.)

CHASTENAY, Victorine de. *Mémoires.* (Paris 1896.)

CLARKE, General. (Reproduced in BOURRIENNE, q.v.)

CLARY-et-ALDRINGEN, Prince Charles de. *Souvenirs: Trois mois à Paris lors du mariage de Napoléon et de Marie-Louise.* (Paris 1914.)

COIGNET, Sergeant. *Les Cahiers du capitaine Coignet.* (Paris 1883.)

CONSTANT. *Mémoires de Constant, premier valet de chambre de l'empereur.*
CUSSY, Chevalier de. *Souvenirs du chevalier de Cussy.* (Paris 1909.)

DENNIÉE, Baron. *Itinéraire de l'empereur Napoleon pendant la campagne de 1812.* (Paris 1842.)
DESGENETTES. *Histoire médicale de l'armée d'Orient.*
'DÉTENU'. *The Journal of a Detenu, An Eye-Witness of the Events in Paris,* etc. (London Magazine, Sept. 1825).
DÉTROYE, Brigadier. Archives Guerre. Armée d'Orient. 22 ventôse–12 mars 1799.
DIVOV, Elisabeth Petrovna. *Journal et Souvenirs.* (Paris 1929.)
DUMAS, General Comte Mathieu. *Souvenirs.*
DURAND, Mme. *Mémoires sur Napoléon et Marie-Louise.* (Paris 1896.)

ECKERMANN. *Conversations with Goethe.* (Tr. Paris 1862.)

FAIN. *Mémoires du baron Fain,* publiés par ses arrière-petits-fils. (Paris 1908.).
FLEURY de CHABOULON. *Mémoires pour servir à l'histoire de la vie privée, du retour et du règne de Napoléon en 1815.*
FOUCHÉ. *Les Mémoires de Fouché.* (Paris 1945.)

GASSICOURT, C. L. Cadet de. *Voyage en Autriche, en Moravie et en Bavière, pendant la campagne de 1809.* (Paris 1818.)
GAUDIN, Duke of Gaeta. *Mémoires, souvenirs, opinions et écrits du duc de Gaète.* (1834 repr. Paris 1926.)
GEORGE, Mlle. *Mémoires inédits de Mlle George,* publiés par P.-A. Cheramy. (Paris 1908.)
GOETHE. *Entrevue de Napoleon I et de Goethe,* suivie de notes et commentaires, par S. Sklower. (Lille 1853.)
GOHIER. *Mémoires de Louis-Jérôme Gohier, président du Directoire au 18 brumaire.* (Paris 1824.)
GONNEVILLE, Colonel de. *Souvenirs militaires.* (Paris 1895.)
GOURGAUD, General. *Sainte-Hélène, Journal inédit de 1815 à 1818.* (Paris, Flammarion, s.d.)

HALÉVY, L. *Notes et Souvenirs.* (Paris 1889.)
HOME, George. *Memoirs of an Aristocrat* (quoted as appendix to MAITLAND, q.v.).
HORTENSE (Beauharnais). *Mémoires de la reine Hortense.* (Paris 1927.)

KIELMANNSEGGE, Charlotte von. *Mémoires de la comtesse de Kielmannsegge sur Napoléon I^{ier}.* (Tr. Paris 1928.)
KOCK, Paul de. *Mémoires.* (Paris 1873.)
KOTZEBUE, August. *My Memories of Paris in 1804.* (Tr. Hague 1805.)
KRETTLY. (In BELLIARD, q.v.)

LA TOUR DU PIN. Marquise de. *Journal d'une femme de cinquante ans.* (Paris 1913.)

LAVALLETTE. *Mémoires et Souvenirs du comte Lavallette.* (Paris 1905.)

LEJEUNE, General Baron. *De Walmy à Wagram.*

LOWE, Sir H. Forsyth, *History of the Captivity of Napoleon at St Helena, from the Letters and Journals of Sir Hudson Lowe.* (1853.)

MACDONALD, Marshal. *Souvenirs.* (Paris 1892.)

MAITLAND, F. L. *The Surrender of Buonaparte, and his Residence on H.M.S. Bellerophon.* (1826.)

MARBOT, General. *Mémoires.* (Paris 1892.)

MARMONT, Marshal. *Mémoires.* (Paris 1857.)

MÉLITO, Miot de. *Mémoires.* (Paris 1873.)

MÉNEVAL. *Mémoires pour servir à l'histoire de Napoléon I^{ier} depuis 1802 jusqu'à 1815.* (Paris 1894.)

MÉRODE-WESTERLOO, Comte de. *Souvenirs.* (Paris 1864.)

METTERNICH, Prince. *Mémoires, documents et écrits divers, publiés par son fils.* (Paris 1880.)

MOLÉ. Marquis de Noailles, *Le comte Molé, sa vie, ses mémoires.* (Paris 1922.)

MOLLIEN. *Mémoires d'un ministre du trésor public.* (Paris 1845.)

MOUNIER. Comte d'Hérisson, *Souvenirs intimes et notes du baron Mounier.* (Paris 1896.)

NADAILLAC, Marquise de. *Mémoires.* (Paris 1912.)

NORVINS. *Souvenirs d'un historien de Napoléon. Mémorial de J. de Norvins,* publié par L. de Lanzac de Laborie. (Paris 1897.)

ODELEBEN, General Baron. *The Campaign in Saxony in 1813.* (Tr. Paris 1817.)

OUVRARD. *Mémoires de G.-J. Ouvrard sur sa vie et ses diverses opérations financières.* (Paris 1826.)

PASQUIER. *Histoire de mon temps. Mémoires du chancelier Pasquier.* (Paris 1893.)

PAULIN, General Baron. *Les Souvenirs du général baron Paulin (1782–1876).* (Paris 1895.)

PELET (de la Lozère). *Opinions de Napoléon sur divers sujets de politique et d'administration.* (Paris 1833.)

PERCY, Baron. *Journal des campagnes du baron Percy,* publié par M. Emile Longin. (Paris 1904.)

PEYRUSSE. *Mémorial et Archives de M. le baron Peyrusse (1809–1815).* (Carcassonne 1869.)

PICHON, L.-A. *De l'état de la France sous la domination de Napoléon Bonaparte.* (Paris 1814.)

PONS (de l'Hérault). *Souvenirs et anecdotes de l'île d'Elbe.* (Paris 1897.)

PONTÉCOULANT. *Souvenirs historiques et parlementaires du comte de Pontécoulant.*

POTOCKA, Countess. *Mémoires de la comtesse Potocka (1794–1820).* (Paris 1897.)

POUGET, General Baron. *Souvenirs de guerre.* (Paris 1895.)

POUMIÈS DE LA SIBOUTIE. *Souvenirs d'un médecin de Paris* (Revue Hebdomadaire 1909).

PRADT, Abbé de. *Histoire de l'ambassade dans le grand duché de Varsovie, en 1812.* (Paris 1815.)

RAPP, General. *Mémoires du général Rapp, écrits par lui-même.* (Paris, Garnier, s.d.)

RÉAL. *Indiscrétions, Souvenirs anecdotiques et politiques,* mis en ordre par Musnier Desclozeaux. (Paris 1835.)

RÉMUSAT, Mme de. *Mémoires de Mme de Rémusat,* publiés par son petit-fils. (Paris 1880.)

RICARD, General de. *Autour des Bonaparte.* Fragments de Mémoires publiés par L.-Xavier de Ricard.(Paris 1891.)

ROEDERER. *Mémoires sur la révolution, le consulat et l'empire.* (Paris 1942.)

ROMAIN, F. de. *Souvenirs d'un officier royaliste.*

ROUSTAM. *La vie privée de sier R.R. jusqu'à 1814. Souvenirs de Roustam mamelouk de l'empereur,* in Jean Savant, *Les Mamelouks de Napoléon.* (Paris 1949.)

SAINT-CHAMANS, General. *Mémoires du général comte de Saint-Chamans, ancien aide de camp du maréchal Soult.* (Paris 1896.)

SAINT-DENIS, L.-E. *Souvenirs du mamalouk Ali sur l'empereur Napoléon.* (Paris 1926.)

SÉGUR, Comte de. *Mémoires du général comte de Ségur.* (Paris 1894.)

STAËL, Mme de. *Mémoires de Mme de Staël (Dix années d'exil).* (Paris 1818.)

STENDHAL. *Les temps héroiques de Napoléon.* (Paris, Nilsson, s.d.)

STURMER, Baron. J. Saint-Cère et H. Schitter, *Napoléon à Sainte-Hélène.* Rapports officiels du baron Sturmer. (Paris, Librairie illustrée, s.d.)

THIARD, General. *Souvenirs militaires et diplomatiques.*

THIBAUDEAU. *Mémoires de A.-C. Thibaudeau, 1799–1815.* (Paris 1913.)

THIÉBAULT, General. *Mémoires du général baron Thiébault,* publiés par Fernand Calmettes. (Paris 1895.)

VANDAL, A. *Napoléon et Alexandre I^{ier}.*

WALDBURG-TRUCHSESS. *Journal du comte de Waldbourg-Truchsess.* (Paris 1815.)

Index

DD